MONTRÉAL

ANDREA BENNETT

CONTENTS

Discover Montréal.....................4

10 Top Experiences..................6

Explore Montréal 12

Planning Your Trip..................21

Neighborhoods.......................28

■ Sights...................................56

■ Restaurants........................98

■ Nightlife 130

■ Arts and Culture..............148

■ Sports and Activities........173

■ Shops 187

■ Where to Stay 211

Day Trips...............................228

Background...........................252

Essentials.............................272

Resources.............................284

Index.....................................296

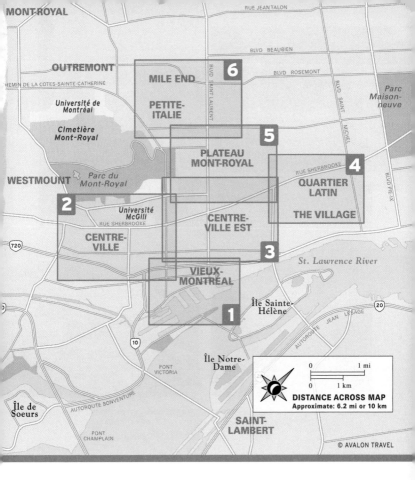

MAPS

1 Vieux-Montréal 312

2 Centre-Ville 314

3 Centre-Ville Est 316

4 Quartier Latin
and the Village 318

5 Plateau Mont-Royal 320

6 Mile End and Petite-Italie 322

7 Greater Montréal 324

1 Parc La Fontaine (page 82)

2 Chapelle Notre-Dame-de-Bon-Secours (page 65)

3 Rue Ste-Catherine Est, the heart of the city's gay neighborhood (page 79)

4 La Ronde, an amusement park at Parc Jean-Drapeau (page 93)

5 Buckminster Fuller's Biosphère at Parc Jean-Drapeau (page 91)

6 A fruit stand at Marché Atwater (page 90)

DISCOVER
MONTRÉAL

Montréal is a place all its own, with its own traditions, architecture, and language. It's known for its bilingualism, its dynamic culture, and its relaxed, laissez-faire attitude.

The city is home to a large population of students, artists, writers, and musicians, drawn by low living costs and support for the arts. You'll see signs of them everywhere—in murals, festivals, and live shows. Famous musical exports include Leonard Cohen and Arcade Fire; branch out and you may discover the city's next big act.

The city has been shaped by Franco-Anglo tensions, influxes of immigrants from all over the world, and an evolving approach to religion. Its roots come directly via 17th-century colonial missions from France—and this is especially visible in Vieux-Montréal—but today this history flavors its diverse culture rather than defining it. Once incredibly Catholic, the city is now known for its social liberalism and hedonistic attitude.

From the vine-covered alleys to the corkscrew staircases to each neighborhood's hidden architectural gems, Montréal should be discovered at the street level. Explore its nooks and crannies, stopping for a coffee in a cozy café or a drink in an up-and-coming microbrewery. Build some time into your travels to stumble across someone playing a public piano or wander through a small summer festival. Serendipity will make you fall in love with Montréal.

10 TOP EXPERIENCES

1 **Basilique Notre-Dame-de-Montréal:** One of the best-known sights in the city, this beautiful church is steeped in history (page 58).

2 **Saint Joseph's Oratory:** Perched on the north side of Mont-Royal, this stunning oratory offers great views and holds regular concerts (page 87).

3 Parc du Mont-Royal: This park is an expansive green respite in the midst of hectic city life (page 86).

>>>

4 Musée des Beaux-Arts de Montréal: Discover an impressive permanent collection alongside major touring exhibitions (page 69).

5 Marché Jean-Talon: Find fresh seafood, cheeses, chocolate, crêpes, and a bounty of local produce at this busy local market (page 83).

<<<

6 **Cycling the City:** Whether by Bixi or bike tour, you'll travel quickly and safely while taking in the sights, sounds, and smells of the city (page 175).

7 **Local Cuisine:** Sample local specialties like **poutine** (page 115) in the Plateau and **bagels** (page 123) in Mile End. Bring your appetite!

8 **Green Alleyways:** Wend your way through the Plateau and Mile End and you'll be rewarded with plenty of urban backyard charm (page 85).

<<<

9 **Festivals:** Dozens of world-renowned festivals, including Just for Laughs, the Festival International de Jazz de Montréal, Les FrancoFolies de Montréal, and Pop Montreal, make their home here (page 165).

>>>

10 **Wining and Dining Alfresco:** Montréal's "picnic law" means you can have a beer or a glass of wine with your picnic dinner. Order takeout and head to your favorite park (page 118).

<<<

EXPLORE
MONTRÉAL

THE BEST OF MONTRÉAL

Montréal is a busy, vibrant city that is very walkable and bikeable. There is plenty to see and do in every neighborhood, and it's fairly easy to get from one side of the city to another by bike or public transit. While you're traveling, keep an eye out for street festivals, especially in the Quartier Latin and the Plateau—they're everywhere in the summer.

This itinerary assumes that you won't be traveling by car. If you'd like to get more exercise, substitute cycling by Bixi for public transit. If you or a traveling partner has mobility issues, skip the Métro (it's often not accessible) in favor of the bus or a cab.

>DAY 1: VIEUX-MONTRÉAL

Arrive in **Montréal** and head to your hotel in Vieux-Montréal. Drop your bags and head out to grab a coffee and a light bite at **Olive & Gourmando.** Then stroll down **rue St-Paul,** the oldest street in the city, and do a little browsing.

Head to the **Basilique Notre-Dame-de-Montréal,** Montréal's beloved landmark and the site

Place d'Armes

BEST VIEWS

- Down at the **Vieux-Port** (page 63) you'll be able to see Silo #5, Habitat 67, the Biosphère, and Parc Jean-Drapeau.

- At the **Au Sommet observation deck** (page 75) at Place Ville-Marie, get a 360-degree view of the city from 185 meters up in the sky.

- **Parc du Mont-Royal** (page 86) has city overlooks at the Kondiaronk and Camillien-Houde belvederes, as well as from the northern side of the park, near the Université de Montréal or the Outremont belvedere.

- Located on the northern side of Mont-Royal, **Saint Joseph's Oratory** (page 87) offers an eastern-facing view that is particularly stunning at sunset.

- Overlooking the Notre-Dame Basilica and the Place d'Armes, the **Terrasse Place d'Armes** (page 133) at the Hôtel Place d'Armes is the perfect spot to grab a scenic drink.

- In Bonsecours Basin, **La Grande Roue de Montréal** (page 177) will give you a panoramic year-round view across the water and back at the city.

of much of the city's early history. Right in front of the church you'll find **Place d'Armes,** a bustling tourist spot home to public art, four centuries of architecture, and, often, talented buskers. Next, walk down to the **Vieux-Port,** stroll along the waterside promenade, and check out **Chapelle Notre-Dame-de-Bon-Secours,** the oldest church in the city, as well as **Habitat 67** and **Silo #5.**

In the late afternoon head out onto Jacques-Cartier Quay to **Terrasses Bonsecours** for a drink on

the patio and a great view of the skyline as the sun begins to dip down. Head past the artists and street vendors on **Place Jacques-Cartier** and up to **Basilique Notre-Dame-de-Montréal** for the nightly light show.

Le Club Chasse et Pêche

Try local French favorite **Le Club Chasse et Pêche** for dinner. After the meal, head to Place d'Armes Hôtel and Suites for a nightcap and a view of the city's twinkling lights at rooftop bar **Terrasse Place d'Armes.** If you're not ready to head back to your hotel, there's always a chance to make a few late-night dance moves at dance club **Wunderbar.**

> **DAY 2:**
PETITE-ITALIE, MONT-ROYAL, AND CENTRE-VILLE

Take the Métro to **Marché Jean-Talon** for breakfast—**La Crêperie du Marché** is a perfect choice—and stroll around enjoying the sights and sounds and gathering snacks for later. Then rent a **Bixi** from the closest stand and head south along the bike paths toward **Parc du Mont-Royal.** Grab a coffee to go at **Café Santropol** and hike up the mountain to one of its four belvederes—**Belvedere Kondiaronk** near the Chalet du Mont-Royal is a favorite.

Aux Vivres

For lunch, try **Aux Vivres,** close to the eastern edge of the park—the healthy vegetarian food will be welcome after all that exercise. Next, hop back on a Bixi or catch bus 435 to the **Musée des Beaux-Arts de Montréal.** Spend the afternoon soaking up art.

When you get peckish, grab dinner and a drink at **Kazu.** Then catch bus 165 up the west side of the mountain and end your evening by walking to **Saint Joseph's Oratory** and climbing the steps for an amazing sunset view.

BEST PEOPLE-WATCHING

- Businesspeople on their lunch breaks, tourists playing with interactive public art, young punks kicking a hacky-sack—**Place des Arts** (page 76) was built to be a meeting place and hangout spot, the perfect place to get a bit of respite or put your feet up after pounding the pavement downtown.

- On Avenue du Mont-Royal, the **Mont-Royal Métro station** (page 81) is a bustling busker favorite and well-used transit hub with a café and flower shop right in the vicinity. Prepare yourself to make new friends—folks are chatty around this station.

- The **George-Étienne Cartier monument** (page 87) in Parc du Mont-Royal is home to the Sunday Tam Tam, an informal festival where locals and visitors come to smoke joints and play drums. Bring pocket change for lemonade or handmade jewelry.

- **Marché Atwater** (page 90) on the Lachine Canal, draws locals, lovers, and tourists from near and far. Buy an ice cream cone from Havre aux Glaces, pull up a chair near the south end of the market or along the canal, and watch the world go by.

- The clientele at **Café Olimpico** (page 128) is young and old, hipster and jock, Anglo and Franco. The *terrasse* is the perfect place to enjoy an espresso and cannoli and get a feel for the Mile End.

> **DAY 3:**
QUARTIER LATIN, MILE END, AND PLATEAU MONT-ROYAL

Take the Métro to rue Sherbrooke and walk north on **rue St-Denis,** taking as many side streets and alleyways as possible to explore the true character of **Plateau Mont-Royal.** Grab breakfast at French bistro **L'Express** and keep your eyes peeled for

BEST FOR ROMANCE

- To most North Americans, **Marché Jean-Talon** (page 83) will immediately give off a European vibe. Share oysters and sample cheeses with your date, take an espresso at Café Saint-Henri, and split dessert at Chocolats Privilège.

- There is something incredibly calming about wandering the **Jardin Botanique** (page 94) and its greenhouses, especially on a weekday when things are quiet. Bring a picnic and a bottle of wine and take your time.

- Another perfect spot for a picnic, **Parc La Fontaine** (page 180) is incredibly picturesque at any time of day, with a bevy of restaurants nearby providing delicious takeout for an alfresco dining experience.

- Packed on the weekends but less busy on weekdays, **Bota Bota** (page 191) is a spa that offers saunas, steam rooms, cold baths, and Jacuzzis—all with breathtaking views of the city and the Vieux-Port.

- **Pierre du Calvet** (page 216) is a hotel and restaurant featuring a lobby bar. Built in 1725, the building is quirky and sumptuous; stay there if your budget allows, or pop in for a drink or dinner if it doesn't.

- Rent a car and leave the city for a day to visit **La Route des Vins** (page 247) in the Cantons de l'Est. Pretty scenery, vineyards, apple orchards, and wine sampling—it doesn't get much better.

the cobblestone avenue Duluth and, farther north, avenue Marie Anne, Leonard Cohen's old haunt. Explore a bit of the French side of avenue Mont-Royal before heading west and north.

Make your way to **St-Viateur Bagel Shop** and eat your hot-from-the-oven treat with a coffee from **Café Olimpico** for lunch.

Check out the **vintage stores** on rue St-Viateur and avenue Bernard. Comic fans should hit up **Drawn & Quarterly.**

Head for **boulevard St-Laurent.** Browse the shops and take in the street's history as you head south. Stop in at **Kitsch 'n' Swell** and **La Centrale Galerie Powerhouse.** Have a beer or cider at **Else's** and get a thick, smoked-meat sandwich at **Schwartz's.** Catch an up-and-coming band or dance the night away to the city's most eclectic DJs at **Casa del Popolo.**

With More Time

DAY 4: THE VILLAGE AND GREATER MONTRÉAL

Head to the Village, get goodies to go from Le Mie Matinale, rent a Bixi, and make your way to the Pont Jacques-Cartier. Built over the St-Lawrence River, the bridge has spectacular panoramic views of the city, and it's a unique way to get to Parc Jean-Drapeau. Once on the island, you can drop your bike off and head off for a day of rides at La Ronde or just ogle the awe-inspiring wonder that is Buckminster Fuller's Biosphère.

Have a picnic on the shores of the river—take advantage of Montréal's picnic law and enjoy a beer with your meal—wander the gardens, then hop the Métro back for an unparalleled dining experience at Toqué! and an evening performance at Cirque du Soleil.

DAY 5: MONT-TREMBLANT

Throw your hiking boots in a bag and leave Montréal on the first bus to Mont-Tremblant National Park for a day in the rugged outdoors. At the largest and oldest park in the province, you can hike, swim, canoe, and kayak to your heart's content. For something a little less taxing, head to Mont-Tremblant Resort for some alpine luging and pedal-boating. Spend the night in Mont-Tremblant's Auberge la Porte Rouge and have dinner at Seb l'Artisan Culinaire.

MONTRÉAL WITH KIDS

Reasonable rents and a good social safety net mean most Montrealers eschew the burbs and stay in the city to raise their kids. Festivals often have kid-friendly options, and there are plenty of parks and fun things to do. Visiting teens can often join their parents on bike tours and other excursions, and if you're with little ones most rental places will offer something to accommodate that—a bike trailer or trail-a-bike, for example, or a pedal boat instead of a kayak.

Many hotels, especially the higher-end ones in Vieux-Montréal, can set up child care if you give them some advance notice. Staying in Vieux-Montréal also means you'll be close to the Vieux-Port, which features a ton of family-friendly activities and museums.

>DAY 1

Arrive in **Montréal** and head to your hotel in **Vieux-Montréal.** Drop your bags and head out to grab a coffee and a light bite at **Crew Café.** Then stroll down **rue St-Paul,** the oldest street in the city, and do a little browsing. Head to the **Basilique**

Notre-Dame-de-Montréal and learn a bit about the city's culture and history to ground your trip— you can take a guided tour of the church, or just a read a little about the church and the **Place d'Armes.**

Next, walk down to the **Vieux-Port** and grab a snack from a food truck or Muvbox—tacos, poutine,

Voiles en Voiles, an elaborate rope course stretching between pirate ships in the Vieux-Port

BEST OUTDOOR FUN

- **Parc du Mont-Royal** (page 86) is the ideal place to jog, walk, or bike in the warmer months. Come winter, you can snowshoe up that same incline or cross-country ski along the mountain's 20 kilometers of trails. Once you get to the top, enjoy skating at **Lac aux Castors** (page 183).

- Biking is the best way to explore the city and get your daily dose of exercise. There are 350 kilometers of bike paths for you to explore. The bike rental program **Bixi** (page 180) makes it simple.

- The **Lachine Canal** (page 175) is great for cycling in summer and an ideal spot to cross-country ski come winter. It's also one of the few places in the city where you can rent a kayak or rowboat.

- On Montréal's south shore you'll find the ski hills **Ski Mont Sutton** (page 249) and **Ski Bromont** (page 248). Both are ideal for skiing in the winter and hiking in the summer.

- **Mont-Tremblant National Park** (page 232) to the north of the city is great for skiing, hiking, mountain climbing, canoeing, and kayaking.

- **Oka National Park** (page 236) has a beach and is ideal for water sports and swimming when it's warm out. The hiking trails can be used for snowshoeing come winter.

- **Parc Jean-Drapeau** (page 91), on an island south of the city, offers an Olympic-sized outdoor pool, tons of biking paths, and even a beach where you can bathe in the St-Lawrence.

- **Parc La Fontaine** (page 82), in the Plateau, is ideal for running or walking in the summer; in the winter, it becomes the ultimate place to lace up your skates.

and lobster rolls are all popular options. After lunch has settled, head to **Voiles en Voiles,** a super-fun ropes course set up on pirate ships in the Vieux-Port—you can stay for an hour or longer. If you find yourself with more time to spend before dinner, check out the **Centre des Sciences de Montréal.**

Try local favorite **Brit and Chips** for dinner. After the meal, head back down to the Vieux-Port and enjoy an evening at the **Bonsecours Basin. La Grande Roue de Montréal,** a giant Ferris wheel, is open till 11pm nightly, or, if you've still got some energy to burn off, the **SOS Labyrinthe** is a fun game for the whole family.

> ## DAY 2

After breakfast at **Le Cartet,** head down to the river and walk east along the **Lachine Canal,** or take transit if you're with young kids. Hook a right and cross the bridge at **Marché Atwater.** Treat the kids to an ice cream at **Havre aux Glaces** and wander the market for a while before you rent a pedal boat at **H2O Adventures.**

When you're done pedal-boating, return to the market for a quick bite to eat—**Pizza Mia** is a safe bet. Then catch the Métro back east to the **Pointe-à-Callière Musée d'Archéologie et d'Histoire.** There's plenty to explore, and this museum always offers a few kid-friendly interactive exhibits.

For dinner, head to **Jardin Nelson,** which offers refined classics for adults alongside kid-friendly choices. After the meal, meander up Place Jacques-Cartier and

the lush, expansive grounds of the Jardin Botanique

make your way to the **Basilique Notre-Dame-de-Montréal** for the nightly light show.

>DAY 3

Today you'll be taking an excursion out to **Greater Montréal**—pack snacks and a picnic—so start your morning with a hearty, healthy breakfast at **7Grains Bakery & Café.** Catch the Métro to the **Space for Life** park out at Pie-IX station—this park includes the **Jardin Botanique, Biodôme, Insectarium,** and **Planetarium.** The best deal—you'll get to experience a whole day of fun—is to purchase the family package allowing you access to all four spaces.

When you're ready for lunch, unpack your picnic at one of the designated picnic areas or the Frédéric Back Tree Pavilion in the botanical garden. Alternatively, order lunch at the botanical garden and find a seat on the lovely *terrasse.* After lunch, head back to **Space for Life** and pick up where you left off.

Just before dinnertime, catch the Métro back into town—specifically, to **La Banquise,** Montréal's most-famous poutine spot. Order your meal to go and take it for a picnic at the nearby **Parc La Fontaine,** where the kids can splash their feet in the pond or play Frisbee after dinner. Take transit back to your hotel when you're feeling tuckered, or if you've got energy to spare, wander back along Ste-Catherine, in the pedestrian-only section of the **Village.**

MONTRÉAL ON A BUDGET

Montrealers are all about having the highest standard of living on the smallest possible budget. That's part of what makes Montréal such an attractive city in the first place. If you're traveling with limited means, no fret—stay in a hostel or an Airbnb, or check out Pensione Popolo. Opt for parks and free sights, enjoy bagels and poutine, and, if you'd like to experience a higher-end French or Québécois spot, check it out at happy hour or see if they have a reasonable lunch menu.

>MORNING

Start your day with a bagel from **St-Viateur Bagel Shop**—grab a half dozen and save some for later—and head to **Café Olimpico**, just down the street, to enjoy a coffee with your breakfast. Check out the **vintage stores** on rue St-Viateur and avenue Bernard, and browse for books and comics at **Drawn & Quarterly.** Meander southward through the Mile End and the Plateau until you're ready for lunch.

The delicious smell of roasting chicken will greet you blocks before you reach Rotisserie Romados.

>AFTERNOON

Hop on a **Bixi** and ride downtown to **Qing Hua Dumpling,** where you can get a veritable feast on the cheap. Once you've had your fill, it's a 20-minute walk or another quick bike ride over to the **Belgo Building,** where entrance is free and you can check out over a dozen contemporary art galleries. From there it's a quick stroll to **Place des Arts,** perfect for afternoon people-watching.

>EVENING

Find the nearest **Bixi** stand and ride over to **Rotisserie Romados.** A half chicken with fries and salad is plenty for two. Pick up a bottle of wine or some beer and head to **Parc La Fontaine** for a picnic dinner. You can hang out until 10pm enjoying buskers and the summer air, or make your way over to **Casa del Popolo** to enjoy their patio or catch a show.

MONTRÉAL IN THE SNOW

Though it gets cold and snowy in the wintertime, that doesn't keep Montrealers indoors. Pull on your coat and boots and explore the city by foot—you may need some skis or snowshoes, but don't let that hold you back.

>MORNING

Start your day in Vieux-Montréal. Grab breakfast at **Crew Café** and wander down rue St-Paul to the **Basilique Notre-Dame-de-Montréal.** Next, browse the shops of the **Marché Bonsecours** to warm up (you may even find some new shearling gloves). Head to the Vieux-Port, grab a snack at the café, and take a spin at **La Grande Roue de Montréal,** a Ferris wheel with gorgeous views that is heated in the wintertime.

>AFTERNOON

Catch the bus up to **Lac aux Castors** (take bus 55 and then transfer to bus 11) or hail a cab and enjoy lunch at the pavilion overlooking the lake. Then, choose your winter sport: You can rent skates and glide along the outdoor rink or grab skis or snowshoes to explore the park.

>EVENING

Catch a bus back down the mountain and grab hearty poutine and burgers for dinner at **Patati Patata.** After you're satiated, head right next door for a cozy evening drink at **Big in Japan Bar.**

COLD COMFORTS

- Bundle up and check out a winter festival. **La Fête des Neiges** (page 165), **Igloofest** (page 165), and **Montréal en Lumière** (page 166) all run in the snowy months.

- Winter means hockey and cheering on the **Montréal Canadiens** (page 178). Grab tickets to a game at the Bell Centre or head to a local bar to catch the game.

- Ice-skating is the ultimate Canadian pastime, and the open-air rink in **Parc La Fontaine** (page 180) is large enough to accommodate hockey players, wannabe figure skating stars, and those just finding their skating legs.

- There are few things in the world as decadent as real hot chocolate. Warm up and indulge in a cup of the good stuff at **Juliette et Chocolat** (page 114).

- Grab a toboggan and slide down **Mont-Royal** (page 86) to avenue du Parc, or head farther into the park and go skating, or rent skis, at **Lac aux Castors** (page 183).

- Enjoy shopping and exploring the linked walkways in Montréal's **Underground City** (page 73). Running 32 kilometers, its size and diversity make it more than just a shopper's paradise.

PLANNING
YOUR TRIP

WHEN TO GO

Though **summer** is the busiest time to visit, it's also the best time to explore Montréal's neighborhoods, and you'll get to experience fun summer festivals like the Festival International de Jazz. **May to September** is generally considered the **high season,** with the peak being from early June to Labour Day.

It's no surprise that prices drop considerably **October-April,** so if you can handle a bit of cold, your pocketbook will thank you. Plus, the cold isn't so bad when it's hockey season and 98 percent of the people—and you—are crowded into bars watching the game. **Winter** can be freezing, but **December-March** is an ideal time to visit if you love skiing or other winter recreational activities. October is particularly pretty thanks to the changing fall foliage, and even February has a bright spot with Montréal en Lumière's all-night art party.

ENTRY REQUIREMENTS

All visitors must have a **valid passport** or other accepted secure documents to enter the country; even those entering from the United States by road or train must have these documents.

Citizens of the United States,

Place des Arts is built for public art and people-watching.

Australia, New Zealand, Israel, Japan, and most Western European countries don't need visas to enter Canada for stays up to 180 days. U.S. permanent residents are also exempt.

Nationals from South Africa, China, and about 150 other countries must apply for a **temporary resident visa** (TRV) in their home country. Full details can be found at **Citizen and Immigration Canada. Single-entry visitor visas** are valid for six months and cost $100, while **multiple-entry visas** last for up to 10 years, as long as a single stay doesn't last for longer than six months, and cost $100. A separate visa is required if you intend to work in Canada.

TRANSPORTATION

Visitors traveling by **air** will arrive at Montréal's **Pierre Trudeau International Airport,** the main hub for both national and international air travel to the province. It's about 21 kilometers from downtown, and shuttles and public transport are available.

If you're traveling by **train** you'll arrive at Montréal's **Gare Centrale** in the downtown core.

Those traveling by **bus** will arrive at the city's main bus terminal, **Gare d'Autocars,** in the Quartier Latin.

The **Montréal public transit system** is run by **STM,** and it includes both the **Métro** (subway) and **buses.** Pay-as-you-go **public bike rentals,** otherwise known as **Bixis,** are available between April and November, and navigating the city's streets by **car** is relatively simple, though parking can be a pain and expensive.

DAILY REMINDERS

- **Monday:** Most museums, except for the Redpath Museum of Natural History (located on-campus at McGill University), are closed on Monday. Smaller restaurants are also often closed on Monday and/or Sunday.

- **Tuesday:** Smaller restaurants are often closed on Monday and/or Tuesday.

- **Wednesday:** The Musée des Beaux-Arts de Montréal offers reduced admission prices to major exhibitions 5pm-9pm; the Musée d'Art Contemporain is half-price 5pm-9pm.

- **Thursday:** The farmers market at the Marché des Éclusiers, in the Vieux-Port, is held 2pm-7pm. Marché Jean-Talon, usually open until 5pm or 6pm, is open until 8pm. The Centre Canadien d'Architecture is free 5:30pm-9pm.

- **Friday:** Marché Jean-Talon and Marché Atwater, usually open until 5pm or 6pm, are open until 8pm.

- **Saturday:** The farmers market at the Marché des Éclusiers, in the Vieux-Port, is held 9am-2pm.

- **Sunday:** On the last Sunday of the month, the Musée des Beaux-Arts de Montréal is free 10am-5pm. On the first Sunday of each theater show run, the Segal Centre for the Performing Arts hosts free general admission lectures and Q&As. Mass is held at 8am, 9:30am, 11am, and 5pm on Sunday at the Notre-Dame Basilica. Smaller restaurants are often closed on Sunday and/or Monday.

RESERVATIONS

Montréal is a foodie's paradise, boasting a wide array of impressive restaurants at varying price points. If you're planning to treat yourself to some fine dining at spots like **Maison Publique, L'Express,** or **Le Quartier Général,** it's best to make reservations. (Some restaurants offer a brunch service that doesn't take reservations, so weekend brunch can be a great way to sneak in if you haven't planned ahead.)

To see the city by boat with companies such as **Croisières AML** and **Le Bateau-Mouche,** especially for brunch or dinner cruises, it's best to make reservations. Same goes for bike tours and walking tours—you might be able to sneak in last minute if there's space, but it's best to avoid disappointment by planning ahead.

Many festivals have free events or are free entirely, but tickets for popular shows at **Just for Laughs** or passes for festivals like the **Osheaga Music and Arts Festival** should be purchased well in advance, as should tickets for **Cirque du Soleil** shows and the **Canadian Grand Prix.**

If you want to catch a **Montréal Canadiens** hockey game—the NHL regular season starts in early October and runs until early April—you'll need to buy tickets well in advance, as games sell out consistently.

In the high season, hotels, hostels, and Airbnbs fill up quickly, especially around festivals or events like the Grand Prix. Book ahead to secure the best options; if you get stuck, try hotels near the airport. If you're thinking of taking a day trip out of town, book your rental car, VIA rail ticket, or bus ticket as soon as you've solidified your plans—bus and ticket prices increase as the economy options sell out, and convenient car rental locations often sell out on the weekends.

PASSES AND DISCOUNTS

Passport MTL is the best game in town when it comes to passes.

World-renowned Cirque du Soleil debuts its shows in Montréal.

A 48-hour pass costs $85 plus tax, and a 72-hour pass costs $99. Passes include unlimited public transportation and get you in at 23 different attractions around town, including the **Musée des Beaux-Arts de Montréal,** the **Jardin Botanique, Au Sommet Place Ville-Marie,** the **Tour Olympique,** and more.

The **Montréal Museums Pass** offers access to 41 museums via three different passes: $75 per person for three days, public transport excluded; $80 per person for three days, public transport included, or $225 for one year, either two visits per person or one visit per two people.

On Wednesday, the **Musée d'Art Contemporain** offers half-price admission 5pm-9pm. The **Musée des Beaux-Arts de Montréal** is free on the last Sunday of the month.

Many festivals held throughout the year are either free or offer free events—the **Festival International de Jazz de Montréal,** for example, holds a ton of free shows around rue Ste-Catherine and the Place des Festivals.

GUIDED TOURS

One of the best ways to see the city in the summer is by bike. Guided tours with **Fitz and Follwell** are a great way to see the city's essential sights, sample local cuisine, learn about culture and history, and bookmark places you'd like to explore further. Eat like a Montrealer with Fitz and Follwell's **food tours,** offering different neighborhood walks, cultural information, and plenty of snacks!

Other popular tours include

WHAT'S NEW

- **Transit extensions:** The STM has extended **bus route 55** farther south, making it easier for city-dwellers and visitors to get between the northern and southern neighborhoods of the city along St-Laurent. The new **711 bus route** will take passengers from the Mont-Royal Métro station all the way to Snowdon station, making it easier to get to Parc du Mont-Royal and Saint Joseph's Oratory—very convenient for visitors looking to hit these two top sights.

- **Up-and-coming neighborhoods: Les Quartiers du Canal,** comprising the Lachine Canal-adjacent parts of **Griffintown, Little Burgundy,** and **Saint-Henri,** have blossomed over the past several years. Veteran favorites like McAuslan Brewery and Nora Gray are joined by new coffee shops, fine dining, and dessert spots.

- **Ferris wheel:** Opened in summer 2017 in the Vieux-Port, **La Grande Roue de Montréal** offers 360-degree views of the city throughout the year—air-conditioned in the summer and heated in the winter—with an on-site restaurant and bar.

the **Hop-On Hop-Off Double Decker Tour,** which visits all the top sights and 'hoods across Montréal, and **Les Fantômes du Vieux-Montréal,** which delves into the seedy and spooky sides of Old Montréal's history.

Monday-Thursday, you can book a **Free Old Montréal Walking Tour** with Free Montréal Tours—just make sure to reserve ahead of time.

CALENDAR OF EVENTS

JANUARY

Montrealers live with winter weather for 4-6 months a year—and we make peace with that by getting outdoors to have fun.

Igloofest (www.igloofest.ca) is a large outdoor rave that runs for four weekends in January and February on the Jacques-Cartier Pier in the Old Port.

If you're traveling with kids, **La Fête des Neiges** (www.parcjean-drapeau.com), which takes place in Parc Jean-Drapeau during four consecutive weekends between January and February, will be a better bet. Bundle the whole family up for a day full of winter activities, including tubing, ice fishing, archery, curling, hockey, and ice sculpture.

FEBRUARY

Montréal en Lumière, an 11-day cultural celebration of food, arts, and music, takes place late February to early March all over the city. It is hands-down the most anticipated of winter festivals, if only because of the closing-night festivities. The festival culminates in Nuit Blanche, an all-night party where people take to the streets and trek from live shows to free museum exhibits well into the wee hours of the morning.

From late February to early March, the **Rendez-vous du Cinéma Québécois** (www.rvcq.com) screens Québécois movies made over the past year. This 10-day festival really has a wide range of offerings—everything from comedies to dramas to experimental films and documentaries, with options in French, English, and First Nations languages.

APRIL

Internationally renowned authors converge on Montréal in late April to take part in the **Blue Metropolis Literary Festival** (www.bluemetropolis.org), a multilingual festival featuring novelists, poets, and journalists. Unique in its vision, each year's event has a specific theme. Previous years have included Yann Martel, Margaret Atwood, and A. L. Kennedy.

MAY

Running in May or June (check the website for details) is **Elektra** (www.elektramontreal.ca), a cutting-edge digital arts festival that features everything from sound and light installations to live performances and interactive exhibits. The latest technologies and futuristic designs, like clothing with GPS tracking, are incorporated into almost every work, and there is an emphasis on new digital media.

The **Festival St-Ambroise Fringe de Montréal** (www.montrealfringe.ca) runs late May to early June, taking over venues around the city with local and international Fringe performances that are randomly picked by lottery. Though the program is released a few days early, the best way to see if there's anything that tickles your fancy is to stop by the Fringe for All a few days before opening to see snippets from upcoming shows.

Beginning in late May and continuing until September, **Piknic Électronik** (www.parcjeandrapeau.com), run by the same organizers as Igloofest, is a daytime outdoor music festival held on Sundays. Revelers—a mixed crowd of youth, family, and old ravers looking for sober dance fun—gather under an Alexander Calder statue first installed for Expo 67.

Tons of festivals, including Les FrancoFolies, take place annually at Place des Arts.

JUNE

Brewers from all over the world converge for Canada's largest beer festival, the **Festival Mondial de la Bière** (www.festivalmondialebiere.qc.ca), which takes place at the Palais des Congrès for five days in early- to mid-June. Entrance is free, and tasting coupons are available for a dollar a pop.

Les FrancoFolies de Montréal (www.francofolies.com) is a massive street festival in celebration of Francophone music that takes over the Place des Festivals for 10 days in early to mid-June. Not all concerts are free—bigger names play to a more contained crowd in venues across the city—but many are.

One of the most recognizable festivals in the world, the **Festival International de Jazz de Montréal** (www.montrealjazzfest.com) attracts thousands of tourists to the city each summer, running from the end of June to early July. The exciting, innovative 11-day festival offers nonstop music with big international acts playing for free in the middle of rue Ste-Catherine.

JULY

Just for Laughs (www.hahaha.com) is now one of the biggest and most well-known comedy festivals in the world. For two weeks from mid- to late July, streets all over downtown are closed off to make room for the street performers stationed throughout the city. Established comedians, including Natasha Leggero, Jerry Seinfeld, Wyatt Cenac, and Flight of the Conchords, also bring their own brand of stand-up to the city.

Heavy MTL (www.heavymtl.com): The name says it all. This two-day festival, which takes place outdoors at Parc Jean-Drapeau in late July, is all about heavy metal. No matter who's playing, you can guarantee it'll be loud.

Running from mid-July to early August, **Fantasia Film Festival** (www.fantasiafestival.com), established in 1996, is North America's premiere genre film festival. From the obscure to the grotesque, the Japanese to the Korean, it offers a wide range of films from all over the globe.

AUGUST

On the first weekend in August, the three-day **Osheaga Music and Arts Festival** (www.osheaga.com) is one of the biggest in Montréal, taking place off-island in the picturesque Parc Jean-Drapeau. Thousands of people of all ages spend the weekend checking out unknown emerging bands, musicians like Robyn and Hot Chip, and big-name acts like Arcade Fire, The Cure, and Snoop Dogg.

Fierté Montréal Pride (www.fiertemontrealpride.com) is a festive 10 days of celebration in early to mid-August, featuring outdoor concerts and dance parties, drag races, and performances by interdisciplinary artists.

SEPTEMBER

Pop Montreal (www.popmontreal.com), which features Francophone, Canadian, and international acts, is one of the most highly anticipated festivals of the year, especially among fans of indie music. It's a must-see if your visit to the city overlaps with the mid-September festival dates.

OCTOBER

The regular NHL season begins in early October and runs until early May. Catching a **Montréal Canadiens** game is a great way to have an intense Canadian hockey experience.

Established in 2000, the **Festival du Monde Arabe** (www.festivalarabe.com) is a two-week dance, visual arts, movie, and music festival that takes place from late October to mid-November. Its aim is to develop a dialogue between Arab and Western cultures in the city. Many of the events are in French, but some are in English.

NOVEMBER

Dedicated to documentary films, the 10-day **Rencontres Internationales du Documentaire Montréal,** better known as RIDM (www.ridm.qc.ca), takes place in early to mid-November. It features the work of international and local documentary filmmakers with the aim of presenting the films in their original languages.

NEIGHBORHOODS

Vieux-Montréal

Map 1

Present-day Montréal is located on what was, in the 16th century, the Iroquoian village Hochelaga. In 1642, French settlers arrived and began to put down roots. Though few buildings are left from the 17th century, **Old Montréal** is still full of cobblestone streets, early-New France architecture, regal Beaux-Arts buildings, and the grandeur of the **Basilique Notre-Dame-de-Montréal.** You'll also find some of the city's trendier restaurants, shops, and hotels—as well

as its tourist traps, so best to be discerning. In the south end, a gradual slope leads to the converted warehouses and green spaces of the **Vieux-Port** and the **St-Lawrence River.** The waterfront offers fun, **family-friendly entertainment** options, including bike rentals in the summer and skating in the winter.

TOP SIGHTS
- Basilique Notre-Dame-de-Montréal (page 58)
- Pointe-à-Callière Musée d'Archéologie et d'Histoire (page 63)

TOP RESTAURANTS
- Crew Café (page 105)

TOP NIGHTLIFE
- New City Gas (page 134)

TOP ARTS AND CULTURE
- DHC/ART (page 151)
- Phi Centre (page 151)
- Cirque du Soleil (page 151)

TOP SPORTS AND ACTIVITIES
- Ça Roule Montréal (page 175)

TOP SHOPS
- Bota Bota (page 191)

TOP HOTELS
- Hôtel Gault (page 216)
- Pierre du Calvet (page 216)
- Hôtel St-Paul (page 217)

GETTING THERE AND AROUND
- Métro stations: Champ de Mars, Place d'Armes, Square Victoria-OACI
- Métro lines: Orange
- Major bus routes: 14, 55, 129, 715

VIEUX-MONTRÉAL WALK

TOTAL DISTANCE: 3.6 kilometers (2.2 miles)
WALKING TIME: 45 minutes

Vieux Montréal is a rabbit warren of cobblestone streets, heritage buildings, and fascinating nooks and crannies. Not everything that looks interesting leads somewhere—sometimes an old archway will bring you nothing but a dead end and a pile of trash—but, as in the Mile End and the Plateau, it's worth following your curiosity. Important note: This walk ends at the Bota Bota spa, so pack a bathing suit and flip-flops!

1 Begin your walk at **Place d'Armes,** facing the Notre-Dame Basilica. To the right of the basilica, you'll see the Séminaire de Saint-Sulpice, the city's oldest building, constructed by Sulpician priests (who used to run the Island) in 1684. On the northeast corner of the square lies the city's first skyscraper, the New York Life building (est. 1888). At the

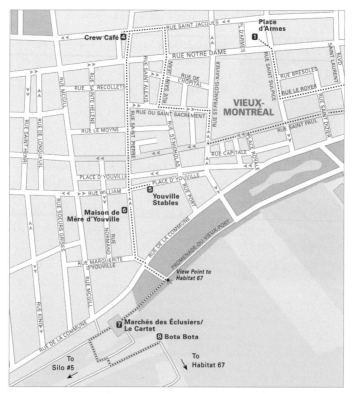

square's center lies the Maisonneuve monument, depicting the founders of Montréal: Paul de Chomedey de Maisonneuve, Jeanne Mance, Charles Lemoyne, Lambert Closse, and an Iroquois warrior (yes, they could have been more specific with that last one).

2 Leave the square from its southeast corner, head two blocks south on rue St-Sulpice, and then take a left and head three blocks east on rue le Royer W. When you hit rue St-Jean-Baptiste, take a right, a left onto rue St-Paul W., and then an immediate left onto rue St-Gabriel, and a right onto rue Ste-Thérèse. A quick jog right on rue St-Vincent, left on rue St-Amable, and you'll reach the **Place Jacques-Cartier,** which is often home to a festival or some artisans and snack shacks. Head north toward Nelson's column—you'll get a great view of the Hôtel de Ville— cross rue Notre-Dame E., and head down the stairs to Champ-de-Mars, a former military parade ground where you can see surviving remnants of Montréal's old fortifications.

3 Head back up the stairs and go east on Notre-Dame E. Walk two blocks and take a right onto rue Bonsecours. At the bottom of the

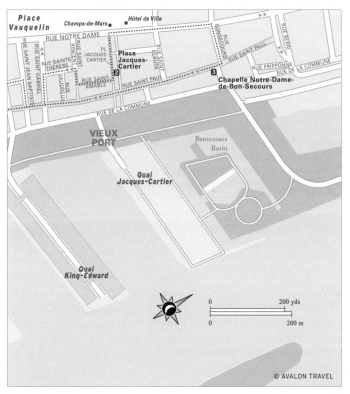

Crew Café

street, you can see the **Chapelle Notre-Dame-de-Bon-Secours** next to the Marché Bonsecours. Around the front of the *chapelle,* you'll see Our Lady of the Harbour, immortalized in the Leonard Cohen song "Suzanne" ("And the sun pours down like honey / On our lady of the harbour"). This chapel, built in 1771, was where sailors used to pray before departing on dangerous journeys. Head inside and you'll see a bunch of gorgeous ship replicas hanging from the ceiling in appreciation of safe passage.

4 Next, take a hike—seven blocks, some long, some short, down the quaint rue St-Paul W. This street, laid along the border of a former fort, is populated with a bunch of kitschy tourist shops, but it's also full of history. Take your time ambling down. When you hit rue St-François-Xavier, turn right, and then take an immediate left on rue du St-Sacrement. Walk two blocks and take a right on rue St-Jean; go three blocks and turn left on rue St-Jacques. One and a half blocks west on St-Jacques, you'll be at **Crew Café,** a gorgeous coffee shop and co-working space located in the gilded former headquarters of the Royal Bank of Canada. Enjoy a coffee, and then be on your way.

5 Retrace your steps half a block to rue St-Pierre and head south toward the water. Walk for six blocks until you reach rue William. Hang a left and cross the street: you'll reach **Youville Stables,** a lovely little courtyard that used to be owned by the Grey Nuns. If you're feeling peckish, stop in at Gibby's steakhouse for a fancy—pricey!—meal.

6 Double back to rue St-Pierre and head half a block to the **Maison de Mère d'Youville** chapel ruins. To your right, you'll see one of the old chapel walls, now populated with bronze strips engraved with a letter from Louis XIV giving his royal assent for the founding of Mère d'Youville's hospital. On the ground, you can see the footprint of the old chapel, which, like many Old Port buildings, used to flood regularly in the spring thaw.

Maison de Mère d'Youville

7 Continue heading south toward the water. When you hit rue Marguerite d'Youville, bear left and cross rue de Commune, heading down to the Promenade-du-Vieux-Port walking trail. Pause here to look out over the water. Directly in front of you, you'll see **Habitat 67,** a concrete structure designed by Moshe Safdie to house foreign dignitaries during Montréal's famous Expo 67. Look to your right and you'll see **Silo #5,** a massive old grain silo, now decommissioned, that used to be one of many along the Old Port. Head west to the **Marché des Éclusiers,** opened in 2016. Named after the canal's locks, this hybrid seasonal market, coffee shop, beer garden, and restaurant is the perfect place to stop for a snack and a drink (it's open May through October; if you visit in the winter, your best bet is **Le Cartet,** nearby at 106 rue McGill).

8 Finally, end your jaunt at **Bota Bota.** This old river ferry was turned into a permanently anchored spa featuring an amazing Norwegian water circuit—cold dunks, scented steam rooms, a sauna, and a bevy of hot tubs to choose from. Prices are reasonable, the clientele is diverse, and you get great views of the harbor.

Centre-Ville

Map 2

By the end of the 19th century, the wealthy had begun to move north of Vieux-Montréal, building **townhouses and mansions** along Sherbrooke Street and leading to the development of the "Golden Square Mile," centered between Sherbrooke and Pine, and Guy and University. Many impressive buildings from this heyday remain. Today, the **downtown core** is the city's **main commercial district.**

Rue Ste-Catherine is lined with everything from historical department stores to trendy boutiques, while **rue Crescent** is popular for clubbing. South of the shopping area is the **Centre Bell,** home of the popular hockey team **Montréal Canadiens,** and to the north,

the **Musée des Beaux-Arts de Montréal** sits among other stately Belle Époque buildings. The area is also home to Montréal's two **English-language universities,** McGill and Concordia. In cold weather, enjoy the shelter of the **Underground City.**

TOP SIGHTS

- Musée des Beaux-Arts de Montréal (page 69)

TOP RESTAURANTS

- Joe Beef (page 106)
- Kazu (page 107)

TOP NIGHTLIFE

- Dominion Square Tavern (page 135)

TOP SPORTS AND ACTIVITIES

- Montréal Canadiens (page 178)

TOP HOTELS

- Fairmont Queen Elizabeth (page 219)
- Ritz-Carlton (page 219)
- Hôtel Le Germain (page 220)

GETTING THERE AND AROUND

- Métro stations: Bonaventure, Gare Lucien-L'Allier, Georges-Vanier, Atwater, Guy-Concordia, Peel, McGill
- Métro lines: Orange, Green
- Major bus routes: 15, 129, 144, 165

CENTRE-VILLE WALK

TOTAL DISTANCE: 5 kilometers (3.1 miles)
WALKING TIME: 1 hour, 5 minutes

In busy downtown, there's tons to see, shop, and snack on. This tour ends at the Musée des Beaux-Arts de Montréal, which is closed on Monday but generally open 10am-5pm; it also heads along Ste-Catherine, a shopping strip—if you anticipate wanting to stop in at H&M or the Apple Store, you may want to allow yourself a little more time. Start the walk at **avenue McGill College and rue Maisonneuve W.**

MCGILL AND THE GOLDEN SQUARE MILE

1 Walk north on the east side of the street. About halfway up the block, look to your right: This sculpture that almost looks like it's made of butter is called *The Illuminated Crowd,* by Raymond Mason, which symbolizes the fragility of the human condition. Two blocks north, you'll reach the gates to **McGill University,** Montréal's oldest English-language university. Head through the gates and explore the campus by

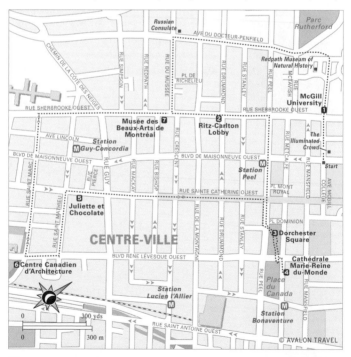

The Illuminated Crowd, by Raymond Mason

walking up toward the **Redpath Museum of Natural History.** At the top of the path, you'll see one of McGill's oldest structures, the **Arts Building:** The urn out front used to contain James McGill's ashes. Turn left and head west in front of the Redpath Museum; walk until you reach rue McTavish. Take a right, then a left onto avenue du Docteur-Penfield.

2 This street forms the northern edge of the Golden Square Mile, home to the early houses of wealthy Montréal merchants. Walk five

monument to Sir Wilfrid Laurier, the seventh prime minister of Canada, at Dorchester Square

blocks west and take a right onto avenue du Musée: Immediately on your right is the former home of Colonel Herbert Molson, who owned Molson brewery; it is now the **Russian consulate.** Head south one block, turn left onto rue Sherbrooke, and continue for almost two blocks. Enter the **Ritz-Carlton**'s Palm Lobby and have a snack or a drink at the Dom Perignon bar. When you're ready, reemerge onto Sherbrooke and head east four blocks to rue Peel.

3 Take a right at rue Peel and walk two and a half blocks to **Dorchester Square,** a bustling little spot of greenery featuring four stone monuments. Head to the kitty-corner of the park—boulevard René-Lévesque W. and rue Metcalfe—and look southwest.

ART, CHOCOLATE, AND RELIGIOUS HERITAGE

4 Across the street, you'll see the gorgeous **Cathédrale Marie-Reine-du-Monde.** Take a few external pictures or head inside to check it out. Next, walk back through Dorchester Square, retracing your steps until you reach rue Peel and rue Ste-Catherine W. Turn left.

5 In almost eight blocks (you may want to stop for some shopping), you'll reach **Juliette et Chocolat**—a great place to take a break and enjoy a brownie, a hot chocolate, or a crêpe. Exit and head west to rue St-Mathieu; take a left and head south one long block to boulevard René-Lévesque W.

6 Cross the street so you're on the southern sidewalk of boulevard René-Lévesque W. and head

Cathédrale Marie-Reine-du-Monde

Centre Canadien d'Architecture

Musée des Beaux-Arts de Montréal

one block west until you reach a strange park overlooking the highway: This is the unconventional sculpture garden of the **Centre Canadien d'Architecture,** designed by Melvin Charney. Charney was a professor and artist whose claims to fame include curating street art to be shown during the 1976 Olympics in Montréal.

7 Head back to the northeast corner of the park and cross the street onto rue St-Marc. Head six blocks north and then take a right onto rue Sherbrooke W. Head east about five blocks, until you reach **Musée des Beaux-Arts de Montréal,** a large art museum home to a solid permanent collection as well as impressive traveling exhibitions.

Centre-Ville Est   Map 3

The **main cultural district** known as the **Quartier des Spectacles** is home to the **Belgo Building,** an arts hub, and the **Place des Arts,** where you can catch the symphony, ballet, and opera and check out the **Musée d'Art Contemporain** next door. Video projections, lighting installations and outdoor art punctuate streets full of bars and venues. In summer, the streets are taken over by the **Festival International de Jazz de Montréal** and the **Just for Laughs** festival. South of the cultural district is **Chinatown,** where'll you find great dim sum, egg custard tarts, and pork buns.

TOP NIGHTLIFE

- Furco (page 136)
- Pullman (page 137)

TOP ARTS AND CULTURE

- Belgo Building (page 155)
- Agora de la Danse (page 156)
- Les Grands Ballets Canadiens de Montréal (page 156)

TOP SHOPS

- Henri Henri (page 195)
- Papeterie Nota Bene (page 196)

TOP HOTELS

- Hotel 10 Montréal (page 222)
- Hotel Zero1 (page 222)

GETTING THERE AND AROUND

- Métro stations: Place-des-Arts, St-Laurent
- Métro lines: Green
- Major bus routes: 55, 80, 747

CENTRE-VILLE EST WALK

TOTAL DISTANCE: 3.5 kilometers (2.2 miles)
WALKING TIME: 45 minutes

Centre-Ville Est is a comparably small neighborhood, but one that contains lots of art and culture. This walk is best taken on a Friday or a Saturday, when the greatest number of galleries are open at the Belgo Building—though you can also opt to sub in the Musée d'Art Contemporain on any day other than Monday.

ART WALK

1 Start your walk at **Pâtisserie Harmonie** in Chinatown—grab a pork bun or egg custard to go, and then head west on the pedestrian street rue de la Gauchetière. Go four blocks west and then take a right onto rue de Bleury.

2 Walk two blocks north and take a left. Half a block in, you'll reach the **Belgo Building,** home to two dozen of the city's best small art

galleries, which are mainly concentrated on the building's third, fourth, and fifth floors.

3 When you leave the Belgo, take a right and head east down Ste-Catherine to Jeanne-Mance. Take a left. You've reached the **Place des Arts,** a great spot to grab a coffee and people-watch by the fountain or check out public art.

4 Continue north to boulevard de Maisonneuve and take a right—you'll pass the Promenade des Artistes. Continue one block to rue St-Urbain and take a left. Head one block north to rue Sherbrooke, take a right, and go two blocks east to St-Laurent. On the southwest corner, you'll see **Hotel 10 Montréal,** a photo-worthy architectural gem whose poured-concrete exterior transports you, momentarily, to Paris.

5 Head almost one block south on the east side of St-Laurent—you'll soon come across **Eva B.** Montrealers are a chic but diverse bunch—those who favor thrift and vintage love this spot. When you're finished, walk a block and a half south on St-Laurent and take a left on boulevard de Maisonneuve.

CHINATOWN

6 Walk about two blocks east and turn right to walk down the pedestrian pathway just past Parc Paul-Dozois. Meet up with rue de Boisbriand and veer right. At the corner of avenue de l'Hôtel-de-Ville and rue Ste-Catherine, one block south, you'll find **Henri Henri,** Montréal's famous hat shop. Browse for a new cap!

7 Walk four blocks west until you reach boulevard St-Laurent, and hang a left. One block south on St-Laurent, at boulevard René-Lévesque, you'll see one of **Chinatown**'s famous gold and red *paifang* (arches). Snap a photo with one of the concrete lions.

8 Next, head to **Chez Bong,** just over a block south of the *paifang*. It's one of the best spots for a Korean lunch or dinner in the city (try the *jap chae* or bibimbap).

9 After you're sated, retrace your steps half a block: You've reached **Le Mal Nécessaire** (you'll know it by the glowing green pineapple), which is sort of a cross between a tiki bar and a speakeasy. Head downstairs and do yourself a favor by ordering a drink in a coconut.

Quartier Latin and the Village

Map 4

Centered around **UQÀM** (Université de Québec à Montréal), the Quartier Latin is home to many Francophone university students. The eastern edge of the Quartier des Spectacles, including the **Cinémathèque Québécoise,** is located within the neighborhood's boundaries. The city's main library, **La Grande Bibliothèque,** is a masterful piece of contemporary architecture, and lively and boisterous bars and restaurants can be found on **rue St-Denis.** To the east is the Village, Montréal's **gay neighborhood,** a mecca for late-night partying, karaoke bars, and antiques shopping. The heart of the Village, **rue Ste-Catherine Est,** turns into a festive pedestrian-only zone in summer.

TOP SIGHTS

- La Grande Bibliothèque (page 79)
- Rue Ste-Catherine Est (page 79)

TOP NIGHTLIFE

- Arcade MTL (page 138)

TOP ARTS AND CULTURE

- Cinémathèque Québécoise (page 158)

TOP HOTELS

- Sir Montcalm (page 224)

GETTING THERE AND AROUND

- Métro stations: Sherbrooke, Berri-UQÀM, Beaudry, Papineau
- Métro lines: Orange, Green
- Major bus routes: 24, 45, 125

Plateau Mont-Royal   Map 5

This **charming artistic enclave** features tree-lined streets, cozy neighborhood bistros, and colorful Victorian homes. The **best restaurants in the city** are located here, and the bars that line **the Main** have secured Montréal's place as a **nightlife destination,** while the bars, cafés, and boutiques on **rue St-Denis** are a quintessential part of the Francophone community. Bounded by parks and squares— Parc La Fontaine to the east, Carré Saint-Louis to the south, Parc Jeanne-Mance to the west—the Plateau is the **picnicking** capital of a picnic-friendly city.

TOP RESTAURANTS

- L'Express (page 116)
- Schwartz's (page 117)
- Chez José (page 118)
- Aux Vivres (page 120)

TOP NIGHTLIFE

- Big in Japan Bar (page 141)
- Casa del Popolo (page 143)

TOP SPORTS AND ACTIVITIES

- Fitz and Follwell (page 179)
- Les Alouettes de Montréal (page 180)

TOP SHOPS

- Kanuk (page 198)
- La Grande Ourse (page 199)
- Kitsch 'n' Swell (page 201)
- Arthur Quentin (page 201)
- Aux 33 Tours (page 201)

GETTING THERE AND AROUND

- Métro stations: Mont-Royal, Sherbrooke
- Métro lines: Orange
- Major bus routes: 55, 80, 129

Mile End and Petite-Italie Map 6

These formerly working-class neighborhoods are now home to hipsters, Hasidic Jews, Italian-Canadians whose roots go back generations, Montréal's younger queer contingent, artists, musicians, writers, and designers. This **vibrant cultural mix** is evident in the Italian cafés, Greek restaurants, and famous **bagel shops,** which mix well with the **chic stores** on avenue Laurier and rue Bernard in **Outremont,** an affluent residential borough. **Bars** hide out in warehouse spaces, **alleyways** offer a green respite, and a **rail trail,** great for biking, bisects the neighborhoods from east to west.

North of Mile End is Little Italy, with the farmers market **Marché Jean-Talon. Mile-Ex,** west of Little Italy and northwest of Mile End, is so named because it feels like an extension of Mile End. It's a **mixed industrial neighborhood** with factories, artist lofts, **hip restaurants,** and coffee shops.

TOP SIGHTS

- Marché Jean-Talon (page 83)

TOP RESTAURANTS

- Dinette Triple Crown (page 124)
- Café Falco (page 128)
- Boulangerie Guillaume (page 128)
- Kem CoBa (page 129)

TOP NIGHTLIFE

- Alexandraplatz Bar (page 144)
- Dieu du Ciel (page 144)
- Notre Dame des Quilles (page 145)

TOP ARTS AND CULTURE

- Never Apart (page 161)

TOP SHOPS

- Boutique Unicorn (page 203)
- Les Étoffes (page 203)
- Drawn & Quarterly (page 207)

GETTING THERE AND AROUND

- Métro stations: Laurier, Rosemont, Beaubien, Jean-Talon, de Castelnau, Fabre
- Métro lines: Orange, Blue
- Major bus routes: 50, 80, 161, 197

MILE END AND PETITE-ITALIE WALK

TOTAL DISTANCE: 4.8 kilometers (3 miles)
WALKING TIME: 1 hour

This walk is designed to give you a religion-infused introduction to
the Mile End and Little Italy, culturally eclectic neighborhoods full
of hot spots and hidden gems. You'll pass through a Hasidic neighborhood, visit some Italian food institutions, and check out two
churches and a temple. Feel free to stray from the route for a time

Parc Outremont

and take an alleyway or side street before you meet up with the route again. This walk is best started around 2pm or 3pm in the afternoon, depending on how much you want to dawdle—Alexandraplatz, the bar at the end, opens at 4pm. In the winter, or if you start the walk sooner, sub in 180g for Alexandraplatz—it's a hip little record store and coffee shop open until 6pm. Begin your walk in **Parc Outremont,** a leafy green oasis just outside the borders of the Mile End.

BAGELS AND COFFEE IN THE MILE END

1 Take a moment to enjoy the fountain and the view of the Victorian houses lining the park. Then head to the northeast end of the park and exit onto rue St-Viateur. Head east five and half blocks until you reach **St-Viateur Bagel Shop.** Step inside and inhale the lovely smell of the wood-burning oven. Grab a bagel or 12—sesame is great, but you may want to choose whatever just came warm out of the oven—and keep heading east on St-Viateur.

2 Three blocks later, cross the street and enter **Café Olimpico,** a bustling Italian coffee shop opened in the 1970s. Order an espresso or cappuccino and enjoy your bagel on the terrace (very good people-watching!).

3 Just a block farther east, pop into the **Church of Saint-Michael and Saint-Anthony** for a quick visit. Look upward and soak in the gorgeous frescos; take a self-guided tour if you'd like to learn more about the church's diverse cultural influences and historical congregations. Next, backtrack for a block and turn right onto rue Waverly, heading north for two long blocks until you hit Van Horne. Cross the street (looking west and admiring the artist studios now making their homes in old industrial buildings) and you'll see **Glen LeMesurier's Twilight Sculpture Garden.** This weird, ad-hoc place—Mesurier, the artist, added pieces secretly, and as he felt like it—epitomizes Montréal's punkish, DIY art approach. To your right, you'll see the **St. Lawrence Warehouse and water tower,** an iconic Mile End architectural anchor.

Glen LeMesurier's Twilight Sculpture Garden is a quirky hidden gem.

PLACES OF WORSHIP IN PETITE-ITALIE (AND A TOAST TO MILE-EX)

4 Cross the street and take the St-Viateur underpass. (This part of the walk is necessarily ugly—sorry. There's a shortcut across the still-working train tracks, but it's not legal to advise you to take it.) St-Urbain turns into Clark after the underpass. Take it for one block, turn right onto Beaubien for a block, and then go left onto St-Laurent for one block—you'll pass under the gateway to Petite-Italie. Take a right and walk five blocks east on St-Zotique. Then turn left for just under one block: You've reached the **Chiesa della Madonna della Difesa,** where you can see a pre-World War II fresco of Benito Mussolini.

5 After you leave the church, rejoin Henri-Julien and head just over two blocks north to **Marché Jean-Talon.** Wander through the market and sample what's on offer (**Fromagerie Hamel, Café Saint-Henri,** and **Chocolats Privilège** are particularly delicious). Exit on the west side of the market and make your way to Casgrain, where you'll cross and join Shamrock. Two blocks later, take a right onto St-Laurent, head one block north to

Café Saint-Henri, at Marché Jean-Talon, serves the best coffee in the city.

the tiny stamped-metal plaque marking the door of Alexandraplatz Bar

Jean-Talon, and then take a left. Continue two blocks west and take a left onto St-Urbain, where you'll see the **Cao Dei Temple of Montreal** almost immediately. Originally a synagogue, this house of worship is now a temple of the Cao Dei faith—a religion that follows many of the teachings of Buddhism.

6 Meander a block south on St-Urbain to Mozart, where you'll turn right. Take a left when you reach Marconi. Pass Beaumont on your left, and then look to your right: You'll see a parking lot. See a bunch of bikes locked up in the near distance? That's the side of **Alexandraplatz Bar,** a sort of hipster beer garden (less in spirit than in its open-air environs). Order a craft beer, a Bicicletta cocktail, or a ginger lime sake.

Greater Montréal

Map 7

Designed by Frederick Law Olmsted in the late 19th century, **Parc du Mont-Royal** is a haven for recreation and provides the best views of the city. Just past the northwest corner of the park, about a 45-minute walk from the Croix du Mont-Royal, lies **Saint Joseph's Oratory,** a striking pilgrimage site with amazing sunset views. To the east of Parc Mont-Royal are the buildings for the 1976 Olympics, including the breathtaking **Stade Olympique. Île Sainte-Hélène** and **Île Notre-Dame** make up **Parc Jean-Drapeau,** a great place for biking, outdoor concerts, and, if you're traveling with children, exploring the **Biosphère.**

TOP SIGHTS

- Parc du Mont-Royal (page 86)
- Saint Joseph's Oratory (page 87)
- Biosphère (page 91)
- Jardin Botanique (page 94)
- Stade Olympique (page 95)

TOP RESTAURANTS

- Tuck Shop (page 129)

TOP ARTS AND CULTURE

- Segal Centre for the Performing Arts (page 164)

TOP SPORTS AND ACTIVITIES

- Jean-Drapeau Aquatic Complex (page 183)
- Canadian Grand Prix (page 186)

GETTING THERE AND AROUND

- Métro stations: Côte-des-Neiges, Pie-IX, Jean-Drapeau
- Métro lines: Green, Blue, Yellow
- Major bus routes: 129, 165, 185, 767, 777

SIGHTS

Vieux-Montréal 58
Centre-Ville 69
Centre-Ville Est 76
Quartier Latin and the Village 78
Plateau Mont-Royal 81
Mile End and Petite-Italie 83
Greater Montréal 86

With its blend of old-world charm and contemporary, diverse cultures, Montréal is one of the most distinctive cities in North America. Old Montréal, Notre-Dame Basilica, the Olympic Stadium, Buckminster Fuller's Biosphère, and the side-streets and alleys of the Plateau and Mile End are all part of what makes the city unique. Home to both French- and English-speakers, it also has a large immigrant community; these cultures inspire and shape the various neighborhoods, and their history is reflected in the sights.

Buckminster Fuller's
Biosphère

Montréal may have the second-largest population in Canada, but geographically it is fairly small, making it ideal to navigate by foot, bike, or Métro (the subway system). Many of the sights, like the Musée d'Art Contemporain, Chinatown, and Basilique Notre-Dame-de-Montréal, are concentrated in the downtown and Vieux-Montréal areas, so even when temperatures drop, it's easy to walk from one to the next.

Spend a day wandering the historic Vieux-Montréal (Old Montréal), brush up on your Canadian history at Pointe-à-Callière Musée d'Archéologie et d'Histoire, then stroll along the waterfront and stop in at the Chapelle Notre-Dame-de-Bon-Secours. While you're there, take a peek at Hôtel de Ville (City Hall) and catch an evening light show at Notre-Dame Basilica. If you're not worn out yet, head to one of Vieux-Montréal's swanky restaurants for a cocktail at the bar.

In the western part of downtown you'll find the Centre Canadien

HIGHLIGHTS

✪ **MOST BEAUTIFUL CHURCH:** The iconic **Basilique Notre-Dame-de-Montréal** has a stunning interior (page 58).

✪ **BEST HISTORY MUSEUM:** Learn about Montréal's history at **Pointe-à-Callière Musée d'Archéologie et d'Histoire,** the site where the city was officially established (page 63).

✪ **BEST ART MUSEUM:** Composed of several linked buildings, the large **Musée des Beaux-Arts de Montréal** houses an impressive and varied permanent collection that makes for a perfect art history tour (page 69).

✪ **BEST STOP FOR KIDS: La Grande Bibliothèque** hosts historical exhibits and an *éspace jeunes*—a spot for youth to read, watch, play, and explore (page 79).

✪ **BEST STREET PARTY:** Closed to traffic for most of the summer, **rue Ste-Catherine Est** is the spot for festivals, food trucks, and fun all summer long (page 79).

✪ **BEST PUBLIC MARKET: Marché Jean-Talon** is a year-round farmers market that offers some of the most diverse and delicious food in the city (page 83).

✪ **BEST VIEWS: Parc du Mont-Royal** offers amazing vantage points to the city and tons of places to stop and admire the view (page 86).

✪ **MOST MIRACULOUS SIGHT:** Built to honor Brother André Bessette and his chosen saint, **Saint Joseph's Oratory** is a place of pilgrimage for those seeking healing (page 87).

✪ **BEST ARCHITECTURE:** Buckminster Fuller's geodesic dome, the **Biosphère,** hovers in the distance like a great architectural puzzle (page 91).

✪ **MOST SPECTACULAR BOTANICAL GARDEN:** Wander for hours through 20 different gardens at **Jardin Botanique** (page 94).

✪ **MOST ICONIC SIGHT:** Built for the 1976 Olympics, the **Stade Olympique** has since become an internationally recognized building (page 95).

d'Architecture; check out the post-modernist facade and then head over to see the latest exhibit at the Musée des Beaux-Arts de Montréal on rue Sherbrooke, which is famous for its stately buildings. From there it's an easy walk to the Musée McCord or the Redpath Museum of Natural History, or, if you're museumed out, you can take a tour of McGill University. Afterward, walk through the campus and head up avenue du Parc to Mont-Royal; it's only a few hundred steps up to a beautiful night view of the city.

Ride the Métro to Marché Jean-Talon and from there make your way through Little Italy to see a fresco of Italian dictator Benito Mussolini at the Chiesa della Madonna della Difesa. Continue south and grab a bagel and a coffee with the locals in Mile End, then keep heading south along St-Laurent to take in the history of one of the city's most famous streets.

Sights that are farther away, like the Stade Olympique (Olympic Stadium) and the Jardin Botanique (Botanical Gardens), are easily accessible by Métro. Plan to dedicate a day to exploring the area, especially if you have kids in tow, since the Biodôme (animals!) and Insectarium de Montréal (bugs!) are all found in the same Olympic grounds.

Marché Atwater, southwest of downtown, is best explored by bike—or cross-country skis in the winter—since it backs directly onto Lachine Canal. Make a morning out of it and head to rue Notre-Dame for breakfast and antiquing, then grab lunch from the market and follow the canal back downtown. Watch a Canadiens game at the Centre Bell or check out the local alt-weeklies to find a live show. Montréal may just be an island, but its varied sights offer something for everyone.

Vieux-Montréal

Map 1

Old Montréal is the city's historical center and remains one of its most charming, most Instagrammable neighborhoods. It's here that you'll find the Basilique Notre-Dame-de-Montréal and rue St-Paul, the oldest street in the city. As you stroll through the area, it's difficult not to swoon at the cobblestone streets, narrow, tin-roofed boutiques, and converted warehouses. All this history, however, means that when you buy anything here, whether it's a lunchtime snack or a drink at a bar, you're paying a slightly augmented fee for the ambience. If you're in search of a reasonably priced, filling lunch or dinner while

exploring, you may do best to hop over to Chinatown in search of some dumplings or pho before resuming your day in the Vieux-Port (Old Port).

TOP EXPERIENCE

✪ Basilique Notre-Dame-de-Montréal

Presiding over Place d'Armes, the Basilique Notre-Dame-de-Montréal is in the heart of Old Montréal. Here, thousands of fans lined the streets to celebrate Céline Dion's wedding and to pay their respects to the funeral processions of former prime minister Pierre Elliot Trudeau, hockey legend Maurice Richard, and, sadly, Dion's husband René Angelil. The basilica is not only the heart of historic Montréal—in many ways it represents the heart of the city.

As you approach the basilica you get a feel for its grandness; its bell towers rise high, and on the building's facade three statues look out over the growing metropolis: the Virgin Mary (representing Montréal), Saint John the Baptist (representing Québec), and Saint Joseph (representing Canada).

Completed in 1830, the Gothic Revival church, the first of its kind in Canada, is set back from the site of the original Notre-Dame parish church, a baroque-style chapel built by the Roman Catholic Sulpician Order in 1672. By 1800, the original chapel was too small to accommodate the population and plans were underway for the basilica. It was designed by James O'Donnell, an Irish-American

Protestant who eventually converted to Catholicism in order to be buried in the basilica's crypt.

Specially ordered and designed by Father Olivier Maurault to celebrate the church's centennial in 1929, the stained-glass windows are entirely unconventional. Depicting the religious and social life of the early Ville-Marie settlement, they show the city's strong ties to the Catholic religion. The deep blue and gold of the ceiling is both particularly striking and unusual. The basilica was viewed as too grandiose for such common events as weddings and funerals, so a second, smaller chapel, Notre-Dame du Sacré-Coeur, was completed in 1891—only to be destroyed by arson nearly 100 years later in 1978. The restoration that took place shortly after drew inspiration from original drawings, but the vault and altar were given a new, modern twist.

Basilique Notre-Dame-de-Montréal

LOOK UP: MONTRÉAL'S ARCHITECTURE

Old Montréal's historic buildings and areas from Expo 67 and the 1976 Olympics stand out as some of the best architecture in the city, but there's a lot of historical and modernist architecture worth a look, too. Beyond singular buildings, make sure to walk through the Plateau to appreciate its triplexes and winding staircases, a key and beloved feature of Montréal architecture.

- **Aldred Building:** Completed in 1931 in the art deco style, this stands as an ode to the architectural style that once dominated the cityscape (507 Place d'Armes).

- **Château Apartments:** Passing this aptly named 14-story apartment block gives you a glimpse into why this section of downtown was referred to as the "Golden Square Mile." Built in 1925, it was home to author Mordecai Richler until his death in 2001 (1321 rue Sherbrooke W.).

- **Gare Windsor:** Headquarters of the Canadian Pacific Railway, this Romanesque Revival building was completed in 1889, and you can still visit its old arrivals terminal (1100 ave. des Canadiens-de-Montréal).

- **Gibeau Orange Julep:** A massive orange just off the Decarie expressway, this restaurant is a Montréal iteration of Canada's obsession with oversized items; more than an architectural delight, it also serves orange milkshakes, hot dogs, and poutine (7700 blvd. Decarie).

- **La Grande Bibliothèque:** From the outside, this massive public library is an impressive wall of glass; from the inside, its incredibly high ceilings and suspended staircases make it even more breathtaking (475 blvd. de Maisonneuve E.).

- **Habitat 67:** Constructed as part of Expo 67, this architectural marvel is loosely based on the idea of a kibbutz; 158 interlocking concrete forms are the basis of the experimental housing complex—a must-see (2600 ave. Pierre-Dupuy).

- **The Linton:** The largest apartment of its kind when it was built in 1906-07, this Beaux-Arts building retains much of its charm and grandeur (1509 rue Sherbrooke W.).

- **Olympic Village:** A sort of flattened, doubled 1970s-style pyramid, this building, designed to house athletes during the 1976 Olympics, saw overwhelming cost overruns and led to fraud convictions for at least one of its architects (511 rue Sherbrooke Est).

- **Palais des Congrès:** Mario Saia's kaleidoscopic extension has put a colorful twist on what could have been another concrete slab (159 rue St-Antoine W.).

- **Saint Joseph's Oratory:** An imposing presence on the north side of the mountain, this is the largest church in Canada. Don't miss Brother Andre's chapel at the back of the oratory—its pressed-metal exterior gives way to a baby-blue interior lined with crutches and often smelling of lilies (3800, chemin Queen-Mary).

- **Sun Life Building:** This 24-story office building was an imposing figure when it was completed in 1931, and it continues to stand its ground as one of the most impressive sights on the Montréal skyline (1155 Metcalfe).

- **Tour de la Bourse:** Erected in 1964, this is the home of the Montréal stock exchange and an example of the international style (800 Place Victoria).

- **Université de Montréal:** The main building, designed by Ernest Cormier, was finished in 1943 and is situated on the northern slope of Mont-Royal (2900 blvd. Edouard-Monpetit).

- **Westmount Square:** Designed by Mies van der Rohe, this is one of the preeminent examples of international style in the city (1 Square Westmount).

Today, the basilica is a site for many high-profile events. Daily mass continues to be held in French, and a 20-minute tour (English and French) is free with entry. If you're interested in classical and religious music, the basilica plays host to concerts throughout the year.

MAP 1: 110 rue Notre-Dame W., 514/842-2925, www.basiliquenddm.org; 8am-4:30pm Mon.-Fri., 8am-4pm Sat., 12:30pm-4pm Sun.; tours daily on the hour and half hour 9am-4pm Mon.-Fri., 9am-4:30pm Sat., 12:30pm-3:30pm Sun.; $6 adults, $4 children, children 6 and under free

NEARBY:

- Head to the pedestrian-friendly Place d'Armes to take in some of the city's most historic architecture (page 61).
- Have some wood-fired pizza at Mangiafoco (page 102).
- Nab a reservation at popular Garde Manger and enjoy meaty French fare (page 104).
- Get an affordable beer or glass of wine at Le Philémon Bar (page 132).
- Sip a cocktail while enjoying the view at Terrasse Place d'Armes (page 133).
- Catch an English-language production at Centaur Theatre (page 152).

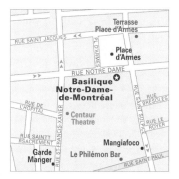

Place d'Armes

As early as 1720, citizens of the Ville-Marie settlement would gather on this site to watch military maneuvers on the Place d'Armes, a French name for the area where a city's defenders would congregate. After the Notre-Dame church was demolished and replaced by the basilica, Place d'Armes became a public square, the site of hay and wood markets and, later, of a Victorian garden and tramway hub.

The site's real significance, however, comes not so much from the spot itself as from what surrounds it. Located in the heart of historic Montréal, it's bordered on all sides by structures that define Montréal's diverse heritage. Directly to the right of Notre-Dame Basilica is the Séminaire de Saint-Sulpice, the city's oldest building. It was constructed in a U-shape by the Sulpician priests in 1684. The building's clock, built in 1701, is the oldest of its kind in North America, and the gardens are said to be among the oldest on the continent. It's still owned and run by the same church order that founded it, the Compagnie des Prêtres de Saint-Sulpice.

Erected in 1888, the New York Life building on the northeast corner of the square became the city's first skyscraper, a whole eight floors up and furnished with an elevator. Kitty-corner to New York Life, the Royal Trust Building and the Duluth Building (to the left of the basilica) are two early-20th-century skyscrapers. They represent a distinct architectural shift around the square, one that was cemented with the arrival of the art deco Aldred Building in 1931. A glass and steel structure, now known as the National Bank Tower, completed the square's architectural timeline in 1968. Directly in front of the National Bank

Tower, at its southern and eastern extremities, you'll find two sculptures—a caricature of an Englishman with an English bulldog, and a caricature of a French woman holding a poodle. The humans stick their noses up in the air and look away from each other, while the dogs just stare longingly, wanting to play.

The square features the de Maisonneuve monument depicting the founders of Montréal: Paul de Chomedey de Maisonneuve, Charles Lemoyne, Lambert Closse, Jeanne Mance, and an Iroquois warrior. The pedestrian-friendly square is surrounded by cobblestone streets and fitted with sprawling benches that are perfect for a rest.

MAP 1: Corner of rue St-Jacques W. and Côte-de-la-Place d'Armes

Quartier International

Linking Old Montréal and downtown, the Quartier International is the result of one of the city's most extensive redevelopment projects. Inaugurated in 2004, the centerpiece of the area is Place Jean Paul-Riopelle, a fountain and public square flanked on one side by the Palais des Congrès (Montréal's convention center). Riopelle, who died in 2002, was a seminal Québécois artist and member of the Automatistes movement. His work was influenced by surrealism and is similar to abstract-expressionism. The fountain at the center of the square incorporates his 1969 sculpture *La Joute,* a tribute to the hockey heroes of his youth.

Square Victoria features a statue of Queen Victoria (very English) facing, across the street, Montréal's only open-air Métro entrance, an art nouveau gift from Paris. On the eastern edge of the square, you'll find the Centre du Commerce Mondial—fairly nondescript, except for the fact that it houses a chunk of the fallen Berlin wall.

MAP 1: Bordered by blvd. René-Lévesque to the north, rue Notre-Dame to the south, blvd. Robert Bourassa to the west, and rue St-Pierre to the east

Maison de Mère d'Youville

Saint Marguerite d'Youville was born Marguerite Dufrost de Lajemmerais in 1701 in Varennes, Québec. Shortly after marrying, she was widowed, and she then founded The Sisters of Charity of Montréal, also called the Grey Nuns.

The Maison de Mère d'Youville, known as the Grey Nuns' Hospital, was built in 1765 and tended to by The Sisters of Charity. This example of early French-Canadian architecture was constructed to last, even if it did happen to be located in a floodplain. Inside, you can visit the inner courtyard, as well as a small exhibit dedicated to Saint Marguerite d'Youville. Outside, take a look at the old chapel ruins—and then look down at the ground, where the footprint of the chapel has been demarcated with cobblestones.

MAP 1: 138 St-Pierre St., www.sgm.qc.ca; 9am-5pm daily; free

Youville Stables

This three-winged building with a courtyard in its center was originally built in 1826 by Jean Bouthillier, a potash inspector. Owned by the Grey Nuns, the building was constructed for use as a warehouse (it was never meant to house horses, as its name implies). The nuns sold the building in the 1960s. Now home to psychology practices and a restaurant, the courtyard features a few wooden benches—a great place for a moment of quiet, surrounded by Montréal greystone.

MAP 1: 300 Place Youville

✪ Pointe-à-Callière Musée d'Archéologie et d'Histoire

It was on this site on May 17, 1642, that Montréal (originally known as Ville-Marie) was established. Founding members of the colony—Paul de Chomedey de Maisonneuve, Jeanne Mance, and Father Vimont—were on hand to mark the occasion at what was then a small point of land that jutted out into the St-Lawrence and St-Pierre Rivers. By 1688 the site was home to Louis Hector de Callière, third governor of Montréal and the museum's namesake. When the settlement began to build fortifications in 1716, the point fell outside of those boundaries, making it an invaluable archaeological site. Dedicated to the various people—indigenous, French, and English—that make up the city's past, Pointe-à-Callière is Canada's only sizable archaeology museum and the quintessential museum on Montréal.

Opened in 1992 as part of the celebrations for the city's 350th anniversary, the museum has distinctly contemporary architecture, standing out in the historic port and disguising the rich history that sits within and beneath its walls. Don't be fooled by the modern reception area: Artifacts and archaeological finds confront you at every turn throughout the six distinct buildings, which include Montréal's first custom house (Ancienne-Douane Building) and first electrically operated wastewater pumping system (Youville Pumping Station). The most fascinating exhibit, however, remains the museum's own archaeological site.

Below the ground level of the main Éperon building, you'll discover traces of Montréal's first Catholic cemetery. Montréal's oldest collector sewer is also on display here: Completed in 1838, it canalized the St-Pierre River underground into one of the first sewer pipes, one that remained in use until 1989.

The number of yearly visitors to the museum has hit the 350,000 mark, so you can almost always expect to find a crowd, especially during the high season (June-Aug.).

MAP 1: 350 Place Royale, 514/872-9150, www.pacmusee.qc.ca; 10am-5pm Tues.-Fri., 11am-5pm Sat.-Sun.; tours 12:30pm, 1:30pm, 2:30pm Mon.-Fri. and 12:30pm, 1:30pm Sat.-Sun.; $20 adults, $18 seniors, $13 students 18-30, $10 students 13-17, $8 children

Vieux-Port

For centuries after the first explorers arrived, Montréal was the final destination of hundreds of thousands of immigrants who made their way for the first time onto Canadian shores. Until 1948, when a series of locks finally connected the St-Lawrence with the Great Lakes, Montréal was the disembarkation point for both trans-Atlantic ships and trains from all over North America. Between 1896 and 1930, Montréal was the major

Vieux-Port

SIGHTS

VIEUX-MONTRÉAL

distribution point for merchandise both into and out of the country. At the west end of the Vieux-Port, Silo #5, which closed for good in 1995, is one of its grandest monuments.

The sheds, grain elevators, and quays that line the port are relics from its heyday, but a major revamp in the 1980s transformed the port into a booming recreation spot. Converted warehouses have turned into quay-side restaurants, cafés, and boutiques. You'll find a labyrinth in shed 16, the Montréal Science Center and IMAX on King Edward Pier, and Cirque du Soleil one pier over.

Rue de la Commune and a thin park are the only things separating Vieux-Montréal from the Vieux-Port. The park runs the entire length of the Old Port Promenade, offering tourists and locals an ideal spot to relax and catch a cool breeze off the water. You can dock your boat in the many marinas, take a boat cruise on the St-Lawrence, or rent a pedal boat for a trip around Bonsecours Basin.

MAP 1: Old Port Promenade, between rue McGill and rue Amherst

Rue St-Paul

Winding and narrow, rue St-Paul is the oldest street in Montréal. Designed by priest, historian, and urban planner François Dollier de Casson, creator of the majority of the street layout of what is now Vieux-Montréal, rue St-Paul was originally paved in 1672 under the direction of city founder Paul de Chomedey de Maisonneuve, whose home, conveniently enough, was also on the same road. Linking Fort Ville-Marie with the Hôtel Dieu (the hospital), the settlement's main thoroughfare remained a vital part of the historic center until the 20th century.

Many of the buildings that line the street date back to the 19th century. They now house some of the city's most modern and contemporary stores and restaurants. Between June and September, rue St-Paul is partially closed to traffic.

MAP 1: Between rue McGill and rue Berri

Marché Bonsecours

When the city of Montréal decided to build a structure to house an indoor market in the 19th century, the site on which Marché Bonsecours now sits was an ideal choice. Since the early days of Nouvelle France, many prominent Montrealers had made their home there, including François Bigot, last intendant of Nouvelle France, and John Molson, founder of the popular Canadian brewery. Charles Dickens and his group of amateur actors performed on this very spot during its incarnation as the Théâtre Royal, whose ruins are buried underneath the existing structure's foundations.

Designed by architect William Footner in 1844, the building was inaugurated with its first public market in January 1847 and remained the city's main agricultural market for over a century. With its tin-plated dome and neoclassical style, it's considered one of the 10 major achievements in the history of Canadian architecture.

From 1852 to 1878 it served as city hall and as such demanded specialized banquet and dining halls to accommodate the social demands of the city. Today, the spirit of a public market remains, with exclusive boutiques selling everything from authentic Canadian crafts to jewelry, leather, and hand-blown glass, all designed and made in Québec. Cafés and restaurants line the facade of the building, and it still hosts events.

MAP 1: 350 rue St-Paul E., 514/872-7730, www.marchebonsecours.qc.ca; 10am-6pm daily; free

Chapelle Notre-Dame-de-Bon-Secours and the Musée Marguerite Bourgeoys

Marguerite Bourgeoys was 33 years old when she arrived in Montréal in 1653, recruited by Paul de Chomedey de Maisonneuve, founder of Montréal, to teach school and religion classes. By 1658, she had traded her skills teaching, mending, and sewing in return for a stone chapel, the first of its kind in the colonial outpost and the only one dedicated to the Virgin Mary, Our Lady of Perpetual Help. It's over the ruins of this original church that the existing Chapelle Notre-Dame-de-Bon-Secours was built in 1771.

With its soft pastels and trompe l'oeil effect, the arched vault of the chapel, an 1886 addition, gives the space a distinctly feminine feel, one that's juxtaposed by a number of ex-votos (a votive offering to a saint) of ships that hang above the pews. Dating back to 1872, the ex-votos give thanks to Mary for a safe passage, a tradition that continues to this day as every September 21 descendants of those who sailed on these ships return to the chapel to pay thanks.

From the chapel, enter the Marguerite Bourgeoys Museum to explore further. Climb the 69 steps up to the tower and the remaining 23 to the belvedere for two great views of the Vieux-Port. Then head down to the crypt. Once used as a school rec room, it now houses treasures that the museum uncovered while excavating the original site of the chapel, which was discovered in 1996.

Elsewhere in the museum, other slices of history illuminate Bourgeoys's life. She is famous for founding the Sisters of the Congregation of Notre Dame, and Bourgeoys's order still exists today. The nuns have made a charming history of her life in doll form. Tours of varied length and focus are available, designed to suit visitors' interests and time constraints. Even if you don't visit the museum, make sure to head around the south, or port, side of the chapel to get a great view of Our Lady, haloed and looking out over her harbor—she was memorialized in Leonard Cohen's song "Suzanne."

MAP 1: 400 rue St-Paul E., 514/282-8670, www.marguerite-bourgeoys.com; 11am-4pm Tues.-Sun. Mar.-Apr., 10am-6pm Tues.-Sun. May-Canadian Thanksgiving, 11am-4pm Tues.-Sun. Canadian Thanksgiving-mid-Jan.; $12 adults, $7 seniors, $6 students, $5 children

Maison Papineau

Builders first broke ground on this house in 1785. In the early 19th century, it was home to Louis-Joseph Papineau, the leader of the Patriote movement, the aim of which was to fight English control of Montréal, restoring French as the language of the legislature and France as the head of government.

The building, typical of the era in which it was built, has a pitched roof with two rows of dormer windows. Recognized as a national cultural heritage site, Maison Papineau is currently occupied by private tenants—though Parks Canada now owns it, and the eventual idea, after the building's tenants have chosen to move on, is to open it to the public.

MAP 1: 440 rue de Bonsecours

Place Jacques-Cartier

Lined with restaurants, inns, and cafés and populated by street artists and

GUIDED CITY TOURS

A great way to discover the city is through a tour that mixes social and historical contexts.

L'Autre Montréal (3680 Jeanne-Mance #331, 514/521-7802, www.autremontreal.com; $15-25 adults) offers guided tours with a focus on history, architecture, urban planning, and sociology and gives you a great vision of the city's unique culture and community. Some of the more interesting options include a tour of Montréal's back alleys and a look at the various immigrant communities.

Cité Mémoire (www.montrealenhistoires.com) offers a downloadable app (designed to work at night, with video projections) as well as a nighttime 90-minute guided visit of Old Montréal. The idea behind the project is to animate the city's history by developing fictional stories based on its architecture, lore, and characters.

Les Fantômes du Vieux-Montréal (360 rue St-François-Xavier, 514/844-4021, www.fantommontreal.com; May-Oct.; $22 adults, $19 students, $13 children) is not for the easily scared. On this ghost tour of Old Montréal, guides in period costume tell you all about the hangings, sorcery, tortures, and spooky sightings that make up the city's past. They also have specialized tours come Halloween.

Fitz and Folwell (115 ave. Mont-Royal W., 514/840-0739, www.fitzandfollwell.co; $55-115), which offers both bike and snowshoe tours come winter, offers three distinct summer walking tours—two food tours (south and north circuits) and one Old Montréal discovery tour. All tours include lunch and/or snacks and range in price, so reserve and budget accordingly.

Guidatour (360 rue St-François-Xavier #400, 514/844-4021, www.guidatour.qc.ca; May-Oct.; $18 adults, $16 students, $9 children) runs walking tours of Old Montréal, the Quartier des Spectacles, the International District, Chinatown, Little Italy, and more.

Héritage Montréal (100 rue Sherbrooke E., 514/286-2662, www.heritagemontreal. qc.ca; Sat.-Sun. May-Oct.; cost varies) is a nonprofit organization that takes visitors on tours exploring the architectural, social, or historical evolution of the city's neighborhoods. Departure points vary depending on the week and the tour, and reservations are recommended.

Free Montréal Tours (5369 blvd. St-Laurent, 514/613-1940, www.freemontrealtours. com; Mon.-Thurs.; free) runs free two-hour walking tours of Old Montréal. Check their website for details, and book ahead to ensure a spot.

The **Hop-On Hop-Off Double Decker Tour** (800/461-1223, www.grayline.com/ montreal; $55 adults, $35 children) is a great way to see a ton of the city—sights in Old Montréal, the Old Port, Chinatown, downtown, the Quartier de Spectacles, and even Saint Joseph's Oratory. This tour does not include snacks or beverages, so bring your own.

seasonal fruit stalls, Place Jacques-Cartier, sloping down toward the St-Lawrence River, remains true to its roots as a natural meeting place. An archaeological dig in 1991 uncovered remains of a First Nations campsite in this exact spot. By the early 1800s, it had become the site of the New Marketplace, surrounded by wooden stalls, inns, and stores. With the creation of Marché Bonsecours, the "New Marketplace" was no longer needed, but it remained the market's outdoor extension and started its transformation into a center for hotels and restaurants.

At the north end of the square you'll find Nelson's Column, erected in 1809. It was the second monument to be built in the city—the first was a bust of King George III, which stood for five years before it was mutilated in 1775—and the first monument in the British Empire to be dedicated to the admiral famous for defeating Napoleon during the Seven Years' War. As in Nelson's Column in London's Trafalgar Square (which was built 31 years after its Montréal counterpart), Nelson faces away from the banks of the river, allegedly to combat his seasickness. The monument was highly controversial, and in 1930 Montréal's Francophone population erected a statue in honor

Nelson's column, at the top of Place Jacques-Cartier

of French naval officer Jean Vauquelin, who fought against the British before being subsequently captured and released. Waging an eternal personal battle, their statues now stare at each other from across rue Notre-Dame.

MAP 1: Between rue Notre-Dame E., rue de la Commune E., and Place Jacques-Cartier

Musée du Château Ramezay

When the governor of Montréal, Claude de Ramezay, started work on his house in 1704, Montréal was a mere colonial outpost, home to approximately 1,500 inhabitants and barely 200 buildings. He chose a plot of land at the edge of the fortified city (it now sits across the street from city hall). De Ramezay, obsessed with having a home that matched his perceived importance, paid for the construction of the property out of his own pocket. The house has gone through many incarnations in its 300-year history, including head offices for the French West India Company (1745-1764), the base for American Revolutionaries including Benjamin Franklin (1775-1776), and a university (1884-1889).

Little of the original structure remains inside the house, though, so if you're expecting a trip back in time,

you'll be a tad disappointed. Though multimedia displays take you through the building's evolution, the real focus is on the history and progression of the city itself. One of the highlights includes the Salle de Nantes, a dark-wood-paneled room from 1725 that is thought to have been carved by Germain Boffrand, chief architect to Louis XIV and Louis XV. The room was part of the French pavilion at the 1967 Expo and was donated to the museum shortly after. Of the entire house, the basement feels the most preserved, with vaulted ceilings and authentic fireplaces that still smell of freshly burned wood. It's also where the life of Montréal's 18th-century inhabitants is depicted, with re-creations of one-room homes, mannequins in traditional dress, examples of farming material, and a room dedicated to the furniture found in homes during the period. From May to October, the museum also boasts an outdoor café that looks out over the house's gardens and that is, in a genius move, catered by the renowned restaurant Le Club Chasse et Pêche.

MAP 1: 280 rue Notre-Dame E., 514/861-3708, www.chateauramezay. qc.ca; 9:30am-6pm daily June-Canadian Thanksgiving, 10am-4:30pm Tues.-Sun. Canadian Thanksgiving-May; $11 adults, $10 seniors, $8.75 students, $5.75 children

Hôtel de Ville

Hôtel de Ville (City Hall) overlooks the port and takes its place alongside other important administrative buildings, including the provincial courts. Its green copper roof and stoic facade lend it an air of old-world nostalgia, but even after 140 years it retains a youthful vitality as the city's political hub. Housing the offices of the mayor and city councillors, it remains the site of countless protests and speeches. In 1967, French president Charles de Gaulle stood on the balcony and shouted to a frenzied crowd, "*Vive le Québec libre!*" (Long live a free Québec!), further fanning the flames of bilingual unrest and leaving an indelible mark on the province's conscience.

Built in 1872-1878, the original building was gutted by a fire in 1922. With only the exterior wall left standing, architect Louis Parant rebuilt from the inside out, reinforcing the building with a self-supporting steel structure from behind the ruins. Taking inspiration from the city hall of Tours in France, he remodeled the roof in a Beaux-Arts style, swapping its slate-tiled roof for the existing copper one.

Inside, you're greeted by the Hall of Honour, an open space full of marble and gold embellishments. Just off the hall is the council room, adorned with five stained-glass windows by John Patrick O'Shea. Installed in 1926, they depict the fundamental aspects of the city: religion, agriculture, the port, commerce, and finance. Open to visitors year-round, the hall plays host to a number of exhibits. Free, hour-long tours are offered throughout the day, though certain areas, such as the protocol room and the mayor's office, are off-limits.

Behind city hall is a wide swath of land known as the Champ-de-Mars. Used for military maneuvers and parades, it was once the site of Montréal's fortifications, which protected the city from invasion. Buried under a municipal parking lot for most of the last century, it was returned to its former

Habitat 67, designed by Moshe Safdie

incarnation in the 1980s, and remnants of the original city walls are now integrated into the landscape of the park.

MAP 1: 275 rue Notre-Dame E., 514/872-0077, www.ville.montreal.qc.ca; 8:30am-5pm Mon.-Fri.; tours 10am-4pm daily; free

Habitat 67

Architect Moshe Safdie was only 24 years old when his master's thesis for McGill University was chosen to be constructed as part of Expo 67. An architectural marvel, Habitat 67 sits on a thin peninsula in the St-Lawrence River just south of the Vieux-Port. Loosely based on the idea of a kibbutz, 158 interlocking concrete forms are the basis of the experimental housing complex, which was supposed to reflect cities of the future, a time when the population would outgrow urban space. Contrary to the original aim of affordable housing, it's now one of the most sought-after addresses in Montréal. This is a private residence, so tours are not possible, but you can get a pretty great view from the pier in the Old Port.

MAP 1: 2600 ave. Pierre-Dupuy, www. habitat67.com; free

Centre-Ville

Map 2

✪ Musée des Beaux-Arts de Montréal

Framed in white marble, Jean-Noël Desmarais Pavilion at the Musée des Beaux-Arts stands out among the limestone and columns of rue Sherbrooke's Golden Square Mile. Designed by Moshe Safdie of Expo 67 fame, and inaugurated in 1991, the modern building stands in contrast to the museum's original Beaux-Arts structure by William Sutherland Maxwell, which sits across the street.

In 1860 a group of art-loving Montrealers convened to create the Art Association of Montréal, with the aim of spreading knowledge of the arts with exhibitions and art classes.

Little was done, however, until 1879, when the association finally got its first building, at the time the only one in the country specifically designed to exhibit and house works of art. By 1909, the association was financially stable enough to live up to its aspirations and it built the Beaux-Arts building, which still exists today.

The pavilions (which are connected through underground walkways), with their distinct designs, speak volumes about the museum's collections and exhibitions. The modern Jean-Noël Desmarais Pavilion is filled with light, the space open and the floors a beautiful black slate. The majority of the museum's permanent collection is found here and includes religious pieces, works by First Nations peoples,

outdoor sculpture garden at the Musée des Beaux-Arts de Montréal

and contemporary pieces by young Canadian and international artists. Spread throughout the building's four floors, the collection takes you on a perfectly balanced art-history tour.

The Beaux-Arts building houses many of the temporary exhibits. With its sweeping marble staircase, maple woodwork, and Victorian light fixtures, it's the perfect environment for viewing exhibits like Tiffany Glass, Van Dongen, and the groundbreaking Yves Saint-Laurent show.

The converted Erskine and American United Church, which opened in late 2010, is the museum's Canadian pavilion, and the building itself is a National Historic Site. After 5pm on Wednesdays admission drops to $11.50.

MAP 2: 1380 rue Sherbrooke W., 514/285-2000, www.mbam.qc.ca; 10am-5pm Tues. and Thurs.-Sat., 10am-9pm Wed.; $23 adults, $15 ages 13-30, children 12 and under free

NEARBY:

- Sample Lebanese cuisine at Boustan—and be sure to try the secret sauce (page 108).
- Recharge with a serious cup of coffee at Café Myriade (page 110).
- Check out Inuit and First Nations art at La Guilde (page 153).

- Browse designer goods at Holt Renfrew, a luxury department store (page 192).
- Purchase something from high-end department store La Maison Ogilvy, and you'll also take home one of their signature tartan bags or boxes (page 192).
- Peruse the creations from Canadian designer Marie Saint Pierre in her eponymous store (page 193).

Grand Séminaire de Montréal

Barricaded by two stone turrets and a high stone wall, the Grand Séminaire de Montréal is well hidden from the busy stretch of Sherbrooke. Built in 1840 as a place to train priests, it is the second seminary to be built in the city—the first is next door to Notre-Dame Basilica—and stands on the same site as the Fort de la Montagne.

Constructed in 1685, the purpose of the fort was to help ward off attacks from the native population; today only the turrets and fieldstone walls remain and are some of the oldest structures in Montréal. Along with the towers, the priests built a series of canals that run along Mont-Royal. The first of these was built in 1675 and remains in use today. The seminary also houses a Romanesque chapel, which boasts hand-carved oak stalls and is one of the best examples of the Beaux-Arts style in the city.

Now the home of a private college, it continues to educate future priests.

MAP 2: 2065 rue Sherbrooke W., 514/935-1162, www.gsdm.qc.ca; check website for guided tour details; free

Centre Canadien d'Architecture

Unique in aim and design, the Centre Canadien d'Architecture (CCA; Canadian Centre for Architecture) is the only cultural institution of its kind in Canada. Founded in 1979 by architect Phyllis Lambert, the aim of the institution is to expand the public's awareness of the role architecture plays in our lives, and to act as a research center for scholars.

Lambert, who convinced her father, Samuel Bronfman, to hire Mies van de Rohe to design the famous Seagram's building in New York, later studied architecture at the Illinois Institute of Technology before going on to design Montréal's Saidye Bronfman Centre for the Arts, which is named after her mother. It was Lambert's vast collection of architectural drawings, photographs, and books that became the founding objects of the center's research collection.

Designing the museum to incorporate a Victorian mansion, the 1872 Shaughnessy House, Lambert stayed true to her vision of modern architecture, one that focused on both preservation and progress. Built 1985-1989 by Montréal-born Peter Rose (Lambert was a consulting architect), the CCA is a perfect example of postmodern architecture. The new wings of the center attach themselves seamlessly to the existing structure, and elements such as the color of limestone, the bay windows, and the windows' placement mimic those of the mansion, preserving and simultaneously mixing the two distinct styles.

From the entrance, however, none of this is visible. Instead you have a view of a thoroughly modern building; it's not until you're inside and past the entrance stairs that you really understand the extent that these two visions have been fused. The fully restored Victorian Devencore Conservatory is one of the museum's highlights and offers a glimpse of the home's past glory.

Each year, the center houses exhibits that examine the effects of modern living on our surroundings, our environment, and ourselves. It also hosts interesting talks as well as family-friendly workshops.

Across the busy boulevard René-Lévesque and just above the highway, you'll find the institute's unconventional garden. Designed by artist and architect Melvin Charney, its use of concrete and unique statues is a comment on the city's architectural and cultural history, and most importantly it offers a great view of the CCA's postmodern facade.

MAP 2: 1920 rue Baile, 514/939-7026, www.cca.qc.ca; 11am-6pm Wed. and Fri., 11am-9pm Thurs., 11am-5pm Sat.-Sun.; $10 adults, $7 seniors, students and children free

McGill University

Built on the southern slope of Mont-Royal on ground that was once owned by James McGill, McGill University is one of the oldest universities in Canada, predating confederation by 46 years.

Born in Glasgow, McGill immigrated to Canada, where he became a successful merchant who also, unfortunately, owned four or five personal slaves—a history that McGill has sometimes struggled to reconcile. Upon his death in 1813, McGill donated his Burnside summer estate to the Royal Institution for the Advancement of Learning, and by 1829, classes were being held in his former home. McGill University granted its first medical degree in 1833; the medical faculty remained the school's only faculty until the addition of the faculty of arts in 1843.

Between 1880 and 1920 the university experienced a huge amount of expansion, thanks in large part

McGill University Arts Building

own self-guided tour on the website. Visitors can pass through the campus any time of day, but the Welcome Center, which offers tours, is only open 9am-4pm Monday-Friday.

MAP 2: 845 rue Sherbrooke W., www.mcgill.ca; free

Musée McCord

Even before David Ross McCord began trolling the country for historical artifacts in 1878, his family, who had been collecting since their arrival in Canada around 1760, had done a good deal of the work for him. By 1921, when the McCord Museum was established, his collection contained 15,000 objects.

Since then the collection has grown, and the museum now has nearly 1.5 million objects, all of which are housed in a classic Arts and Crafts building adjacent to McGill University. Designed by Percy Erskine Nobbs in the early 20th century, it has been the museum's home since 1971. The facade leads to a modern interior—in fact the original structure is almost completely unrecognizable once you pass through the foyer.

Anyone who enjoys looking at stuff will enjoy the McCord. The ephemera from bygone eras allows the viewer to understand the cultural and social aspects of the city's life. And much of its life is represented here, from crossbows, helmets, and armor from the explorer days to the Montréal of the 1920s through the 1940s, when American Prohibition turned it into a swinging hot spot—the cocktail napkins and menus are here to prove it.

Interactive multimedia features can be found throughout the museum and offer a unique way to look at the exhibitions. At lunchtime from Tuesday to Friday, the Café Bistro serves up delicious European fare. Admission

to the financial backing of the city's wealthiest men—William Molson (beer), Sir Peter Redpath (sugar), Lord Strathcona (Hudson's Bay Company), and Sir William Macdonald (tobacco). Much of the architecture from this time still exists today, including the Arts Building, which sits as the focal point of the university's campus as you're looking north from rue Sherbrooke. The Roddick Gates, which so nicely frame the entrance, are themselves a gift, donated by Lady Amy Redpath Roddick in memory of her doctor husband in 1924.

The campus with its sprawling tree-lined lawns is an ideal place to take a rest from downtown, and it also offers an ideal shortcut to the Plateau Mont-Royal, which is reached by wandering through the McGill Ghetto, a nice quiet neighborhood full of gorgeous townhouses and university students.

Historical tours covering the rise and development of the university and campus are provided to the general public but require an email request (welcome@mcgill.ca) at least a week in advance, or you can download your

THE UNDERGROUND CITY

Montréal's Underground City, the RÉSO, has turned from legendary to legend. Though it is true that below the city's streets and skyscrapers there are 32 kilometers of underground tunnels to explore, it is not true that there are entire apartment buildings that exist exclusively within this subterranean matrix, or that the city's inhabitants never have to go outdoors.

In 1957, urbanist Vincent Ponte was the first to envision this underground metropolis when his underground pedestrian walkways were included in developer William Zeckendorf's plans for Place Ville-Marie. At the time, the plan only covered seven acres, but Harvard-educated Ponte's self-sufficient pedestrian complex would soon lead to his nickname: the "multilevel man." What started as a solution to cover old railway tracks soon became an integral part of the city's urban planning. Since Ville-Marie opened in 1962, the subterranean city has grown to include 120 exterior access points and over 12 square kilometers.

Universities, banks, museums, Métro stations, condos, and hotels are all accessible through the underground complexes, but its most important and obvious function is as a huge underground mall. Linking three major shopping tunnels, it is the bloodline of winter commerce, allowing consumers to browse and buy in a temperature-controlled environment. Exploring the many tunnels and passageways can be interesting—especially when you realize just how far you can go—but the main draw of Montréal's underworld is that it allows you to avoid the bitter, freezing cold. In fact, for many Montrealers figuring out how to get from point A to point B without going outside has become something of an art.

to permanent exhibitions is free Wednesdays after 5pm.

MAP 2: 690 rue Sherbrooke W., 514/398-7100, www.mccord-museum.qc.ca; 10am-6pm Tues. and Thurs.-Fri., 10am-9pm Wed., 10am-5pm Sat.-Sun.; $20 adults, $17 seniors, $14 students 18-30, $13 students 13-17, children free

the Boer War Memorial in Dorchester Square

Dorchester Square

Inaugurated in 1878, Dorchester Square became a central meeting point and a prestigious address for a number of large companies. The largest was Sun Life Insurance, whose Sun Life Building continues to preside over the east side of the square. Completed in 1931, after 24 years of on-and-off construction, its architectural presence is rivaled only by the Dominion Square Building at the north end. Designed as both a shopping arcade and an office tower, Dominion Square Building opened in 1930 and now houses the offices of the *Montréal Gazette*, the city's English-language newspaper and one of Canada's oldest.

The square's monuments honor the Boer War, Canadian prime minister Sir Wilfrid Laurier, and Scottish poet Robert Burns. Another is a stone reproduction of the Lion of Belfort.

Though it is now surrounded by some of the more interesting architecture in the downtown area, between 1799 and 1854 the square was the site of a Catholic cemetery, an ideal burial spot at the end of the 18th century when it would have been situated in open countryside. And it is the final resting place of many victims of the

1832 cholera epidemic. During renovations, archaeologists examined the remains before exhuming the bodies and moving them to Notre-Dame-des-Neiges Cemetery on Mont-Royal. To honor those who were laid to rest in this spot, 60 crosses have been installed in the brickwork of the walkways.

Across the street you'll find Place du Canada, inaugurated at the same time. It too was the site of cemeteries until the late 1800s. Today, it's one of a few green spaces in the downtown core and home of the Macdonald Monument, honoring Canada's first prime minister, John A. Macdonald. In 1995, 100,000 Canadian citizens gathered here as part of the Unity Rally to protest Québec's referendum and persuade the province to vote against separating from the rest of Canada.

MAP 2: Blvd. René-Lévesque W. and rue Peel

Cathédrale Marie-Reine-du-Monde

After Saint James Cathedral burnt down in 1852, Ignace Bourget, the first bishop of Montréal, decided he wanted to re-create a smaller version of Rome's Saint Peter's Basilica. After drawing up the plans, architect Victor Bourgeau quit, saying he could not replicate Saint Peter's on a smaller scale. The project went ahead without him (though he subsequently returned), and the first cornerstone for the existing church was laid in 1870. It opened to the public in 1894 and became a cathedral in 1919. Bourget got his wish, though he wasn't around to see it; the sizable church is a perfect replica, right down to the red copper baldachin that was hand-carved in Rome.

Unsurprisingly, the cathedral appears older than its years; behind the facade, the limestone on the outer part of the nave of the church looks distinctly aged. In a delightfully modern move, however, the wrought iron and glass front doors open automatically, sweeping out and ushering you into the narrow narthex. Columns with gilded crowns and the otherwise modest ceiling moldings inlayed with gold support the high, arched ceilings of the nave. Hues of soft green and blush decorate the cathedral, giving it a gentle and slightly feminine touch. Rising 80 meters in height, the cupola is surrounded with stained-glass windows. Similar to Notre-Dame Basilica, the cathedral's main works of art are dedicated to the city's devout Catholics and include depictions of Marguerite Bourgeoys teaching native children and Grey Nuns founder Marguerite d'Youville aiding the sick. Bourget's remains are buried beneath one of the pillars, but there is a mortuary chapel in his honor; the floor and walls are covered in Italian marble, and his tomb takes center stage.

Like St. Peter's, the cathedral has 13 statues that adorn the facade, but breaking with tradition they do not represent Jesus and the 12 apostles. Instead they represent the patron saints of parishes that offered them to the diocese and include Saint Hyacinthe, Saint Francis of Assisi, and Saint John the Baptist.

MAP 2: 1085 rue de la Cathédrale, 514/866-1661, www. cathedralecatholiquedemontreal.org; 7am-7pm Mon.-Fri., 7:30am-7pm Sat.-Sun.; free

Place Ville-Marie

One of the most controversial projects the city has ever encountered, Place Ville-Marie was part of Mayor Jean Drapeau's plan to create a new, modern metropolis. Designed by I. M. Pei (who would go on to become one of the most recognized architects of the 20th century) and Henry N. Cobb, the international-style tower was completed in 1962 and was originally the head offices of the Royal Bank. Its construction marked the move of the city's financial district from Old Montréal's rue St-Jacques to downtown. Rising 47 stories, the four cross-shaped towers made up the world's largest and most complex office building—indeed, the complex itself has 52 different postal codes.

Place Ville-Marie

Though no longer the only skyscraper in the downtown core, it remains one of the most recognizable. Inside, over 40 stores and boutiques connect the tower to the railway station and Métro. This is the starting point of the mythical and complicated Underground City. Since it allows access to the Métro, the concourse is open later than the shops.

At the top of Place Ville-Marie, you'll find the 360-degree Au Sommet observation deck, which offers unprecedented views of the city (very good Instagram fodder). It's also home to a restaurant, boutique and café, and cultural exhibits.

MAP 2: 1 Place Ville-Marie, 514/866-6666, www.placevillemarie.com; shops 9:30am-6pm Mon.-Wed., 9:30am-9pm Thurs.-Fri., 9:30am-5pm Sat., noon-5pm Sun.; free (entrance fee to Au Sommet extra)

Centre Bell

Even those who know little about Montréal have probably heard of the city's passionate relationship with their beloved Montréal Canadiens. Partially hidden on the southern edge of downtown, the enormous red-brick and concrete Centre Bell (Bell Centre) building is not the most inspired of sports arenas—at least not from the outside. Home of the Canadiens since 1996, it replaced the history-laden Montréal Forum (now a movie theater) and seats 21,273 fans, alternately olé-ing and booing.

Originally called the Molson Centre—the arena changed hands and names in 2002, though Molson still owns the team—it is the largest hockey arena in North America. The interior is dedicated to Canadiens history and features team photographs and bronze busts of many players. History is present outside the arena in Centennial Plaza with statues honoring the team's four greatest players: Howie Morenz, Guy Lafleur, Maurice "Rocket" Richard, and Jean Béliveau.

When not packing the house with hockey fans, the center hosts stars of a different kind; entertainers like U2, Céline Dion, Lady Gaga, and Justin Timberlake have performed here.

MAP 2: 1909 ave. des Canadiens-de-Montréal, 514/932-2582, www.centrebell.ca; noon-6pm Mon.-Sat. hockey season, 10am-6pm Mon.-Fri. summer, tours daily; $20 adults, $12 seniors and children

Musée d'Art Contemporain

Established in 1964 at the height of Québec's Quiet Revolution and abstract art boom, the Musée d'Art Contemporain (MAC) had various homes before settling into its own modern building in 1992. Part of the Place des Arts, Canada's only cultural complex devoted to both visual and performing arts, the MAC's subtle concrete facade is the perfect foil for the columns and glass of Salle Wilfrid Pelletier next door.

Entering through the unassuming door, you're bathed in light from a domed skylight around which the museum's restaurant is placed. With over 7,000 works in the permanent collection, including pieces by some of the biggest names in Québec art—like Paul-Émile Borduas, Claude Tousignant, and Jean-Paul Riopelle—it also hosts some of the most exciting, interesting, and boundary-pushing exhibits by Canadian and international artists, such as Marcel Dzama and Bruce Nauman. Grab a drink, catch a live up-and-coming local act, and see the latest exhibit on the first Friday of every month at Friday Nocturnes. Admission is half price after 5pm on Wednesdays.

MAP 3: 185 rue Ste-Catherine W., 514/847-6226, www.macm.org; 11am-6pm Tues. and Thurs.-Fri., 11am-9pm Wed., 10am-6pm Sat.-Sun.; $15 adults, $12 seniors, $10 students 18 and over, $5 youth 13-17, free 12 and under

Place des Arts

Taking up an entire block of the downtown core, Place des Arts is a multivenue arts center and the home of four of the city's largest production companies—Orchestre Symphonique de Montréal, the Opéra de Montréal, Les Grands Ballets Canadiens de Montréal, and the Jean-Duceppe theater company. The Musée d'Art Contemporain is right next door. The site has undergone major reconstruction in order to include a sixth concert hall, La Maison Symphonique de Montréal, dedicated to musical performances by the Montréal Symphony, and to remodel the Grand Foyer, which greets visitors to the complex.

crowd beginning to gather for Les FrancoFolies, one of many festivals held at the Place des Arts

Place des Arts opened in September 1963, just four years shy of Expo 67, at the height of Montréal's construction and architectural boom. The inauguration concert featured Canadian conductor Wilfrid Pelletier and Indian conductor Zubin Mehta.

Running along rue Ste-Catherine, the Esplanade is the site of many of the city's outdoor cultural happenings, including the Festival International de Jazz de Montréal's main stage, free movie screenings during the Montréal World Film Festival, and

With a history that dates to American Prohibition, the **Quartier des Spectacles** (www. quartierdesspectacles.com) used to be the city's red light district—until Mayor Jean Drapeau bulldozed its gambling spots and favorite houses of sin. The Quartier des Spectacles has been revived and today it has over 80 cultural venues, from performance halls to art galleries. The area stretches between rue City Councillors, boulevard St-Laurent, rue Sherbrooke, and boulevard René-Lévesque.

The **Place des Arts** complex is the centerpiece of the Quartier des Spectacles, and the area encompasses many venues, like the **SAT (Société des Arts Technologiques)**, as well as sleek arts hub **Le 2-22**, with galleries, radio stations, arts associations, and a bookstore. The district is also the center of attention during festival season. From **Les FrancoFolies de Montréal** in early June to **Just for Laughs** in mid-July, this square kilometer of the city has been the hub for shows and performances for over a century.

a host of other free summer festival events. Indeed, the block in front of the Esplanade is virtually shut down to regular traffic and even bikes from June to September. The Esplanade's stairs are a choice spot for a meeting point or to simply sit and people-watch, and the fountain at the top is often surrounded by office workers and visitors cooling off, their feet dangling in the basin.

MAP 3: 175 rue Ste-Catherine W., 514/842-2112, http://placedesarts.com; hours vary

Chinatown

Dating back to the 1860s, Montréal's Chinatown is far smaller than many of those found in other parts of North America, but, despite its size, it remains a vital and culturally important neighborhood. The center of traditional festivals and holidays for several of the city's Asian communities, it also has its own Chinese hospital and community center.

An exquisite red *paifang* (arch) on the corner of St-Laurent and René-Lévesque marks the entrance to Chinatown, which borders downtown and the Quartier International and sits just north of Vieux-Montréal. Originally a residential neighborhood, it is now a commercial district with restaurants, bakeries, stores, and

traditional crafts—this is the place to pick up Japanese and Chinese china—many of which are concentrated on rue de la Gauchetière. In the summertime this pedestrian-only street fills up with outdoor stalls.

exterior of a shop on rue de la Gauchetière in Chinatown

Though Chinatown was originally established by Chinese immigrants who came to Canada to work on the railway and in the mines (even during Canada's anti-Chinese head tax era), the area later also became home to Vietnamese-Chinese refugees, many of them French-speaking because Vietnam was under French colonial rule until 1941. As a result, there are now many Vietnamese restaurants throughout the area. It's a great place to pick up some of the best banh mi and pho in the city. (A smaller Vietnamese community has also popped up farther north, near rue Jean-Talon and rue St-Denis.)

A Holiday Inn at the edge of Chinatown designed in the style of a pagoda is a slightly kitschy but nonetheless sweet homage to the community and culture.

MAP 3: Bordered by blvd. René-Lévesque, ave. Viger, blvd. St-Laurent, and rue Jeanne-Mance

Quartier Latin and the Village

Map 4

UQÀM

Architect and urban designer Dimitri Dimakopoulous was one of the most sought-after architects in the country, having designed award-winning buildings from coast to coast. In 1974, along with his ACORP associates, he undertook the project to create an urban campus for the Université du Québec à Montréal (commonly referred to as UQÀM). It subsequently won the city's Prix d'Excellence award in Architecture for that year.

Situated in the Quartier Latin, the campus Dimakopoulous created is an urban one, seamlessly integrated into the city's existing architecture. As such, the school features two former churches that have been incorporated into the design—this can be seen as

La Grande Bibliothèque

an embodiment of the "quiet revolution" of secularization that took place in Québec in the 1960s. Vastly different in styles and even materials, the churches stand out among the modern brick structures that Dimakopoulous added. The unique campus architecture can be seen and explored on Ste-Catherine and St-Denis.

Established in 1969, UQÀM is the product of a merger between the fine-arts-focused École des Beaux-Arts de Montréal and the classics college Collège Sainte-Marie. It continues to be the preeminent Francophone arts university in the province, with special schools in fashion, feminist studies, and environmental studies.

MAP 4: Rue Ste-Catherine E., 514/987-3000, www.uqam.ca; free

✪ La Grande Bibliothèque

One of the most interesting buildings in the city, La Grande Bibliothèque (the National Library, also known as BAnQ) was completed in 2005. Set on the former site of the Palais de Commerce, a serious concrete eyesore, the library invigorated the area and gave it a much-needed boost of elegance.

It was designed by the architectural team of Patkau from Vancouver and Croft-Pelletier/Gilles Guité from Québec City; the two architectural studios beat out 36 other international firms to win the contract. The 6,000 U-shaped plates of frosted glass create the glacial green color seen on the outside of the building, which is reminiscent of the glacial ice found in the far north. It was the first time this type of glass was used in North America.

Light filters into the great hall, which is supported by three concrete pillars and runs the length of the structure. From the great hall you enter into the working area of the library, featuring sleek, glass elevators and elongated stairs that are the centerpiece of the building. Yellow birch wood, one of Québec's official emblems, is used throughout to separate areas and diffuse sound.

With close to three million annual users, it's one of the most popular libraries in the French-speaking world. Ninety-minute tours are available free of charge, but check before you go since the schedule changes monthly. Self-guided tours are also available for download from the library's website.

MAP 4: 475 blvd. de Maisonneuve E., 514/873-1100, www.banq.qc.ca; 10am-10pm Tues.-Fri., 10am-6pm Sat.-Sun.; free

✪ Rue Ste-Catherine Est

This is the heart of one of the largest gay villages in North America. People of all sexual orientations flock to the bars and clubs along Ste-Catherine Est, making it one of the liveliest nightlife spots in the city.

Occupying what was once a poor, working-class neighborhood, the Village first started to grow during the late 1960s and early '70s, with the opening of many gay-owned and gay-friendly businesses. At the time, however, it was kept rather discreet, and in the lead-up to Expo 67 and the 1976 Olympic Games, Mayor Jean Drapeau conducted raids on bathhouses and saunas, further relegating the gay community to the margins—or at least out of the public eye.

By the early 1980s, though, things started to change, with gay bars opening up and drawing a new generation of LGBTQ folks to the neighborhood. The historic heart of queer culture in the city (other areas in the Plateau, the Mile End, and Saint-Henri have emerged as well), its importance is still recognized by all levels of government.

Between June and September Ste-Catherine is closed to vehicular traffic and decorated with a "roof" of thousands of bright spheres strung above it. This pedestrian-only strip hosts festivals, food trucks, and lots of other fun activities.

MAP 4: Between rue Berri and ave. Papineau

Rue Amherst

In the heart of the Village this delightful street—second only to rue Ste-Catherine—is an excellent place to browse and grab a bite. The stunning finds in the antiques stores here span from the 1930s to the 1960s. Fans of midcentury modern design, beware; there's an assortment of it here and at some of the best prices you'll find on the East Coast. Boutique Spoutnik tops the lists for best kitsch, but for old rotary phones, stackable cafeteria chairs, and Expo 67 memorabilia—the perfect gift for any fan of design—Antiquités Seconde Chance is unrivaled.

Alongside the antiques are stores featuring up-and-coming designers; Québécois designer Dinh Bà's store can be found on this strip. Follow the street all the way south toward the port and check out the 200-year-old walls of the Molson Brewery, which look sturdy enough to defend an entire city, let alone a beer factory.

MAP 4: Between blvd. de Maisonneuve E. and rue Ontario E.

Église St-Pierre-Apôtre

With its flying buttresses, stained-glass windows, and open nave, this neo-Gothic Catholic church constructed in 1851 is one of the most traditional in the city. Inspired by Brooklyn's Holy Trinity, it was the first church to be designed by Victor Bourgeau—who would go on to become one of the most prolific church architects in Québec. It is still considered his masterpiece.

Église St-Pierre-Apôtre

Bourgeau's materials were unusual; he used stone throughout, and even the pillars are made of limestone. Step inside, however, and you realize just how nontraditional this church really is. Decorated with rainbow banners, it's known for its gay-friendly Sunday services as well as its overall support of the gay community. Set alight in July 1996, a flame burns permanently in the Chapel of Hope, the first chapel in the world dedicated to the memory of victims of AIDS.

MAP 4: 1201 rue de la Visitation, 514/524-3791, www.diocesemontreal.org; 10:30am-4pm Mon.-Fri., noon-5pm Sat., 9:30am-4pm Sun.; free

Avenue du Mont-Royal

By the end of the 1800s, avenue du Mont-Royal was a bustling thoroughfare linking two smaller villages, De Lorimier and Coteau-Saint-Louis. Once marked with only nine homes, including two dairies, a cart-maker, and a cobbler, it's now the main, and hippest, artery of the Plateau, lined with trendy bars, restaurants, and boutiques.

Made famous by novelist and playwright Michel Tremblay and his depiction of the area as a mostly working-class French-Canadian neighborhood, it has maintained a Francophone population but is no longer as working-class as it once was. Residents today are sometimes chided for being "bobo," a sort of French hipster—simultaneously bourgeois and bohemian. This population, however, likely has a lot to do with the impeccably preserved traditional houses and the area's numerous great restaurants.

Between rue Rivard and rue Berri is the Mont-Royal Métro station, a great spot for people-watching.

MAP 5: Between ave. du Parc and ave. Papineau

The Main

Affectionately called the Main by locals, boulevard St-Laurent was first cobbled together from streets that were established by both the French and the British regimes. When Montréal was still a fortified city, the Main was located inside the walls; it was only with the advent of the Grand Porte St-Laurent, which provided a single route out of the walled city, that it became known as St-Laurent road. In 1792, it became the official division between east and west—a division it still marks today—and the street was renamed as St-Laurent du Main.

Though it is the physical division of east and west, historically, it has also divided the city by language—French to the east, English to the west. Over 11 kilometers long, it runs nearly the entire width of the island of Montréal, which is 14 kilometers from north to south, and it is to this long street that immigrants from outside France and Britain have flocked (caught between the "two solitudes" of French and English, these folks wished to seek out neutral ground).

From the mid-1900s onward the Main became the home of the Jewish community, which migrated north from what is now Chinatown. As trends in immigration changed, Italians, Portuguese, Poles, Greeks, Chinese, Latin Americans, and most recently Africans and people from the Caribbean have settled on the strip, influencing its vibrant, *méli-mélo* (mishmash) culture.

Once the center of industry, with factories and retail businesses stretching along the Main from one end to the other, this National Historic Site is now best known for its restaurants, bars, indie shops, and live music venues.

MAP 5: Blvd. St-Laurent between blvd. René-Lévesque and blvd. St-Joseph

Carré Saint-Louis

This old-world-reminiscent square links boulevard St-Laurent and rue St-Denis and is bordered by colorful, grandiose 19th-century houses.

During that period, the area attracted wealthy French-Canadian families, whose legacy remains today—the majority of the Second Empire rowhouses retain their charm even 200 years later.

Artists were also drawn here, including important French-Canadian poet Émile Nelligan, who was influenced by French Symbolists like Charles Baudelaire and Paul Verlaine. More recently, novelist Heather O'Neill's fiction was inspired by the time she spent sipping cherry colas here as a child with her father. (Keep an eye out in the southeastern corner of the park for a poem, written in yellow text over green, by Michel Bujold.)

Great for people-watching, the square has a nice fountain and pathways lined with trees and park benches. In the summer, the kiosk on the west side of the square sells ice cream and other refreshments, making it a great place to stop and take in the scenery.

MAP 5: Bordered by rue St-Denis, ave. Laval, and rue du Square Saint-Louis

Rue St-Denis

A few blocks east of the Main is rue St-Denis, a largely Francophone street that traverses virtually the whole north-south length of the island. It is filled with restaurants, independent boutiques, and cafés—with some semi-residential areas—and the vibe is a bit more French-Canadian, though the boundaries blur year after year.

Though only a few blocks apart, the architectural contrast between boulevard St-Laurent and rue St-Denis is vast. Where St-Laurent's buildings have been informed by immigration and industry, St-Denis's remain relatively unchanged and stereotypically Montréal. Limestone buildings with steep, outdoor staircases and peaked roofs make St-Denis feel much more residential than St-Laurent.

This street is the center for performing arts in the French-language community. You'll find some of the biggest theaters here, including Théâtre du Rideau Vert and, farther north, the renowned National Theatre School of Canada. Farther south, the street is chock-a-block with bars and clubs, many of them student-centered.

MAP 5: Between rue Sherbrooke and ave. du Mont-Royal

In the summer, the kiosk at Carré Saint-Louis serves snacks and drinks.

Parc La Fontaine

An oasis in the middle of the Plateau, Parc La Fontaine's 40 hectares have everything from tennis to *pétanque* courts, outdoor skating to baseball fields. Bordering the Village in the south and directly in the middle of the *quartier,* the park draws people from all over the city no matter the season.

The houses that border the park might look fancy, but most of them, and indeed most of the buildings in the city, don't have gardens, so Montrealers flock, or more precisely, bike to the green space to picnic with

Parc La Fontaine

friends, catch a performance at the outdoor theater, or jog along its shaded paths.

It was originally named Logan Park and located on an old farm that was perhaps used as military training grounds, but by 1909 the city had turned the land into a public park that looked not unlike the one that exists today. Contrary to popular belief, the park was not named after the fountain in the center of the lake—it takes its moniker from Louis-Hippolyte Lafontaine, a politician and the first prime minister of the United Province of Canada (a precursor to today's nation), whose writings contributed to the founding of the confederation.

MAP 5: Rue Rachel E. and ave. du Parc La Fontaine; 6am-10pm daily; free

Mile End and Petite-Italie   Map 6

✪ Marché Jean-Talon

Constructed in the 1930s as a make-work project during the Depression (Marché Atwater was, too), Jean-Talon is as busy and central nowadays as it was then. Open seven days a week and nearly 365 days a year, this market exceeds expectations, especially for North American visitors—it has a decidedly French approach to the necessity of good food. With permanent stores surrounding the market (among them a fishmonger, two bakeries, two cheese shops, a wine store, several butchers, and numerous specialty shops), you need not shop elsewhere.

It's an ideal place to browse in the summer; you can snack as you pass by the various stands, tasting many of the fruits and vegetables before you

flowers at the Marché Jean-Talon

buy. If you're looking to sample locally grown produce, pick up Québec sausage or cheese, buy some maple syrup or freshly roasted corn on the cob, or eat a crêpe (La Crêperie du Marché has the absolute best in the city), this is the place to do it. Come winter the market moves indoors but stays just as busy. At the start of sugaring-off season in early March the crowds are out in droves drinking in the sunshine, listening to street performers, and happily eating maple syrup off a stick. MAP 6: 7070 ave. Henri Julien, www. marche-jean-talon.com; 7am-6pm Mon.-Wed. and Sat., 7am-8pm Thurs.-Fri., 7am-5pm Sun.; free

NEARBY:

- Try one of the 41 types of pizza offered at popular Pizzeria Napoletana (page 125).
- Dine on Syrian and Armenian dishes at Le Petit Alep (page 125).
- Sip one of 13 house-made draught beers at Harricana (page 145).
- If you're visiting the market on a Saturday, stop by Never Apart

afterward to see contemporary art that spans genres (page 161).

- Buy a bag of coffee beans from Café Saint-Henri as a gift for your favorite caffeine addict (page 209).
- Purchase freshly made chocolate treats at Chocolats Privilège (page 209).
- Browse the collection of teas at Maison de Thè Camellia Sinensis (page 210).

Chiesa della Madonna della Difesa

Built in 1919 by Italian immigrants from Molise, in the southern part of Italy, the Madonna della Difesa (Our Lady of Protection) commemorates a miracle said to have occurred in Casacalenda, Italy, at the end of the 19th century. The creation of the church, built in a Romanesque style and in the shape of a Greek cross, was instrumental in drawing the Italian community northwest, from where they'd originally settled in what's now known as Centre-Sud.

The design of the church, a designated National Historic Site of Canada, was based on drawings by artist Guido Nincheri, who decorated churches across North America. It was built by architect R. Montbirant. Inside, the church is decorated with

MONTRÉAL'S GREEN ALLEYWAYS

Hidden behind Montréal's major (and minor) streets there exists a warren of alleyways. Some have been designated "green alleyways" *(ruelles vertes),* which means pedestrian traffic only; others are, less formally, spots where neighborhood children play and people grow flowers and vegetables in planters. Alleyways are a great way to get a vantage point on how locals live. Keep an eye out, too, for tin-clad structures (converted or not)—they used to house coal and other household necessities in the 19th and early 20th centuries, and some of them have been converted to house additions, garages, and art spaces.

Some of the best neighborhoods to seek out alleyways are Plateau Mont-Royal, Mile End, and Petite-Italie. Most alleyways run north-south, so you can find them easily if you're traveling along rue St-Denis or boulevard St-Laurent between rue Jean-Talon and boulevard Rosemont.

one of Montréal's many leafy, inviting alleyways

Nincheri's frescoes, one of which features a pre-World War II Benito Mussolini signing the Lateran Treaty, signed in 1929 by the Holy See and the Italian government, which recognized the sovereignty of the Holy See in Vatican City.

Next door to the church is Dante Park, dedicated to the 14th-century *Divine Comedy* poet. It features a bocce court, where you'll often find groups of older Italian men playing from noon to midnight.

MAP 6: 6800 ave. Henri Julien, 514/277-6522; 9:30am-12:30pm Tues.-Fri., masses in English, French, and Italian on Sun.

Church of Saint-Michael and Saint-Anthony

The most prominent landmark in Mile End, this Byzantine-style Roman Catholic church stands out thanks to its unique architecture. Inspired by Istanbul's Hagia Sophia (though now a mosque, it was originally a Greek Orthodox basilica), architect Aristide Beaugrand-Champagne integrated

many different styles, including Roman and Gothic elements, in the design and topped it off with a dome and a minaret-style tower typical of Islamic mosques.

Steps lead up to the front door, and inside the dome is decorated with a Guido Nincheri fresco depicting Saint-Michael watching the fall of the angels.

Built in 1915 for the large Irish Catholic population, it was originally called Saint-Michael's; by the mid-1960s, however, the Mile End's Polish population had grown so large that it merged with the existing congregation and Saint-Anthony was added to the name to mark this change. Today, the church is mainly frequented by the area's Polish, Italian, and Greek communities, and services are given in a number of languages. Standing on the corner of St-Urbain and St-Viateur, it's commonly, though incorrectly, called St-Viateur Church by the locals.

MAP 6: 5580 rue St-Urbain, 514/277-3300; 10am-6pm daily, services in English and Polish; free

MONT-ROYAL

✪ Parc du Mont-Royal

Montréal's namesake and an integral part of city life, Mont-Royal rises out of the heart of the metropolis. The first European to climb Mont-Royal was French explorer Jacques Cartier, who climbed it with the help of the Hochelaga First Nations tribe in 1535. When writing about it to the king of France, he referred to it as Mount Royal and the name stuck. Though it was often used as a spot for recreation, it wasn't until 1876, after a mass culling of trees for firewood outraged citizens, that the area was designated a park.

Consisting of 200 hectares, and 234 meters tall at its highest point, the park was designed by famous American landscape architect Frederick Law Olmsted, an integral figure in the development of the U.S. national park system who also designed New York's Central Park.

From the late 1880s to 1920, the Mount Royal Funicular Railway carried sightseers to the top. What was once the site of the old track is now a popular lookout spot—**Belvédère Camillien-Houde.** Known as "Lovers Lookout," this place is a popular stop for couples, who like to canoodle here once the sun sets. Looking out east over the city, you'll see both Olympic Stadium and the oil refineries in Anjou.

the Sunday Tam-Tam at Parc du Mont-Royal

Crisscrossed by trails, the mountain is frequented by runners, bikers, dog-walkers, and, in winter, cross-country skiers and snowshoers. It's also a popular sledding place. The Sunday Tam-Tam is a tradition that started in the late 1970s with an African drumming workshop that is still going strong. In the summer, the public congregates weekly at the base of the Sir George-Étienne Cartier statue, near avenue du Parc and Duluth, to drum, dance, and generally indulge their inner hippie. To explore more of what the park has to offer before your visit, head to the website, where an interactive map and downloadable podcasts guide your trip planning and park discovery.

MAP 7: Via voie Camillien-Houde (from east) or via rue Remembrance (from west), foot access along ave. du Parc, 514/843-8240, www.lemontroyal.qc.ca; 6am-11pm daily; free

NEARBY:

- Visit the Chalet du Mont-Royal, which is bedecked with paintings that trace the city's history (page 89).
- Check out the Croix du Mont-Royal, a massive steel cross that's illuminated at night (page 89).
- Pay your respects at Cimetière Mont-Royal, the final resting spot

of many of the city's Anglophone founders (page 89).
- Skate your heart out at Lac aux Castors, one of the city's most popular ice rinks (page 183).

✪ Saint Joseph's Oratory

Set into the Westmount summit—one of the three peaks of Mont-Royal—this Roman Catholic minor basilica, the largest church in North America, can be seen from various points in the city, though it stands out the most when you catch it from the window of an airplane. It was built by Brother André Bessette, who attributed his healing powers to Saint Joseph.

Frail all his life, and wanting to honor Saint Joseph, Brother André began building a small chapel in 1905. It was soon too small for the number of visitors that came, so they started work on a second, larger chapel, which was completed in 1917, and today it is still part of the basilica and is known as the Crypt. Somehow, though, the Crypt was not enough, and in 1924,

Saint Joseph's Oratory

LA COEUR DE FRÈRE ANDRÉ
(THE HEART OF BROTHER ANDRÉ)

Brother André Bessette, who was sainted in 2010, performed miracles on the sick in Montréal. He died after helping to found and build Saint Joseph's Oratory as a lay brother of the Congregation of the Holy Cross. His body rests in a tomb in the oratory, and his heart has mostly spent its time preserved in a reliquary in the oratory—except for a brief period in 1973-1974 when it was stolen. Its return was brokered by a moderately shady criminal attorney, who claimed that it arrived in his office with a note on its origins.

work on the basilica was officially underway. It was completed over 40 years later in 1967—30 years after Brother André's death.

Built in the Italian Renaissance style, its dome was modeled on the Duomo in Florence. There are 233 steps from the gates to the doors of Saint Joseph's Oratory; shuttles are available for those who are unable to make the journey themselves, while pilgrims take the steps on their knees. As you enter at crypt level you'll find the Votive Chapel, a hallway linking the crypt church and the basilica's upper levels where visitors may light one of 10,000 candles and take in the ex-votos left by previous pilgrims. The Crypt Church itself features low, arched ceilings and a statue of Joseph instead of a cross over the altar. Above, the basilica is a stark, late-1960s architectural gem, including a tracker action grand organ crafted by Rudolf von Beckerath.

Out back you'll find Oratory Gardens (open May to October), with oversized Stations of the Cross and a lush green surrounding. Brother André's press-metal chapel is still on the premises. Open to the public, it contains plaques and prayers for healing; one wall is lined with crutches, and it often smells like the lilies left by visitors and church members. In 1910 the chapel underwent renovations, and a room was added on top that would become Brother André's living quarters; they are today as he left them.

The oratory hosts musical and cultural events; check the calendar for details. Ninety-minute guided tours are offered in several languages; call for times. If possible, time your visit so you catch a view both of and from the oratory at sunset. There is a snack bar in the Main Gift Shop building.

MAP 7: 3800 chemin Queen Mary, 514/733-8211, www.saint-joseph.org; 7am-8:30pm daily; tours 10am and 2pm daily June-Aug., 10am and 2pm Sat.-Sun. Sept.-Oct.; by donation

NEARBY:

- Visit **Cimetière Notre-Dame-des-Neiges,** the largest cemetery in Canada (page 90).
- Spend a few hours at the **Montréal Holocaust Memorial Museum** and take in the moving exhibits (page 163).
- Catch an English-language productions at **Segal Centre for the Performing Arts** (page 164).

Chalet du Mont-Royal

Sitting on the top of Mont-Royal and looking out over downtown, this structure was a make-work project during the Depression. Commissioned by then-mayor Camillien Houde, the chalet was inaugurated in 1932 and is decorated with paintings tracing the history of the city. The impressive artworks, along with the chalet's spacious interior and exposed wood beams, make it look more like a vast dining hall than a mountaintop chalet. Reward your climb to the top with a cold water or popsicle from one of the vendors who hang around out front (the chalet is only equipped with vending machines). Before you head back outside, look up: The chalet's wooden beams are decorated with distinctive midsize squirrel sculptures.

Just in front is the Belvedere Kondiaronk, named after a Huron chief who signed the Great Peace Treaty. It is the biggest lookout on the mountain, with sweeping views of downtown and beyond. On a clear day, you can see parts of Old Montréal, the bridges that traverse the St-Lawrence, and the mountains southeast of the city, including Mont-Saint-Bruno and Mont-Saint-Grégoire.

MAP 7: 1196 voie Camillien-Houde, 514/872-3911; 8am-8pm daily; free

Croix du Mont-Royal

On the eastern side of the mountain in Parc du Mont-Royal you'll find a massive steel cross. At night, illuminated, it acts as a way-finding beacon. If the city's laissez-faire cultural attitude allowed you to forget its Catholic roots, this giant monument acts as a pretty good reminder.

In December 1642, the city, then Ville-Marie, a small, fortified settlement on the banks of the St-Lawrence, experienced what could've been a disastrous flood. To ward off disaster, founder Paul de Chomedey de Maisonneuve and others prayed to the Virgin Mary, pleading with her to make it stop and promising to erect a cross in her honor if she intervened. Divine or not, the flood receded and the settlement was saved. Keeping his word, de Maisonneuve carried a large wooden cross from the settlement all the way to Mont-Royal, where it was erected on January 6, 1643—perhaps closer to what is now rue Sherbrooke rather than the top of the mountain, but impressive for the time period.

In 1924, Sulpician priest Pierre Dupaigne decided to re-create the cross; the Société Saint-Jean Baptiste installed the new cross, assuming responsibility for its upkeep before giving it to the city in 1929. Today, the cross is illuminated in LED lights—usually lit in white, it changes color for events such as the death of a pope, Saint-Jean-Baptiste Day (Québec's national holiday), and even AIDS awareness. Every March, the lights on the cross are turned off for Earth Hour.

Rising 251 meters above sea level, the cross is made of 26 tons of steel and is visible from 80 kilometers away.

MAP 7: East side of Parc du Mont-Royal

Cimetière Mont-Royal

One of the first rural cemeteries in North America, Mont-Royal Cemetery was incorporated in 1847. Though the first burial took place here in 1852, two years before the opening of its Catholic counterpart, Mont-Royal is the smaller of the two, taking up 165 acres of the mountain. In 1901 it became the site of Canada's first crematorium.

Predominantly Protestant, it is the final resting spot of many of the city's English-speaking founding fathers, including John Molson (whose family has a prominent set of mausoleums) and John Redpath. Other famous Canadians, including hockey player Howie Morenz and author Mordecai Richler, are also buried here. One of the more famous graves is that of Joe Beef—now the namesake of a popular restaurant—otherwise known as Charles McKiernan, who owned a canteen on the port and was known for giving food to the homeless and housing them in his 100-bed dorm. He died in 1889.

Though they're distinctly different, you can access both Notre-Dame-des-Neiges and Mont-Royal cemeteries through a small path found behind the war monument and marked with two cannons. It's a particularly popular spot for joggers, cyclists, and those delving into their family's past. The cemetery houses an arboretum and has been designated a National Historic Site.

MAP 7: 1297 chemin de la Forêt, 514/279-7358, www.mountroyalcem.com; 8:30am-4:30pm daily; free

Cimetière Notre-Dame-des-Neiges

Covering a fair portion of Mont-Royal and following the mountain's natural landscape is Notre-Dame-des-Neiges Cemetery, the biggest in Canada and the third largest in North America. It is traditionally Catholic and Francophone, while its smaller counterpart, Mont-Royal Cemetery, is Protestant and Anglophone. It was founded in 1854, and more than one million people have been interred here.

Because of its garden-like character, it is a great place to have a stroll, be it on a hot summer day or on freshly fallen snow. You can enjoy the flora

(it has almost 6,000 trees), the fauna (squirrels, groundhogs, raccoons, foxes, and more), and, of course, the quietness of the dwellers. Among them, you'll come across the tombs of various prominent Montrealers, from doomed poet Émile Nelligan to hockey star Maurice Richard and some of the most important Canadian politicians.

The direction of the main chapel and office is indicated by the white dots on the ground from three access points: entrance Côte-des-Neiges, entrance Decelle (by the university), and entrance Camillien-Houde (the other side of Beaver Lake). There you can get maps and information. Like its English counterpart, Notre-Dame-des-Neiges is a great place for an afternoon walk through history.

MAP 7: 4601 chemin de la Côte-des-Neiges, 514/735-1361, www.cimetierenotredamedesneiges.ca; 8am-7pm daily Apr.-Oct., 8am-5pm daily Nov.-Mar.; free

LACHINE CANAL
Marché Atwater

A public market since it opened in 1933—another one of Montréal's Depression-era make-work projects—this art deco building designed by Ludger Lemieux is one of the most striking in the area. Located on the Lachine Canal, the market is home to butchers, bakeries, general-food stores, fresh produce stalls, and food vendors like Pizza Mia and ice cream spot Havre aux Glaces. Many vendors migrate outside during the summer. Though it has long been the community's home for daily staples, it's also been the site of social and sporting events, including wrestling, as well as political speeches. Mayor Camillien Houde and Québec premier Maurice Duplessis both spoke here to roaring crowds. A large room on the second floor, which seats up to 1,000 people, can still be rented.

MAP 7: 138 rue Atwater, www. marche-atwater.com; 7am-6pm Mon.-Wed., 7am-7pm Thurs., 7am-8pm Fri., 7am-5pm Sat.-Sun.; free

ÎLE SAINTE-HÉLÈNE AND ÎLE NOTRE-DAME

These two islands in the stream of the St-Lawrence River have a curious history. Île Notre-Dame is fully artificial, having been built with the soil excavated while building Montréal's Métro; for its part, Île Sainte-Hélène is named after Samuel de Champlain's wife, Hélène Boulé. Both islands are easily reached in a number of different ways. By Métro, the stop is Parc Jean-Drapeau; by car, the direction is Parc Jean-Drapeau; by bike, see www.route-verte.com for directions.

✪ Biosphère

Designed by visionary architect R. Buckminster Fuller—who later went on to design Spaceship Earth at the Epcot Center—this geodesic dome is the most iconic structure left from Expo 67. Fuller was seen as an eccentric for his philosophical approach to design and his views on creating a synergy between the environment and technology, but his works were beyond their time. Because he had successfully built a few geodesic domes across the United States, when he approached the U.S. government in 1963 with his plans for the American Pavilion for the 1967 World's Fair, they immediately responded.

With the invention of the geodesic dome, Fuller created the most efficient structure ever, using one-fiftieth of the materials normally used in conventional architecture. This perfect form would become one of the biggest attractions at the fair—a futuristic monorail that originally passed through it also added to its appeal—and is still one of the most breathtaking sights in the city. It was originally covered in thin acrylic panels, but repairs to the structure in 1976 set the whole of the skin ablaze in a matter of minutes. The panels were never replaced.

Popular with architecture buffs and kids alike, the 20-story-high building remained empty until 1995, when a new structure was built inside the Biosphère that would become an environmental museum of the same name. The only one of its kind in North America, this unique museum, which caters to children, is aimed at raising awareness of environmental issues such as air and water quality, biodiversity, and sustainable development. The structure itself uses sustainable energy resources, such as solar panels, wind turbines, and a geothermal heating system.

MAP 7: 160 chemin Tour-de-Isle, Île Ste-Hélène, 514/283-5000, www.ec.gc. ca/biosphere; 10am-5pm Thurs.-Sun. mid-Jan.-late May, 10am-5pm daily June-Oct.; $15 adults, $12 seniors, $10 students, children 17 and under free

Parc Jean-Drapeau

Named after the at-times controversial mayor who turned Expo 67 into a reality, Parc Jean-Drapeau consists of two islands, Île Sainte-Hélène and Île Notre-Dame. A green paradise on the Métro line, the islands were the site of Expo 67, and though you'll find some relics remaining—like Buckminster Fuller's geodesic dome and the Québec and French Pavilions, now the site of the city's casino—most

SAILING UP THE ST-LAWRENCE

One of the most inspired ways to travel from Montréal to Québec City and beyond is by boat cruise. Sure, it's not the most cost- or time-effective (a single trip lasts about eight hours), but it is one of the most romantic. And the views of the St-Lawrence and the villages that dot its banks easily beat out those of the highway.

When it comes to choosing a company or cruise there are a few different options. **The CTMA Group** (www.ctma.ca) offers a week-long trip from Montréal with stops in other regions of the province, like Gaspé and the Îles-de-la-Madeleine, as well as Québec City. **Croisières AML** (www.croisieresaml.com), meanwhile, offers a great option for a simple day-long cruise with an early-morning Montréal departure that gets you to Québec in time for dinner.

All companies offer a variety of cruise times and types—everything from a brunch cruise and a bus ride back to Montréal to a night in Québec with a cruise back the following day—allowing flexibility in your travels. The trips, however, do not take place every day, so make sure to plan well in advance and check the websites for exact dates and schedules.

the Alexander Calder sculpture *L'Homme* in Parc Jean-Drapeau

and the like. The 25 hectares of gardens were originally created for the 1980s Floralies Internationales horticultural fair. The grounds were designed by some of the world's best landscape architects and boast 5,000 rose bushes. In the summer, Piknic Électronik—a daytime dance festival—takes place every Sunday 2:30pm-9:30pm under the Alexander Calder sculpture *L'Homme*. Cyclist? Parc Jean-Drapeau can be accessed by the separated bike lane on the Jacques Cartier bridge, and the ride makes for a fun, scenic day trip.

MAP 7: Île Ste-Hélène and Île Notre-Dame, 514/872-6120, www. parcjeandrapeau.com; 6am-11pm daily; free

of the pavilions were destroyed in the 1970s to make room for a large basin used for water events during the 1976 Olympics. Today the basin still exists and is a great place to try your hand at rowing, canoeing, and dragon boating. Just beside the Jean-Drapeau Métro station you'll find the Jean-Drapeau Aquatic Complex, with an Olympic-size pool and diving board to match. They're open for public swims May-September.

The park also has a beach, which includes boat rentals, beach volleyball,

Stewart Museum

This former British army garrison now serves as a museum dedicated to Canada's past. Built in 1820, the fort is the most important historical military site in Montréal. During the summer months, daily military parades and demonstrations are given on the fort's grounds, and in a nod to both French and English heritage, both the Franche de la Marie and Olde 78th Fraser Highlanders are represented.

The permanent collection History

and Memory draws a picture of the old and new worlds by establishing links in technological and societal advances with events in early Canada. Using artifacts like navigational tools, prow figureheads, sedans, and playing cards, the museum also tells us of our ancestors' daily lives. Guides in period costume help us envision the fort's daily life, and the old barracks are still open to visitors. Temporary exhibits have included retrospectives on Expo 67 and the 375th anniversary of Montréal.

MAP 7: Vieux Fort, Île Ste-Hélène, 514/861-6701, www.stewart-museum.org; 10am-5pm Tues.-Sun. late June-early Sept., 10am-5pm Wed.-Sun. early Sept-late June; $15 adults, $12 students, 18-25, $10 children 13-17, children under 12 free

La Ronde

Situated on the eastern tip of Île Sainte-Hélène, La Ronde opened as part of Expo 67 and has since grown to become the second-largest amusement park in Canada—lots of rides for kids, families, and those looking to test the limits of their stomachs. Previously owned by the City of Montréal, it was bought by Six Flags in 2001. Though little of the quaint, original park remains, the frontier town of "Fort Edmonton" is still in use and is now the entrance to Le Monstre (The Monster), the highest double wooden roller coaster in the world.

Throughout June and August the park plays host to an international fireworks competition, with countries from all over the world competing for top spot, judged by a public jury. Though you don't have to be at the park to see the fireworks—anywhere near the river will do—it's fun to sit on the Ferris wheel and watch the explosions in the night sky.

As at most amusement parks, much

La Ronde, an amusement park on Île Sainte-Hélène.

the arid regions greenhouse at the Jardin Botanique

of the food is overpriced, and though it's close to downtown and easily reached by Métro, there are no other dining options in the area.

MAP 7: 22 chemin Macdonald, Île Ste-Hélène, 514/397-2000, www.sixflags.com/larondeen; hours vary late-May-Oct.; $66 adults (54 inches and taller), $49 seniors and children (shorter than 54 inches), children 2 and under free

Casino de Montréal

Housed in the former French and Québec Expo 67 Pavilions, this casino is the largest in Canada, with over 3,200 slot machines and 115 gaming tables. At night, you can catch a glimpse across the water from the Vieux-Port—bathed in golden light, the casino is a sparkly mirage floating above the St-Lawrence and the trees of Île Notre-Dame.

The French Pavilion was criticized for its numerous tall fins, which appeared to critics to have been tacked on as an afterthought. The Québec Pavilion meanwhile was made of glass and by night acted as an illuminated display case. Today it is these exact traits that contribute to the casino's impressive exterior.

If you get tired of the game of chance, there are plenty of other things to keep you occupied, including four restaurants, three bars, and a cabaret. For upscale dining in a casual atmosphere, check out the eatery of three-Michelin-star chef Joël Robuchon at l'Atelier Joël Robuchon. And be sure to catch a bit of Vegas in Montréal—take in a show at the cabaret, which has regular musical and dance performances.

MAP 7: 1 ave. du Casino, Île Notre-Dame, 514/392-2746, http://casinos.lotoquebec.com/fr/montreal/accueil; 24 hours daily; free

HOCHELAGA-MAISONNEUVE
✪ Jardin Botanique

Facing Montréal's Olympic Park is the Jardin Botanique, 185 acres of outdoor gardens. Founded in 1931

In the late 1960s, Montréal was thrust onto the world stage as an example of the "City of the Future." Held from April 27 to October 29, 1967, Expo 67 was the most well-attended and most successful world's fair of the 20th century—which, rightfully, put a spotlight on the city. Mayor Jean Drapeau, a stubborn, quixotic mayor known for his championing of the Expo as well for some less well-received municipal policies (raiding and bulldozing gay clubs and other underground venues, for example), was instrumental in securing the city the attention it deserved. Montréal had so impressed the world that it won the bid for the 1976 Summer Olympics.

What started as an ambitious project soon became too much for the city to handle. Partway through preparations for the games, the provincial government stepped in to take over. Bad management and planning, coupled with corruption and contractor scandals, led to a loss of three years' worth of building, and by 1973 the project was already behind. Though the Olympics themselves went off without a hitch, they left the city and its citizens reeling from a massive deficit.

Drapeau famously said that the Olympics could no more incur a deficit than a man could have a baby; on both counts, he was wrong—transgender men can have babies, and the Olympics saddled Montréal with $1.3 billion of debt. The Olympic Stadium, which Drapeau himself was involved in designing, cost $1.1 billion alone. Montrealers take our Olympic nosedive in grudging, chuckling stride—if you can't be the best, you may as well be notable for something!

by Mayor Camillien Houde, it was the brainchild of Brother Marie-Victorin, a De La Salle brother and noted botanist who established the Botanical Institute at the Université de Montréal in 1920—he's also a relative of writer Jack Kerouac and was born Conrad Kirouack. After years of tirelessly campaigning, Marie-Victorin got his garden and Houde used out-of-work Montrealers to make the garden a reality. Designed by Henry Teuscher, a Berlin-born landscape architect and horticulturalist, it consists of 30 thematic gardens and 10 exhibition greenhouses. Its goal is to educate the general public as well as students of horticulture and to conserve endangered plant species.

Though all the gardens are worth a visit, the most popular are the Chinese and Japanese gardens, both of which were designed by architects from their respective countries. Pieces used in the Chinese garden were even shipped over from China. Every September and October, the Chinese gardens are the site of a wonderful exhibition of Chinese lanterns. The show is so popular that the gardens are open until 9pm to accommodate the crowds. Admission to the gardens is free November through mid-May.

MAP 7: 4101 rue Sherbrooke E., 514/872-1400, www.espacepourlavie. ca/en/botanical-garden; 9am-5pm Tues.-Sun. Nov.-mid-May, 9am-6pm daily mid-May-early Sept., 9am-9pm daily early Sept.-Oct.; $20.25 adults, $18.50 seniors, $14.75 students, $10.25 children 5-17, children 4 and under free

✪ Stade Olympique

Built as the main stadium for the 1976 Olympics, the Stade Olympique hosted both the opening and closing ceremonies as well as equestrian and athletic events. The structure, designed by French architect Roger Taillibert, is one of the most impressive sights in the city and considered one of the best examples of organic architecture in the world. As impressive as it is, however, it doesn't quite erase the fact that its construction put the city into some serious debt.

With its saucer-like shape and swooping roof, the stadium is a looming reminder of the problems that plagued its construction and the debt the city incurred in the process. Its nickname, The Big O, refers not only to the stadium's doughnut-like shape but also to the amount of money it cost the city. Even after the city finally paid off its stadium debt in 2006, Montrealers continue to refer to it as The Big Owe.

The former home of the much-missed Montréal Expos baseball team, the stadium now stands mainly empty, hosting the occasional concert or sporting event when the city's smaller stadiums can't accommodate the crowds. Guided tours of the stadium are also available—sometimes as part of other exhibits occurring at the park.

MAP 7: 4141 ave. Pierre-du-Coubertin, 514/252-4737, www.parcolympique. qc.ca; check website for rates, hours, and events

Tour Olympique

Though the Olympic tower, with its moving funicular and observation deck, was built for the 1976 Olympics, it didn't open until 1987, 11 years after the last Olympian went home from the games. At the time, the malfunctioning only added to the city's Olympic hangover, but today it's a unique way to see the city. Built at a 45-degree angle, the tower is 175 meters high and accessible only by a two-level funicular that rides the rails to the top at 2.8 meters per second and works using hydraulics. Once you get to the top, you enter the observatory, exhibition hall, and reception hall, which occupy the three upper floors of the tower. The view from the observation deck is unique, offering a near-panoramic view of the city and its surroundings; on a clear day you can see as far as 80 kilometers away, even catching sight of the Laurentians.

Though the stadium and tower are connected, they operate as separate entities, which means admission to one won't get you into the other.

MAP 7: 4141 ave. Pierre-du-Coubertin, 514/252-4141, http://parcolympique.qc.ca; hours vary by season; $23.25 adults, $21 seniors, $18.75 students, $11.50 children 5-17, children 4 and under free

Biodôme

Part of the former Olympic complex, the Montréal Biodôme is housed in the old velodrome, where cycling and judo events took place in 1976. It was designed by French architect Roger Taillibert, who developed the entire plan for Montréal's massive Olympic park. From above the shape is reminiscent of a stingray with its flat, aerodynamic shape.

Opened in 1992, the Biodôme re-creates ecosystems found in the Americas: the tropical rainforest, the Laurentian maple forest, the gulf of the St-Lawrence, the Labrador coast, and the sub-Antarctic islands. In these re-created environments the animals live in partial freedom, adding a dimension of reality that you don't always find in a zoo. The ecosystems also blend into one another so that you slowly migrate from one area to the next—from the hottest to the coldest—as you explore them. The Laurentian forest, in particular, is worth visiting as it represents the diverse vegetation and wildlife surrounding Montréal. Unlike the other ecosystems, it also changes with the seasons.

Biôdome

The Biodôme and the Insectarium closed for major renovations in 2018, with an expected reopening in 2019. MAP 7: 4777 ave. Pierre-du-Coubertin, 514/868-3000, www.biodome.qc.ca; 9am-5pm Mon.-Fri., 9am-6pm Sat.-Sun. June-Aug., 9am-5pm Tues.-Sun. Sept.-May; $20.25 adults, $18.50 seniors, $14.75 students, $10.25 children 5-17, children 4 and under free

Insectarium de Montréal

Established in 1990, directly inside the city's Jardin Botanique, this is one of the largest insectariums in North America. The collection features both live and mounted insects. Bugs from Africa; Australia; North, South, and Central America; and Asia. Spiders, walking sticks, and beetles can be observed in the Live Collection room, and a number of butterflies are displayed among the Mounted Collection. Entrance to the Jardin Botanique is bundled with a ticket to the Insectarium. The Insectarium and the Biodôme closed for major renovations in 2018, with an expected reopening in 2019.

MAP 7: 4581 rue Sherbrooke E., 514/872-1400, www.ville.montreal. qc.ca/insectarium; 9am-5pm Tues.-Sun. early Nov.-mid-May, 9am-6pm daily mid-May-early Sept., 9am-9pm Sun.-Thurs., 9am-10pm Fri.-Sat. early Sept.-late Oct.; $20.25 adults, $18.50 seniors, $14.75 students, $10.25 children 5-17, children 4 and under free

Planétarium Rio Tinto Alcan

The Planétarium Rio Tinto Alcan is part of Space for Life, the largest natural sciences museum complex in Canada, which includes the Biodôme, Insectarium, and Jardin Botanique. The planetarium's architecture is impressive; its dome is an oversized silo covered in luminescent steel. Inside, it's all about light wood and slate floors. Designed by local architectural firm Cardin Ramirez Julien, it's also one of the city's greenest buildings, using sustainable material and incorporating the latest green initiatives.

Visitors can explore the universe in two different ways—through poetry and science, thanks to the planetarium's shows Continuum and From the Earth to the Stars. Both explore the cosmos and the universe, but each has its own take. Both shows are included with the price of admission.

MAP 7: 4801 ave. Pierre-du-Coubertin, 514/868-3000, www.espacepourlavie.ca/ en/planetarium; 9am-5pm Tues.-Wed. and Sun., 9am-8pm Thurs.-Sat.; $20.25, adults, $18.50 seniors, $14.75 students, $10.25 children 5-17, children 4 and under free

RESTAURANTS

Vieux-Montréal 100
Centre-Ville 106
Centre-Ville Est 110
Quartier Latin and the Village 112
Plateau Mont-Royal 114
Mile End and Petite-Italie 122
Greater Montréal 129

Montréal is known for its amazing restaurants and range of diverse culinary delights, with more varied and rough-and-tumble options than Québec City.

Dépanneur Le Pick-Up is a popular sandwich spot.

Strong ties to French cuisine remain, so many eateries offer a table d'hôte, and a café is a place where you can drink your espresso standing up, sit down with a café au lait, or grab a hearty bite to eat.

Boundaries are blurred between café, bar, and restaurant, with a lot of places serving all three functions, depending on the time of day. Most cafés follow the French model and serve breakfast, lunch, and dinner, so don't be surprised if you find a place that makes a great cappuccino and croissant in the morning and duck confit at night. Restaurant as late-night-party-bar is a long-standing tradition in the city, so remember that when heading out you might need to only head to one place. Liquor licensing can be bizarre in the city; some restaurants serve full meals but not alcohol, while other places can only serve alcohol as long as it's accompanied by a snack, like nachos or nuts. Many restaurants also have a bring-your-own policy, which allows diners to bring their own store-bought vintage to the table.

Diverse cuisines are available throughout the city and, depending on where you're staying, they're often your best late-night bet—that or fast food. Petite-Italie (Little Italy) is obviously best for high-end pasta and pizza, and Chinatown offers Chinese as well as Vietnamese and Korean cuisines, but both a Koreatown and a second Chinatown are growing on the western edge

HIGHLIGHTS

✪ **SWANKIEST COFFEE SHOP:** Visit **Crew Café** for its location—a grand, cavernous old bank (page 105).

✪ **MOST QUINTESSENTIAL MONTRÉAL RESTAURANT:** The rustic, hearty, over-the-top dishes at **Joe Beef** have become synonymous with the city's cuisine (page 106).

✪ **BEST** *IZAKAYA:* Stepping into **Kazu**, an *izakaya* (Japanese gastropub), is like entering a tiny back-alley eatery in Shibuya, complete with soju (rice liquor) cocktails and cramped seating (page 107).

✪ **BEST PLACE FOR A DATE:** Its classic Parisian vibe, impeccably seasoned steak, and perfect French desserts make **L'Express** the ideal spot for an intimate, decadent dinner for two (page 116).

✪ **BEST SMOKED MEAT:** A Jewish deli in business for over eight decades, **Schwartz's** is a must-visit. The line-up is part of the experience (page 117)!

✪ **BEST BREAKFAST:** Tiny **Chez José** offers filling omelets (or scrambled tofu) and tasty hot sauce with fresh salad and satisfying roasted potatoes (page 118).

✪ **BEST VEGETARIAN:** With West Coast vibes and delicious dragon bowls, **Aux Vivres** is the ideal spot to take in your veggies and tempeh (page 120).

✪ **MOST UNIQUE DINING EXPERIENCE:** At **Dinette Triple Crown,** pick up your picnic basket filled with Southern staples, then head to a park to chow down (page 124).

✪ **BEST JAPANESE LUNCH:** Just east of rue St-Laurent, **Café Falco** serves up delicious homemade *onigiri* and soups (page 128).

✪ **BEST CROISSANTS:** For an authentic taste of Europe, look no further than **Boulangerie Guillaume** (page 128).

✪ **BEST ICE CREAM:** A small, seasonal ice cream and sorbet shop, **Kem CoBa** offers both creative and traditional flavors—all homemade on-site (page 129).

✪ **MOST WORTHWHILE SPLURGE:** Leave the well-worn tourist path behind for the cornflower blue walls and delectable menu of **Tuck Shop** (page 129).

PRICE KEY

$	Entrées less than CAN$15
$ $	Entrées CAN$15-25
$ $ $	Entrées more than CAN$25

of downtown. Moreover, wherever you find yourself, it's probably possible to find a half-decent healthy, hearty bowl of pho. The best Indian and Pakistani food can be found in Parc Extension (known locally as Parc-Ex), northwest of Little Italy, while Greek cuisine is a Mile End staple. Caribbean, Mexican, and Japanese options exist, but they're a little tougher to find and aren't as concentrated in particular neighborhoods.

Montréal also excels at rustic Québécois fare in an exciting, boisterous atmosphere. There has always been a real emphasis on market fresh in the city, and though it can sometimes translate to higher prices, it's worth it. At times it seems Montréal suffers from a lack of good midrange restaurants, but that's not exactly true. Many neighborhood bistros—or bars for that matter—offer delicious and affordable meals that are likely to exceed your expectations.

Though menus are often written in French, they are usually accompanied by an English translation, and servers will gladly translate anything on the menu. Although you might originally be greeted by the wait staff in French, it is perfectly fine, and normal, to switch to English. If you're comfortable, adding a French word here or there, like *merci,* is always welcome.

Many restaurants are closed on Sunday or Monday. Diners start late, especially later in the week or on weekends; it's not unusual to sit down to a meal at 10 o'clock at night. In fact, some of the city's best restaurants keep their kitchens open past midnight. There's no smoking in restaurants or cafés or on outdoor *terrasses* (patios).

When dining in Vieux-Montréal and the Old Port, watch out for tourist traps. Go for something a little more pricey or very low-key to avoid over-paying. There are enough top-notch restaurants in the area for every budget, so resist resorting to the first place you see. For delicious and affordable options—or if you're tired of steak frites, foie gras, and cheese—trek over to Chinatown.

The food choice in Montréal is expansive, and as you get to know the city you'll recognize a few of its own chain restaurants, as well as international ones, but the real culinary wizardry is found in the neighborhood bistros. Take a chance on smaller, intimate eateries; you won't be disappointed.

Vieux-Montréal   Map 1

QUÉBÉCOIS
Toqué! $$$

Since opening in 1993, Normand Laprise's Toqué! has almost single-handedly changed the culinary landscape of Montréal. Laprise's restaurant is known around the globe for his use of Québécois ingredients, partnerships with local producers, and boundary-pushing creations. The menu includes such notable dishes as pork shoulder with black pudding and beet mousse with caramel sorbet. The subtle and minimalist decor only adds to the overall sophistication of the atmosphere. The website may note attire as casual but ignore it; this is your opportunity to dress up.

There's also a more affordable lunch menu. Reservations are a must.

MAP 1: 900 Place Jean-Paul-Riopelle, 514/499-2084, www.restaurant-toque. com; 11:30am-1:45pm and 5:30pm-10pm Tues.-Fri., 5:30pm-10:30pm Sat.

FRENCH
Chez L'Épicier $$$

Chef and owner Laurent Godbout opened this cozy, storefront restaurant in 2000. Since then, Godbout and his restaurant have received glowing reviews from diners and critics alike, citing his *terroir* cooking as some of the best in the city. Local produce is a main ingredient, but Godbout also likes to incorporate more unusual, less-local flavors like kumquat, wasabi, and mango-curry sorbet. (Unlike at many of the high-end restos in the area, you should be able to find vegetarian and vegan options here.) The atmosphere is cozy and casual. For a real treat, try the seven-course tasting menu for $85.

MAP 1: 311 rue St-Paul E., 514/878-2232, www.chezlepicier.com; 5pm-10pm Tues.-Sat.

Le Club Chasse et Pêche $$$

On an unassuming side street in Old Montréal, Le Club Chasse et Pêche looks more like a forgotten Portuguese diner than one of the best restaurants in the city. All that changes when you enter its warm, cavernous, and clubby interior with its quasi-famous animal-inspired lighting fixtures by Antoine Laverdière. With a focus on great meat and fish, as the name suggests, the restaurant has an ambience that is decidedly grown up and sophisticated—with a boys' club edge. The menu changes weekly, but there are a few constants, such as scallops and risotto (though the preparation never stays the same).

MAP 1: 423 rue St-Claude, 514/861-1112, www.leclubchasseetpeche.com; 6pm-10:30pm Tues.-Sat.

Les 400 Coups $$$

A nod to both the address and to the François Truffaut film of the same name, Les 400 Coups is also a French expression meaning to push the limits. Having been voted one of Canada's best restaurants, this bistro lives up to its name. Chef Jonathan Rassi seeks out new ways to present local produce and flavors—try the kohlrabi with watermelon relish, or shell out the worthwhile $75 for the tasting menu. Pair your choices with wine suggestions, and then sit back and let the black walls, white marble bar, and mural of Parisian neighborhood St-Germain-des-Prés transport you directly to Paris.

MAP 1: 400 rue Notre-Dame E., 514/985-0400, www.les400coups.ca; 5:30pm-10:30pm Tues.-Sat.

Jardin Nelson $$

Conveniently located on Place Jacques-Cartier in a historic building that dates back to 1812, this seasonal restaurant's real gem is its courtyard. Enormous parasols save diners from the occasional rain shower and, along with the overflowing gardens and nightly live jazz, heighten the restaurant's intimate atmosphere. The menu offers everything from crêpes to pizza, and poke to tuna ceviche, but the ambience and surroundings are the real draw.

MAP 1: 407 Place Jacques-Cartier, 514/861-5731, www.jardinnelson.com; 11:30am-10pm Mon.-Fri., 10am-11pm Sat.-Sun. mid-Apr.-Canadian Thanksgiving

Jardin Nelson

INDIAN
Gandhi $$

Quiet and relaxed—populated with bistro-style seating, lots of natural light, and white, sparsely decorated walls—Gandhi is perfect for couples craving a romantic Indian meal. The tandoori chicken, lamb tikka, and homemade chutney are particular standouts, but there are no wrong choices when it comes to this restaurant's comprehensive menu. Prices are reasonable, especially for the neighborhood.

MAP 1: 230 rue St-Paul W., 514/845-5866, www.restaurantgandhi.com; noon-2pm and 5:30pm-10:30pm Mon.-Fri., 5:30pm-10:30pm Sat.-Sun.

ITALIAN
Graziella $$$

Chef and owner Graziella Baptista creates memorable northern Italian dishes in her namesake restaurant on the west extremity of Old Montréal. Simple, honest, and prepared to perfection, the house specialties include osso bucco, risotto, and smoked ricotta gnocchi. The dining room itself is light-filled and airy with modern minimalist decor, appealing to mature diners and those looking for a quiet, refined meal. Save room for dessert: Graziella serves an orange-perfumed ricotta cannoli, perhaps the best in the city.

MAP 1: 116 rue McGill, 514/876-0116, www.restaurantgraziella.ca; noon-2:30pm and 6pm-10pm Mon.-Fri., 6pm-10pm Sat.

Mangiafoco $$

This pizza joint and "mozzarella bar" is in a stunning Beaux-Arts building on rue St-Paul. The art nouveau-inspired typography immediately catches the eye, as does the decor, which is totally unique thanks to its molded steel seating, light wood bar, and numerous hanging lights. Luckily, the food lives up to the decor—the wood-fired pizzas are some of the best in the city. Fun fact: It's owned by Jean-François Stinco, the lead guitarist for local pop punk band Simple Plan.

MAP 1: 105 rue St-Paul W., 514/419-8380, www.mangiafoco.ca; 11:30am-2pm and 5pm-11pm Mon.-Fri., 5pm-11pm Sat.-Sun.

POLISH
Stash Café $$

Since its opening over 30 years ago the Stash Café has become a veritable Montréal institution—the best place to get your fill of borscht, pierogies, and *wódka*. With low-hanging red-shaded lights, exposed brick walls, bench seating, and a nightly pianist, this restaurant is a cozy place to spend a winter night. With hearty portions at a reasonable price for Vieux-Montréal, Stash is also perfect if you're starving after a long day of touring around the heritage neighborhood.

MAP 1: 200 rue St-Paul W., 514/845-6611, www.stashcafe.com; 11:30am-10pm Mon.-Thurs., 11:30am-11pm Fri., 11am-11pm Sat., 11am-10pm Sun.

MARCHÉ DES ÉCLUSIERS

In 2016, doors opened on the **Marché des Éclusiers** (400 rue de la Commune W., 438/795-8265, www.marche514.com), a small, seasonal hybrid market (named for the nearby locks) and restaurant location close to Bota Bota spa and Silo #5 in the Old Port. On the second floor, you'll find **Pastaga** (514/688-0412, 4pm-11pm Mon.-Fri., 2pm-11pm Sat.-Sun.), an upscale snack bar with fresh seafood and inspired cocktails. On the ground level, **Burgers Royal** (11am-8pm daily) serves milkshakes and burgers made from ethically raised beef, and **Volcanic Organic** (514/805-2815, 7am-7pm daily) serves fair-trade coffee. Every spot here offers a bunch of seating. On the weekends, a farmers market shares the space. Check the website for more specific info.

A Segway tour glides by Muvbox Homard, near the Marché des Éclusiers.

Nearby—right next to the Marché des Éclusiers, and scattered throughout the Vieux-Port during the late spring, summer, and early fall—a bunch of shipping containers have been converted into food stands. (The containers are manufactured by local company Muvbox, and their brand name is often emblazoned on the side of the containers.) Favorites include the **Taco Box** and **Muvbox Homard** (514/627-8452, http://muvboxrestos.com, 11:30am-9pm daily May-Sept.), the latter of which serves lobster rolls, but you'll also find street food staples like poutine and crêpes. There's bench seating at the trucks, as well as communal picnic tables inside open-sided shipping containers.

Dining in the Old Port can be quite pricey, so these spots can be particularly helpful for lunch or an afternoon snack.

SPANISH
Barroco $$$

The menu of this upscale joint takes inspiration from all over Europe—with a distinctly Spanish bent. The paella is one of its most popular offerings; stuffed with squid, shrimp, and scallops, it's got a freshness not always found in this dish. The restaurant has

Barroco

a great ambience, with its stone walls and beamed ceiling giving the baroque touches a rustic feel. Staff are helpful and accommodating. Note that, because of its liquor license, this restaurant only allows patrons age 18 and over.

MAP 1: 312 rue St-Paul W., 514/544-5800, www.barroco.ca; 6pm-10:30pm Mon.-Wed. and Sun., 6pm-11pm Thurs.-Sat.

SEAFOOD
Le Bremner $$$

Run by culinary whiz-kid Chuck Hughes, the man behind Garde Manger, Le Bremner continues to keep the party and excellent food coming. Situated on the eastern edge of Vieux-Montréal in an inconspicuous location down a few steps, the restaurant has a cavernous vibe, with stone walls, dark wood tables, low ceilings, and a hidden back patio. Everything on the menu is fresh from the sea (or just about) and cooked to perfection; you can't go wrong with the snowcrab kimchee or the hot lobster sandwich.

MAP 1: 361 rue St-Paul E., 514/544-0446, www.crownsalts.com/lebremner; 6pm-11pm Mon.-Sat.

Garde Manger $$$

A former sailor's bar, this restaurant retains its working-class charm with shabby-chic decor and a rough-and-tumble menu that includes meaty staples done perfectly—executive chef Chuck Hughes, host of the show *Chuck's Day Off,* once beat Bobby Flay on *Iron Kitchen.* Reservations are a must, since this place is always hopping. Check out sister restaurant Le Bremner if you can't find a spot here.

MAP 1: 408 rue St-François-Xavier, 514/678-5044, www.crownsalts.com/gardemanger; 5:30pm-11pm Tues.-Sun.

STEAKHOUSE
Gibby's $$$

Located in the Youville Stables, the setting for this classic Montréal steakhouse dates back to 1740. Stone walls, original beamed ceilings, and numerous fireplaces are dotted throughout the six separate dining rooms, which include a cocktail lounge and a secluded outdoor courtyard. If your preference is for surf, not turf, they've also got an excellent seafood selection. With its cozy atmosphere and classic fine-dining service, Gibby's tends to be popular for special family get-togethers, weddings, and romantic dinners.

MAP 1: 298 Place d'Youville, 514/282-1837, www.gibbys.com; 5:30pm-10pm Mon.-Fri., 5pm-11pm Sat.-Sun.

COMFORT FOOD
Brit and Chips $

With its old-school stools, blackboard menu, and white-shirted, bow-tied staff, Brit and Chips offers the charm of a lost era. This tiny neighborhood chip shop, which has only six tables and counter space for about 20, serves five kinds of fish as well as English staples like steak and kidney pie and Scotch eggs. Takeout is wrapped in newspaper-print wax paper, and the traditional mixes with the modern—there are gluten-free options, a curry fish pie, and tandoori shrimp, too.

MAP 1: 433 rue McGill, 514/840-1001, www.britandchips.com; 11am-10pm Sun.-Wed., 11am-11pm Thurs.-Sat.

CAFÉS AND BAKERIES
Café Titanic $

Serving the 9-5 crowd, this bustling café is filled with dark wood, exposed brick walls, and reclaimed Métro chairs and diner accessories. Arrive before or after the lunch rush to secure your seat. True to its name, the sandwiches are "titanic," so bring your appetite or share with a friend. For something lighter, try the soup of the day, often served with a crispy oil-drenched baguette. Coffee here is some of the best in the area and always elegantly served. If it's chilly, treat yourself to the baked three-cheese macaroni.

MAP 1: 445 rue St-Pierre W., 514/849-0894, www.titanicmontreal.ca; 7am-4:30pm Mon.-Fri.

Le Cartet $

This open-concept dining hall offers a great selection of hot (grilled salmon, seafood lasagna) or cold (salade Niçoise, grilled chicken sandwiches) lunches. Take out or eat in at one of their long, inviting communal tables. The ambience is one of fever pitch during the week, when office workers are meeting for a quick business lunch. The weekend crowd is much more diverse, with families and friends meeting up before an afternoon in Vieux-Montréal. The popular brunch features mimosas and dishes like the hearty Brunch des Cantons, which comes with scrambled eggs, three types of meat, beans, potatoes, and toast.

MAP 1: 106 rue McGill, 514/871-8887; 7am-7:30pm Mon.-Fri., 9am-4pm Sat.-Sun.

Olive & Gourmando $

From the fresh-from-the-oven bread to the array of mouthwatering goodies (the Valhrona chocolate brioche is divine) that greet you at the front counter, Olive & Gourmando has earned its spot as an Old Montréal lunchtime institution. It was started by two former chefs from Toqué!, and the atmosphere is casual but chic, with heavy wood tables, comfy seats with leather accents, and deep red walls. The dining room is always packed. In fact, on weekdays just getting takeout can be chaotic, but the food, including panini, salads, breakfast, and brunch, is worth the wait. Gluten-free and vegan options are available.

MAP 1: 351 rue St-Paul W., 514/350-1083, www.oliveetgourmando.com; 9am-5pm daily

7Grains Bakery & Cafe $

Cute, hippie-ish, and centrally located across from the Marché Bonsecours, this café and bakery serves soups, sandwiches, crêpes, Greek dishes, and lots of baked goods. Gluten-free and vegan-friendly, with a focus on organic food, this spot offers a respite for travelers whose stomachs aren't quite ready to eat poutine, tartare, and foie gras at every meal.

MAP 1: 393 rue St-Pierre E., 514/861-8181, www.7grains.ca; 10am-8pm Sun.-Fri., noon-midnight Sat.

COFFEE
✪ Crew Café $

Rue St-Jacques used to be known as Canada's Wall Street, and this café is in the swank surrounds of the former headquarters of the Royal Bank of Canada—gilded, cavernous, and the fanciest place to get a cup of coffee in Montréal. Also a co-working space, Crew rents their meeting rooms by the hour. If you'd just like to stop in to eat a croissant and Instagram photos of the impressive ceiling, they also have a communal area with couches, tables, and chairs.

MAP 1: 360 rue St-Jacques, www.crewcollectivecafe.com; 8am-8pm Mon.-Fri., 10am-7pm Sat.-Sun.

QUÉBÉCOIS

✪ Joe Beef $$$

Named after Charles "Joe Beef" McKiernan, a popular 19th-century innkeeper, Joe Beef is one of the hottest places to dine in Montréal, and with good reason. Its name has become synonymous with fresh, hearty fare. The oysters are popular, as are dishes like lobster spaghetti, when it's available—regional ingredients mean the menu changes often. It made the list of World's Best Restaurant in 2016, and was featured on *Anthony Bourdain: Parts Unknown,* in 2011. The atmosphere is casual chic: brick walls, simple dark-wood tables, and a huge blackboard menu.

MAP 2: 2491 rue Notre-Dame W., 514/935-6504, www.joebeef.ca; 6:30pm-10:30pm Tues.-Sat.

FRENCH

Europea $$$

Executive chef Jérôme Ferrer holds the title of Grand Chef Relais et Châteaux (a chef who's been recognized by the French governing body of top chefs), and Europea is one of the few places that offer a contemporary French menu untouched by current food fads. The three-floor restaurant is a sprawling affair in a grand old brownstone downtown. Service is impeccable, and offerings include a delectable lobster bisque and foie gras expertly seared on a sizzling rock. It's all about the tasting menu, and the selection is generous, even at lunchtime. Dress code is business casual.

MAP 2: 1227 rue de la Montagne, 514/398-9229, www.europea.com; 6pm-9:30pm Sun.-Mon., noon-1:30pm and 6pm-9pm Tues.-Fri., 6pm-10pm Sat.

AMERICAN

Dunn's Famous Deli $

Opened in 1927, Dunn's is a Montréal staple. The long narrow dining hall, banquette seating, and wood ceiling beams give the place the feel of an old ski chalet. Open 24 hours, seven days a week, this is a late-night or early-morning staple. A favorite with downtown shoppers, pre- or post-movie diners, and those just leaving the bars, Dunn's has a no-nonsense staff; they can be a little short at times. The deli counter selections offer a great choice of classic deli fare, and you can't go wrong with any one of their five club sandwiches.

MAP 2: 1249 rue Metcalfe, 514/395-1927, www.dunnsfamous.com; 24 hours daily

Joe Beef

CHINESE
Qing Hua Dumpling $

This hole-in-the-wall eatery situated on a small side street—south of rue Sherbrooke and north of boulevard de Maisonneuve—is a local favorite. The decor is unassuming, but it doesn't need to be fancy; the food speaks for itself. The dumplings are fried or steamed and stuffed with just about any combination you can imagine, including vegetarian; the pork and cabbage ones are some of the best.

MAP 2: 1676 ave. Lincoln, 438/288-5366; 11am-11pm daily

Qing Hua Dumpling

JAPANESE
✪ Kazu $$

Montrealers are virtually starving for great Japanese food, so when this place popped up in 2010 it was no surprise that it became an instant hit. From the hurried pace of the staff to the cold beers and the hamburger patties, Kazu is a little slice of Japan in the heart of Montréal. Because it has only three tables and a handful of stools, you may be forced to wait in line before sitting down and digging in to your 48-hour pork bowl—but it's wholly worth it.

MAP 2: 1862 rue Ste-Catherine W., 514/937-2333; 12:30pm-3pm and 5:30pm-9:30pm Mon. and Thurs.-Fri., 5:30pm-9:30pm Sat., 12:30pm-3pm and 5:30pm-9pm Sun.

VIETNAMESE
Miss Bánh Mì $

Miss Bánh Mì, conveniently located next to the Guy-Concordia Métro stop, offers meat and vegetarian sandwich options, as well as noodle soups, vermicelli, and, for a bit of a Thai twist, pad thai. The atmosphere at this long spot with an exposed brick wall, single-stool seating, and a handful of tables leans toward students—but, then again, so do the reasonable prices!

MAP 2: 1452B St-Mathieu, 514/379-1088; 11am-8pm daily

Pho Saigon VIP $

There are a lot of reasonably priced pho restaurants (you'll see signs for Soupe Tonkinoise) in the student-filled downtown areas, and this is one of the best for your money. Ample seating, quick and friendly service, and flavorful pho, vermicelli, and fresh rolls make this one of the best places to grab a healthy lunch or dinner in the downtown area.

MAP 2: 1850 rue Ste-Catherine W., 514/934-2168; 11:30am-11pm Mon.-Thurs., 11:30am-midnight Fri.-Sun.

ITALIAN
Liverpool House $$$

A large, glowing L will most likely be the first thing you notice about this restaurant, whose entrance features old-school shop display windows. This unaffected atmosphere is reflected inside with original moldings, antique hooks on which to hang your coat, and old brass lighting fixtures. The second venture by the people who brought us Joe Beef, Liverpool House, despite the name, serves a good amount of Italian fare, as well as a handful of French classics.

MAP 2: 2501 rue Notre-Dame W., 514/313-6049, www.liverpoolhouse.ca; 5pm-10:30pm Tues.-Sat.

Nora Gray $$$

Co-owned by Emma Cardarelli, Ryan Gray, and Lisa McConnell (alumni of Liverpool House), Nora Gray is a must-visit, immediately noticeable by its discreet hand-painted sign. This chic and cool vibe continues inside, where the decor is sleek with dark, paneled walls, banquettes, and low lighting, all working in tandem with chef Cardarelli's modern take on Italian cuisine. The pasta is near perfect, flavorful and filling but never heavy, and the cocktails are divine. With capacity topping out at 50, the place is almost always packed.

MAP 2: 1391 rue St-Jacques W., 514/419-6672, www.noragray.com; 5:30pm-11:30pm Tues.-Sat.

LEBANESE

Boustan $

There are a lot of Lebanese restaurants in Montréal, but nothing comes close to Boustan, smack-dab in the center of downtown, barely a block from Concordia University and on the main clubbing strip. You'll find everyone from students to office workers and late-night revelers stopping in to this fluorescently lit, three-table fast-food counter. The standbys, like falafel, shawarma, and shish kebabs, are all as tasty as the next; even the vegetarian pita is worth a try. But no matter what you order, make sure to say "yes, please" to the secret sauce.

MAP 2: 2020 rue Crescent, 514/843-3576, www.boustan.ca; 11am-4am daily

Garage Beirut $

There's an authentic feel to Garage Beirut, from its simple decor—white walls and wood tables and chairs—to its delicious grilled meats and delectable mezes (small dishes); everything feels and tastes homemade. The grilled meats are a must, as is the hummus, which will never quite taste as good elsewhere. Portions are reasonable, not huge, which just means that there's more room for their homemade baklava. Located near Concordia University, this place is popular with students and locals grabbing an affordable bite before heading to the cinema.

MAP 2: 1238 rue Mackay, 514/564-2040; 11:30am-2:30pm and 5pm-10pm Mon.-Fri., 11am-10pm Sat.-Sun.

TURKISH

Avesta $

The first thing you'll notice about this restaurant is a woman methodically rolling out dough in the storefront window. What she's rolling, and what features in almost all of the dishes, is lavash, a thin, doughy flatbread that'll just about melt in your mouth. Dip this bread into any of a large selection of mezes (small dishes) or try it folded around some spinach and feta in *gozleme* (Turkish crêpes). The atmosphere is casual, comfortable, and inviting, with traditional crafts accenting the seating and walls. Relax after your meal with a strong Turkish coffee and some baklava.

MAP 2: 2077 rue Ste-Catherine W., 514/937-0156; 11am-11pm daily

VEGETARIAN

Bonny's $

Dedicated to organic, vegetarian meals, this eatery also caters to vegans and those with other similar dietary restrictions. An open kitchen and a wall covered with logs add to the restaurant's charm. The soup of the day

NAVIGATING DIETARY RESTRICTIONS

Montréal is an eater's paradise—one that often focuses on rich French cuisine. But never fear: We also have a bevy of cuisines to suit other tastes, requirements, and palates!

VEGETARIAN AND VEGAN

Many Montréal faves offer great vegetarian and vegan options: **La Banquise** and **Chez Claudette** have vegan poutine (and **Patati Patata**'s is vegetarian). **Dépanneur le Pick-Up** has a killer "pulled tofu" sandwich. **La Panthère Verte** offers pitas stuffed with tempeh or tofu steak. **Aux Vivres, ChuChai,** and **Le Cagibi** are all (amazing) vegetarian restaurants that offer vegan options. **7Grains Bakery & Cafe** is vegan-friendly.

You'll probably be fine making requests in English, but, just in case: *végétarien* means vegetarian ("without meat" is *sans viande*), and *végétalien* means vegan (*sans viande,* and without eggs and dairy—*sans oeufs ni produits laitiers*).

GLUTEN-FREE

If you eat gluten-free, then Montréal's bagel shops and delis may not work well for you—and you'll need to seek out specialty poutine. The gravy in **La Banquise**'s vegan poutine is also gluten-free; most Vietnamese restaurants, plentiful in the city, offer gluten-free options as well. **Dépanneur le Pick-Up** will make their sandwiches on corn tortillas, and **Aux Vivres** and **7Grains Bakery & Cafe** have gluten-free, vegetarian choices. **Sophie Sucrée** is a gluten-free-friendly, vegan bakery. **Chez José, La Panthère Verte, Les Oubliettes, Brit and Chips,** and **Olive & Gourmando** all offer gluten-free dishes. At crêperies, ask if they offer pure-buckwheat crêpes.

Gluten-free is *sans gluten* in French—you may see "SG" instead of, or in addition to, "GF" on menus.

is served in a giant teacup. Burgers, sandwiches, and salads make up the majority of the menu, but there are daily specials for more dinner-like fare. The desserts tend to be simple but no less inviting—try the brownies with coconut milk ice cream for a decadent, shareable treat. A takeout counter serves those on the run.

MAP 2: 1748 rue Notre-Dame W., 514/931-4136, www.bonnys.ca; 11:30am-9pm Mon.-Fri., noon-9pm Sat.

PUB GRUB
Burgundy Lion $$

At this classic-style British pub—it even has popular Brit-Pop nights—the people are always warm, welcoming, and drinking a pint. Typical public house grub like shepherd's pie, bangers-and-mash, and fish-and-chips are all on the menu. But as at modern British counterparts, expect gastropub fare: less grease, more cuisine. The weekend brunch is a treat and can be served with a choice of English muffins or crumpets and even a serving of Scotch eggs. The decor features dark wood, exposed brick, and a fire in winter.

MAP 2: 2496 rue Notre-Dame W., 514/934-0333, www.burgundylion.com; 11:30am-3am Mon.-Fri., 9am-3am Sat.-Sun.

COMFORT FOOD
Le Boucan $$

An American smokehouse in the heart of Little Burgundy, Le Boucan serves up Stateside classics like mac-and-cheese, Cajun shrimp, pork ribs, and barbecue chicken, all available to be washed down with bourbon. The decor is fairly casual, with repurposed wood on the walls, banquettes, bar stools, and diner-style napkin dispensers on each table, which you'll need for their 5 Napkin Burger. This place is often busy, so call ahead for reservations, and if you're visiting in summer try to nab a table on the outdoor patio.

MAP 2: 1886 rue Notre-Dame W., 514/439-4555, www.leboucan.com; 11:30am-10pm Mon.-Wed., 11:30am-11pm Thurs.-Fri., noon-11pm Sat., noon-10pm Sun.

COFFEE
Café Myriade $

Serving blends from Canada's top roaster, 49th Parallel, and using a Mirage coffee maker—the only one of its kind in Canada—Café Myriade takes coffee seriously, but in taste, not pretension. The decor is well thought out, with lots of wood and large, open windows letting in a ton of light, which is needed in the winter months. During the summer there's a small terrace out front. The vibe is friendly and the baristas are eager to please. As it's surrounded by Concordia University, expect to find yourself among students during the school year.

MAP 2: 1432 rue Mackay, 514/939-1717, www.cafemyriade.com; 7:30am-7pm Mon.-Fri., 9am-7pm Sat.-Sun.

Centre-Ville Est   Map 3

QUÉBÉCOIS
SAT Labo Culinaire $

On the top floor of the Société des Arts Technologiques (the SAT), the Labo Culinaire is run by über-talented chefs Adrien Renaud and Maude Rochette. The mind-blowing menus, based on a dedicated seasonal theme, offer a few choices for appetizers and mains, and one dessert. The no-frills decor ensures you get a great view of the open kitchen where the chefs work their magic. Portions are reasonable, so order more than one dish. A summer rooftop terrace is almost always packed. It's one of the best places to grab a drink and a bite downtown.

MAP 3: 1201 blvd. St-Laurent, 514/844-2033, ext. 225, www.sat.qc.ca/en/evenements/labo-culinaire; 5pm-10pm Tues.-Sat.

FRENCH
Brasserie T! $$

Brasserie T!, the bistro brainchild of Toqué!'s Normand Laprise, is housed in a sleek, all-glass, corridor-like building. It cozies up to the Musée d'Art Contemporain and looks out onto the sleek low fountains of the Quartier des Spectacles. Serving dishes like cheeseburgers and shrimp *guédille* (shrimp-stuffed hot dog roll), this place has been packed since it opened with businesspeople, curious tourists, and young professionals. It provides an excellent alternative to Laprise's super good and super expensive usual fare—try the post-9:30pm menu for a real deal. Reservations are recommended.

MAP 3: 1425 rue Jeanne-Mance, 514/282-0808, www.brasserie-t.com; 11:30am-10:30pm Sun.-Wed., 11:30am-11:30pm Thurs.-Sat.

CHINESE
Maison Kim Fung $

Hidden in a nondescript, all-purpose complex on the edge of Chinatown, Maison Kim Fung is the go-to place for dim sum, but it also offers Cantonese and Szechuan dishes. Maison Kim Fung takes up prime real estate on the corner unit, and you can often see the packed house before you even step in the building. No matter the time, this place is always bustling, so expect a line for Sunday morning dim sum.

MAP 3: 1111 rue St-Urbain, 514/878-2888, www.restaurantchinatownkimfung.com; 11am-10pm daily

Chez Bong

KOREAN
Chez Bong $

Half a flight of stairs leads down to this eatery in the heart of Chinatown. You'll find a menu full of Korean cuisine. The modest decor consists of a few long, communal tables, wood-paneled walls, and lighting that gives the place a yellowish hue. It is usually packed with locals, and the atmosphere is decidedly relaxed. Favorites include bibimbap (a rice dish), *jap chae* (stir-fried noodles), and spicy stir-fried pork and kimchi.

MAP 3: 1021 blvd. St-Laurent, 514/396-7779; 11am-3pm Mon., 11am-3pm and 5pm-9pm Tues.-Fri., noon-9pm Sat.

COFFEE
Pikolo Espresso Bar $

Pikolo is an apt name for this sliver of an espresso bar. With a few stools and tables along the walls and a teeny mezzanine with seating at the back, Pikolo is a great place to grab a coffee to go or drink an espresso (though you can also often nab a seat on the bench out front). Located on the edge of downtown and the McGill University Ghetto (where most McGill students live), it's one of the best bets for great coffee in the area.

MAP 3: 3418B ave. du Parc, 514/508-6800, www.pikoloespresso.com; 7:30am-7pm Mon.-Fri., 9am-7pm Sat.-Sun.

DESSERT
Pâtisserie Harmonie $

Fifty different sweets are on offer at this Chinese bakery. It's an ideal spot to pop in and grab a mango cake, a few rounds of egg custard, or a deliciously moist slice of Japanese cheesecake. Buns are their hallmark, though, so sample both the savory (barbecue pork, curried beef) and the sweet (red bean cake, taro, and sesame). With no seats and no counter space, this is a take-out place—keep your eyes open and you'll see the area's shoppers digging into their sweets as they wander the streets.

MAP 3: 85 rue de la Gauchetière W., 514/875-1328; 8:30am-9pm Mon.-Thurs., 8:30am-10pm Fri., 9am-10pm Sat.-Sun.

Quartier Latin and the Village

Map 4

QUÉBÉCOIS

Mâche $$

Serving up Québécois comfort food in the heart of the student-strewn Quartier Latin, Mâche offers provincial classics like poutine (fries, gravy, cheese curds), *ragoût de pattes de cochon* (pork meatballs and potatoes), and *pâte chinois* (ground beef, mashed potatoes, etc.), as well as North American faves like mac-and-cheese and grilled cheese. Wood-paneled walls, stools reminiscent of hockey benches, and a couple of flat screens give it a slight sports bar feel. It's a few steps below street level, and during the summer there's a sidewalk patio.

MAP 4: 1655 rue St-Denis, 514/439-5535, www.restaurantmache.com; 11:30am-10pm Mon.-Wed. and Sun., 11:30am-11pm Thurs.-Sat.

Mâche

FRENCH

O'Thym $$

This BYOB restaurant in the Village offers a nice alternative to some of the more boisterous eateries in the area. Situated on an unassuming strip of de Maisonneuve not far from Amherst, O'Thym has high ceilings, lots of banquette seating, and picture windows that let in tons of light. The daily market menu is written on the chalkboard walls, and offerings include staples like Îles-de-la-Madeleine scallops and *magret de canard* (duck breast). With seating for approximately 50 people, the atmosphere is inviting but not the best choice for larger groups.

MAP 4: 1112 blvd. de Maisonneuve E., 514/525-3443, www.othym.com; 6pm-10pm Mon., 11:30am-3pm and 6pm-10pm Tues.-Thurs., 11:30am-3pm and 6pm-10:30pm Fri., 11:30am-2:30pm and 6pm-10:30pm Sat., 11:30am-2:30pm and 6pm-10pm Sun.

Au Petit Extra $$

Though the menu varies depending on the season, Au Petit Extra always features classic French staples like steak frites, *confit de canard* (duck), and *terrine de foie gras.* The atmosphere is casual but elegant and often full of lively clientele; the venue has the feel of a great neighborhood bistro. If you're in the mood for a full meal, opt for the table d'hôte, available at either lunch or dinner and always a great deal. Reservations are never a bad idea.

MAP 4: 1690 rue Ontario E., 514/527-5552, www.aupetitextra.com; 11:30am-2:30pm and 5:30pm-10pm Mon.-Wed., 11:30am-2:30pm and 5:30pm-10:30pm Thurs.-Fri., 5:30pm-10:30pm Sat., 10am-2pm and 5:30pm-9:30pm Sun.

BE YOUR OWN SOMMELIER

Montréal is home to BYOBs and BYOWs, otherwise known as Bring Your Own Bottle (or Wine) restaurants, where diners are invited to bring their own instead of choosing from the restaurant's wine list—and you won't be charged a corkage fee. These restaurants are popular with groups and, it has to be said, young university students. But it doesn't have to be a rowdy night; many BYOBs have some of the best chefs in the city, and depending on where you go, the atmosphere can be either casual or refined.

Bring-your-owns can be found around the city, but Duluth and Prince Arthur, both charming cobblestone streets, have the highest concentration. Duluth has the most choices in the city, but some options are mediocre. One standout is **La Colombe,** a great, elegant corner bistro. Farther north on rue Rachel, you'll find seafood restaurant **Le Poisson Rouge.**

Up in the Plateau, Gilford is a picturesque street full of irresistible BYOBs; **Le Quartier Général** is one of the best on the scene and is almost always packed. One of the most popular with locals and visitors alike is **Pizzeria Napoletana,** a lively, busy pizza parlor and Italian eatery in Little Italy. They don't take reservations for groups under eight, however, so you might be in for a wait.

AMERICAN
Kitchenette $$$

The relaxed atmosphere and minimal and welcoming decor—dark wood bar, antique white columns, and lots of windows—are the backdrop for dishes like sea bream tartare, trout gravlax, lobster ravioli, and rabbit saddle. For a special treat, try the evening tasting menu for $89.

MAP 4: 1353 blvd. René-Lévesque E., 514/527-1016, www.kitchenette-montreal. ca; 11am-2:30pm Mon., 11am-2:30pm and 5:30pm-10pm Tues.-Fri., 5:30pm-10pm Sat.

BAKERIES
La Mie Matinale $

This artisanal bakery offers your morning bread—everything from muffins to croissants, all buttery and impeccably good, made from untreated flour without preservatives. At Christmastime, stop by the café, with its exposed brick walls, bistro chairs, and welcoming staff, for some of their stollen, a German Christmas cake. It's so popular with the local community that it can be ordered online. One quirk about this place is its dedication to Dalida, a popular French singer from the early 1960s; her images completely fill one long wall, and her music is on heavy rotation.

MAP 4: 1654 rue Ste-Catherine E., 514/529-5656, www.lamiematinale.ca; 10am-3:30pm Mon., 8:30am-8:30pm Tues.-Sat., 9am-8pm Sun.

COFFEE AND TEA
Camellia Sinensis $

Started by four men who, quite simply, just love tea, the aim of Camellia Sinensis was to bring quality teas from all over the world to tea lovers in Montréal. Each year the four head off to different corners of the world to find the best tea there is, and each year, the menu changes accordingly. The salon is a cozy spot full of red cushions on which to sit cross-legged and enjoy a pot of one of their unique, high-quality brews. Check out its Marché Jean-Talon location if you're in the north end of the city.

MAP 4: 351 rue Emery, 514/286-4002, www.camellia-sinensis.com; 10am-6pm Mon.-Wed. and Sun., 10am-9pm Thurs.-Sat.

Pourquoi Pas Espresso Bar $

This snug spot on rue Amherst is owned by Tony (a Francophone) and Tyler (an Anglo). The café has a gender-neutral bathroom, vegan-friendly desserts, and an overall welcoming vibe. The beans are from roaster Te Aro, delicious as espresso or as a latte or cappuccino. Stop in for a pick-me-up while visiting the Village and, if it's not too busy, pull up a chair and enjoy the ideal Montréal atmosphere before you mosey on your way.

MAP 4: 1447 rue Amherst, 514/419-9400; 7:30am-6pm Mon.-Fri., 8:30am-6pm Sat., 11am-5pm Sun.

DESSERT
Juliette et Chocolat $
Perfect for late breakfast, lunch, or dinner, Juliette et Chocolat is known for its sweet and savory crêpes, brownies, and other chocolate desserts—including plenty of gluten-free options. Whatever your choice, be sure to top it off with a thick Grandma's Style hot chocolate. The popular business has grown apace since the sweet-loving Juliette opened her first location on St-Denis in 2003; you can now find several more locations in Outremont, the Plateau, Mile End, Marché Jean-Talon, and Centre-Ville.

MAP 4: 1615 rue St-Denis, 514/287-3555, www.julietteetchocolat.com; 11am-11pm Mon.-Thurs. and Sun., 11am-midnight Fri.-Sat.

Plateau Mont-Royal   Map 5

QUÉBÉCOIS
Maison Publique $$$
Maison Publique, or "Public House" in English, sums up its French-English mash-up perfectly from the get-go. Ranked #11 by Canada's 100 Best Restaurants, this gastropub's decor is all down-home charm—dark wood paneling, warm wallpaper, open kitchen. Its ambitious menu, crafted by chef Derek Dammann, mixes classic British (he worked at Jamie Oliver's Fifteen in London and the celeb chef backed the project) and French flavors to create some truly unique dishes like horse carpaccio, strawberries with cheddar, and delicacies served on toast. Eating here is an absolute must.

MAP 5: 4720 rue Marquette, 514/507-0555, www.maisonpublique.com; 6pm-10pm Wed.-Fri., 10:30am-2pm and 6pm-10pm Sat.-Sun.

Le Chien Fumant $$$
On a quiet street corner, this long, narrow restaurant is virtually all windows, but it stays cozy even in the deepest of winter with hearty fare like Cuban hanger steak, Rossini quail, and cod served with tabbouleh. Using local, market-fresh ingredients, the menu changes regularly—and the dishes are influenced by chef Maxim Morin's travels. The youthful atmosphere invites a youthful crowd, but it's also a popular family spot for brunch. Start your meal with one of the cocktails—the bar is artfully hung from the ceiling. Make reservations.

MAP 5: 4710 rue de Lanaudière, 514/524-2444, www.lechienfumant.com; 6pm-2am Tues.-Sat., 10am-3pm and 6pm-2am Sun.

Au Pied de Cochon $$$
This bustling Plateau bistro specializes in hearty, nose-to-tail Québécois

POUTINE

Poutine—piping-hot, crispy French fries covered with fresh cheese curds and smothered in gravy—is the unofficial food of Québec.

It can be found on menus throughout the province, from upscale restaurants (where it's likely served with foie gras) to fast-food places. Despite the dish's popularity, its origins remain hotly debated, with a number of greasy spoon owners declaring themselves the true inventor.

Whether the first poutine was created in the town of Drummondville or Warwick, no one will ever know for sure. But one part of the origin story remains the same: The invention of poutine hinges on customers adding fresh cheese curds to their fries.

Cheese is one of the province's biggest industries, and because of this fresh cheese curds are found in greasy spoons and corner grocery stores all over the province. The curds have a slightly rubbery texture and a mild but salty taste. You can tell whether the cheese is fresh or not by the sound of the squeak it makes when chewed—the squeakier, the fresher.

Since the fries and cheese together taste a little dry, gravy is added to the mix—enough so that you taste it, but not so much that it looks like a stew. The gravy also helps melt the cheese and turn the whole thing into a glorious mess.

The dish is popular across Montréal, especially in the winter. You can find fancy, pricey versions at **Au Pied de Cochon** (page 114), a down-to-earth iteration at **Patati Patata** (page 116), and a massive range of options, including vegan and gluten-free choices, at **La Banquise** (page 116). You really can't go wrong ordering poutine in Montréal—even McDonald's carries it here, and city chain Frite Alors offers it up on the cheap in most neighborhoods.

fare, catering to a fairly carnivorous crowd. Anthony Bourdain, visiting for *No Reservations,* called chef Martin Picard "one of the best chefs in Canada" and Au Pied de Cochon a "temple to everything fatty, porky, and duck-related." Picard is now a household name in the province, thanks to outrageous dishes like Foie Gras Poutine, Duck in a Can, and maple crème brûlée. Always lively, this warmly lit casual spot is popular for group get-togethers—plan ahead to snag a table.

MAP 5: 536 ave. Duluth E., 514/281-1114, http://aupieddecochon.ca; 5pm-midnight Wed.-Sun.

Le Quartier Général $$$

Le Quartier Général offers local (meaty!) ingredients cooked perfectly and served with artistic flair. Think chalkboards and minimal, though nice, decor; the perfect spot for dinner with friends. Dishes vary by week and season, but often feature perfectly cooked rabbit and duck, two Québec staples. Call ahead for dinner reservations, or stop in to treat yourself to lunch.

MAP 5: 1251 rue Gilford, 514/658-1839; 11:30am-3pm and 6pm-11pm Mon.-Fri., 6pm-11pm Sat.-Sun.

La Banquise $

Poutine capital of Montréal, La Banquise serves 28 different kinds of poutine, 24 hours a day, seven days a week. Initially opened in 1968 as an ice cream shop, La Banquise soon started to serve typical *casse-croûte* (Québécois snack bar) fare; today, it offers an impressive variety of fried delicacies, including poutines for vegan and gluten-free diners. You'll find brightly painted walls, wooden banquettes, and boisterous company, no matter the time of day. Open all night, this bright-blue-and-yellow building acts as a siren call for midnight revelers looking to temper their beer consumption with a snack.

MAP 5: 994 rue Rachel E., 514/525-2415, www.restolabanquise.com; 24 hours daily

Patati Patata $

This *"friterie de luxe"*—a "luxurious" Québécois-style chip shop—is a tiny, colorful spot on the corner of St-Laurent and rue Rachel, right next door to the Big in Japan Bar (don't get the lines confused!). The ambience is warm, the service is brisk, and you'll be elbow to elbow with your neighbors; grab a seat at the counter, if you can, and watch the skilled cooks pull together near-slider-size burgers, huge poutines (including veg-friendly options), and cheap breakfasts using a tiny bank of fryers and a flat-top grill. Cash only.

MAP 5: 4177 blvd. St-Laurent, 514/844-0216; 8am-2am daily

FRENCH

La Colombe $$$

Located on the end of a busy restaurant strip, this bring-your-own-wine restaurant is romantic and elegant. Popular with both gourmet and classical diners, this peace-loving restaurant (La Colombe means "dove") serves a prix fixe menu of upscale French food with a bit of Moroccan influence—and amazing local cheese. With exposed brick walls, low lighting, and seating topping out at 45 people, it's a small restaurant with a neighborhood feel.

MAP 5: 554 ave. Duluth E., 514/849-8844; 5:30pm-10pm Tues.-Sat.

✪ L'Express $$

L'Express ranks among the best French bistros in the city. From the unnamed facade—look down, the restaurant's name is spelled out in the sidewalk tiles in front—to the arched floor-to-ceiling front window, it looks exclusive and inviting all at once. Inside, the place feels like a classic subway car-style resto—long and narrow, black-and-white tile floor, bar stools on one half and small square tables on the other. The service is impeccable, the food is classic French bistro, and the ambience is perfect for date night. Many of the city's chefs come for late-night bites.

MAP 5: 3927 rue St-Denis, 514/845-5333, www.restaurantlexpress.ca; 8am-3am Mon.-Fri., 10am-3am Sat., 10am-2am Sun.

Laloux $$

This casual but elegant bistro features high-end food and an extensive wine list. The menu, which changes seasonally, is focused on Québécois and Montréal flavors, using local produce and artisanal suppliers for creations like veal *tataki,* foie gras with brioche, and guinea fowl with *beurre noisette* (brown butter) pureed carrots. Save room for dessert—the chefs' creativity extends to smoked meringue, clementine mousse, and a host of other zany, simultaneously rich and delicate creations. Slightly off the beaten path, it's a neighborhood staple, appealing mostly to those with discerning palates.

MAP 5: 250 ave. des Pins E., 514/287-9127, www.laloux.com; 11:30am-2:30pm and 5:30pm-11:30pm Mon.-Fri, 5:30pm-11:30pm Sat.-Sun.

AMERICAN
L'Anecdote $$

This all-purpose diner is inviting and unpretentious, featuring mismatched chairs, checkerboard floors, and old-style counter seating. The menu is extensive, offering everything from filling and delicious crêpes and omelets to fried fish and fancier dishes like ravioli. Locals recommend the classic diner grub—the club sandwich and the perfectly seasoned burger. Like all favorite Plateau spots, it's bustling on the weekends.

MAP 5: 801 rue Rachel E., 514/526-7697; 11am-9pm Mon., 11am-10pm Tues.-Fri., 9am-10pm Sat., 9am-9pm Sun.

✪ Schwartz's $

This is the oldest deli in Canada; so when the term "Montréal institution" is used to describe this place, it is warranted. Opened in 1928, Schwartz's Hebrew Delicatessen remains largely unchanged, right down to its location, placemat menus, banquette seating, gruff waiters, fast service, and fluorescent lighting. Using tried-and-true-methods, the cooks smoke the meat daily in a special blend of spices to give it that Schwartz's taste. The basic smoked-meat sandwich, coleslaw, and fries combination—washed down with a cherry Coke—is the only way to go. You should, however, expect to wait, no matter the weather: Be it -30°C or 30°C, there is always a line down the block.

MAP 5: 3895 blvd. St-Laurent, 514/842-4813, www.schwartzsdeli.com; 8am-12:30am Sun.-Thurs., 8am-1:30am Fri., 8am-2:30am Sat.

Beauty's $

Founded in 1942, this neighborhood favorite offers all-day breakfast, pitch-perfect bagels and lox, melts, and luncheonette fare. Beauty's offers fresh, homemade, unpretentious food in a quaint diner atmosphere that's packed on the weekend; your best bet for a quick brekkie is to join the regulars on an early-morning weekday.

MAP 5: 93 Mont-Royal W., 514/849-8883, http://beautys.ca; 7am-3pm Mon.-Fri., 8am-4pm Sat.-Sun.

SOUTHERN
Icehouse $$

It's a tight squeeze into this corner Tex-Mex restaurant full of wood-paneled walls, heavy-duty benches, and wall-mounted paper towel dispensers, which you'll need since Icehouse has dispensed with plates. Your order of chicken and waffles, popcorn shrimp, fish tacos, or juicy ribs is served either in a paper container or in a bucket that is promptly dumped on your table for you to attack hands-on. The place is bound to be jumping, with bartenders serving up cold Micheladas and bourbon lemonade to just about every customer. Hit this place in summer when the patio allows for more breathing space.

MAP 5: 51 rue Roy E., 514/439-6691; 5pm-11pm Sun.-Thurs., 5pm-midnight Fri.-Sat.

KOREAN
Négasaké $$

This cute split-level restaurant can be easily missed on Prince Arthur, but it's worth stopping in—especially if

WINING AND DINING ALFRESCO

It's illegal to consume alcohol in public places in Montréal—unless you're having a picnic in the park! Montrealers have their so-called **"picnic law"** to thank for this fun custom. On a warm summer night when the wait times are long, consider picking up a bottle of wine or a couple beers on the way to a resto on the top of your list; order your food to go and decamp to one of Montréal's leafy, abundant parks. (Once the food is gone, put the alcohol away to avoid a ticket.) Try one of the spots below, or find your own hidden gem—they're abundant across the city.

PLATEAU MONT-ROYAL
Take your **La Banquise** poutine (page 116) or **Rotisserie Romados** chicken (page 118) to **Parc La Fontaine** (page 82). Farther west, check out **Parc Jeanne-Mance** (page 179).

PETITE-ITALIE
Grab a picnic basket from **Dinette Triple Crown** (page 124) and nestle into the tiny **Parc de la Petite-Italie** (page 181).

picnickers in the park

you're a bibimbap fan. The rice dish arrives in a hot stone bowl, perfectly spicy. Very filling, it makes the perfect lunch or dinner on a rainy day. Try cold soba noodles on a hot summer day, or, if you're feeling adventurous, snack on the beef tartare.

MAP 5: 70 rue Prince Arthur E., 514/564-5850; 11:30am-3pm and 5pm-10:30pm Tues.-Sun.

PORTUGUESE

✪ Chez José $

This tiny café with outdoor summer seating serves up my favorite breakfast in the city, Le Kurt Belair, an omelet with chorizo, potatoes, and cheddar served with their very good hot sauce. Gluten-free-friendly and offering foamy cappuccinos, José is a colorful spot popular with students, artists, and locals. At lunchtime, grab a smoothie, soup, or salad—or just have an afternoon latte at a window table, people-watching as you sip.

MAP 5: 173 ave. Duluth E., 514/845-0693; 7am-6pm Mon.-Fri., 8am-6pm Sat., 9am-6pm Sun.

Rotisserie Romados $

Rotisserie Romados serves the best grilled chicken in town. It's cooked just right—salty, spicy, and juicy—and you can smell the smoky tastiness all the way down the block. Seating is tight and it's hot as Hades in summer, so consider ordering to go and heading to Parc Jeanne-Mance for some alfresco dining. While decor is spare and reminiscent of a Midwest bus station, the vibe's still good—everyone's stoked to get their dinner. Not terribly vegetarian-friendly, Romados does serve perfectly baked Portuguese buns and egg tarts (natas).

MAP 5: 115 rue Rachel E., 514/849-1803; 11am-8pm daily

SPANISH
Pintxo $$

Pintxo is the Basque word for bite-size, flavor-packed food, which is what this restaurant does best. The subdued setting—white tablecloths, exposed brick walls, and large works of art—makes it an ideal place for a leisurely meal, but things get lively later in the evening. Though they serve a variety of mains, you may want to skip them in favor of cocktails and shared small bites. Try the *txori-pulpo* (grilled chorizo and octopus) or scallops in maple bacon to kick-start your palate. Popular with small groups who are ready to share, Pintxo attracts young professionals and mature diners.

MAP 5: 330 Mont-Royal Ave E., 514/844-0222, www.pintxo.ca; 6pm-11pm Mon., noon-2pm and 6pm-11pm Tues.-Fri., 11:30am-3pm and 6pm-11pm Sat.-Sun.

Khyber Pass

La Sala Rosa $$

Frequented by hipsters and elders of the Spanish community alike (it's owned by the same folks who run Casa del Popolo), this trendy restaurant represents the diversity of the neighborhood. Tapas are the main draw, though they also make a mean paella. Every Thursday diners are treated to a live flamenco performance; if you stay at the Pensione Popolo, you'll get 25 percent off their already reasonably priced tapas.

MAP 5: 4848 blvd. St-Laurent, 514/844-4227, www.lasalarosa.com; 5pm-11pm Sun.-Thurs., 5pm-midnight Fri.-Sat.

MIDDLE EASTERN
Kaza Maza $$

On the first floor of what was once a residential building, Kaza Maza is a comfortable, low-key eatery that also doubles as a performance space. Open and sparsely decorated, it serves up some of the best Middle Eastern food in the area. Mezes (small dishes) are their forte, with a selection of both hot and cold; though the *basturma* (dried, seasoned aged beef) and the thick *muhammara* (red pepper and walnut dip) are the standouts. For something a bit different, try the pistachio *kefta*, which mixes the nut with minced lamb, walnuts, and spices.

MAP 5: 4629 ave. du Parc, 514/844-6292, www.kazamaza.ca; 5pm-10pm Tues.-Thurs., 5pm-11pm Fri., 1pm-11pm Sat., 1pm-10pm Sun.

Khyber Pass $$

With its instantly recognizable exterior—a curved wooden facade makes it look like you're about to enter the Ark—and a warm interior chockablock with textiles, Khyber Pass is the perfect spot to bring a date or a few friends for an intimate meal. Serving meaty Afghan dishes and scented rice (you can't go wrong with the lamb kebab), this spot also caters to vegetarians and serves soothing after-dinner teas and desserts.

MAP 5: 506 ave. Duluth E., 514/844-7131, www.kazamaza.ca; 5pm-11pm daily

For Montrealers, there's nothing quite like the **Gibeau Orange Julep** (7700 Décarie, 514/738-7486, 24 hours daily summer, 7:30am-3am daily winter), a huge, two-story orange ball that sits near the Décarie highway and serves classic Québécois fast food—poutine, club sandwiches, hot dogs, and the eponymous orange drink, a delicious concoction that tastes like a creamsicle. It was started in 1932 by Hermas Gibeau, who constructed the first orange—a smaller version of the one we know today, which opened its doors in 1966—in 1945. Rumor has it he wanted to move both his business and his family into it (who wouldn't want to grow up in a giant ball?). A symbol to many Montrealers, it draws both curious tourists and long-time residents. (Note to those with bee and wasp allergies: The juleps are popular with your flying nemeses, so it may be best to stay in the car while a non-allergic family member tracks down takeout.)

VEGETARIAN
✪ Aux Vivres $$
Located in a bright, open, large space on the Main with a nice backyard terrace, Aux Vivres serves wholesome and filling vegan food at brunch, lunch, and dinner. It's not just vegans and vegetarians who frequent the joint, however; carnivores craving a healthy, satisfying meal also stop by for tempeh, veggies, and whole grains. Everyone will enjoy the Thai Bowl with grilled tempeh and the BLT Caesar, but you really can't go wrong. They also offer very good gluten-free options. For dessert, share a slice of the *gâteau choco-pomme* (chocolate apple cake). If you're in a rush, visit the take-out counter next door and take a bowl or wrap to go.
MAP 5: 4631 blvd. St-Laurent, 514/842-3479, www.auxvivres.com; 11am-11pm daily

ChuChai $$
ChuChai is the grande dame of vegetarian and vegan restaurants in the city, specializing in vegetarian Thai cuisine. There's nothing you can get here that you couldn't have in a regular Thai restaurant, but with about triple the taste. Fake duck, chicken, and shrimp (most are "wheat meat," so not suitable for gluten-free diets) are all on the menu and supremely

delicious, and the same goes for the melt-in-your-mouth fried spinach. The choice of diehard vegans wanting to indulge in a refined meal, ChuChai also appeals to all Thai-food lovers, since, meat or not, they serve some of the best Thai in the city.
MAP 5: 4088 rue St-Denis, 514/843-4194, www.chuchai.com; 11am-2pm and 5pm-10pm Tues.-Thurs., 11am-2pm and 5pm-11pm Fri.-Sat., 2pm-9pm Sun.

SEAFOOD
Le Poisson Rouge $$$
This bring-your-own-wine restaurant is a rich, deep red, with cozy seating and a wall of near floor-to-ceiling windows facing out onto rue Rachel. Specializing in seafood—the name means "red fish"—they offer a prix-fixe menu with house-smoked salmon as well as dishes like a daily terrine, ceviche, sweetbreads, fried calamari, and seared tuna. The intimate setting, relaxed familiar ambience, and attentive staff will make you feel like you've been here for years.
MAP 5: 1201 rue Rachel E., 514/522-4876, www.restaurantlepoissonrouge.com; 5:30pm-10pm Wed.-Sun.

STEAKHOUSE
Moishes $$$
Founded in 1938 by Moishe Lighter, a Jewish-Romanian immigrant, Moishes

is a true institution. Lighter was part of the immigrant community that helped shape the Main, and his tradition of smoking meat turned his restaurant into the best steakhouse in Montréal. The menu is meat-heavy—"lighter" options include steak frites and filet mignon poutine. The elegant atmosphere and upscale prices mean you will feel most comfortable if you dress up a little. If you like the idea but hate the price, a fabulous After 9 menu is well worth your hard-earned cash and there's a $45 prix-fixe Sunday dinner.

MAP 5: 3961 blvd. St-Laurent, 514/845-3509, www.moishes.ca; 5:30pm-10pm Sun.-Tues., 5:30pm-11pm Wed., 5:30pm-midnight Thurs.-Fri., 5pm-midnight Sat.

CAFÉS

Le Café des Chats $

Wash your hands and leave your boots in the foyer—then settle in for coffee, tea, and snacks including croissants, *pain au chocolat* (chocolate croissants), and grilled cheeses. The café's atmosphere and fare are on par with the Plateau's high bar for quality, but the real draw of this cat café is its nine felines, all adopted from the SPCA. Whether you're missing Fluffy or looking for a moment of respite from the busy city, this concept café—the first of its kind in North America—will deliver.

MAP 5: 3435 St-Denis, 514/289-2428, www.cafedeschats.ca; 11am-8pm Tues.-Thurs., 11am-10pm Fri.-Sat., 11am-8pm Sun.

Café Santropol $

Santropol bills itself as Montréal's first café—it was founded in 1976 as part of an effort to stop a neglected building from being torn down. Now a neighborhood staple with a beloved

summer patio (snag a seat with a view of Mont-Royal!), Santropol serves up quality soups, sandwiches, and coffee in a laid-back, old-school-hippie-ish atmosphere. The coffee is fair-trade organic, and it's so popular, you can now pick up a pound or two on your way out the door or at the local grocery store.

MAP 5: 3990 rue St-Urbain, 514/842-3110, www.santropol.com; 11:30am-10:30pm daily

Café Santropol

COFFEE

Café Névé $

In a corner spot that used to belong to a bike repair shop, Café Névé is a great addition to this strip of rue Rachel, linking St-Laurent and St-Denis. The large, open space with huge windows and cozy nooks and crannies is sparsely decorated with shabby-chic decor. The vibe is youthful and cool, but it's also a favorite for families—no one's going to be uptight about your tantrum-throwing four-year-old. Everything is reasonably priced and the coffee will satisfy even the snobbiest of coffee snobs. Check out other locations on Mont-Royal and in the Mile End.

MAP 5: 151 rue Rachel E., 514/903-9294, www.cafeneve.com; 8am-10pm Mon.-Thurs., 8am-9pm Fri., 9am-9pm Sat.

Café Replika $

Take a break from your busy day touring the city and *prend un café* (have coffee) at this homey spot across the street from Café Névé. Though it's popular with freelancers and students—recall the sound of many fingers typing—Replika somehow retains a chill, laid-back feel. It's the perfect place to put your feet up for a minute while you decide which corner of Montréal you'll head to next.

MAP 5: 252 rue Rachel E., 514/903-4384, www.cafereplika.com; 8am-6pm Mon.-Fri., 9am-6pm Sat.-Sun.

DESSERTS

Pâtisserie Kouign Amann $

This bakery specializes in *kouign amann,* a hard-to-pronounce layered cake from Brittany that takes a ratio of 40 percent dough, 30 percent butter, and 30 percent sugar—100 percent delectable. (Cronut fans—this is your fave's great-grandparent.) Cozy and welcoming, this bakery also serves coffee, sandwiches, croissants, and quiches, and is a great place for a light lunch. The whole operation takes place directly behind the counter—if you manage to lay claim to one of the relatively few chairs, you can watch the chefs work as you bite into your little piece of French heaven.

MAP 5: 322 ave. du Mont-Royal E., 514/845-8813; 7am-7pm Mon.-Fri., 7am-6pm Sat.

Sophie Sucrée $

This vegan, gluten-free-friendly bakery stands out like a pink beacon on the otherwise stark Avenue des Pins. Decadent yet healthy, Sophie Sucrée caters to pretty much any dietary requirement you can think of. The atmosphere is quaint, like a cozy teahouse, and the proprietors are friendly. Share a tart in-house and then take some goodies to go. (Traveling with non-vegan, gluten-loving friends? They won't even notice you're tricking them out of wheat and butter.)

MAP 5: 167 ave. des Pins E., 514/823-5865; 11am-6pm Sun.-Thurs., 11am-9pm Fri., 11am-8pm Sat.

Mile End and Petite-Italie   Map 6

FRENCH

Leméac $$$

Open and spacious, this is one neighborhood bistro that can, and does, accommodate a crowd. Built on great bistro fare like steak frites, beef tartare, and blood pudding, Leméac goes just that little bit further with homemade desserts and Québec specialties like local cheese. Depending on when you go, the clientele varies from ladies who lunch to young professionals having a late bite before heading out on the town. The atmosphere is always a little reserved, however, in that classic French way. A little on the pricier side, it's popular for its $27 menu, available after 10pm.

MAP 6: 1045 ave. Laurier W., 514/270-0999, www.restaurantlemeac.com; noon-midnight Mon.-Fri., 10am-midnight Sat.-Sun.

Lawrence $$

At Lawrence, chef Marc Cohen adds to the restaurant's casually chic

MONTRÉAL BAGELS

Unlike the big, doughy New York bagel, Montréal bagels are smaller, denser, sweeter, and, traditionally, covered in sesame seeds. The city's most famous bagelries, **St-Viateur Bagel Shop** (page 123) and **Fairmount Bagel** (page 123), both operate 24 hours a day, seven days a week—with only a 10-minute walk between them. Made around the clock, using a wood-fired oven and hand-rolled dough, the bagels are always hot and delicious and are best when dipped in whipped cream cheese.

Together, St-Viateur and Fairmount Bagel form the contemporary legacy of Montréal's bagel dominance. They also share similar histories.

Founded in 1957 by Myer Lewkowicz, who brought his recipe with him when he emigrated from Eastern Europe, St-Viateur has since expanded to include cafés in the Plateau, Notre-Dame-de-Grâce, and Monkland neighborhoods, as well as a second, smaller bakery about half a block down from the original.

The origins of Fairmount Bagel, however, go much further back. Opened in 1919 by Isadore Shlafman, off a back alley on the Main, it was the first bagel bakery in Montréal. When it moved to its current location on Fairmount in 1949, it was renamed "The Original Fairmount Bagel Bakery." Shlafman's grandchildren continue to run the business to this day.

Since the early days, there has been a silent but ongoing competition between the two shops, and both have their diehard customers. To an outsider the differences between the two are negligible, but ask any Montrealer and they'll likely have a preference.

atmosphere with his simple and delicious dishes and a classic brunch on weekends. The evening and lunch offerings feature everything from lamb with kohlrabi to stewed chicken, fennel, and clams. Lawrence is ideally located in a cozy corner spot, with windows on both sides of the restaurant, allowing light to come in at all times of the day. Inside, plaid banquettes and long wooden tables complement the soft gray walls.

MAP 6: 5201 blvd. St-Laurent, 514/503-1070, www.lawrencerestaurant.com; 11:30am-3pm and 5:30pm-11pm Tues.-Fri., 10am-3pm and 5:30pm-11pm Sat., 10am-3pm Sun.

BAGELS

Fairmount Bagel $

Opened in 1919 under a different name, Fairmount Bagel claims the title of first-ever Montreal bagel bakery. Like its closest competitor, St-Viateur, Fairmount uses traditional methods, including a wood-fire oven, to craft its bagels. Unlike St-Viateur, however, they'll apply your cream cheese in-store for you. The small storefront is lined with baked goods, and its dark-wood and subway-tile decor gives it a classic, age-old institution feeling. The line-up, which moves quickly, often snakes out the door and around the side of the building. No indoor seating is available.

MAP 6: 74 Fairmount W., 514/272-0667, www.fairmountbagel.com; 24 hours daily

St-Viateur Bagel Shop $

Located on Mile End's busiest cross street, this long, narrow storefront and bakery pumps out bagels 24 hours a day, 365 days a year. Boiled in honey water and then cooked in a wood-fire oven, the bagels are very fresh, and often still warm when you buy them. Drinks and cream cheese, as well as St-Viateur swag—mugs, T-shirts, tote bags—are available, but you'll need to apply the cream cheese yourself. Very limited seating is available, so visitors often find a bench along St-Viateur in the summer months, or head to Café Olimpico, just down the street, to buy a cappuccino and snack on their bagels indoors.

MAP 6: 263 rue St-Viateur, 514/276-8044, www.stviateurbagel.com; 24 hours daily

SOUTHERN
✪ Dinette Triple Crown $$

The experience you'll get at Dinette is unlike any other. The brainchild of an ex-chef of Dépanneur le Pick-Up (another excellent, quirky restaurant), it's all about Southern comforts and alfresco dining. Dinette offers traditional Southern dishes like pulled pork, fried chicken, collard greens, and pan-fried cornbread. You can eat in their warm dining room, or, in the summer, the staff will pack your order up in a picnic basket, complete with checkered tablecloth, and send you on your way. Luckily, there's a park kitty-corner to the restaurant where you can enjoy your meal under the stars. All of this makes for a memorable dinner—just remember to return the basket after your meal.

Map 6: 6704 rue Clark, 514/272-2617, www.dinettetriplecrown.com; 11am-9pm Thurs.-Tues.

CHINESE
Étoile Rouge $

A smallish spot in Little Italy, this restaurant offers great wonton soup, General Tao chicken, and spicy cabbage salad, but its crowning jewel is

its wide variety of vegetarian and meat dumplings. Opened in 2016, Étoile Rouge has not quite caught on yet, which means that it's a great place to go on a busy Friday or Saturday night.

MAP 6: 6707 blvd. St-Laurent, 438/386-9788 or 514/507-3474, www.comptoir21.com; 11:30am-11pm Sun.-Thurs., 11:30am-midnight Fri.-Sat.

VIETNAMESE
Pho Tay Ho $

In Montréal, pho tends to be called Tonkinese soup, or soupe Tonkinoise. Pho Tay Ho, a midsized restaurant on a nondescript part of rue St-Denis, is one of the best places to get a reasonably priced bowl of steaming-hot beef, chicken, or vegetarian soup on a cold winter's day, or a vermicelli bowl (try the lemongrass beef) on a warm day in summer, when the patio is open. It's not fancy, but it's the perfect place for lunch or dinner if your stomach needs a break from rich French food.

MAP 6: 6414 rue St-Denis, 514/273-5627; 10am-8:45pm Wed.-Mon.

GREEK
Milos $$$

Located on a stretch of avenue du Parc that isn't exactly swanky, Milos is a pricey hidden gem—its luxurious taverna interior feels almost yacht-like (which is apt, because the restaurant, which has locations in New York, Athens, and Miami, also offers catered cruises of the Mediterranean). Serving what is considered by some to be the best seafood in the city, Milos is well-known for its pricey dishes and cool surroundings. Try the wine-marinated octopus, crab cakes, and *tsipoura* (sea bream), fresh from the Aegean Sea. Affordable prix-fixe lunch and after-10 specials are also available.

MAP 6: 5357 ave. du Parc,
514/272-3552, www.milos.ca; noon-3pm
and 5:30pm-midnight Mon.-Fri.,
5:30pm-midnight Sat., 5:30pm-11pm Sun.

ITALIAN
Lucca $$$

Classy and rustic all at once, this is the
swankiest of restaurants in the area,
with the prices to prove it. The deceptively simple cuisine is what customers come back for, such as the seafood
linguine with clams, shrimp, and fish.
Because they use market-fresh ingredients, dishes often change (check out
the chalkboard menu), but staples like
risotto, pasta, and meat dishes are always available, as is their heavenly ti-
ramisu for dessert. The dress code isn't
too fancy, but you might want to pull
on a collared shirt and leave the cargo
pants at home.

MAP 6: 12 rue Dante, 514/278-6502,
www.restaurantlucca.ca; noon-2:30pm
and 6pm-10:30pm Mon.-Fri., 6pm-10pm
Sat.

Bottega Pizzeria $$

This modern upscale setting is welcoming, with the heat of a real wood
fireplace burning in the background.
Using traditional Neapolitan methods,
Bottega makes some of the most authentic pizza in the city, and their wine
list is exquisite. Following tradition,
they offer *sfizis,* typical Neapolitan
appetizers; try the giant meatball and
you won't be disappointed. For dessert, go for a gelato—the perfect cap to
a Neapolitan meal. Allow your server
to pair your wines for you—the wine
list perfectly complements the meals
on offer.

MAP 6: 65 rue St-Zotique E., 514/277-8104,
www.bottega.ca; 5pm-10pm Tues.-Wed.
and Sun., 11:30am-2:30pm and 5pm-11pm
Thurs.-Fri., 5pm-11pm Sat.

Pizzeria Napoletana $$

Located in the heart of Little Italy
since 1948, Pizzeria Napoletana is everyone's favorite bustling, boisterous,
bring-your-own-wine pizza joint—
it was even featured on the Food
Network's *You Gotta Eat Here* a few
years ago. They don't take reservations
and there's usually a line, but things
move quickly inside. They serve 41
types of pizza and 15 kinds of pasta,
including their signature Napoletana
with anchovies. Service is fast and efficient if not totally attentive, though
they'll happily uncork two bottles of
wine at once.

MAP 6: 189 rue Dante, 514/276-8226,
www.napoletana.com; 11am-10:30pm
Mon.-Thurs., 11am-11:30pm Fri.-Sat.,
noon-10:30pm Sun.

MEXICAN
Fortune $

Slightly hipsterish but super-friendly,
this spot serves tacos, *guédilles* (hot
dog rolls stuffed with meat or veggies),
and great cocktails. Pricier than you'll
be used to if you live in, say, California,
Fortune uses high-quality ingredients,
including a few—daikon, marinated
cucumber, roasted cauliflower—you
might not often see. As far as cocktails
go, their Arnold Palmer and Hibiscus
Bucks both take the cake, but you can't
go wrong with a bottle of Red Stripe or
Tecate, either.

MAP 6: 6488 blvd. St-Laurent,
514/303-3111, www.fortunemtl.com;
11:30am-10pm Tues.-Wed. and Sun.,
11:30am-11pm Thurs.-Sat.

MIDDLE EASTERN
Le Petit Alep $

Simply delicious—there's no better way to describe the Syrian and
Armenian food on the menu here,
from their coffee to their meats, which

are always tender and juicy, to the *fattouche* salad that comes with a nice kick. The relaxed atmosphere is reflected in the magazines that hang on the wall and the newspapers nearby that you are welcome to bring to your table while you dig into a filet brochette. If you're feeling fancy, pop next door to big Alep (199 rue Jean-Talon E., 514/270-6396) and enjoy your dinner in slightly more romantic and upscale surroundings.

MAP 6: 191 rue Jean-Talon E., 514/270-9361, www.petitalep.com; 11am-11pm Tues.-Sat.

VEGETARIAN
Le Cagibi $

Situated on the corner of St-Laurent and St-Viateur, Le Cagibi is one of the coziest, most down-to-earth cafés in the area, serving affordable vegetarian meals and good coffee all day long. At night, the back room transforms into a performance space with everything from live shows to stand-up comedians and public talks. If you drink, however, you must eat, so make sure to bring an appetite. Though Montréal is queer-friendly, Le Cagibi is especially so for a younger LGBT crowd. Cash only.

MAP 6: 5490 blvd. St-Laurent, 514/509-1199, www.lecagibi.ca; 6pm-midnight Mon., 9am-midnight Tues.-Fri., 10:30am-midnight Sat.-Sun.

La Panthère Verte $

This panther has eschewed its carnivorous ways for a vegan lifestyle featuring falafels, tofu steak, tempeh, and veggie burgers—get them wrapped up in a half- or full-size pita, or, if you're gluten-free, request the fillings in a salad-style plate. Wash it all down with some kombucha or natural soda. Local, organic, and green, the Green

Panther has five other locations to check out, in the Plateau, downtown, the Quartier Latin, Côte-des-Neiges, and Snowdon.

MAP 6: 160 rue St-Viateur E., 514/508-5564, www.lapanthereverte.com; 10am-10pm Mon.-Sat., 11am-7pm Sun.

La Panthère Verte

COMFORT FOOD
Le Ballpark $

"J'<3 tes balles," reads a sign posted outside this restaurant at the corner of Clark and St-Zotique. As the name suggests, menu items tend toward round edibles: meatballs, croquettes, chicken, and blue cheese balls. But they also serve $1 oysters at happy hour, perfectly salted fries, and meaty poutine. The cozy ambience and happy hour make it a great place for a casual date (but not if you're about to propose, or need to talk about anything serious—most of the seating is at communal tables).

MAP 6: 6660 rue Clark, 438/384-6660, www.leballpark.com; noon-2pm and 5pm-11pm Mon.-Sat.

Comptoir 21 $$

This fish-and-chips shop is a reclaimed-wood paradise, featuring U-shaped counter seating, blue-and-white checkerboard linoleum, and vinegar in spray bottles. The batter is light, greasy, and salty, just the way a fried fish should be. Of course, they have other items on the menu, like fried calamari, burgers, salads, and the requisite poutine, but the real star is the fish-and-chips served with coleslaw, a slice of lemon, and a tasty tartar sauce. This spot is so popular there are now four more locations across the city, in the Plateau, Verdun, Quartier Latin, and Square Victoria.

MAP 6: 21 rue St-Viateur W., 514/507-3474, www.comptoir21.com; 11:30am-11pm Sun.-Thurs., 11:30am-midnight Fri.-Sat.

BREAKFAST AND BRUNCH

La Croissanterie Figaro $

Full of round, marble-topped tables, gilded light fixtures, and wrought-iron chairs, this corner café and bistro is a little bit of Paris in Outremont. The long, wooden counter adds to the art deco interior and Old World feel, and the menu, too, is decidedly Parisian, offering homemade croissants, coffees, and a reasonably priced lunch and dinner table d'hôte with selections like quiche Lorraine and roast beef. The spacious, leafy outdoor terrace is a great place to meet friends for drinks in the evening.

MAP 6: 5200 rue Hutchison, 514/278-6567, www.lacroissanteriefigaro.com; 7am-1am daily

Vieux Vélo $

Vieux Vélo is an updated (read: slightly hipsterish) meeting between café and diner, replete with Formica-topped tables, old wooden school chairs and little *vélos* (bicycles) dotting the decor. If you're not a fan of Benedicts (the menu has a number of them, and they're very popular), try le Marin, which consists of fluffy, cheesy eggs with a side of smoked salmon, salad, and toast. Montrealers like this place so much that Vieux Vélo opened Café Odessa (65 rue Beaubien E.) next door, making it even more convenient to grab one of their perfect lattes.

MAP 6: 59 rue Beaubien E., 514/439-5595; 8:30am-4pm Tues.-Fri., 9am-4pm Sat.-Sun.

LUNCH COUNTERS

Dépanneur Le Pick-Up $

In Québec a *dépanneur* is a corner store, and that's exactly what this place is: a corner store with a vintage lunch counter and outdoor seating in the summer. Located in Mile-Ex (a stone's throw from Alexandraplatz Bar), Dépanneur Le Pick-Up is known for its amazing pulled pork and faux pulled pork (vegetarian!) sandwiches as well as its weekend brunches, *haloumi* cheese sandwiches, and gluten-free chocolate chip cookies. Le Pick-Up is in the running for the best sandwich in town.

MAP 6: 7032 rue Waverly, 514/271-8011, http://depanneurlepickup.com; 7am-7pm Mon.-Fri., 9am-6pm Sat.

Wilensky's Light Lunch $

Not much has changed since Moe Wilensky opened this lunch counter in 1932, housed in the current location since 1952. Nine counter stools make up the only seating, and the decor can only be described as nonexistent. If timelessness were an ambience, they'd have it in spades. Act like a regular and get the house special, a double grilled salami and bologna sandwich with mustard—mustard is compulsory, as a sign inside makes clear—on a kaiser bun, which tastes as delicious as it sounds. The old-fashioned sodas are mixed by hand. Wilensky's was immortalized by Mordecai Richler in *The Apprenticeship of Duddy Kravitz.*

MAP 6: 34 ave. Fairmount W.,
514/271-0242, www.wilenskys.com;
9am-4pm Mon.-Fri., 10am-4pm Sat.

LATE-NIGHT EATS
Chez Claudette $

There's nothing quite like Chez Claudette, a 24-hour diner that caters to late-night revelers of any persuasion, including vegans. Tucked away on a quiet part of one of the city's fancier strips, it's a bright-yellow corner spot popular for fried snacks, including poutines, hamburgers, and onion rings. A few years ago, it was featured on the Food Network's *You Gotta Eat Here*.

MAP 6: 351 ave. Laurier E., 514/279-5173; 7am-11pm Sun.-Wed., 24 hours Thurs.-Sat.

COFFEE
✪ Café Falco $

You might get the sense that Café Falco exists solely thanks to a concentration of tech companies in the Mile End—and you wouldn't be wrong. If Falco's high ceilings and great coffee don't win you over, though, their *onigiri* (rice balls stuffed with delicious fillings like barbecued pork, salmon, and edamame) and homemade soups surely will. Stop in for an early lunch (the lunch rush can be bananas) before exploring the rest of the Mile End.

MAP 6: 5605 ave. de Gaspé, 514/272-7766, www.cafefalco.ca; 8am-5pm Mon.-Thurs., 8am-4pm Fri.

Café Olimpico $

A neighborhood staple, Olimpico was opened in 1970 by Rocco Furfaro, who'd immigrated to the city from Rome a decade earlier. To this day, the café is dedicated to coffee (espresso, cappuccino, sweet iced lattes in summer), though you can also get cold drinks, cannoli, biscotti, and lemon cake. Olimpico brings a diverse crowd together—you're as likely to see a sports fan as you are someone buried in a Leonard Cohen novel. No one will bat an eye if you savor a hot sesame bagel from St-Viateur with your coffee.

MAP 6: 124 rue St-Viateur W., 514/495-0746, www.cafeolimpico.com; 6am-midnight daily

Café Olimpico

CAFÉS AND BAKERIES
✪ Boulangerie Guillaume $

Opened in 2010 by the cool and tattooed namesake Guillaume, this bakery has been serving the city's best baguettes, croissants, sourdough, and *pain au chocolat* (chocolate croissants) to clients ever since. The selection of breads is marvelous, with both organic and non-organic options. And the French goodies—*chaussons aux pommes* (apple turnovers), brioche rolls, *chouquette* pastries—rival any you'll find in France. They also serve coffee to wash down those treats and have delectable sandwiches to grab on the go—which you may be, if the seating is chockablock on a weekend.

MAP 6: 5134 blvd. St-Laurent, 514/508-3199, www.boulangerieguillaume. com; 7am-7pm daily

Les Oubliettes $

Set in what feels like the middle of nowhere—an industrial stretch just off Bellechasse east of St-Denis—this café is an oasis for lunch, coffee, and snacks. Slightly forgetful service (order at the counter and your meal will be brought out to you, fingers crossed), but the staff makes it up by being incredibly friendly. Try the homemade cookies or treat yourself to a sandwich—they have great gluten-free options.

MAP 6: 6201 rue St-Vallier, 438/384-6688; 8am-6pm Mon.-Fri., 9am-6pm Sat., 10am-4pm Sun.

DESSERT
✪ Kem CoBa $

Those who didn't already know that ice cream could come in butter flavor are in for a treat. As at most ice cream shops in the city, the line can be long (in 2015, someone even started a Twitter account to document it!), but it moves quickly. Pastry chefs and chocolatiers Diem Ngoc Phan and Vincent Beck craft delicious, creamy ice cream right on location, offering a mix of classic flavors as well as new creations like butter, lychee, and *la dua* (pandan). Cash only (to keep the line moving!).

MAP 6: 1311 ave. Bernard, 514/276-0414, http://kemcoba.com; noon-8pm Tues.-Sun. late Apr.-early Nov.

Greater Montréal   Map 7

AMERICAN
✪ Tuck Shop $$$

Going off the beaten tourist path to this restaurant in the up-and-coming Saint-Henri neighborhood is totally worth it. Not only will you get to see a different side of the city, but you'll get to indulge in some incredible food. In a narrow storefront, Tuck Shop has the vibe of an old French farmhouse, with cornflower-blue wood-paneled walls and a giant blackboard announcing wine and cocktail options. The menu changes almost daily, but staples include a fish taco starter and homemade ravioli, both guaranteed to please. Check their Twitter (@TuckShopMTL) for daily menu updates.

MAP 7: 4662 rue Notre-Dame W., 514/439-7432, www.tuckshop.ca; 6pm-11pm Tues.-Sat.

NIGHTLIFE

Vieux-Montréal 132
Centre-Ville. 135
Centre-Ville Est 136
Quartier Latin and the Village 138
Plateau Mont-Royal. 141
Mile End and Petite-Italie. 144

Montréal is known for its nightlife. Whether you're catching the latest emerging bands, dancing till the early morning, or sharing drinks with friends on a *terrasse,* there's no shortage of places or things to keep you busy. Many cafés, restaurants, and live venues double as nightlife hot spots when the sun goes down. If you're looking for something unpretentious and fun, these are the kinds of joints that you should seek out.

Looking for dance club ecstasy? Look no further than Stereo.

Those looking for a flashy night out at the club should head directly to boulevard St-Laurent; the lower part of this strip on the boundary of downtown and the Plateau has long been one of the top places to see and be seen. Restaurants that double as nightlife hot spots are especially popular in this area; servers are even known to get in on the party at these types of venues.

Chockablock with bars and nightclubs, rue Crescent may be enticing but should be avoided—unless you're an 18-year-old out-of-towner enjoying your first taste of freedom (in which case, party on). As on any popular strip, there are definitely some more sophisticated and worthwhile spots, but migrating farther east to St-Laurent will give you a more authentic Montréal experience. The lower part of rue St-Denis also offers some options—generally a mix of large student-oriented clubs and smaller pub-like venues.

The legal drinking age in Québec is 18. Kids who are from the province are usually well behaved, but because the drinking age is much lower than that

HIGHLIGHTS

✪ **BEST DANCE CLUB:** Amazing views of the city skyline and some impressive architecture make **New City Gas** the best place to go dancing (page 134).

✪ **BEST GASTROPUB: Dominion Square Tavern** is one of the oldest taverns in the city. It has now been renovated into a sleek gastropub that serves a great mix of food and drink (page 135).

✪ **BEST HAPPY HOUR:** The laid-back atmosphere and high-school cafeteria feel make **Furco,** hidden on a quiet downtown side street, the place to hit after the office (page 136).

✪ **BEST WINE BAR: Pullman** boasts a stunning interior and extensive wine list featuring 300 wines (with 50 wines by the glass), making this the best spot in the city for a classy but laid-back night out (page 137).

✪ **BEST FOR BEER AND PAC-MAN:** Located on a strip of St-Denis more famous for brewpubs, **Arcade MTL** is fun, busy, and just slightly nerdy (page 138).

✪ **MOST SURPRISING:** A nondescript red door leads you into the wonderful speakeasy **Big in Japan Bar** (page 141).

✪ **MOST VERSATILE VENUE:** Drink, dance, and catch the latest bands at **Casa del Popolo,** where there is always something happening and it's always fun (page 143).

✪ **BEST BEER GARDEN:** Only open during the summer, **Alexandraplatz Bar** is a fleeting pleasure that shouldn't be missed (page 144).

✪ **BEST MICROBREWS:** Taste real Québécois beer at **Dieu du Ciel,** an unpretentious neighborhood staple (page 144).

✪ **UNIQUE DECOR:** At dive bar **Notre Dames des Quilles,** you can drink and bowl (page 145).

in the United States or even neighboring provinces, many teenagers come to Montréal for the clubs, especially during New Year's and spring break. They tend to stick to the same area, however, like the aforementioned rue Crescent, so if you head off the beaten path, you'll soon lose them.

Live music is a big part of going out, especially in a city known for its indie rock scene. Whether you're into minimal electro, hip-hop, metal, or even bluegrass, there's a club or a DJ night for you. The Plateau is the best area to catch emerging or lesser-known bands, both Canadian and international. If you're wandering the area at

night, you'll likely come across a show or three. Most venues have a small cover charge, under $20, so if you like what you hear, it is usually worth it.

Since it is such a nightlife spot, Montrealers tend to go out late. It's not unusual to head out for an evening at midnight, or even later. Montrealers also love a good after-work drink. Happy hour is referred to as *cinq à sept*, or 5 à 7, meaning cheaper drinks between five and seven in the evening.

No matter what you're up for—a quiet night sipping scotch, or hitting the clubs until the wee hours of the morning—Montréal's got you covered.

Vieux-Montréal

Map 1

BARS

Le Confessionnal

With a richly decorated interior enhanced by soft lighting, Le Confessional has the cozy feel of an old-time pub. Hosting diverse events, everything from stand-up comedy to live performances, rock nights to R&B, Le Confessional has something to offer everyone, and the crowd reflects that. Depending on the night's event, the place might be packed with old-school hip-hop fans or young professionals winding down after work.
MAP 1: 431 rue McGill, 514/656-1350, www.confessionnal.ca; 5pm-3am Wed.-Fri., 9pm-3am Sat.; no cover

Le Philémon Bar

This bar is popular with locals and known for its warm, friendly staff. Cocktails are a popular choice, but they also serve reasonably priced beers, wine, and bubbly. Delicious

and affordable snack options include king oyster mushrooms with parmesan, Moroccan ribs, and a cheese plate. The unique layout has the bar in the middle of the room, surrounded by bar seating, banquettes along the walls, and window seats, but it can be

Le Confessional

a bit difficult to dance when the place picks up around 10pm.

MAP 1: 111 rue St-Paul W., 514/289-3777, www.philemonbar.com; 5pm-3am Mon.-Wed., 4pm-3am Thurs.-Sat., 6pm-3am Sun.; no cover

Taverne Gaspar

Taverne Gaspar is the go-to spot at the Auberge du Vieux-Port. Young and fresh, it brings a needed bit of relaxed fun to the district, offering top-quality wines and locally brewed beer on tap. This is a popular after-work destination, so expect it to be especially crowded on Thursday and Friday nights. In summer, Taverne's *terrasse*, also known as Terrasse Sur L'Auberge, is a great place to grab a drink and take in the sights of the river and Vieux-Port from five stories up.

MAP 1: Auberge du Vieux-Port, 89 rue de la Commune E., 514/392-1649, www. tavernegaspar.com; 5pm-10pm Sun.-Wed., 5pm-midnight Thurs.-Sat.; no cover

Terrasse Nelligan

During the summer, this rooftop *terrasse* in Hôtel Nelligan is one of the best-kept secrets when it comes to terrace cocktails. It's on the roof of a boutique hotel, so drinks are on the pricier side ($13 for a cocktail, $7 for a draft beer), but you can't beat the 200-degree view of the city, which encompasses the Aldred Building, Habitat 67, and Notre-Dame Basilica. If you visit in April, check out the Terrasse des Sucres, a sky-high sugar shack.

MAP 1: Hôtel Nelligan, 100 rue St-Paul W., 514/788-4000, www.terrassenelligan.com; noon-10pm Mon.-Fri., 10:30am-10pm Sat. Apr.-Oct.; no cover

Terrasse Place d'Armes

This swank cocktail bar on the roof of Place d'Armes Hôtel overlooks the Place d'Armes and couldn't give you better views of the city's skyline. A DJ pumps tunes throughout the day, everything from Top 40 to bossa nova, for the mostly local clientele who slip on their best dancing shoes for an evening of open-air dancing. The service is attentive and efficient, and the drinks are great. If the weather turns, you can take refuge in the adjoining indoor lounge.

MAP 1: Place d'Armes Hôtel and Suites, 701 Côte de la Place d'Armes, 514/904-1201, www.terrasseplacedarmes.com; 11:30am-10pm daily May-Oct., weather permitting; no cover

LOUNGES

Terrasses Bonsecours

Just past the Cirque du Soleil, surrounded by water, are the four floors of Terrasses Bonsecours. A great place to rent ice skates in the winter, it transforms into a bistro and a jumping, open-air hot spot come summer. Avoid the cover and get to the nightclub early to enjoy a cocktail and watch the sun set behind the city. By midnight, the place is packed with suburban revelers; stay and dance to the techno and R&B, or head for a late-night waterfront stroll.

MAP 1: 364 rue de la Commune E., 514/969-9716, www.terrassesbonsecours. com; noon-3am daily May-Sept.; $5-25 (nightclub)

WINE BARS

Dolcetto

Terra-cotta floor tiles, blue-and-white-striped banquettes, exposed beams, and gleaming white walls evoke a seaside retreat in this wine bar. Serving Italian tapas along with its cocktails, Dolcetto is all prosciutto, calzones, lobster cannelloni, and a good time. Crowds and couples in their early

Velvet Speakeasy

thirties can be found taking part in the establishment's delights during the week, while a slightly more sophisticated crowd shows up on the weekends.

MAP 1: 151 rue St-Paul W., 514/419-8522, www.dolcettomontreal.com; 11:30am-2pm and 5pm-11pm Mon. and Thurs.-Fri., 11:30am-2pm and 5pm-10pm Tues.-Wed., 5pm-11pm Sat.-Sun.

DANCE CLUBS
✪ New City Gas

This EDM-focused club in the heart of Griffintown, an old working-class area that's quickly transforming into one of the city's coolest neighborhoods, takes full advantage of the building's history. Built in 1859, the original facade remains intact, as does the name. Once the headquarters of a gas company, the venue now hosts up to 3,000 people a week who come to party and to sip on cocktails, such as Birds of Paradise (vodka, blood orange juice), created by mixologist Lawrence Picard.

MAP 1: 950 rue Ottawa, 514/879-1166, www.newcitygas.com; 10pm-3am Fri.-Sat.; $16-35 for shows

Velvet Speakeasy

Enter the cavernous, candle-lit bar through a long hallway that feels like it might just be leading you toward the catacombs—not the foundations of a 17th-century basement that has been converted into a bar. Despite the mysterious setting, Velvet is all about contemporary beats, and electro, pop, and disco tunes keep the crowd moving. Velvet specializes in vodka; the drinks are affordable and the atmosphere is a far cry from the black-light glitz of other Old Montréal clubs.

MAP 1: 426 rue St-Gabriel, 514/995-8754, www.velvetspeakeasy.ca; 11pm-3am Thurs.-Sat.; free-$15

Wunderbar

With a roster that includes some of the city's top DJs playing everything from Top 40 mash-ups to old school slow-jams, the dance floor at Wunderbar is always packed. The clientele is decidedly diverse—everyone from college kids to high rollers—and in keeping with the Montréal ethos, everyone is impeccably dressed. Unlike at many clubs, the bar snacks are actually pretty delicious.

MAP 1: 901 rue du Square-Victoria, 514/395-3100, www.wunderbarmontreal.com; 5pm-midnight Mon.-Tues., 5pm-3am Wed.-Fri., 10pm-3am Sat.; no cover

LIVE MUSIC
Les Deux Pierrots

If you're looking for a truly Québécois experience, head to Les Deux Pierrots on a Friday or Saturday night. Since opening its doors in 1974, it has become one of the most well-known *boîtes à chansons* in Montréal. First springing up in the mid-1950s, *boîtes à chansons* combine well-known and home-grown songs with live

Les Deux Pierrots

entertainment in a bar setting, a phenomenon specific to Québec. Featuring some of the best singers *(chansonniers)* and entertainers in the province, the atmosphere is rowdy in the best way.

MAP 1: 104 rue St-Paul E., 514/861-1270, www.lespierrots.com; open 24 hours Thurs.-Sun.; shows begin at 8:30pm on Fri. and Sat.; $7

Centre-Ville   Map 2

BARS
✪ Dominion Square Tavern

Built in 1926, Dominion is one of Montréal's oldest taverns. Renovated by its owners, Alex Baldwin (of Baldwin Barmacie) and Alexander Wolosianski (of Whisky Café), it is now an old-timey, chic gastropub. Serving fare like bangers and mash, Welsh rarebit, and roasted Cornish hen, it draws everyone from Canadiens fans to moviegoers and more than a few hipsters. Tastefully decorated with a good amount of historical grit, it's also just a great place to grab a cocktail.

MAP 2: 1243 rue Metcalfe, 514/564-5056, www.tavernedominion.com; 11:30am-midnight Mon.-Fri., 4:30pm-midnight Sat.-Sun.; no cover

Bar George

In the heart of the Golden Square Mile, Bar George is inside Le Mount Stephen hotel, a drop-dead gorgeous old heritage building. Reopened in 2017 after a six-year hiatus, this classy bar is already amassing loyal fans. Chef de cuisine Kevin Ramasawmy serves up modern British fare, including Scotch eggs, Earl Grey salmon, and smoked haddock hash. Cocktails, infused with British flavors, are a must-try.

THE HEIGHT OF COCKTAIL HOUR: ROOFTOP BARS

Montréal is in winter's clutches for what feels like eight months of the year, so when the thermometer finally shows a positive number, everyone is out drinking in the sunshine.

- **Taverne Gaspar:** This rooftop terrace offers a great view of the Vieux-Port as you sip an old-fashioned (page 133).

- **Terrasse Place d'Armes:** Looking out onto Notre-Dame Basilica and Place d'Armes, you can enjoy your port while contemplating the great architecture (page 133).

- **Les Trois Brasseurs:** This popular local microbrewery chain has the best patio of any bar in the Latin Quarter (page 139).

MAP 2: 1440 rue Drummond, 514/669-9243, www.bargeorge.ca; 7am-1am daily; no cover

Brutopia

The microbrew selection at this well-liked brewpub consists of classic beers all year, including an IPA and a Raspberry Blonde, while seasonal brews include the Chocolate Stout, the Maple Rousse, and the Scotch Ale. It takes up three floors (with three outdoor terraces) of an old stone building on Crescent, and the vibe can definitely steer toward student at times. Happy hours extend from opening till 8pm daily, and they regularly host open mic nights and smaller, local bands.

MAP 2: 1219 rue Crescent, 514/393-9277, www.brutopia.net; 2pm-3am daily; no cover

Centre-Ville Est   Map 3

BARS
✪ Furco

In an old fur warehouse tucked on a quiet side street, Furco is a go-to spot for after-work drinks. The bar, which serves food (cheese plates, beef *tataki*, bread pudding) until 11pm or midnight, has an industrial-chic vibe (exposed pipes, wood, and steel stools). The crowd is a bit more mature than at some downtown places, and the vibe is distinctly French, though the bartenders are all bilingual. It also draws a crowd on weekends, so come early and expect to stay late.

MAP 3: 425 rue Mayor, 514/764-3588, www.barfurco.com; 4pm-3am Mon.-Sat.; no cover

La Distillerie no. 1

This small neighborhood bar has quickly grown into a small chain of neighborhood bars. The downtown location is the original and has a welcoming laid-back vibe. The interior is fairly bare-bones, with saloon-style chairs and tables. The drinks are definitely out of the ordinary, and they come in Pinterest-worthy mason jars. Come early for happy hour (4pm-7pm), when the drinks are a bit cheaper and the snacks are free. Service is friendly and prompt, even on super-busy nights.

MAP 3: 300 rue Ontario E., 514/488-2461, www.pubdistillerie.com; 4pm-3am daily; no cover

Le Mal Nécessaire

Right in the heart of Chinatown, down a flight of stairs—look for the glowing neon green pineapple—you'll find Le Mal Nécessaire. This bar is half speakeasy, half tiki bar. You can order your drinks in coconuts or pineapples, as well as order delicious, if pricey, snacks—fried wontons, pork dumplings, Chinese broccoli. This bar gets increasingly packed as the night goes on, so it's best to go early if you don't love crowds.

MAP 3: 1106B blvd. St-Laurent, www.lemalnecessaire.com; 4:30pm-2am Sun.-Wed., 4:30pm-3am Thurs.-Sat.

Nyks

Just south of rue Ste-Catherine, surrounded by big, flashy venues, you'll find Nyks, an unpretentious, rustic haven in which to kick back and have a drink. This is a serious gem with great food, after-work drink specials, and a great atmosphere with brick walls and heavy wood tables and chairs. It's a nice alternative to the crowded bars in the rest of the downtown core. Grab a bite from the varied menu; the kitchen is open until 11pm and never disappoints.

MAP 3: 1250 rue de Bleury, 514/866-1786, www.nyks.ca; 11:30am-3am Mon.-Fri., 3pm-3am Sat.-Sun.; no cover

Le Sainte-Élisabeth

Le Sainte-Élisabeth's nondescript 1930s exterior hides a magnificent beer garden, lush and green in the summer and surrounded by tall, ivy-covered walls. It's always hard to find a seat. Inside, there's an old tavern atmosphere. Even in the winter this place gets packed, and you'll sometimes find yourself yelling over the music, which ranges from Top 40 hits to Québécois rock. If you can't find a seat in the garden, a second-floor glassed-in terrace overlooks the outdoor one.

MAP 3: 1412 rue Ste-Élisabeth, 514/286-4302, www.ste-elisabeth.com; 4pm-3am Mon.-Sat., 7pm-3am Sun.; no cover

WINE BARS
✪ Pullman

The huge, crystal chandelier is likely the first thing you'll notice about this wine bar. Situated on a strip of avenue du Parc, it faces a grocery store and is next to a student residence, but if you're heading to a show in the Quartier de Spectacles, it's a perfect place to start your evening. The high ceilings make for a dramatic interior, full of chic, minimal furniture and stark walls. The extensive wine list features 300 wines, 50 available by the glass.

MAP 3: 3424 ave. du Parc, 514/288-7779, www.pullman-mtl.com; 4:30pm-1am Tues.-Sat., 4:30pm-1am Sun.-Mon.; no cover

LIVE MUSIC
Coop Katacombes

This co-op punk club has been going for years, though it only recently moved into its black-brick digs on St-Laurent and Ontario. Catering to mainly punk, hard-core, and metal crowds, Katacombes features bands from all three genres as well as industrial DJs. The club sometimes branches out into one-off events like dress-up disco night. The venue has also hosted comedians and other performers.

MAP 3: 1635 blvd. St-Laurent, 514/861-6151, www.katacombes.com; hours vary depending on shows; $5-15

Les Foufounes Électriques

Les foufounes électriques means "electric ass." Lovingly called Foufs by locals, this bar opened in 1983 with the aim of showcasing art, and a large metal spider still hangs over the entrance. This artists' hangout has turned into a club and bar, with bands like Nirvana, L7, and The Misfits taking the stage. It's still one of the best places to catch bands and drink a cold beer, but it's also become a popular dance spot, attracting young and old punks and students to the dance floor.

MAP 3: 87 rue Ste-Catherine E., 514/844-5539, www.foufouneselectriques. com; 4pm-3am daily; no cover, $5-30 shows

Quartier Latin and the Village

Map 4

BARS

✪ Arcade MTL

Opened in 2016, Arcade MTL is the perfect place to go if you're looking for something to do while enjoying your microbrew. A $7 cover will get you access to more than 20 retro arcade games and video consoles. This fun spot can be packed on the weekends—it's not the best place for a quiet, romantic date—and special events include participatory arcade tournaments.

MAP 4: 2031 rue St-Denis, info@ arcademtl.com; 5pm-1am Tues.-Wed., 5pm-3am Thurs.-Fri., noon-3am Sat., noon-1am Sun.; $7 cover

L'Amère à Boire

Three stories tall, this artisanal microbrewery is one of the best places to grab a drink in the Latin Quarter, and not only because of the 22 brews to choose from. Patrons include university students and office workers, and L'Amère has a convivial atmosphere. Almost labyrinthine in design, the bar has multiple levels throughout, and the stairs are seemingly endless. There's usually one corner or another available. L'Amère serves tasty tapas, including home-made pretzels and pogos (corn dogs).

MAP 4: 2049 rue St-Denis, 514/282-7448, www.amereaboire.com; 1pm-2am Mon.-Thurs., noon-3am Fri., 1pm-3am Sat., 1pm-midnight Sun.; no cover

L'Amère à Boire

Le Cheval Blanc

Le Cheval Blanc is unlike any other bar in Montréal. It's a long-time family-run business located in a turn-of-the-20th-century building; the green Formica on the walls, bar, and tabletops is the main aspect of the decor. In 1986 it became the first brewpub in the city, and its white beer Cheval Blanc is famous throughout the province. Everyone comes here, from young artists to old regulars, and the staff is friendly. It's mainly a Francophone

Only a few hours from the U.S. border, Montréal has always had a tortured history with its neighbors to the south. For generations, out of work Quebeckers would head across the border, looking for work in small New England towns close to the frontier. After World War I, however, roles reversed and it was the Americans who came north, though they were seeking something different.

Between 1920 and 1933, Prohibition turned Montréal into a paradise for many Americans who came north in search of alcohol and found the jazz clubs, burlesque shows, gambling rooms, and brothels that went along with it. With this kind of "entertainment" unrivaled by any other North American metropolis, it quickly picked up the nickname "Sin City." The city continued its reign well into the 1940s and 1950s, even attracting popular burlesque performers like Lili St-Cyr to the town.

Despite the fact that the city is no longer a mecca for jazz clubs or gambling, it still retains that Sin City vibe, though one that's on the right side of the law, thanks mainly to the city's joie de vivre—as well as semi-secret loft parties, live venues that double as someone's living room, and the city's numerous strip clubs.

hangout, and you'd be hard-pressed to find a more down-to-earth bar in Montréal.

MAP 4: 809 rue Ontario E., 514/522-0211, www.lechevalblanc.ca; 3pm-3am daily; no cover

Le Saint-Sulpice

Occupying four floors of a 19th-century house, the immense Saint-Sulpice has 10 bars in summer and 7 in winter, all with a university-student vibe. Each floor has its own style: There's the library, the cabaret, and the cave and annex; the basement and top floors both double as dance floors. Outside, a massive terrace attracts summer patrons and features a babbling fountain and its own back alley entrance. This place asks for ID, so don't forget to bring yours, regardless of age.

MAP 4: 1680 rue St-Denis, 514/844-9458, www.lesaintsulpice.ca; Tues.-Sun. 3:30pm-3:30am; no cover

Les Trois Brasseurs

This local microbrewery has branches throughout the city (in Vieux-Montréal at 105 St-Paul E., 514/788-6100, and downtown at 732 rue Ste-Catherine W., 514/788-6333), as well as throughout Québec and Ontario, but this is the only location with a year-round rooftop terrace. It's popular with university students and office workers off the clock. The vibe is always lively and relaxed, and the service is like that, too, with servers happy to bring you another pitcher and freshly chilled beer mugs. The interior isn't much—wooden tables, beer vats—but the view of St-Denis at night is perfect.

MAP 4: 1658 rue St-Denis, 514/845-1660, www.les3brasseurs.ca; 11:30am-midnight Mon.-Wed. and Sun., 11:30am-1am Thurs., 11:30am-2am Fri.-Sat.; no cover

Les Trois Brasseurs

DANCE CLUBS

Circus After-Hours

Three different rooms catering to three different sounds make up the biggest after-hours club in Canada. The club features circus performers wandering around the crowd as they dance well into the morning. DJs spin mainly house, dark house, hip-hop, tribal, and R&B, though celebrity DJs often bring their own sounds. Dress code is less formal than in most clubs in the city, but since the majority of the clientele have already been out all night, dress as though you have, too.

MAP 4: 917 rue Ste-Catherine E., 514/844-3626, www.circusafterhours.com; 2am-8am Thurs. and Sun., 2am-10am Fri., 2am-11am Sat.; cover varies

Stereo

This world-renowned after-hours club bills its purpose as "pure dance floor ecstasy." Still one of the best places in the world to party late into the night and early morning, it is known for playing house music and attracting some of the world's top DJs, including deadmau5 and Cesar Romero. There's a no-gum rule, though, so leave yours at home and bring mints instead.

MAP 4: 858 rue Ste-Catherine E., 514/286-0325, www.stereonightclub.net; 2am-10am Fri.-Sun.; $40

GAY AND LESBIAN

Cabaret Mado

The grande dame of Montréal drag, Mado Lamothe is the proprietor and star attraction of this cabaret showcase. Performances always include silliness, dancing, music, and a little improv. Showcasing some of the best drag acts from across the city and internationally, Mado always attracts a diverse crowd. The setup isn't particularly flashy, with a small(ish) stage, regular bar seating, and lots of black lights. Each performance is followed by a night of dancing, so come ready to bust a move.

MAP 4: 1115 rue Ste-Catherine E., 514/525-7566, www.mado.qc.ca; 4pm-3am daily; $10-25

Club Unity

Featuring three floors, a VIP lounge, and a rooftop terrace, Club Unity is one of the bigger clubs in the Village. The casual atmosphere, epitomized by the lounge with its long benches and friendly environment, extends to the dress code as well. The music tends toward house, Top 40, and hip-hop, with local and international DJs taking over the decks nightly. It also plays host to special events, including drag shows, karaoke nights, and even the occasional dance troupe.

MAP 4: 1171 rue Ste-Catherine E., 514/523-2777, www.clubunitymontreal. com; 10pm-3am Thurs.-Sat.; $7, free before 11pm

Complexe Sky

This absolutely massive complex—a bit of a trend in the Village—has a ground-floor pub (open for dinner 4pm-9pm), a male strip club, a dinner and drag cabaret, a hip-hop room, a huge disco, and even an outdoor terrace with a pool. Though it caters to a mostly gay male clientele, it also features lesbian nights. It's a great place for dancing, especially if you're part of a large group.

MAP 4: 1478 rue Ste-Catherine E., 514/529-6969, www.complexesky.com; 3pm-3am Thurs.-Sat.; free 1st floor, $4 2nd-4th floors

Le Date Karaoke

Situated in the heart of the Village, this place is known for the intense level of commitment shown by die-hard karaoke fans. Seat yourself at the bar or at one of the more intimate tables near the front window, which opens onto the sidewalk in the summer. Musical selections are vast and range from Led Zeppelin to Céline Dion. This spot is stripped-down when it comes to their drink menu, but the show is worth it. Cash only.

MAP 4: 1218 rue Ste-Catherine E., 514/521-1242, www.ledatekaraoke.com; 8pm-3am daily; no cover

Plateau Mont-Royal   Map 5

BARS

✪ Big in Japan Bar

Step through the unassuming red door and head down a long corridor—one sweep of a heavy velvet curtain, and you're inside Big in Japan Bar. The atmosphere is at its best when the spot is busy and buzzing, lending a real 1970s James Bond feel. Head to the right of the room when you enter, pulling up a stool at the wooden bar, and do yourself a favor by ordering the Paso Doble—gin, chartreuse, and lime, finished off with a giant square ice cube and a sprig of thyme.

MAP 5: 4175 blvd. St-Laurent, 514/380-5658; 5pm-3am daily; no cover

Barfly

This dive bar—a tiny hole in the wall with a black brick exterior and well-worn interior—is known for its bluegrass nights and dingy charm. Full of regulars (including some dogs), it's a popular place to play pool, drink cheap beer, and watch the Canadiens on TV when hockey's in season. What this bar lacks in size, it makes up for in authenticity.

MAP 5: 4062 blvd. St-Laurent, 514/284-6665; 4pm-3am daily; no cover, $5-15 shows

Bar Plan B

Designed to feel like an airport lounge, this modern bar (try their eponymous cocktail) is in the heart of the Plateau. Leather banquette seating, club chairs, and a sizable outdoor terrace all lend themselves to a comfortable, casual atmosphere. Snacks on the menu include mixed nuts, gravlax, and a cheese plate, so it's a perfect place for a pre-dinner aperitif. Check out the private terrace in the summertime.

MAP 5: 327 ave. du Mont-Royal E., 514/845-6060, www.barplanb.ca; 3pm-3am daily; no cover

Barraca

Barraca, the city's only *rhumerie* (rum bar), offering more than 50 different types of rum, cocktails, tapas, and a $5 snack menu. Stepping in here on a chilly spring or fall night is sure to warm you up. The bar itself feels a little like a friend's den—long and narrow with warm lighting, tin walls, and weathered wooden floors. Once the summer hits, patios open in the back and on the street out front.

MAP 5: 1134 ave. du Mont-Royal E., 514/525-7741, www.barraca.ca; 3pm-3am daily; no cover

Bily Kun

Meaning "white horse" in Czech, Bily Kun is named after a bar of the same name found by Fabien Lacaille and Bruce Hackenbeck during a trip to the Czech Republic. Charmed by the bar's quiet but cool ambience and the rumor that Goethe used to go there, they returned to Montréal determined to create something similar. Mounted ostrich heads make this one of the most distinctive bars in the city. Intimate tables and a chic but unpretentious crowd make this place a must.

MAP 5: 354 ave. du Mont-Royal, 514/845-5392, www.bilykun.com; 3pm-3am Mon.-Sat., 3pm-midnight Sun.; no cover

Else's

Serving beer, hot cider, and cocktails, Else's is the perfect place to meet a friend for a sleepy Sunday afternoon catch-up. Founded two decades ago by a Norwegian immigrant named—you guessed it—Else, this homey neighborhood favorite serves fantastic polenta, satisfying vegetarian chili, and tasty tacos. In the summer, opt for the mojito; in the winter, opt for a cider, served hot, with cloves.

MAP 5: 156 rue Roy E., 514/286-6689; noon-3am daily; no cover

Pit Caribou

This down-to-earth oasis of Canadiana brews its own beer (try the Gaspesienne no. 13, which won a silver medal at the Canadian brewing awards) and offers dry cider as well—though you won't find many wine options. Bring a friend and try out one of their planchettes, featuring local smoked fish and seafood, or delicious French cheeses (the menu's in French, so if you haven't downloaded a translation app, now might be the time to do it).

MAP 5: 951 rue Rachel E., 514/522-9773; 2pm-3am daily; no cover

LOUNGES
Blizzarts

One of the first places in the city to exclusively play electro-techno, Blizzarts now plays various kinds of music all week long. Large, rounded banquettes give the space a retro-futurist feel. Art exhibitions are often held here, and the *vernissages* (typically private previews, but in Montréal, the term often just means "opening") can go late into the night. The attitude and crowd are generally laid-back, and you're welcome to come dancing in your sneakers, or your winter boots for that matter—whatever suits.

MAP 5: 3956A blvd. St-Laurent, 514/843-4860; 10pm-3am Mon.-Sat.; no cover most nights

Else's

WINE BARS
La Buvette Chez Simone

On the border of Mile End and the Plateau is this very popular wine bar offering a great selection of local charcuterie. Traditionally, *buvette* means a place to grab a drink and a light snack while you wait for your train; though Chez Simone is nowhere near the station, the bare tabletops, low lighting, and terrace give it a similar ambience.

Casa del Popolo

Relaxed elegance nicely describes the feel of the place, which attracts younger, sophisticated patrons. No matter the day of the week, the parties go late.
MAP 5: 4869 ave. du Parc, 514/750-6577, www.buvettechezsimone.com; 4pm-3am daily; no cover

DANCE CLUBS
Le Salon Daomé
Dedicated to electronic music, this dance club is set in a sparsely decorated loft with high ceilings and a few sofas here and there. The electronic music is more varied and off-the-beaten-track than what you'll find elsewhere in the city—check out the month's *programmation* ahead of time to see if any of your faves will be in town at the same time as you. Patrons are usually die-hard electronic fans seeking out the latest music in the scene.
MAP 5: 141 ave. du Mont-Royal E., 514/982-7070, www.lesalondaome.com; 10pm-3am Tues.-Sun.; cover varies (sometimes free)

LIVE MUSIC
✪ Casa del Popolo
Started by Godspeed You! Black Emperor's bassist and his wife, this venue hosts both obscure and more well-known bands—it's probably best known for giving Arcade Fire its start.

A vegetarian café during the day, later in the evening it transforms into a bar. True to its roots on the Main, it has authentic tin ceilings and a lot of old, dark wood. There's always something happening—check the calendar and pick up tickets in advance to snag a spot. In summer, head out back to the bustling terrace.
MAP 5: 4873 blvd. St-Laurent, 514/284-3804, www.casadelpopolo.com; noon-3am daily; no cover, $5-20 shows

Café Campus and Petit Campus
Café Campus has become one of the most frequented venues in the city. The clientele draws from the student sector, but it is no longer as closely associated with the Université de Montréal; instead, university kids from all over the city come here for their dance and DJ nights or to check out an indie rock show. Divided into two venues, with three floors and four bars, Café Campus and Petit Campus are busy most days of the week. Drinks are quite reasonably priced.
MAP 5: 57 rue Prince Arthur E., 514/844-1010, www.cafecampus.com; 8:30pm-3am Tues.-Sat. (Café Campus), check show calendar for Petit Campus hours; $5-15, dance nights are often free before 10pm or 11pm

Divan Orange
Effortlessly bilingual and run by a workers collective, Divan Orange attracts patrons from both sides of Québec's famed two solitudes. Despite its small stage, it's one of a few places to hear bands as diverse as Fleet Foxes and Coeur de Pirate; the venue hosts 300 shows featuring 1,000 acts every year.
MAP 5: 4234 blvd. St-Laurent, 514/840-9090, www.divanorange.org; check the calendar for showtimes; $5-20

L'Escogriffe

This intimate, stone-walled basement bar with a close-knit, friendly staff is one of the best places to see emerging bands, which is what makes it so popular with the *branchée* (hip) Francophone crowd. Though it has a decidedly rock edge, it also showcases jazz, indie rock, and electro bands. Even the occasional dance night focuses on lesser-known tunes. If you're passing by during the day, grab a drink and sit on one of their two terraces.

MAP 5: 4467 rue St-Denis, 514/842-7244, www.lescobar.com; 4pm-3am daily; no cover, $5-20 shows

O Patro Vys

One level above the ostrich heads at Bily Kun is O Patro Vys (the Czech phrase, translated into English, means "upstairs"), their live-venue counterpart, which showcases more jazz and minimal-electro than punk bands. The cool elegance of the downstairs bar continues upstairs, making it a more adult venue than some. The atmosphere is always super relaxed, and it draws an interested, interesting crowd.

MAP 5: 356 ave. du Mont-Royal E., 514/845-3855, http://opatrovys.com; check Bily Kun calendar for showtimes; $5-25

Mile End and Petite-Italie   Map 6

BARS

✪ Alexandraplatz Bar

This open-air bar is tucked away in a labyrinthine industrial neighborhood; check out the map on their site before heading over. One of the most enjoyable bars in the city, Alexandraplatz is open only in summer, when the large garage door is raised to reveal a sparse, high-ceilinged space filled with long communal benches, a diagonal bar in the corner, and revelers galore. Serving everything from fancy cocktails (try the Bicicletta) to beer and wine by the bottle, the bar also features a taco cart.

MAP 6: 6731 ave. de l'Esplanade, www.alexandraplatzbar.com; 4pm-midnight Mon.-Wed., 4pm-1am Thurs.-Fri., 4pm-1am Sat., 4pm-midnight Sun. May-Oct.; no cover

✪ Dieu du Ciel

This microbrewery and brasserie is one of the best places in the city to experience real Québécois beer. Full of dark wood, tiny round tables, heavy velvet curtains, and a view of the beer vats themselves, Dieu du Ciel evokes a relaxed, friendly atmosphere. Beer menus change often but usually include at least 15 choices, some seasonal. Try the Péché Mortal (Mortal Sin), an imperial coffee stout, in

Dieu du Ciel

winter. Unlike some breweries, it has some gluten-free options.

MAP 6: 29 ave. Laurier W., 514/490-9555, www.dieuduciel.com; 3pm-3am Mon.-Thurs., 1pm-3am Fri.-Sun.; no cover

⊙ Notre Dame des Quilles

A nice little dive bar just off of St-Laurent between Mile End and Petite-Italie, Notre Dame des Quilles has something not all dive bars have: its very own bowling lane. In fact, directly translated, the name means "Our Lady of Bowling." Drink prices are more than reasonable, the atmosphere completely relaxed, and the bowling pretty fun. The decor is bare-bones (Formica tables, bingo-hall chairs, the walls an unsubtle shade of mint), but the vibe is pure Montréal and the grilled-cheese sandwiches are great.

MAP 6: 32 rue Beaubien E., 514/507-1313; 5pm-3am Mon.-Fri., 4pm-3am Sat., 4pm-midnight Sun.

Le Bar Sans Nom

This mystery bar—it began life with no name, no website, no phone number—is now sometimes called "The Emerald," though you still won't find a sign outside. The decor is a mix of giant birds of paradise, slow-churning fans, slightly worn cane chairs, and downright ratty couches, but the cocktails are some of the best in the city, and the bar's rear room, decorated with low leather sofas and black *tadelakt* (Moroccan plaster) walls, looks like something out of a kasbah in Marrakech.

MAP 6: 5295 ave. du Parc, 514/508-5295; 5pm-3am daily; no cover

Harricana

A spacious brewpub and restaurant with high wooden ceilings and subway tile floors, Harricana is just west of the Marché Jean-Talon—the perfect place to take a break after an afternoon of cheese-shopping. With 13 house-made beers on tap, each served at its optimal temperature, Harricana also offers gluten-free options, ciders, tasting flights, and cocktails, all at reasonable prices.

MAP 6: 95 rue Jean-Talon W., 514/303-3039, www.brasserieharricana.com; noon-2am Mon.-Fri., 10am-2am Sat.-Sun.; no cover

HELM

HELM, a slightly bro-ish but sleek and friendly micropub, is a popular place, and in summer patrons often sit on the bar's street-level window ledge swigging a beer. Beer prices change depending on size and time of day, so if you want a real bargain, get here early and grab a bite off the bar menu. Eleven micro-beers, brewed on-site and named mostly after Montréal streets, feature on the menu, alongside ciders, wines and spirits, and a few regular domestic brews.

MAP 6: 273 rue Bernard W., 514/276-0473, www.helmmicrobrasserie.ca; 4pm-1am Mon.-Tues. and Sun., 3pm-3am Wed.-Sat.; no cover

Ping Pong Club

Located on a busy stretch of the Mile End just down the street from the bookstore Drawn & Quarterly, the Ping Pong Club has fine cocktails, good beer, and a nice enough ambience—but the real draws are the Ping-Pong and foosball tables: There is only one of each, so visit early to practice with friends, or come prepared at peak times to cheer on spirited strangers.

MAP 6: 5788 blvd. St-Laurent, 514/272-7464; 5pm-3am daily; no cover

CRAFT BEER BARHOPPING

The Mile End, Mile-Ex, and Little Italy are almost as popular for craft breweries as they are for hip coffee shops. One great way to spend a sunny afternoon or warm evening is by craft-beer hopping—making your way from brewpub **Dieu de Ciel** to **HELM, Vices et Versa, Alexandraplatz Bar,** and **Harricana,** perhaps with stops at **Casa del Popolo** and the **Ping Pong Club** along the way. Plot out a route, check opening times, plan for snacks (Alexandraplatz has a taco stand!), and take advantage of taster flights and half pints for a responsibly fun, extraordinarily tasty walk of the neighborhood.

Sparrow

The bird motif wallpaper, church pews, and fireplace make Sparrow one of the Mile End's coziest bars. (Check out the bathrooms—with their warm light and wallpaper, they're popular for selfies.) The Sparrow (in French, Le Moineau) serves brunch, small plates (try the devils on horseback appetizer and the tandoori chicken wings), and delicious cocktails. Perfect for a dinner date or a small group hangout, Sparrow transforms into one of the busiest bars in the neighborhood after the dinner rush, with standing room only on weekends.

MAP 6: 5322 blvd. St-Laurent, 514/690-3964, www.sparrow-lemoineau. com; 5pm-3am Mon.-Fri., 10am-3pm and 6pm-3am Sat.-Sun.; no cover

Vices et Versa

This neighborhood brewpub, on the cusp of Mile End and Petite-Italie, has a definite laid-back atmosphere, though things often get rowdy later in the night. The high tin ceilings give the impression that the bar is bigger than it actually is, with its built-in wooden banquettes and long, narrow terrace. Thirty-five Québécois beers are always on tap, including Vices et Versa's own IPA and Cream Ale. Selections change regularly, so if you loved the Framboise (raspberry) last time, they might not have it this time.

MAP 6: 6631 blvd. St-Laurent, 514/272-2498, www.vicesetversa.com; 3pm-3am Mon.-Wed., 11:30am-3am Thurs.-Sun.; no cover

LOUNGES

Whisky Café

The Whisky Café is a favorite of cigar and whisky aficionados. The opulent surroundings—think lush leather club chairs and rich wood—give off a private club atmosphere. Just separate from the main bar is the adjoining cigar lounge, one of the last places in the city where you're allowed to smoke indoors. Though food is served, it is more a tasting menu than a full meal. This place is all about the 150 Scotch whiskys, and they even have designated drivers to make sure you arrive home safely.

Sparrow

MAP 6: 5800 blvd. St-Laurent, 514/278-2646, www.whiskycafe.com; 5pm-1am Mon.-Thurs., 5pm-3am Fri., 6pm-3am Sat., 7pm-1am Sun.; no cover

LIVE MUSIC

Bar Le Ritz PDB

A wheelchair-accessible venue with gender-neutral washrooms, Le Ritz PDB serves delicious cocktails and brews and hosts shows organized by creative, well-loved local promoters Blue Skies Turn Black—think punk, indie, and everything in between. The atmosphere is down-to-earth cool, with a social justice-informed lens. Seating can be tight, so come early. Cash only.

MAP 6: 179 rue Jean-Talon W., 514/274-7676; 5pm-3am daily; no cover before 9pm, $5-20 after 9pm on show nights

ARTS AND CULTURE

Vieux-Montréal 150
Centre-Ville. 153
Centre-Ville Est 155
Quartier Latin and the Village 157
Plateau Mont-Royal. 159
Mile End and Petite-Italie. 161
Greater Montréal 163
Festivals and Events 165

Ever since the city's musical explosion of the early 2000s, Montréal has become synonymous with up-and-coming artists, be it internationally known indie rock

the Centre d'Histoire de Montréal

musicians (Arcade Fire, Grimes) or visual masters (David Altmejd, TAVA). The city attracts some of the best and brightest in a number of disciplines.

This richness translates to a thriving arts scene. No matter which neighborhood you're exploring, you're likely to find both galleries and theaters. The city is full of small commercial galleries representing established and emerging artists. Independent galleries show work from both local and international artists and offer an abundance of different styles and genres. Many hold *vernissages* (art openings) with complimentary drinks on Thursday evenings, making it a great time for a gallery crawl.

Fans of French theater can enjoy some of the best this side of Paris. Though not as big, Montréal's English theater scene offers diverse plays and performances by both established and independent production companies. The city even has its own Fringe festival, the Festival St-Ambroise Fringe de Montréal, one of the largest in North America.

If the province of Québec is known for one thing, it's the circus, a theatrical event you can enjoy no matter your mother tongue. Unconventional circuses in the city range from Cirque du Soleil to TOHU.

Museums tend to be concentrated in the downtown core, with some dotted throughout Vieux-Montréal and the Plateau. Many offer free or half-price entry at least once a week.

HIGHLIGHTS

○ **BEST GALLERY:** Dedicated to the contemporary arts, **DHC/ART** is one of the most sophisticated galleries in the city, featuring work by contemporary arts stars like Jenny Holzer, Sophie Calle, and Cory Arcangel (page 151).

○ **MOST LIKELY TO OFFER AN ART/FASHION/MUSIC MASH-UP:** Calling itself a "gathering place for art," the **Phi Centre** more than lives up to its motto with events and exhibits that explore a range of disciplines (page 151).

○ **BEST PLACE TO SEE THE CIRCUS:** From April to July, internationally renowned circus performers **Cirque du Soleil** debut their spellbinding shows in the Vieux-Port (page 151).

○ **BEST ART COMPLEX:** Get all your art viewing out of the way at the **Belgo Building.** Once a warehouse, it has since turned into a hive of artistic activity and now has five floors of independent galleries (page 155).

○ **BEST PLACE TO SEE FANCY FOOTWORK:** The country's preeminent school and performance venue for contemporary choreography, **Agora de la Danse** is where to catch the work of ground-breaking dancers and choreographers (page 156).

○ **BEST DANCE PERFORMANCE:** With both classical and contemporary pieces, **Les Grands Ballets Canadiens de Montréal** brings classical dance into the 21st century (page 156).

○ **BEST PLACE TO THRILL A FILM BUFF:** Home to celluloid classics and the bravest and boldest in documentary film, the **Cinémathèque Québécoise** is an absolute must (page 158).

○ **WEIRDEST ART SPACE:** Open on Saturday afternoon, **Never Apart** is a sprawling, unique gallery that features work across genres, all with a social justice focus, and also hosts events (page 161).

○ **BEST THEATER: Segal Centre for the Performing Arts** offers some of the best new plays in the city. Architecture buffs will also get a kick out of the Mies van der Rohe-designed complex (page 164).

ARTS AND CULTURE

VIEUX-MONTRÉAL

MUSEUMS

Centre des Sciences de Montréal and IMAX Telus Theatre

Taking up an entire quay-side warehouse in the Vieux-Port, the Centre des Sciences de Montréal (Montréal Science Center) aims to woo 9- to 14-year-olds with interactive exhibitions focusing on the environment and technology. Permanent exhibits include Science 26, which invites you to learn about scientific concepts through trial and error, and Fabrik, which presents you with materials and tools to use to build new inventions. The IMAX and temporary exhibits draw the biggest crowds; if you're looking to catch either, get your tickets in advance.

MAP 1: 2 rue de la Commune W., 514/496-4629, www.montrealsciencecentre.com; 9am-4pm Mon.-Fri., 10am-5pm Sat.-Sun.; $15 adults, $13 seniors and teens, $8.50 children, rates vary for IMAX and temporary exhibitions

Centre d'Histoire de Montréal

This converted firehouse, built in 1904 and decommissioned in 1972, now holds the Centre d'Histoire de Montréal (Montréal Historical Center) and its three stories of civic history. Dating as far back as the first contact with the indigenous people in 1535 and extending to the cultural boom of the 1960s and '70s, the permanent collection looks at five important eras in the city's history through archival footage, interactive exhibits, and reconstructions. The museum also offers guided walking tours throughout the year focusing on different aspects or areas of the city.

MAP 1: 335 Place d'Youville, 514/872-3207, www.ville.montreal.qc.ca/chm; 10am-5pm Wed.-Sun.; $6 adults, $5 seniors, $4 students and children

Sir George-Étienne Cartier National Historic Site

One of the founders of the confederation, George-Étienne Cartier originally practiced law before being elected co-prime minister of the province of Canada alongside John A. MacDonald in 1858 (nine years before confederation). Home to the Cartier family from 1848 to 1872, this historic site is the only Victorian house open to the public in Montréal. Tour guides in period dress show you through the house, which has been restored to match the customs of the bourgeoisie of 1860.

MAP 1: 458 rue Notre-Dame E., 514/283-2282, www.pc.gc.ca/cartier; 10am-5pm Wed.-Sun. and holidays mid-June-early Sept., 10am-5pm Fri.-Sun. and holidays early Sept.-mid-Dec.; $3.90 adults, $3.40 seniors, $1.90 children

Sir George-Étienne Cartier National Historic Site

GALLERIES

✪ DHC/ART

Since opening in fall 2007, the DHC/ART Foundation for Contemporary Art has exhibited the work of some of the world's biggest contemporary artists, including Jenny Holzer, Sophie Calle, Marc Quinn, and Cory Arcangel. Located in two heritage buildings, the gallery has an ultramodern interior. In keeping with their dedication to dynamic programming, group visits, interactive projects, and workshops are available. Their opening parties (known as *vernissages* in Québec) are, hands-down, some of the best in the city.

MAP 1: 451 rue St-Jean, 514/849-3762, www.dhc-art.org; noon-7pm Wed.-Fri., 11am-6pm Sat.-Sun.; free

✪ Phi Centre

Part contemporary art gallery, cinema, recording studio, and concert hall, the Phi Centre cultivates, produces, and disseminates every possible kind of contemporary art. Whether you want to watch a hard-to-find movie, enjoy an intimate concert, or check out an artist talk, you'll find your niche. The Phi Centre is unlike anything else in the city and should make it onto your to-do list, if only for you to get a glimpse of its architecturally diverse rooftop patios.

MAP 1: 407 rue St-Pierre, 514/225-0525, www.phi-centre.com; hours vary according to events; cost varies

Darling Foundry

Known for its ambitious installations and industrial surroundings—much of the foundry remains unchanged—the Darling Foundry is both an exhibition space and artists' residence, situated in what was once the industrial heartland of the city. Part of the gallery's aim was to help rejuvenate the area, something it has accomplished with the addition of the Cluny Art Bar. Exhibiting the work of both Canadian and international contemporary artists, the Foundry approaches the work on a big scale and often holds outdoor and sight-specific exhibits. Admission is pay-what-you-can on Thursdays.

MAP 1: 745 rue Ottawa, 514/392-1554, www.fonderiedarling.org; noon-7pm Wed. and Fri.-Sun., noon-10pm Thurs.; $5

CIRCUS

✪ Cirque du Soleil

The now infamous blue-and-yellow-striped Grand Chapiteau (Big Top) stands out among the rest of the more somber-colored buildings of the Vieux-Port. Started in the town of Baie-Saint-Paul by stilt-walker Guy Laliberté, Cirque's first big gig was in 1984 in celebration of Jacques Cartier's discovery of Québec, and now they have reached near world domination with shows on almost every continent and a permanent show in Las Vegas. This is the only Cirque du Soleil venue in Montréal and the premiere spot to see their latest productions: They debut new shows here every April to July before heading out on tour.

MAP 1: Quai Jacques-Cartier, 800/450-1480, www.cirquedusoleil.com; $39-295

Cirque Éloize

Following in the footsteps of fellow Québec-founded circus Cirque du Soleil, Cirque Éloize also boasts a big top in the Vieux-Port and a worldwide audience (nearly 4,000 performances in 30 countries). Founded in 1993 by Jeannot Painchaud, Daniel Cyr, and Julie Hamelin, the performance group combines circus arts with music, dance, and theater. Éloize, which is an

THEATER EN FRANÇAIS

Montréal has some of the best French theater this side of Paris. Here are some of the city's top theaters.

- **Espace Go** is committed to showing plays by women playwrights. It opened as Théâtre Expérimental des Femmes in the 1980s and remains true to its roots (4890 blvd. St-Laurent, 514/845-4890, www.espacego.com).

- **Espace Libre,** dedicated to experimental theater, is considered one of the best theater companies in the city (1945 rue Fullum, 514/521-4191, www.espacelibre.qc.ca).

- **Théâtre d'Aujourd'hui,** founded in 1968, is focused on showing new work from Québécois playwrights (3900 rue St-Denis, 514/282-3900, www.theatredaujourdhui.qc.ca).

- **Théâtre de Quat'Sous** is a great venue to catch up-and-coming talent. The modern building is as daring as the company itself (100 ave. des Pins E., 514/845-7277, www.quatsous.com).

- **Théâtre du Nouveau Monde** stages traditional and modern classics and is better known as **TNM** (84 rue Ste-Catherine W., 514/866-8668, www.tnm.qc.ca).

- **Théâtre du Rideau Vert** is the oldest professional theater company in Québec, and it has a faithful fan base (4664 rue St-Denis, 514/844-1793, www.rideauvert.qc.ca).

Acadian word referring to the heat and lightning before a storm, breaks away from the traditional circus mold and pushes the boundaries of the art with a youthful flair.

MAP 1: Quai de l'Horloge, 514/596-3838, www.cirque-eloize.com; $30-50

THEATER

Centaur Theatre

Founded in 1969, the Centaur Theatre is Montréal's preeminent English-language theater company. Located in the Old Stock Exchange, which was built in 1903 by American architect George B. Post, the theater went through two major renovations in 1974 and 1996. As one of only a handful of English-language theater companies, Centaur's mandate is to present the plays of Montréal and Canadian playwrights. The company also consistently produces English-language productions of French-language plays by such noted Québécois playwrights as Michel Tremblay.

MAP 1: 453 rue St-François-Xavier, box office 514/288-3161, www.centaurtheatre.com; $28-45

MUSEUMS
Redpath Museum of Natural History

The Redpath Museum, completed in 1882, is the oldest museum in Canada. Located on the McGill campus, it's one of the few museums in the city open on Mondays. The building itself is gorgeous, and the museum offers a sometimes-uncomfortable window into Canada's colonial past—it's unsettling, for example, to come face to face with mummies on the top floor. The Redpath has opted to retain and recontextualize its ethnological displays. It also has quite a number of stuffed animals, dinosaur bones, and extinct animal exhibits. Indoor shoes are recommended for winter.

MAP 2: McGill University, 859 rue Sherbrooke W., 514/393-4086 ext. 00549, www.mcgill.ca/redpath; 9am-5pm Mon.-Fri. year-round, 1pm-5pm Sun. early June-late Aug., 11am-5pm Sun. fall and winter; suggested fees: $10 adults, $20 for a family

GALLERIES
La Guilde

Founded in 1906, with the aim to preserve and promote Inuit and First Nations art, the Canadian Guild of Crafts has one of the most important permanent collections of aboriginal art in Canada. Prints, tapestries, and sculpture make up the majority of the collection, along with fine ceramics, glass work, and handmade jewelry. Temporary exhibits by Canadian artists are displayed throughout the year.

CENTRE-VILLE

Redpath Museum of Natural History

MAP 2: 1460-B rue Sherbrooke W., 514/849-6091, www.laguilde-theguild.com; 10am-6pm Tues.-Fri., 10am-5pm Sat.; free

Parisian Laundry

Spacious, with floor-to-ceiling windows, exposed wood beams, and a cavernous exhibition space referred to as the "Bunker," Parisian Laundry is a massive space dedicated to contemporary art. Though focused on Canadian artists—they represent some of the best up-and-comers in the country, like Kim Dorland and Rick Leong—they are also monumental in bringing top international artists to Montréal, like Kalup Linzy and Alex Da Corte. The sheer size of the gallery allows for a unique use of space.

MAP 2: 3550 rue St-Antoine W., 514/989-1056, www.parisianlaundry.com; noon-5pm Tues.-Sat.; free

CONCERT VENUES

Corona Theatre

Opened in 1912, when silent movies and light comedy shows were the kings of entertainment, the Corona Theatre with its elaborate moldings and gold touches retains much of its century-old charm. Located on a bustling strip of the city, across the street from the renowned Joe Beef, it has balcony seating and a former orchestra pit, making it perfect for getting up close with musicians like Japandroids, Animal Collective, and Big Wreck.

MAP 2: 2490 rue Notre-Dame W., 514/931-2088, www.theatrecorona.ca; $15-40

CINEMA

Cinéma Banque Scotia

A three-floor movie complex in the heart of downtown, this is your typical

Cinéma Banque Scotia

North American movie theater that plays the latest Hollywood releases and little else. Lines can be long, especially for highly anticipated films, so buy your tickets early. Viewing options include 3-D and IMAX.

MAP 2: 977 rue Ste-Catherine W., 514/842-0549, www.cineplex.com; $13.50 adults, $10.99 seniors, $10.50 children under 14

Cineplex Odeon

Montréal's Cineplex Odeon theater (AMC in the United States) may be part of a chain, but this particular cinema is different for one reason and one reason only: the Canadiens. The theater took up residence in the Forum, the hockey team's former beloved rink. The Canadiens' logo can still be seen at center ice, and a few authentic stands still remain. The theater also shows 3-D and IMAX movies for slightly higher ticket prices.

MAP 2: 2313 rue Ste-Catherine W., 514/904-1250, www.cineplex.com; $13.50 adults, $10.99 seniors, $9.99 children under 14

GALLERIES
❂ Belgo Building

Once an old industrial building, the Belgo has been given a new life, thanks to the various art galleries, dance studios, and cultural organizations that have opened here. What started as a haven for struggling artists in the 1980s and '90s is today an artistic hub with five floors housing over two dozen art galleries—the real draw of the place. Some of the city's most respected galleries make their home here, like Galerie Dominique Bouffard (Ste. 508, 514/678-7054, www.galeriedominiquebouffard.com) and the Galerie Visual Voice (Ste. 421, 514/873-3663, www.visualvoicegallery.com).

MAP 3: 372 rue Ste-Catherine W., no phone; hours vary; free

the Belgo Building

Le 2-22

Le 2-22 is both an architectural joy—all right angles and glass—and a hub for contemporary arts. The flagship building of the Quartier des Spectacles, it houses La Vitrine (Ste. 101, 514/285-4545, www.lavitrine.com), the one-stop shop for all your cultural informational needs:

tickets, events, calendars, and more. In addition to offering last-minute deals and cultural expertise, the building is home to contemporary art galleries, including Vox Centre d'Image Contemporaine (Ste. 401, 514/390-0382, www.voxphoto.com), art archives, and a radio station that broadcasts from its street-level studios.

MAP 3: 2 rue Ste-Catherine E., www.artactuel2-22.com; free

THEATER
Gesù Centre de Créativité

Though it is adjacent to the Église du Gesù (Jesus in Italian), one of the oldest baroque churches in Montréal, don't expect many religious performances. Being in the middle of the Quartier des Spectacles means the venue plays host to events and performances, everything from stand-up comedy to contemporary dance, visual arts, and events featuring traditional African and Native American music. Depending on the event, you'll find yourself in either the roomy theater below the church or in the impressive sanctuary.

MAP 3: 1202 rue de Bleury, 514/861-4378, www.legesu.com; $10-50

Théâtre Sainte-Catherine

This cozy, independently run theater is a great place to catch various, usually more experimental, acts. Emerging Montréal-based playwrights often stage new work here, but you could also find yourself chuckling along with a stand-up comedian—though you may not recognize the name on the marquee. Improv nights happen regularly, with a stellar lineup of local talent that invites audience members to get in on the action every Sunday.

MAP 3: 264 rue Ste-Catherine E., 514/284-3939, www.theatresaintecatherine. com; $5-20

DANCE
✪ Agora de la Danse

With over a hundred performances a year, Agora de la Danse is the place to see contemporary dance in Montréal. Started in the 1980s, it continues to present interesting works from both local and international choreographers and is the only venue in all of Canada dedicated to the presentation and creation of contemporary dance.

MAP 3: 1435 rue de Bleury, 514/525-1500, www.agoradanse.com; $15-30

✪ Les Grands Ballets Canadiens de Montréal

Founded in 1957 by young choreographer and dancer Ludmilla Chiriaeff, Les Grands Ballets continues to be the only ballet company in the city and one of the most boundary-pushing in North America. Presenting both classical and more contemporary works, which have included *Tommy*, Les Grands remains vibrant.

MAP 3: 175 rue Ste-Catherine W., 514/842-2212, www.grandsballets.com; $50-150

OPERA
Opéra de Montréal

In the years since its founding in 1980, the Opéra de Montréal has presented 98 operas, including *La Boheme, Salome,* and four world premieres. In a city full of bilingual arts, the opera is one of the few places the two languages come together. The opera house presents a handful of operas a year. There are often specials for 18- to 30-year-olds.

MAP 3: 260 blvd. de Maisonneuve W., 514/985-2258, www.operademontreal.com; $20-110

SYMPHONY
Orchestre Symphonique de Montréal

Currently led by world-renowned conductor Kent Nagano, the Montréal Symphony Orchestra was founded in 1934 and continues to be the leading company of classical music in the province. It is one of the biggest and most respected in Canada. The orchestra's specialized hall, which was inaugurated at the Place des Arts in spring 2011, ensures the sound is impeccable and is quite the feast for the eyes. Those ages 34 and under should check the website for ticket deals.

MAP 3: 1600 rue St-Urbain, 514/842-9951, www.osm.ca; $30-165

CONCERT VENUES
L'Astral

Found in the heart of the Quartier des Spectacles, L'Astral is situated in the building that now houses the Festival International de Jazz de Montréal. It's fitting then that L'Astral is mainly a jazz venue, with performances from international musicians throughout the week. The venue has a club atmosphere, with tables and chairs set up on the floor around the room for a more intimate setting. It also hosts music-related art exhibits featuring the jazz festival's collection, so give yourself time to pop in and take a look.

MAP 3: 305 rue Ste-Catherine W., 514/288-8882, www.sallelastral.com; $15-50

Club Soda

Around since the 1980s, this two-floor venue has a 900-person capacity and plays host to well-known international bands whose music you'd likely recognize on the radio. Frank Ocean, Amy Winehouse, and Oasis are just some of the musicians who have graced the stage. A second-floor balcony, which is quite flashy with accents of neon blue and LCD screens, accommodates more patrons, and bars on both levels ensure the beer keeps flowing.

MAP 3: 1225 blvd. St-Laurent, 514/286-1010, www.clubsoda.ca; $15-30

Métropolis

This is the biggest venue in the city other than the Centre Bell, and tickets to shows usually sell out fast. The large venue still manages a little charm with balconies and richly hued walls. Bars line the walls, and TVs are in place around the venue for those whose view of the stage is obscured by a tall person.

MAP 3: 59 rue Ste-Catherine E., 514/844-3500, www.metropolismontreal.ca; $25-80

SAT

Founded in 1996, SAT is dedicated to the research, creation, production, education, and conservation of digital culture. La Société des Arts Technologiques, or the Society for Arts and Technology, is one of the most interesting and diverse venues in Montréal, hosting everything from fashion shows to electronic music nights and holiday craft fairs. The sparsely decorated, simple, modular seating is forever shifting places. Its open-concept space has floor-to-ceiling windows that let passersby in on the action. If it's innovative, new, and cutting edge, it's happening here.

MAP 3: 1201 blvd. St-Laurent, 514/844-2033, www.sat.qc.ca; $15-40

Quartier Latin and the Village
Map 4

MUSEUMS
Éco Musée du Fier Monde

Housed in a former public bath, the Éco Musée du Fier Monde is dedicated to the city's industrial and working-class history. Though the exhibit is fairly straightforward, it is worth the price of admission alone to see the refurbished public bath, a historic building in itself and part of the area's history. The now empty pool is one of the first things you notice about the space, which was built in 1924 for the area's working-class residents, who didn't have access to showers or bathtubs. It was later used for recreation

and remained popular and in full use into the 1970s.

MAP 4: 2050 rue Amherst, 514/528-8444, www.ecomusee.qc.ca; 11am-8pm Wed., 9:30am-4pm Thurs.-Fri., 10:30am-5pm Sat.-Sun.; $8 adults, $6 seniors, students, and children

CONCERT VENUES
Le National

On the cusp of the Village and the Quartier Latin, Le National is a great old venue on an unassuming strip, with an austere blink-and-you-miss-it marquee. The names range from popular French and English indie rock bands to acid jazz. Audience members who are lucky enough to get up to the balcony are welcome to a seat; the rest of the venue is standing room only.

MAP 4: 1220 rue Ste-Catherine E., 514/845-2014, www.lenational.ca; $20-35

L'Olympia

L'Olympia

Built in 1925, the Olympia theater remains one of the most majestic in the city. Once the place to go for "cinematic theater," it is now a great place to catch a band or a stand-up show. The main theater still has seats on both the main floor and the balcony, a rarity in the city.

MAP 4: 1004 rue Ste-Catherine E., 514/845-3524, www.olympiamontreal.com; $25-50

Theatre Berri

Theatre Berri is in the east end of downtown, near the Quartier Latin. Performers tend toward the R&B, hip-hop, and electronic dance music end of the spectrum—and there are drag shows, too. The modern building has some flashy features, like LEDs illuminating the entrance and an impressive sound system, which many venues in the city lack.

MAP 4: 1280 rue St-Denis, 514/764-2680 or 888/608-1280, www.theatreberri.com; $15-40

CINEMA

✪ Cinémathèque Québécoise

Dedicated to preserving cinema, the Cinémathèque Québécoise is the place to catch celluloid classics, hard-to-find international titles, or Kenneth Anger's experimental gems. The schedule often includes a month dedicated to a single director or type of cinema. The modern architecture of the space adds to the overall ambience of the theater and evokes Paris's Cinémathèque Française. This is a must for cinema buffs.

MAP 4: 335 blvd. de Maisonneuve E., 514/842-9763, www.cinematheque. qc.ca; $10 adults, $9 seniors, students, and children

MUSEUMS

Musée des Hospitalières de l'Hôtel Dieu

Tucked inside the stone walls of l'Hôtel-Dieu de Montréal, the Musée des Hospitalières looks at the history of the hospital and its medical practices. Visitors are greeted by a 17th-century staircase before learning about early treatments and practices administered by the nurses, as well as the history of national health care and the hospital. If you are visiting in summer, take a detour into the garden. The museum is closed from mid-December to mid-January, and reservations are required in January and February. Cash only.

the Musée des Hospitalières

MAP 5: 201 ave. des Pins W., 514/849-2919, www.museedeshospitalieres.qc.ca; 10am-5pm Tues.-Fri., 1pm-5pm Sat.-Sun. mid-June-mid-Oct.; 1pm-5pm Wed.-Sun. mid-Oct.-mid-Dec. and Mar.-mid-June; reservations required Jan.-Feb.; $10 adults, $6 students, $5 seniors and students, children free (cash only)

GALLERIES

La Centrale Galerie Powerhouse

Opened in 1973, La Centrale Galerie Powerhouse is an artist-run center that focuses on the work of contemporary female artists and aims to expand on the history of feminist art practices. The works displayed are often witty and humorous as well as thought-provoking.

MAP 5: 4296 blvd. St-Laurent, 514/871-0268, www.lacentrale.org; noon-6pm Wed., noon-9pm Thurs.-Fri., noon-5pm Sat.-Sun.; free

THEATER AND DANCE

MAI

Promoting multidisciplinary and multicultural contemporary artists, the MAI (Montréal, Arts Interculturels) is the only venue in the city to focus on work by artists who have diverse origins and inspirations—meaning you could catch a traditional Thai dance performance one night and a psychedelic Middle Eastern post-rock band the next. The modern surroundings make it a nice place to have a drink or a coffee while you wander from the gallery into the theater to catch a play by a young, emerging playwright.

MAP 5: 3680 rue Jeanne-Mance, 514/982-1812, www.m-a-i.qc.ca; box office 3pm-6pm Tues.-Sat.; $10-35

MainLine Theater

The MainLine was originally established to produce the Festival St-Ambroise Fringe de Montréal, an event it continues to support. Nowadays, however, it is a theater company known

Cinema L'Amour

for presenting more cutting-edge English theater and hosting events during festivals like Just for Laughs. It's directly above a grocery store on the Main, and the surroundings tend toward the dingy, but the shows are still worth checking out.

MAP 5: 3997 blvd. St-Laurent, 514/849-3378, www.mainlinetheatre.ca; $15-30

CONCERT VENUES
La Sala Rossa

Sitting atop super-cool Spanish restaurant La Sala Rosa is super-cool venue La Sala Rossa (see the difference? Two S's). Locals often grab a bite downstairs before heading upstairs to catch an indie rock band. The open space is nothing fancy, with chairs stacked in the corner. Though mainly a live music venue, it also hosts dance nights, film screenings, and weddings.

MAP 5: 4848 blvd. St-Laurent, 514/284-0122, www.casadelpopolo.com; $15-50

La Tulipe

La Tulipe has one of the most interesting histories of any theater in the city. Built in 1913, it was a traditional music hall and movie theater (its domed ceiling makes for great acoustics) until the early 1960s, when it became a popular place to see burlesque and stand-up comedy. Today, it has returned to its roots as a music hall, with popular bands playing here from all over the world. If you've had a long day, snag a seat in the balcony, sit back, and enjoy the show.

MAP 5: 4530 ave. Papineau, 514/529-5000, www.latulipe.ca; $15.75-35

CINEMA
Cinema du Parc

Found in the basement of an out-of-place shopping complex (so many McGill students!), Cinema du Parc is the best repertory theater in Montréal. Playing everything from well-known American directors like Jim Jarmusch and Woody Allen to lesser-known Québécois directors like Xavier Dolan, the best in international contemporary cinema is always on view here. Films are subtitled in both English and French; if it is an international title, double-check the language before heading off to the showing.

MAP 5: 3575 ave. du Parc, 514/281-1900, www.cinemaduparc.com; $12.50 general admission, $11 youth 14-25, $9 youth under 13, $11 seniors

Cinema L'Amour

Profiled by media outlets VICE and Maisonneuve, Montréal's foremost adults-only cinema started off as a theater hall/movie house in 1914, called Le Globe. Located at the time in the heart of Montréal's Jewish community, in the 1920s and '30s locals would flock here to catch the latest Yiddish films. After a stint as a regular movie house (1930-1960s), it turned to adult films in the late-1960s; lately, they've started hosting live music for festivals like Pop Montreal. The interior remains virtually unchanged and is as opulent and, oddly, as beautiful as in its heyday.

MAP 5: 4015 blvd. St-Laurent, 514/849-2727, www.cinemalamour.com; $10.50 adults, $9.50 seniors

Mile End and Petite-Italie   Map 6

GALLERIES

✪ Never Apart

This sprawling gallery space—they even have an outdoor pool in the summer!—takes up 12,000 square feet of space in Mile-Ex. Technically open only noon-5pm on Saturday, it also holds events, including music shows, screenings, and talks. Never Apart consistently features the best contemporary work across genres, all with a social justice focus. It's a uniquely Montréal spot, made possible by affordable space, intense creativity, and the blending of many different cultures and perspectives.

MAP 6: 7049 rue St-Urbain, no phone, www.neverapart.com; noon-5pm Sat.; free

Articule

This artist-run center, established in 1979, often showcases the work of local Montréal artists. Situated in the heart of the Mile End, it takes up the street level storefront of a grand old townhouse, but the bright-green facade sets it apart from the otherwise quiet street. Exhibits range from video and performance art to installations, and the center also offers talks and workshops. It closes for a month during the summer, but it always has a window installation for passersby.

MAP 6: 262 ave. Fairmount W., 514/842-9686, www.articule.org; noon-6pm Wed.-Fri., noon-5pm Sat.-Sun.; free

Battat Contemporary

Though "contemporary" is in its name, Battat is one of a few places outside a museum where you can occasionally see older works from the owner's private collection. Occupying the second floor of an old warehouse in Mile-Ex, the collection includes the work of masters like Gustave Courbet and Francisco de Goya. The single-room format allows for an intimate viewing of the work, which also includes exhibitions by established and emerging

MURALS GALORE

Montréal is a city of artists, and one of the ways that manifests is in its abundance of murals. In 2016, the city invested half a million dollars to finance 21 murals in 10 different boroughs. Moreover, rue St-Laurent is transformed into the open-air **Mural Festival** (page 168) every summer in mid-June.

The result of this public-art-friendly activity is that a walk around downtown, Chinatown, the Plateau, or Mile End will bring many Instagram-worthy moments. My favorites include an extraordinarily vibrant painting by Bicicleta Sem Freio featuring a toucan and a pair of chattering teeth in a parking lot off St-Laurent, north of Milton, and an impossible-to-miss giant painting of a Chinese opera singer by Brian Beyung and Gene Pendon flanking the northern gate of Chinatown on boulevard René-Lévesque—but keep your eyes peeled to find your own delights, as murals change every few years, and there are always new gems to discover.

Canadian and international artists. (Check ahead to make sure the gallery isn't closed between exhibitions.)
MAP 6: 7245 rue Alexandra, 514/750-9566, www.battatcontemporary.com; noon-6pm Tues.-Fri., noon-5pm Sat.; free

Galerie Simon Blais

Initially founded to exhibit abstract works and those done on paper, Simon Blais is now recognized as one of the most diverse galleries in the city, representing both established international artists like Betty Godwin as well as known Québécois artists like Claude Tousignant and Guido Molinari. Given the wide range of work exhibited, shows can be hit or miss. The Guest Artist series, which invites emerging artists to exhibit in the two-story space, is usually more rewarding.
MAP 6: 5420 blvd. St-Laurent, 514/849-1165, www.galeriesimonblais.com; 10am-6pm Tues.-Fri., 10am-5pm Sat.; free

Galerie Yves Laroche

This avant-garde gallery exhibits work that is influenced by subcultures, like graffiti, tattooing, comics, and cartoons, and art movements like pop-art and surrealism (think of Dali's melting clocks but with melting Mickey Mouses). Cutting edge and provocative, the work is often both dark and darkly funny. Opened in 1991, the gallery has moved from its old digs in Vieux-Montréal to a modern space in Petite-Italie, the perfect backdrop for the dynamic pieces on show.
MAP 6: 6355 blvd. St-Laurent, 514/393-1999, www.yveslaroche.com; 11am-7pm Tues.-Fri., 11am-5pm Sat.; free

CONCERT VENUES

Rialto Theatre

Designed after the Palais Garnier in Paris, the Rialto Theatre is an absolutely gorgeous venue. Opened as a movie theater in 1924, its dark red-and-gold interior and near-vertical balcony seating set it apart from any other theater in Montréal. Once relegated to yearly showings of *The Rocky Horror Picture Show*, it now hosts theater and music and acts as a venue for large local festivals like Pop Montreal.
MAP 6: 5723 ave. du Parc, 514/770-7773, www.theatrerialto.ca; $15-50

Théâtre Outremont

This art deco theater opened in 1929, and its music hall was subsequently filled with the voices that defined the eras that followed. Renovated to include a cinema in the 1970s, it soon became a popular repertory cinema. Today, it's a venue for live music, film festivals, comedy shows, and circus events—check the calendar for tickets while you're planning your trip.

MAP 6: 1245 ave. Bernard W., 514/495-9944, www.theatreoutremont.ca; $7.50-70

Greater Montréal   Map 7

MUSEUMS

Maison Saint-Gabriel

Situated in Pointe-Saint-Charles, a working-class neighborhood west of Old Montréal, the grounds that are now Maison Saint-Gabriel were given to Marguerite Bourgeoys in 1668. Bourgeoys used the land to start a farm and built the house to accommodate the *filles du roi,* young French women who came to Canada in the early days of the settlement to help populate the new colony.

Interpreters re-create the everyday tasks of the 17th and 18th centuries, and in the summer artisans re-create traditional trades on the museum's grounds. This interpretive museum is well worth the trip, especially if you have your own transportation. Tours are offered.

MAP 7: 2146 Place Dublin, 514/935-8136, www.maisonsaint-gabriel.qc.ca; 1pm-5pm Tues.-Sun. mid-Jan.-mid-June and early Sept.-late Dec., 11am-6pm Tues.-Sun. mid-June-early Sept.; $15 adults, $10 seniors, $5 students and children

Montréal Holocaust Memorial Museum

With over 7,000 documents, photographs, and objects in its collection, the Holocaust museum reconstructs the life of Jewish communities before, during, and after World War II, exploring the rise of Nazism, life in the ghettos, and the diaspora communities after the war. The museum was founded in 1979 by Holocaust survivors, and the history of Montréal's Jewish community is explored here as well as in the testimonials and life stories of those who eventually chose Montréal as their home.

Found off of the beaten path in the residential area of Côte-des-Neiges, it was the first major museum dedicated to the Holocaust in the country, and it will take visitors a couple of hours or more to browse the museum and take in the multimedia displays. The personal artifacts (which include everything from suitcases and postcards to stars of David and identity cards) and moving testimonials of nearly 500 survivors make for a profound experience. The permanent exhibition may not be suitable for children under 8.

MAP 7: 5151 chemin de la Côte-Ste-Catherine, 514/345-2605, www.museeholocauste.ca; 10am-5pm Mon.-Tues. and Thurs., 10am-9pm Wed., 10am-3pm Fri., 10am-4pm Sun.; $8 adults, $5 seniors, students, and children

Le Musée Dufresne-Nincheri

Not far from the modern organic architecture of the Olympic Stadium is Le Musée Dufresne-Nincheri, the complete antithesis to its surroundings with its classic Beaux-Arts style. Designed by Parisian architect Jules Renard in 1915, the museum was originally two houses owned by brothers Marius and Oscar Dufresne, who were wealthy entrepreneurs. The

Montréal Holocaust Memorial Museum

interior of the house remains virtually untouched, right down to murals and ceiling paintings by Florentine artist Guido Nincheri, best known for his ecclesiastical works. The museum now also includes one of the oldest stained-glass workshops in Canada, where Nincheri created over 5,000 stained-glass windows for clients across North America between 1925 and 1996.

MAP 7: 4040 rue Sherbrooke E., 514/259-9201, www.chateaudufresne. com; 10am-5pm Wed.-Sun., tours 1:30pm and 3:30pm; $14 adults, $13 seniors and students, $7 children

CIRCUS
TOHU

Montréal is a city full of circuses, but the TOHU is a little bit different. Founded in 2004 by En Piste, the National Circus School, and Cirque du Soleil, TOHU is one of the largest training grounds for performers of the circus arts in the world. Shows might lack the pomp and circumstance (and the awesome costumes) of Cirque du

Soleil, but you'll be hard-pressed to find performers who are more dedicated and astounding in their art.

MAP 7: 2345 rue Jarry E., 514/376-8648, www.tohu.ca; $25-55

THEATER
✪ Segal Centre for the Performing Arts

With a focus on creating a nurturing environment for developing performers and playwrights, the Mies van der Rohe-designed Segal Centre has different stages and programs that make it one of the most exciting places to see English theater in the city. Independent companies use the Segal Stage as a place to refine and perform, while bigger productions are found on the larger stage. The Dora Wasserman Yiddish Theatre, part of the Segal, has been nurturing and supporting plays that dramatize the Jewish experience since 1958.

MAP 7: 5170 chemin de la Côte-Ste-Catherine, 514/739-2301, www.segalcentre. org; $25-50

Festivals and Events

Montréal has never met a festival or party it did not like. The summer is a particularly high season for festivals and outdoor events, but Montrealers don't stay cooped up all winter—they pull on parkas and head outside for winter carnivals, too.

WINTER

La Fête des Neiges

The biggest winter festival in Montréal, La Fête des Neiges takes place in Parc Jean-Drapeau during four consecutive weekends between January and February. It's a great festival for the kids. Bundle the whole family up for a day full of winter activities, including tubing, ice fishing, archery, curling, hockey, and ice sculpture.

Face paint, kid-friendly tunes, and hot chocolate are also on the agenda.

Greater Montréal: Parc Jean-Drapeau, www.parcjeandrapeau.com; four weekends in Jan.-Feb.; free

Igloofest

At its base, electronic music festival Igloofest (run by the same folks who run Piknic Électronik) is a large outdoor winter rave full of trippy beats, mesmerizing visuals, an enormous igloo, and audience members dancing around in snowsuits. It takes over Jacques-Cartier Pier for four weekends between January and February—it takes a lot of dancing to get rid of the chill that blows in off the St-Lawrence. DJs pack their mittens and

TOP EXPERIENCE

CITY OF FESTIVALS

Montréal prides itself on hosting the world's largest number of festivals. Some, like the Sunday drum circle in front of the George-Étienne Cartier monument on the east side of Parc du Mont-Royal, are informal. Public pianos, dotted throughout the city in the summer, host piano lessons and occasionally draw virtuosos. Visitors with an open mind and an ear cocked to the ground will likely stumble across an impromptu gathering or two.

Other festivals are more formal. If your trip overlaps with any of the top celebrations listed below, be sure to check them out.

- **Les FrancoFolies de Montréal** (page 167)

- **Mural Festival** (page 168)

- **Festival International de Jazz de Montréal** (page 168)

- **Just for Laughs** (page 169)

- **Pop Montreal** (page 171)

Festival International de Jazz de Montréal

toques (woolen hats) and come from all corners of the world to keep revelers moving.

Vieux-Montréal: Jacques-Cartier Pier, www.igloofest.ca; four weekends Jan.-Feb.; from $10

Rendez-vous du Cinéma Québécois

Québécois cinema is celebrated annually from late February to early March during the Rendez-vous du Cinéma Québécois, which screens films made in the last 12 months. This 10-day festival is fascinating, whether or not you're familiar with Québécois movies. The range on view is spectacular, everything from mediocre comedies to astounding documentaries full of emotion and surprise. Though the festival's name is in French, selections are not limited to the French language; this is really dedicated to any and all films made in Québec, so there are English and First Nations selections as well.

Various locations: 514/526-9635, www. rvcq.com; late Feb.-early Mar., $12/film, $99 pass

Montréal en Lumière

Montréal en Lumière, an 11-day cultural celebration of food, arts, and music, takes place from late February to early March all over the city. It is hands-down the most anticipated of winter festivals, if only because of the closing-night festivities. The festival culminates in Nuit Blanche, an all-night party where people take to the streets and trek from live shows to free museum exhibits well into the wee hours of the morning, refueling with flasks of hot chocolate and stronger stuff as they go.

Citywide: www.montrealenlumiere.com; late Feb.-early Mar.; free

SPRING

Blue Metropolis Literary Festival

Internationally renowned authors converge on Montréal in late April to take part in the world's first multilingual literary festival. Writers of fiction, nonfiction, poetry, and journalism come to be a part of the panel discussions, interviews, Q&A periods, book signings and launches, and of course to read their work to a captive audience. Unique in its vision, each year's event has a specific theme, with the discussions and authors invited tying into that theme. Previous years have included Yann Martel, Margaret Atwood, and A. L. Kennedy.

Various locations: 661 rue Rose-de-Lima Ste. 201, 514/932-1112, www. bluemetropolis.org; late Apr.; individual events $10-30, $60 pass

Festival St-Ambroise Fringe de Montréal

Though not as big as the Edinburgh Fringe, Montréal's version, the Festival St-Ambroise Fringe de Montréal, comes close, with over 55,000 attendees at the week-long festival. Running late May to early June, the festival takes over venues around the city with local and international Fringe performances that are randomly picked by lottery; if your play makes it to the stage, it is all about luck. Though the

Montréal en Lumière

program is released a few days early, the best way to see if there's anything that tickles your fancy is to stop by Fringe for All a few days before opening to see snippets from upcoming shows.

Various locations: 514/849-3378, www. montrealfringe.ca; late May-early June; $10-25, $275 unlimited Fringe Pass

Festival TransAmériques

Contemporary dance and theater are the focus of Festival TransAmériques, which runs late May to mid-June. Though it shares the stage with theater, this is the most important contemporary dance festival in the city, and the works on view are usually standouts. Drawing talents from across Canada and the world, Festival TransAmériques is known for some audience participation in its works—a public dance performance, for example, or a play that invites the audience to join the cast, if only for a fleeting moment.

Various locations: 514/842-0704, www. fta.qc.ca; late May-mid-June; $25-60

Elektra

Elektra is a cutting-edge digital arts festival that takes place sometime in May or June (check the website for details). It offers some of the most unusual experiences you're likely to come across at a festival. Internationally renowned and drawing artists from such diverse nations as Japan and Mexico, the exhibits range from sound and light installations to live performances and interactive exhibits. The latest technologies and futuristic designs, like clothing with GPS tracking, are incorporated into almost every work, and there is an emphasis on new digital media, though the artists themselves come from varied backgrounds, like contemporary dance and musical composition.

Various locations: www. elektramontreal.ca; May or June; $12-20

SUMMER

Festival Mondial de la Bière

Canada's largest beer festival, the Festival Mondial de la Bière takes place for five days in early June at the Palais des Congrès. Local and international microbreweries share the stage with giants like Molson and Stella Artois. Brewers from all over the world converge, allowing visitors to taste hundreds of different types of beers. Entrance is free, but a full pint will set you back about $8. Tasting coupons are also available for a dollar a pop.

Vieux-Montréal: Palais des Congrès, 201 rue Viger W., 514/722-9640, www. festivalmondialbiere.qc.ca; early June; free entry, tasting $1-5

Piknic Électronik

Piknic Électronik is an outdoor music festival held on Sundays during the day from late May through to September. Revelers—a mixed crowd of youth, family, and old ravers looking for sober dance fun—gather under an Alexander Calder statue first installed for Expo 67. No alcohol is allowed on-site, but picnics are encouraged.

Greater Montréal: Parc Jean-Drapeau, www.parcjeandrapeau.com; most Sundays May-Sept.; tickets $13.50, pass $116

Les FrancoFolies de Montréal

Les FrancoFolies de Montréal is a massive street festival in celebration of Francophone music that takes over the Place des Festivals for 10 days in early to mid-June. A whole strip of rue Ste-Catherine is blocked off to make way for the throngs of fans who

Les FrancoFolies de Montréal

come out in force to check out emerging and established Francophone bands and musicians. Not all concerts are free, however; bigger names play to a more contained crowd in venues across the city. It's a great way to check out the latest in the Québécois and Francophone music scenes.

Centre-Ville Est: 514/876-8989, www. francofolies.com; early-mid-June; free-$120

Mural Festival

For two weeks in mid-June, the Montréal Mural Festival invites artists from across the world to paint giant murals across the city. Founded in 2012, the festival has supported the creation of 80 murals in almost as many different painting styles. Mostly-free outdoor music and art events are also often part of the festival, and the festival partners with a local tour guide company to offer $20 guided tours of the murals—check the website for details.

Various locations: www.muralfestival. com; mid-June; free

Suoni per il Popolo

As the name suggests, Suoni per il Popolo, which takes place throughout June, is organized by the same people behind café/bar/venue Casa del Popolo and is aimed at underground and experimental music. Started in 2001, the festival has since grown and is now one of the foremost festivals of experimental music of all kinds. If weird and wonderful is your thing, Suoni per il Popolo is the place for you. Past editions have seen the likes of Lillian Allen, The Microphones, Vic Chesnutt, and Jandek.

Various locations: 514/282-0122 ext. 222, www.suoniperilpopolo.org; June; $8-35, $295-330 festival pass

Festival International de Jazz de Montréal

One of the most recognizable festivals in the world, the Festival International de Jazz de Montréal attracts thousands of tourists to the city each summer, running from the end of June to early July. Some of the biggest names in music have played here, including Tony Bennett, B. B. King, and Norah Jones. The 11-day festival offers non-stop music with big international acts playing for free in the middle of a shut-down rue Ste-Catherine. The outdoor atmosphere and huge crowds make it one of the most exciting festivals in the city.

Various locations: 514/871-1881, www. montrealjazzfest.com; late June-early July; free-$150

Week-ends du Monde

For two weekends in early to mid-July, Week-ends du Monde invites Montrealers of all ethnicities and heritages to share and celebrate their cultures through music, food, and dance. A family segment offers activities for kids 12 and under, including singing, dancing, games, live music shows, and creative and sports workshops. Characters in costume entertain the kids.

Greater Montréal: Parc Jean-Drapeau, www.parcjeandrapeau.com; two weekends in early-mid-July; free

Just for Laughs

What started as a two-day Francophone comedy event, Juste pour Rire (Just for Laughs), has since grown into one of the biggest comedy festivals in the world. For two weeks from mid- to late July, streets all over downtown are closed off to make room for the street performers stationed throughout the city. Each year established comedians, such as Natasha Leggero, Jerry Seinfeld, Wyatt Cenac, and Flight of the Conchords, bring their own brand of stand-up to the city. The recently launched Zoofest, also part of Just for Laughs, has a younger take on funny and features more obscure (sometimes funnier) acts.

Various locations: 514/845-4000, www. hahaha.com; mid-late July; $15-120

Festival International Nuits d'Afrique

Fans of African music will rejoice at the Festival International Nuits d'Afrique, which focuses on music with African roots. From Ethiopian jazz to Algerian *raï* and even sounds from Latin America, this festival has it all. Established in 1987, it has become the springboard for African music in North America and has helped introduce many international groups to Canadian audiences. Happening throughout mid- to late July, it is the city's premiere world music festival.

Various locations: 514/499-9215, www. festivalnuitsdafrique.com; mid-late July; $12.50-40

Heavy MTL

Heavy MTL: The name says it all. This two-day festival, which takes place outdoors at Parc Jean-Drapeau in late July, is all about heavy metal. Offering a mix of old-time metalheads like Megadeth, Danzig, and Rob Zombie with new kids on the block like Mastadon, Avenged Sevenfold, and Baroness, it keeps fans from all generations pleased. No matter who's playing, you can guarantee it'll be loud.

Greater Montréal: Parc Jean-Drapeau, www.heavymtl.com; late July; $150 weekend pass

Fantasia Film Festival

Running from mid-July to early August, Fantasia Film Festival is North America's premiere genre film festival. From the obscure to the grotesque, the Japanese to the Korean, it offers a wide range of films from all over the globe. Established in 1996, it has since grown to become the place where distributors come to scope out the best of the weird and the strange. Popular with moviegoers, it has become a destination festival for die-hard genre fans.

Various locations: www.fantasiafestival.com; mid-July-early Aug.; $11/film, $100 for 10 films

Osheaga Music and Arts Festival

The three-day Osheaga Music and Arts Festival is one of the biggest in Montréal, taking place off-island in the picturesque Parc Jean-Drapeau. Thousands of people of all ages spend the weekend checking out unknown emerging bands, musicians like Robyn and Hot Chip, and big-name acts like Arcade Fire, The Cure, and Snoop Dogg. Local art collectives set up installations in a designated area of the site and you can often check out the work in progress. Among leafy-green forests, it is a great way to spend the first weekend in August.

Greater Montréal: Parc Jean-Drapeau, www.osheaga.com; first weekend in Aug.; $120/day, $320 weekend

Fierté Montréal Pride

Montréal Pride is quite the celebration. Nonprofit Fierté Montréal hosts a celebration that includes a parade, community day, and 10 days' worth of gay pride activities, including outdoor concerts and dance parties, drag races, and performances by interdisciplinary artists in early to mid-August.

Various locations: www.fiertemontrealpride.com; early-mid-Aug.; free-$35

Mutek

Celebrating digital creativity and electronic music, Mutek is a generally sweaty six days of dancing and chilling

Fierté Montréal Pride parade

out to the latest electronic sounds, while magical worlds are created on a screen behind a stage. Taking place in late August, it is presented by Mutek, a not-for-profit organization leading the way in digital sounds and visual arts. It draws talent from emerging and established international scenes and is a great festival for anyone drawn to the digital age and all that comes with it.

Various locations: www.mutek.org; late Aug.; $27-35, pass $265

Montréal World Film Festival

With the aim of supporting cultural diversity in cinema, the Montréal World Film Festival supports many emerging filmmakers. The public festival invites viewers to be the jury, and audience members participate in the process by voting for films in various categories—like the Oscars but without Hollywood. That's not to say bigger name directors don't show here; they do, but they rarely come from Hollywood. During its 12-day run from late August to early September, the festival also offers free viewings of films out under the stars in front of Place des Arts.

Various locations: 514/848-3883, www. ffm-montreal.org; late Aug.-early Sept.; $10/film, $100 pass

FALL

Pop Montreal

Pop Montreal is an annual five-day festival occurring in mid-September that features Francophone, Canadian, and international acts. It's one of the most highly anticipated festivals of the year, especially among fans of indie music. Emerging and underground artists might outnumber other bands on the schedule, but industry pioneers include Burt Bacharach, Swans, and Os Mutantes. Though primarily a music festival, it has grown to include offshoots like Puces Pop, Art Pop, Film Pop, Fashion Pop, and Kids Pop.

Various locations: 514/842-1919, www. popmontreal.com; mid-Sept.; $10-60, $225 Pop Pass

Festival du Nouveau Cinéma

Founded in 1971, the Festival du Nouveau Cinéma is an independent film festival dedicated to showing independent films from the world over. Taking place over 12 days in October, it has become a huge draw for cinephiles and is viewed as one of the most prestigious festivals for films of this kind. It is even a qualifying festival for the Academy Awards in the category of short film. Directors such as Kenneth Anger, Wim Wenders, and Atom Egoyan have attended the festival.

Various locations: 514/282-0004, www. nouveaucinema.ca; Oct.; $13/film adult, $9/film senior and student, $200 pass adult, $160 pass senior and student

Festival du Monde Arabe

Established in 2000, the Festival du Monde Arabe is a two-week festival that takes place from late October to mid-November. It aims to develop a dialogue between Arab and Western cultures in the city. Featuring everything from dance to visual arts and music to movies, it attempts to present every aspect of the culture. Many of the events are in French, though English events also exist; check the website for details.

Various locations: www.festivalarabe. com; late Oct.-mid-Nov.; $15-50

Rencontres Internationales du Documentaire Montréal (RIDM)

Dedicated to documentary films, the 10-day Rencontres Internationales du Documentaire Montréal, better known as RIDM, takes place in early to mid-November. The festival was founded in 1998 by filmmakers who wanted to create a new platform for perspectives in the discipline. It now features the work of international and local documentary filmmakers with the aim of presenting the films in their original languages. Alongside the films, the festival includes panel discussions, workshops, and master classes.

Various locations: 514/499-3676, www.ridm.qc.ca; early-mid-Nov.; $12/film adult, $9.50/film senior and student, $120 adult pass, $90 pass senior and student

Image+Nation

Held at the end of October, Image+Nation is the preeminent LGBTQ film festival in the city. With international titles and 11 days of screenings, and thanks to the collapse of independent film distribution, it has become one of the most important festivals of its kind. Titles by and for the LGBTQ community are on view, and the films include animation and shorts.

Various locations: www.image-nation.org; late Nov.-early Dec..; $12.75/film adult, $9.50/film senior and student

SPORTS AND ACTIVITIES

Vieux-Montréal 175
Centre-Ville. 178
Plateau Mont-Royal. 179
Mile End and Petite-Italie. 181
Greater Montréal 182

When it comes to sports, Montréal can be summed up in one word: hockey. There's little the city loves more than a good hockey game, whether it's a quick game of shinny (ice hockey) on an outdoor rink or cheering on the Canadiens at the Bell Centre. From late December until early March, skating rinks pop up in public parks (and private backyards) across the metropolis and are ideal if you have skates on hand. If skating is new for you, test your skills at one of the larger outdoor rinks across the city, where you can rent skates at a nearby pavilion.

Since winter feels like it lasts forever, winter sports are a huge part of a Montrealer's daily routine. As soon as there's snow on the ground, cross-country skis are brought out of hibernation and put to good use navigating the unplowed city streets.

The city's many green spaces allow urban dwellers to indulge in snowshoeing and skiing throughout the winter. Of course, these parks provide the perfect opportunity to run, roller-blade, or do yoga once the winter has disappeared.

Montréal Canadiens fan

Though all outdoor sports are popular in this city, cycling is the most prevalent. Biking is a huge part of city life, and you'll see cyclists battling the elements even in the middle of winter. The city's bike share scheme, Bixi, has helped to make cycling even more popular, not just for recreation but as an alternative to public transportation. As such, Montréal has 700 kilometers of designated bike lanes crisscrossing the city. Look for the painted bikes on the asphalt or follow fellow cyclists to find your way.

HIGHLIGHTS

✪ **BEST WAY TO SEE THE CITY:** Get yourself a bike from **Ça Roule Montréal** and explore the city on two wheels (page 175).

✪ **BEST SPORTING EVENT:** The **Montréal Canadiens** have won the most Stanley Cup championships of any team in the National Hockey League. Montrealers are extremely devoted to the team, so the fan spirit at any of their games is palpable (page 178).

✪ **BEST TWO-WHEELED TOUR:** Offering everything from family tours to hidden neighborhood gems, **Fitz and Follwell** is your best biking tour bet (page 179).

✪ **BEST TASTE OF CANADIANA:** The Canadian Football League was founded in 1958, but its roots go back to 1878. Catch **Les Alouettes de Montréal** in action to see one of the country's oldest sports (page 180).

✪ **BEST PLACE TO GET WET:** Located on a lush island a Métro stop from downtown, **Jean-Drapeau Aquatic Complex** is the ideal place to take a dip (page 183).

✪ **MOST LIKELY TO GET YOU REVVED UP:** Since the 1960s, the **Canadian Grand Prix** has brought the world's top drivers to the city for a week of cars and champagne, with a distinctly European flair (page 186).

BIKING
BIKE RENTALS AND TOURS
✪ Ça Roule Montréal

If you want to explore the city's waterfront, biking is the most accessible and fastest way to do it. If you're in the Vieux-Port, Ça Roule Montréal provides a great option for hourly or daily rentals. They rent hybrid, road, tandem, and touring bikes, as well as children's bikes, so you can pick the style you're most comfortable with. If you'd prefer a more structured approach, check out their three- and four-hour tour options.

MAP 1: 27 rue de la Commune E., 514/866-0633, www.caroulemontreal.com; 10am-6pm daily; rentals $28/day, tours $22-65

BIKE PATHS
Lachine Canal Bike Path

Running along the base of the Vieux-Port and continuing west, this bike path is one of the longest and most popular in the city. Following the river for 15 kilometers (over 9 miles), the path enables riders to get a view of the city skyline and take in what was once a bustling port. It also runs past Marché Atwater and McAuslan Brewery, both great places to stop for a snack or beverage. Open for cycling from April to when the snow flies, it becomes a cross-country skiing path in winter. It can get crowded, especially on summer weekends.

MAP 1: From Vieux-Port to chemin du Musée in Lachine

CYCLING THE CITY

Montréal is incredibly bike-friendly. Whether tooling around the **Plateau Mont-Royal** neighborhood, traversing the **rail trail** that bisects Mile End and Petite-Italie, or biking along the **Lachine Canal** to Marché Atwater for lunch, there are many ways to explore the city and its environs on two wheels. You can even pick up the **Route Verte** if you're looking for a more ambitious trip out of the city.

If you're bringing your bike with you, plan ahead to store it safely—**L'Hôtel de l'Institut de Tourisme et d'Hôtellerie du Québec** is a great place to stay, as they've got bike parking. And make sure to pick up a **bike route map** as soon as you arrive or rent a bike—they're available at bike shops and bike cafés (visit **Maison des Cyclistes,** near Parc La Fontaine, for even more detailed info). To get a great overview of the city, book a **bike tour** with the friendly, knowledgeable staff at **Fitz and Follwell,** on Mont-Royal in the Plateau.

cycling along the Lachine Canal

HANG 10 ON THE RIVER

Montréal may be surrounded by water, but anyone who's visited the city would be hard-pressed to think of it as surf heaven. There are no beachfront properties, no surf shacks, no sun-bleached beach babes. But in recent years the sport has exploded, and it's now one of the fastest-growing recreational activities in the city.

It works like this: Montréal is on the St-Lawrence River, and part of that river includes the Lachine Rapids, which create large standing waves. It is on these waves that surfing has become popular. In contrast to regular surfing, the standing wave doesn't really move—the surfer does.

Between late May and early September, you can ride the wave yourself! **Kayak Sans Frontiéres** (7770 blvd. Lasalle, Lachine, 514/595-7873, www.ksf.ca) offers 3- to 6.5-hour courses as well as board and equipment rental. If you want to check out the scene before you sign up to ride the rapids, **Surf Montréal** (www.surfmtl.com) is a great resource, offering suggestions about surf spots, water levels, and how to get started river surfing.

BEACHES

Clock Tower Beach

This urban beach on the eastern edge of the Old Port is not for swimming—its warm sand, lounge chairs, and umbrellas are instead designed to bring a bit of vacation to the city. As a bonus, you'll get great lounging views of the Jacques-Cartier bridge and Île Sainte-Hélène. When you get thirsty, check out the Bar L'Horloge for a snack and beverage.

MAP 1: Place de l'Horloge, 514/496-7678, www.oldportofmontreal.com/activity/clock-tower-beach; opening hours vary (9am or 10am to between 6pm and 11pm late Apr.-mid-Oct.); $2

Sunbathe and get great city views at Clock Tower Beach.

BOAT TOURS

Le Bateau-Mouche

Departing from the Old Port, Le Bateau-Mouche takes you on a boat tour of the Vieux-Port and the surrounding islands, including sites such as the Biosphère, La Ronde amusement park, and Habitat 67. Hour-long tours depart three times daily, with a 90-minute cruise departing once a day around noon. Evening dinner cruises are also available, as are specialty cruises during popular events like the jazz festival.

MAP 1: Quai Jacques-Cartier, 514/849-9952, www.bateaumouche. ca; 11am, 2:30pm, and 4pm daily mid-May-mid-Oct.; $29 adult, $27 senior and student, $15 child, children under 5 free

Saute Moutons

This is the wettest and wildest of boat tours on offer in Montréal. This hour-long tour takes you from the heart of the Old Port out onto the St-Lawrence River and the Lachine Rapids for an unparalleled experience on the water. An integral part of the city's history, the rapids are part of the reason explorers stopped in Montréal. The tours offer a unique view of the city and are guaranteed to get you soaked.

MAP 1: 47 rue de la Commune W., 514/284-9607, www.sautemoutons.com; 10am-6pm daily May-Oct.; jet boating $69 adult, $59 adolescent (13-18), $49 child (6-12); spin boating $27 adult, $22 adolescent (13-18), $20 child (6-12)

ICE-SKATING

Bonsecours Basin

Depending on the winter weather, skaters are either lucky enough to skate free on the larger open-water basin—it's approximately one and a half times the size of a regular rink—or are restricted to a smaller pond. Either way,

it's a great family or date activity on lovely cold and crisp days. Keep an eye out for winter festivals in the area. La Grande Roue de Montréal (www.lagranderouedemontreal.com; 4pm-11pm Mon.-Fri., 10am-11pm Sat.-Sun.; $20-25), a giant Ferris wheel (heated in the wintertime), opened in 2017.

MAP 1: Bonsecours Basin, 514/496-7678; 10am-9pm Mon.-Wed., 10am-10pm Thurs.-Sun. Dec.-Mar.; $6.95 adult, senior, and student, $4.60 child, free for under age 6; $8.70 skate rental, $3.48 helmet rental

FAMILY ADVENTURES

SOS Labyrinthe

Located in an old port warehouse building, this labyrinth, established in 2015, is fun for the whole family. At two kilometers (just over a mile) long, the maze, which requires participants to search for treasure, is full of tricky bits and obstacles. June-August, SOS Labyrinthe also offers "mystery evenings," if you're looking for a slightly enhanced maze experience. Bundle the outing with one at Voiles en Voiles or a participating Old Port activity to save a bit of money.

Bonsecours Basin

MAP 1: Hangar 16, 360 rue de la Commune E., 2nd floor, Old Port, 514/499-0099, www.oldportofmontreal. com/activity/sos-labyrinthe; hours vary May-early Oct.; $16.50 adults, $14.50 seniors and youths 13-17, $12.50 children 4-12

Voiles en Voiles

Right in front of the Marché Bonsecours, you'll find an immersive, kid-friendly rope course. Based out of an 18th-century pirate ship—you can't miss it—Voiles en Voiles features seven aerial courses and 61 different games kids can play. If you're traveling with a particularly energetic set of young 'uns, you might want to look into a combo deal with the SOS Labyrinthe or the **Mtl Zipline** (Hangar 16, 363 rue de la Commune E., 514/947-5463, https:// mtlzipline.com; hours vary seasonally; $20 adults, $17 children under 13).

MAP 1: Place des Vestiges (Quai de l'Horloge), 514/473-1458, www. voilesenvoiles.com; opening hours vary (9am or 10am to between 6pm and 11pm late Apr.-mid Oct.); rates start at $35 pp for 2 hours

Centre-Ville   Map 2

ICE-SKATING
Le Atrium 1000

Open year-round, this indoor skating rink in the atrium of a large office tower is a great place to bring the family or enjoy a little winter sport in the middle of a heat wave. Special times are reserved for younger skaters and their parents, so if you are traveling with kids make sure to check the site for days and times.

MAP 2: 1000 rue de la Gauchetière, 514/395-0555, www.le1000.com; 11:30am-6pm Wed.-Fri., 12:30pm-9pm Sat., 12:30pm-6pm Sun. June-Sept.; 11:30am-6pm Mon., 11am-9pm Tues.-Fri., noon-9pm Sat.-Sun. Oct.-May; $7.50 adult, $6.50 senior and student, $5 child, skate rental $7, helmet rental $1

SPECTATOR SPORTS
HOCKEY
✪ Montréal Canadiens

One of the original six teams to play in the National Hockey League, the Canadiens have won the Stanley Cup 24 times, more than any other team. To say that the city supports the "Habs" is an understatement; Montrealers of all stripes are devoted to the team. Despite the fact that they haven't won the cup since 1993, games routinely sell out, so if you would like to catch a game, buy your tickets well in advance.

MAP 2: Centre Bell, 1909 ave. des Canadiens-de-Montréal, 877/668-8269, www.nhl.com/canadiens; $22-270

The Montréal Canadiens, one of the original six NHL teams, are well-loved.

CATCH HABS FEVER: THE MONTRÉAL CANADIENS

A fast way to make friends in this town is to strike up a conversation about the city's beloved hockey team, the Montréal Canadiens. One of the oldest and most storied franchises, in not only hockey but in all North American sports, the Canadiens are one of the original six teams to make up the National Hockey League and have been around since 1909. Also known as the Habs (short for *habitant*, a term used to describe early French settlers), the Canadiens hold the record for the most Stanley Cup wins: The team has won the title 24 times, though the cup has been elusive since last having been hoisted here in 1993.

During the season (September to April), most of the bars in town will be showing the game. Water cooler talk, newspapers, and entire radio stations are dedicated solely to discussing last night's game and dissecting coaching strategies. Passionate is an understatement when describing Hab fans, who are known to voice their opinions about anything Hab related. Sit down next to one for a game and you'll see for yourself.

The team plays out of the centrally located Centre Bell, and tickets are a hot commodity. Having sold out every season since 2004, tickets can most easily be bought from scalpers around the arena or on sites such as Craigslist. Seeing a game live, you'll find out why this city lives and dies with this team; the atmosphere is infectious and insane, and even the most lax of supporters will be olé-ing with the best of them by the end of the third period.

Plateau Mont-Royal   Map 5

PARKS

Parc Jeanne-Mance

Adjacent to Parc Mont-Royal on its eastern edge, this leafy rectangular 35-acre park, named after one of Montréal's co-founders, is popular with picnickers. Home to baseball diamonds and a splash pad in the summer, it houses a seasonal ice rink in the winter (it's a bring-your-own-skates spot). The park is easily accessible by bus, has a great view of the eastern side of Mont-Royal, and offers great people-watching opportunities.

MAP 5: Corner of ave. du Parc and ave. Duluth W.

BIKING

BIKE RENTALS AND TOURS

✪ Fitz and Follwell

This popular bike rental shop and tour company is open year-round—when it's snowy, check out their snowshoe treks—but their bike tours are by far the most popular. Drawing a diverse crowd from families to bachelorette parties to seniors, Fitz has a tour, and a bike, that will work for you. Take the South Tour and make your way through Mont-Royal and down to the Old Port, or try the North Tour for a deep dive into the hidden gems of the Plateau, Mile End, Little Italy, and Mile-Ex. Their fleet consists of Linus roadsters and cruisers, with a few touring bikes thrown in for good measure. Book ahead to ensure your spot.

MAP 5: 115 Mont-Royal W., 514/840-0739, www.fitzandfollwell.co; 10am-6pm Mon.-Sat. (hours vary by season); rentals $40/day, tours $55-115

Maison des Cyclistes

Run by Velo Québec, a provincial cycling advocacy agency, Maison des Cyclistes is a three-in-one café, boutique, and travel agency. Grab a coffee

BIXI-ING THE CITY

The **Bixi** is a public bicycle sharing system with 5,000 bikes and 500 stations located in and around Montréal. Available from April to November, Bixis are an ideal, super convenient way to get around the city—they can often be your fastest option to get from A to B.

Getting in on the Bixi action is simple; subscriptions can be purchased at any Bixi station (or online at www.bixi.com), located on street corners in just about every neighborhood. Swipe your credit card to get a number code, type that number code into the bike of your choice to unlock it, and voilà, you're ready to ride. When you get to your destination, push the Bixi into an empty slot and check for the red light to make sure it is locked in.

Bixis are ideal for short rides and the payment scheme promotes that. A single-day subscription will cost you $5—which means you can take an unlimited number of under-30-minute trips. Trips that last longer than 30 minutes incur a charge of $3 to $6 for each subsequent 30-minute period. If you're in town for a week or longer and use the Bixi bikes daily to get around, opt for the $30 monthly pass.

If this is your first time using a Bixi, take it for a spin before you head out on the road; they're nearly indestructible, so the movement is stiffer than a regular bike. And if you're more comfortable riding with a helmet, bring your own—Montréal doesn't have a mandatory helmet law, and Bixi stands don't provide them.

Maison des Cyclistes

and plot your day of biking using their Wi-Fi; pick up bike lights in the boutique; or sign up for a cycling trip through one of their travel agents (go to www.veloquebecvoyages.com/e/quebec-bike-tour to join them on a trek around Québec). If you're unsure about cycling or traffic laws, or need a map or route suggestions, these friendly folks can help.

MAP 5: 1251 Rue Rachel E., 514/521-8356, ext. 344, www.velo.qc.ca/en/Maison-des-cyclistes; café 7:30am-6:30pm Mon.-Fri., 9am-7:30pm Sat.-Sun.; boutique noon-6pm Mon.-Fri.

ICE-SKATING
Parc La Fontaine

The most idyllic place to go for a skate in the city, Parc La Fontaine's large pond offers a huge rink on which to meander and practice your camel spins and backwards technique. Hockey enthusiasts can usually be found shooting the puck off in their own corner, and beginners are able to find their own spot of ice on which to get their balance. Skate and equipment rental is available on-site at a minimal cost. Those with their own skates can skate for free.

MAP 5: Middle of Parc La Fontaine; 11am-10pm Mon.-Fri., 10am-10pm Sat.-Sun. Dec.-Mar. (varies yearly); free

SPECTATOR SPORTS
FOOTBALL
✪ Les Alouettes de Montréal

The team was originally founded in 1872, playing a hybrid of English rugby and football, but a game against Harvard University in 1874 changed the rules and created Canadian football. Rechristened the Montréal Alouettes in 1946, the team has since

The **Route Verte** (www.routeverte.com) is an impressive 5,000-kilometer-long network of designed bike trails, roads, and multi-use trails linking many different parts of Québec—including Montréal. For a day trip in the city, explore the route along the river in Verdun, and then head over the Estacade-du-Pont-Champlain to access La Voie Maritime. Or, if you've got more time, bike out to Oka Beach in the west or head north to the ski town of Saint-Jerome. Explore the Route Verte maps online to create your cycling itinerary and, if you're planning an overnight trip, to find bike-friendly hotels.

gone on to win three Grey Cups (the Canadian Football League's equivalent of the Super Bowl). The Alouettes are popular, and the screams of the crowd can be heard far across the Plateau.

MAP 5: Percival Molson Stadium, 475 ave. des Pins W., 514/871-2266, www. montrealalouettes.com; June-Nov.; $16-130

CYCLING
Grand Prix Cyclistes

Part of the UCI World Tour, this elite cycling race has been taking place in Montréal on the second Sunday in September since 2009. Not quite as popular as the car-related Grand Prix or tennis's Rogers Cup, the race nevertheless draws a large crowd, particularly near the end. Most spectators camp out near the start/finish line, which riders cross on each lap of the circuit; large screens broadcast the televised version of the race so you can keep up even when the cyclists are not in your sight-line.

MAP 5: Ave. Parc, in front of the George-Etienne Cartier monument, 514/350-0000, http://gpcqm.ca; second Sun. in Sept.; $500 VIP package (or free to watch from just outside the barriers!)

Mile End and Petite-Italie   Map 6

PARKS
Parc de la Petite-Italie

This tree-lined park packs a lot into a small space. Replete with picnic tables and benches, it is a popular neighborhood hangout for those who live and work nearby. In the evenings, the gazebo often hosts groups dancing waltzes or salsas; the music and energy fills the streets and draws twilight picnickers. In winter, you'll find an ice-skating rink; in the summer, the main park activity is rest and relaxation, with some squirrel-watching thrown in for good measure.

MAP 6: Corner of St-Zotique and St-Laurent

CROSS-COUNTRY SKIING AND SNOWSHOEING

La Cordée

Québec's answer to Mountain Equipment Co-op or REI, La Cordée specializes in cycling and skiing equipment as well as clothing and other gear from midrange and high-end quality brands. They also rent ski equipment, including avalanche equipment, and snowshoes, at reasonable daily and weekly rates. In the summer, they rent fat bikes.

MAP 6: 5190 blvd. St-Laurent, 514/271-0773, www.lacordee.com; 10am-6pm Mon.-Wed., 10am-9pm Thurs.-Fri., 9am-5pm Sat., 10am-5pm Sun.; $45/day for skis, boots, skins, and poles, $10/day for snowshoes

Greater Montréal   Map 7

BIKING

BIKE RENTALS AND TOURS

Ma Bicyclette

Located on the Lachine Canal near the Atwater Market, Ma Bicyclette offers hourly and daily rates for adult and children's bikes. One of the best locations in the city for bike riding, the canal path is 15 kilometers long and runs from the Old Port to Lake Saint-Louis in the west. All bike rentals come with a helmet and a map of the city.

MAP 7: 2985 rue St-Patrick, 514/317-6306, www.mybicyclette.ca; 10am-6:30pm Mon.-Sat., 10am-6pm Sun.; rentals $30-60/day

Ma Bicyclette

BEACHES

Jean-Doré Beach

A modest beach in a secluded bay near the Casino de Montréal, this spot is ideal for families with kids. There's an area to swim and paddle, of course, and then an aquatic obstacle course called Aquazilla floating farther out on the water. Stand-up paddle boards and kayaks are available to rent.

MAP 7: Parc Jean-Drapeau, Île Notre-Dame, 514/872-0199, www. parcjeandrapeau.com; 10am-7pm daily mid-June-late Aug.; $9 adult, $4.50 children 3-13, free children 2 and under

KAYAKING

H2O Adventures

Located along the bank of the Lachine Canal, H2O Adventures rents sea kayaks, pedal boats (*pedalos* in Montréal parlance), and electric boats. They also offer Saturday-morning tours of the Lachine Canal and two-hour lessons in sea kayaking. It's a popular place in the summer. Reserve a rental 24 hours in advance online, or arrive early—some boats are available on a first-come, first-served basis.

MAP 7: 2985B rue St-Patrick, 514/842-1306, www.h2oadventures.com; 9am-9pm daily June-Sept., noon-8pm Mon.-Fri., 10am-8pm Sat.-Sun. Sept.-close; kayak rental $20/hour; kayak lessons $50

SWIMMING

✪ Jean-Drapeau Aquatic Complex

Cool off from the summer heat in one of three pools—a lane pool, a diving pool, and a recreational pool—at this massive aquatic center, a good option for families. A strong bonus? You'll be surrounded by park greenery, in the shadow of R. Buckminster Fuller's geodesic dome. Open throughout the summer, the off-island location gives it an edge over the competition, and it's less frequented throughout the week than those in the heart of the city.

MAP 7: Parc Jean-Drapeau, Île Sainte-Hélène, 514/872-7368, www. parcjeandrapeau.com; 10am-8pm daily mid-June-late Aug.; $6 adult, $3 child

CROSS-COUNTRY SKIING

Jardin Botanique and Parc Maisonneuve

When the flowers are no longer in bloom, the Montréal botanical gardens become an urban winter wonderland. Situated out by the Olympic Stadium, the Jardin Botanique and the adjacent Parc Maisonneuve are some of the most picturesque places to cross-country ski. The mostly flat terrain includes 20 kilometers of trails that weave through both the park and the gardens and offer great views of the Biodôme and stadium. But you are required to bring your own gear.

MAP 7: 4101 and 4601 rue Sherbrooke E.; Jardin Botanique 9am-5pm Tues.-Sun., Parc Maisonneuve 6am-11pm daily; free

Parc du Mont-Royal

Ideally located in the heart of the city, Mount Royal Park transforms into one of the best places in the city to cross-country ski and snowshoe when the snow falls. Twenty-two kilometers worth of trails are easily accessible by public transport and offer both flat and inclined terrain, making it a perfect choice for beginners and old pros alike. Skis are available for rent from the Beaver Lake Pavilion (9am-9pm Sun.-Thurs., 10am-9pm Fri.-Sat. Dec.-Mar.), but those with their own equipment are invited to simply enjoy the trails.

MAP 7: Beaver Lake Pavilion, Parc du Mont-Royal, 514/872-6559; 6am-11pm daily; free

ICE-SKATING

Lac aux Castors

Near the top of Mont-Royal, you'll find Lac aux Castors (Beaver Lake), an artificially constructed, donut-shaped skating rink. It isn't the biggest or the most diverse in Montréal, but Mont-Royal provides a beautiful backdrop and makes it one of the most popular outdoor rinks in the city.

Facing the lake is a pavilion where you rent skates in the winter and boats in the summer. Its zigzagged roof and glass facade make it a modern-day

Cross-country skiing is a popular winter activity.

MONTRÉAL BIKE RIDE

Total Distance: 13 kilometers (8 miles)
Cycling Time: 1 hour
Montréal is a very bikeable city—especially in the summer. Pick up a route map at a local bike shop or wherever you rent your bikes, and take some time to acquaint yourself with symbols and routes. Some designated bike routes share lanes with cars, others have painted lanes, and still others have separated bike lanes, which may be preferable if you're a bit of a nervous rider or you're riding with kids. This route is designed to let you soak up the sights in a fairly broad swath of Montréal, often right from your saddle.

LACHINE CANAL BIKE PATH

1. Start your trip at **Marché Atwater** in Saint-Henri. Atwater was a make-work project in Depression-era Montréal—one of many that saved workers and families while simultaneously coming close to bankrupting the city. On the south end of the market, across the street from the main market area, you'll find ice cream shop **Havre aux Glaces.** You can roll right up to the window and fuel up on some dulce de leche before heading out.

2. Next, cross the pedestrian bridge and join the bike path on the opposite side of the canal. Head left (east) on the bike path. Keep an eye out for old industrial buildings—many have been turned into gorgeous loft apartments, and one has been converted into a climbing gym, complete with an outdoor route. In about 800 meters, when you reach the **Ecluses Saint-Gabriel (Saint Gabriel Locks),** stop and visit for a moment: these locks are what allowed the Lachine Canal to be used as a shipping route in Montréal's industrial heyday. Now they are open to pleasure craft—if you're lucky, you just might catch them in action.

3. Continue to follow the bike path as it curves along the canal. Eventually, you'll reach the Bassins Peel, or Peel Basin: Ahead, you'll see grain silos, and the first hint of the **Farine Five Roses** sign. Take a left and head under the Bonaventure highway to keep following the path. When you emerge from the underpass, look up and to your right: this is the best view you'll get of Montréal's iconic Farine Five Roses sign.

4. Keep following the bike path—you'll head over a rattly old train trestle—and eventually, you'll dip below a city street and then curve around onto a small bridge with a bike path. Follow it to cross to the northern shore of the canal, and then pick up the bike path on the other side. Navigate your way through the Old Port on the bike path, passing the Silo #5, Habitat 67, and the Montréal Science Centre. When you reach the Quai de L'Horloge, pause for a moment and turn to face the city: you'll get a great view of both **Marché Bonsecours,** with its giant silver dome, and **Chapelle**

landmark, one that stands in stark contrast to its bucolic surroundings. The second floor houses a cafeteria. Though the public is still encouraged to bring their own snacks, the various food options are a plus, especially if you've just walked all the way up. In the winter, Beaver Lake is an ideal winter date spot—go skating, or follow one of the several skiing and snowshoeing trails that start from the lake and spread out along the mountain, and then return to warm up over a hot chocolate.

This place can get packed on weekends—head here on a weeknight for a calmer atmosphere. Rental equipment is available from the pavilion, which also offers storage lockers as well as a café and a cafeteria. Hours and dates vary depending on weather conditions, so check before heading out.

MAP 7: Beaver Lake Pavilion, Parc du Mont-Royal, 514/843-8949; 9am-9pm Sun.-Thurs., 10am-9pm Fri.-Sat. Dec.-Mar.; free

GOLF

Club de Golf Sainte-Rose

North out of the city in the suburb of Laval is the Sainte-Rose Golf Club. Located on the Rivière des Mille-Îles and inaugurated in 1996, it was designed by course architect John

Notre-Dame-de-Bon-Secours, where the giant Our Lady of the Harbour used to look out for sailors—and now looks out over the St. Lawrence River.

5. Take the bike path one more block east to rue Berri, and then, when the coast is clear, take a left and join rue Berri's separated bike lane. Head seven city blocks north—and be ready to gear down a bit, because this part of the ride is a bit hilly. As you pass rue St-Catherine, look right and to the sky to see the bright spheres hovering over the Village. When you reach Maisonneuve, the block after St-Catherine, dismount and soak up the architectural wonder of **La Grande Bibliothèque.**

A BIRD'S-EYE VIEW OF MILE END AND PETITE-ITALIE

6. Rejoin the bike path and keep heading north three blocks. Take a right at rue Cherrier and join the separate bike lane on the north side of the street. Ride three blocks until you reach Avenue de la Parc Fontaine. Hang a left onto the bike lane and either cut your way through the park or keep to its eastern edge. **Parc La Fontaine** is one of the best and most well-loved parks in the city, so I'd suggest cutting through—you'll see picnickers, a fountain, and a bunch of Canadian flora and fauna.

7. When you're done exploring the park, head to rue Brebeuf on its northern edge (if you've stuck to the bike path, it'll spit you out right where you need to be). Head north on rue Brebeuf for six blocks (for the entire sixth block, you'll be on the eastern edge of Parc Sir Wilfred Laurier). Take a left at rue Gregoire, a right onto avenue Christophe-Columb, and hug left to stay in the separate bike lane. Continue to follow the bike lane as it curves left into Parc des Carriers, then take a left on rue Boyer. At the end of the street, cross the road and join the **rail trail.** Head right.

8. The rail trail makes quick work of an east-west stretch between Mile End and Little Italy—and it offers some great views. Follow the rail trail until it ends at rue Beaubien. When it's safe, cross the street, jog east just a bit, and head north on rue St-Urbain two blocks until you reach avenue Beaumont. Head left for two blocks, then right on rue Marconi for one block, and right on avenue Mozart for one block. Head left on rue Waverly, and **Dépanneur le Pick-Up** will appear on your left. They have some of the best sandwiches—including a vegetarian "pulled tofu"—in town (opt for tortillas for a gluten-free option). Snack outside on the picnic tables, or take your sandwiches to go—your next stop is close.

9. Outside Dépanneur le Pick-Up, take a left on avenue Alexander and then a left onto rue Marconi. Follow rue Marconi until it curves around to meet rue Waverly. Take a right, then a right onto St-Zotique. A final, immediate right will bring you onto avenue l'Esplanade, where you'll see **Alexandraplatz Bar** on your right. There's plenty of bike parking in the parking lot, along with lots of delicious craft beers and cocktails inside.

Watson, one of the most renowned architects in the province. This 18-hole par-70 course has a rustic feel to it, with weather-worn pines lining the fairway and natural ponds along the course. Deceptively challenging, it's 6,400 yards in length and includes three par-5 holes.

MAP 7: 1400 blvd. Mattawa, Laval, 450/628-6072, www.groupebeaudet. com/en/clubs/ste-rose; dawn-10pm daily May-Nov.; $26-51 for 18 holes

Meadowbrook Golf Club

Located in the west-end borough of Côte-Saint-Luc, this 18-hole course

got its start as part of the Canadian Pacific Recreation Club of Montréal in the early 20th century. Opened as a course in 1949, it's now tucked behind houses and railway tracks, though the tree-lined fairways and occasional babbling brook do a nice job of transporting players off the island. Although not the most challenging of courses, it's convenient to get to and offers a bit of an oasis without leaving the city.

MAP 7: 8370 rue Côte Saint-Luc, 514/488-6612, www. clubdegolfmeadowbrook.com; dawn-10pm daily May-Nov.; $23-35 for 18 holes

The **Montréal Roller Derby League** (various locations, www.mtlrollerderby.com, May-Oct., tickets $10 adults, $5 kids 6-12, free 5 and under) was founded in 2006. Over the last few years, roller derby has made a comeback in cities all across North America, and Montréal is no exception. Consisting of six home teams—New Skids, Montréal Sexpos, Les Contrabanditas, Les Filles du Roi, La Racaille, and Smash Squad—and a revolving cast of visiting teams, the league always sees a lot of action. The season runs May-October. During that time, unused ice rinks around the city fill with fans cheering on their favorite players. The matches attract so many people that the lines to get in are often down the block.

SPECTATOR SPORTS

CAR RACING

✪ Canadian Grand Prix

A yearly event since 1961, now held every June, the Canadian Grand Prix is part of the Formula One World Championship and takes place on the Gilles Villeneuve circuit off island on Île Notre-Dame near Parc Jean-Drapeau. Drivers cover the 2.7-mile-long circuit 70 times before crossing the finish line. One of the most-watched sporting events in the world, the race attracts visitors from all over, and the three-day event has street parties and events in its honor. Book your hotel early and expect to pay a little more than usual.

MAP 7: Circuit Gilles Villeneuve, Parc Jean-Drapeau, 514/350-0000, www.grandprixmontreal.com; $37-465

SOCCER

Montréal Impact

We may not have a player as internationally recognizable as Cristiano Ronaldo or Mia Hamm, but the Montréal Impact still bring in the crowds. In a city full of citizens with strong ties to their soccer-loving family heritage, it is no surprise that soccer pulls at our heartstrings, and a subculture around the club has even started to emerge. Founded in 1992, the Impact joined Major League Soccer (MLS) in 2012.

MAP 7: Saputo Stadium, 3750 rue Sherbrooke E., 514/328-3668, www.montrealimpact.com; $29-89

TENNIS

Rogers Cup

Otherwise known as the Canadian Masters, and formerly called the Canadian Open, the Rogers Cup is the country's preeminent tennis tournament and annually hosts the world's top players. Established in 1881, the weeklong competition in August is the third longest-running tennis tournament in the world after Wimbledon and the U.S. Open. Montréal splits the duty with Toronto, and the cities annually take turns hosting the men's and women's championships.

MAP 7: Uniprix Stadium, Parc Jarry, 514/273-1234, www.rogerscup.com; $25-200

SHOPS

Vieux-Montréal 189
Centre-Ville 191
Centre-Ville Est 195
Quartier Latin and the Village 197
Plateau Mont-Royal 198
Mile End and Petite-Italie 203

Back in the early 20th century, Montréal was a chic travel hub. Passengers traveling to and from Europe would disembark here, bringing the latest fashions from the Continent before traveling on to places like New York and Toronto. Today, Montréal's style is still influenced by Europe and North America.

Even before the words sustainability and eco-friendly became part of everyday parlance, the city's shops featured made-in-Québec goods. Montréal is a hotbed for up-and-coming designers. Montrealers are fond of simple leather goods and handmade pieces from local jewelers.

The city has a torrid love affair with antiques and kitsch, one that's led to an overabundance of both bizarre back-room family-run affairs and huge, engrossing warehouses.

Montréal has great record stores that carry a spectrum of musical styles from classic albums by Québécoise singers like Céline Dion and Isabelle Boulay to acid jazz and prog-rock. Most bookstores in the city are French. There are a couple English-language bookstores, though most are large chains.

Founded in 1929, J. Schreter sells mid-range shoes, clothes, and backpacks.

The main shopping district is concentrated in the downtown core, along and underneath rue Ste-Catherine, where you'll find shopping malls, department stores, popular chain stores, electronics shops, and the legendary Underground City that lets you explore the entire area without stepping outside. For a bit of chic, head for upscale rue Sherbrooke, with its high-end fashion boutiques and department stores.

HIGHLIGHTS

✪ **BOURGIE ON A BUDGET: Bota Bota,** a spa on a boat, has an extensive outdoor/indoor water circuit and numerous treatments to choose from—all at reasonable prices (page 191).

✪ **BEST HAT STORE: Henri Henri** has barely changed since it opened in 1932. It remains a dapper hat store with selections for men and women for all types of weather (page 195).

✪ **BEST PAPETERIE:** Lovers of stationery could spend hours browsing the notebooks, agendas, and colorful pens at **Papeterie Nota Bene** (page 196).

✪ **BEST PLACE TO PULL ON A PARKA:** Quebeckers flock to **Kanuk** to keep properly warm in the wintertime (page 198).

✪ **MOST INSPIRED CHILDREN'S STORE:** The wooden toys at **La Grande Ourse** will capture the imagination of kids of all ages (page 199).

✪ **BEST KITSCH: Kitsch 'n' Swell** is a great place to find a unique gift or that perfect item you've been wanting for your home. And it's just really fun to browse (page 201).

✪ **BEST KITCHEN SUPPLIES:** If you're crazy about cooking or collecting fancy stuff for your kitchen, **Arthur Quentin** is the place to pick up oyster knives and Le Creuset cookware, among other things (page 201).

✪ **BEST MUSIC STORE:** It's all about the vinyl, both new and used, at **Aux 33 Tours** in the Plateau. Warning: You could be here for a while (page 201).

✪ **BEST QUÉBÉCOIS FASHION:** The women behind **Boutique Unicorn** have a keen eye for style, stocking work by local designers (page 203).

✪ **BEST MEN'S BOUTIQUE:** Though not exclusively a men's store, **Les Étoffes** has an impeccable men's section full of the latest from some of the coolest labels around (page 203).

✪ **BEST BOOKSTORE:** The brick-and-mortar store of independent comic publisher **Drawn & Quarterly** stocks both new and classic literature and a fine selection of comics and graphic novels (page 207).

CLOTHING AND SHOES

Boutique Denis Gagnon

Known for his modern approach to clothing shapes and design—and his love of leather—Denis Gagnon is one of Canada's best and most well-renowned Canadian designers working today. Gagnon's boutique, in the heart of Vieux-Montréal, carries a well-curated handful of lines from other designers—think Harakiri, Rubbercraze, Catrie, and Panache—as well as accessories and handbags. If you'd like your next little black dress to be *très* recherché, this is the place to come.

MAP 1: 170B rue St-Paul W., 514/935-6360, www.denisgagnon.ca; 11am-6pm Mon.-Thurs., 11am-5pm Fri.-Sat.

Cahier d'Exercices

This upscale boutique (whose name means "school notebook" in English) offers only the most coveted of labels, an eclectic and avant-garde mix of internationally recognized as well as up-and-coming designers. It's a few steps up to the grand old space in Vieux-Montréal, whose interior has been transformed into a contemporary heaven full of sleek white shelves, a high, open ceiling, and simple, suspended steel racks, stocked with pieces by the likes of Vetements, Jacquemas, and Issey Miyake.

MAP 1: 369 rue St-Paul W., 514/439-5169, www.cahierdexercices.com; 11am-7pm Mon.-Fri., 10am-5pm Sat.

Clusier Habilleur

More than just a store, this menswear boutique in Old Montréal offers made-to-measure pieces that range from suits and tuxes to jeans, dress shirts, and even cashmere coats. Since they offer bespoke services, the staff knows their stuff and can guess your neck size just by looking. Sip a coffee in the espresso lounge as you wait for them to get your size in a pair of multicolored Lacoste topsiders. Alongside well-known brands, the store has its own in-house Clusier line.

MAP 1: 432 rue McGill, 514/842-1717, www.clusier.com; 10am-7pm Mon.-Wed., 10am-8pm Thurs.-Fri., 10am-5:30pm Sat., noon-5pm Sun.

Dubarry Fourrures

Dubarry Fourrures

Best avoided if you're a card-carrying PETA member, Dubarry Furs was founded in Europe in 1935 and came to Montréal in 1978. They sell a wide range of furs, leathers, capes, and shearlings, from sizes XS to XXXL. Treat yourself to a pair of warm mitts, or, if you live in a chilly climate (Montréal qualifies!) splurge on a fur coat to keep you toasty all winter.

MAP 1: 206 rue St-Paul W., 514/844-7483, www.dubarryfurs.com; 10am-6pm Tues.-Fri., 11am-5pm Sat.-Sun.

Espace Pepin

Owner and artist Lysanne Pepin has created a unique space where her artwork serves as a backdrop to a carefully selected array of clothing, jewelry, accessories, and lingerie. Created by local and international designers, the pieces are affordable and have a classic, relaxed appeal. White walls and shabby-chic decor invite you into the open-concept boutique that's as welcoming as a friend's apartment.

MAP 1: 350 rue St-Paul W., 514/287-5005, www.espacepepin.com; 10am-6pm Mon.-Sat., 11am-5pm Sun.

Harricana by Mariouche

First Nations designer Mariouche Gagné first started working with fur as a struggling fashion student. Having entered a competition with the Fur Council of Canada, she used her mother's old coat to create a piece and her business was born. Working with recycled fur, she transforms pieces into hats, mittens, a chic *gilet,* or a new coat entirely. The store space is modern and clean, and, though it's slightly below street level, huge windows let in lots of light.

MAP 1: 416 rue McGill, 514/287-6517, www.harricana.qc.ca; 10am-6pm Mon.-Wed., 10am-8pm Thurs.-Fri., 10am-5pm Sat.-Sun.

SSENSE

This is the flagship store of online luxury retailer SSENSE (pronounced "essence"). Pieces from Alexander McQueen, Balmain, and Lanvin stand out against the high-gloss black walls and well-worn gray floorboards. The boutique is filled with light from the

Espace Pepin

store's high windows. Menswear can be found down a set of burnished steel stairs that lead to a dimly lit basement bunker, complete with stone walls and the latest from Comme des Garçons and Maison Margiela.

MAP 1: 90 rue St-Paul W., 514/289-1906, www.ssense.com; 10am-6pm Mon.-Wed. and Sat., 10am-9pm Thurs.-Fri., noon-5pm Sun.

U&I

Focusing on outerwear, this chic shop offers stylish, high-quality Canadian brands. The modern, open concept design of the store is welcoming, and the racks are perfectly balanced—not too much, not too little. Whether you're looking for a full-scale parka or a chic leather jacket, U&I has something that will work for you. For menswear, check out the clean, classic lines of Mackage; for women, try Soia & Kyo.

MAP 1: 215 rue St-Paul W., 514/508-7704, www.boutiqueuandi.com; 10am-6pm Mon.-Sat., 11am-5pm Sun.

GIFT AND HOME

Espace Pepin Maison

Part home decor and furniture shop, part café, this sister store of Espace Pepin, owned by artist Lysanne Pepin, is warm and calming, with an industrial *hygge* vibe. You can buy everything from unique handbags to shoes, mugs, plates, and modern chandeliers—or, if your suitcase is already stuffed, you can settle in for a vegan meal and order online later. Pepin's hand-crafted salt and pepper mills, carved from branches, make a great non-hokey Canadian gift.

MAP 1: 378 rue St-Paul W., 514/844-0114, www.thepepinshop.com; 10am-6pm Mon.-Sat., 11am-5pm Sun.

BATH, BEAUTY, AND SPAS

✪ Bota Bota

Once a ferry, this spa is a permanently docked boat that has been converted in a luxe experience that epitomizes Montréal culture. The water circuit, which features cold showers and baths, scented steam rooms, Finnish saunas, and hot tubs, offers a quaint garden area and gorgeous views. Water circuit prices start at a very reasonable $39 at off-peak hours. They offer standard spa treatments, too.

Bring a bathing suit, flip-flops, and a desire to relax.

MAP 1: Corner of rue McGill and rue de la Commune W., 514/284-0333, www.botabota.ca; 10am-10pm daily

Scandinave Les Bains Vieux-Montréal

Taking over a large 19th-century building directly across from the Vieux-Port, the Scandinave Les Bains focuses its attention on hydrotherapy, relaxation, and massages. Modeled after traditional Scandinavian spas, the surroundings are as natural as possible, with stone walls, wood floors, and an earthy color scheme. Massages, which start at $135 for 60 minutes and include access to the baths, are from the Nordic mold and include deep tissue ($145), *lomi atsu* ($145), and hot stone ($267).

MAP 1: 71 rue de la Commune W., 514/288-2009, www.scandinave.com; 8:30am-9pm daily

Centre-Ville   Map 2

SHOPPING DISTRICTS AND CENTERS

Centre Eaton

Four floors of shops, kiosks, restaurants, and exhibition spaces make up the Centre Eaton. You'll find North American staples like Aritzia, the Gap, Levi's, Old Navy, and Aldo. The largest shopping mall in downtown Montréal, it boasts 175 boutiques, services, and restaurants.

MAP 2: 705 rue Ste-Catherine W., 514/288-3710, www. centreeatondemontreal.com; 10am-9pm Mon.-Fri., 10am-6pm Sat., 11am-5pm Sun.

Les Cours Mont-Royal

The crème-de-la-crème of brands can be found in this upscale shopping center—DKNY, Harry Rosen, Ethan Allen. It's a former hotel, and the original ceiling mosaic and dazzling chandelier add elegance to the main hall. Independent boutiques carrying local and well-known international brands can be found here, as well as one of the city's top spas and salons. It connects to the Métro system and other shopping centers through the Underground City. Hours vary depending on the boutique.

Rue Ste-Catherine is the city's central shopping hub.

MAP 2: 1445 rue Peel, 514/842-7777, www.lcmr.ca; 10am-7pm Mon.-Wed., 10am-9pm Thurs.-Fri., 10am-6pm Sat., noon-5pm Sun.

Rue Ste-Catherine

This is the main commercial shopping district for the city. Starting at rue Bishop in the west, stores, shopping centers, and department stores run the length of the street till about Bleury. Name-brand stores include Apple, Indigo, Urban Outfitters, H&M, Banana Republic, and Zara. Belowground, the various malls and department stores of the Underground City are all connected through walkways, and you can walk about a third of the Ste-Catherine strip below street level.

MAP 2: Rue Ste-Catherine W. between rue Bishop and rue de Bleury

DEPARTMENT STORES

Holt Renfrew

This luxury department store is housed in an illustrious art deco building. It has all the top-name designer brands from around the world. Established as a furrier in 1849 in Québec City, Holt Renfrew opened the Montréal store in 1910 and continues to be one of the few places you can find the labels Marni, Marchesa, and Balenciaga. The Holt Renfrew Café on the ground level is a chic place to grab an open-faced sandwich.

MAP 2: 1300 rue Sherbrooke W., 514/842-5111, www.holtrenfrew.com; 10am-6pm Mon.-Wed., 10am-9pm Thurs.-Fri., 9:30am-6:30pm Sat., 11am-6pm Sun.

La Maison Ogilvy

Established in 1866 by Montréal linen merchant James A. Ogilvy, La Maison Ogilvy is a timeless Montréal institution, and its tartan bags and boxes are ubiquitous throughout the city. The only high-end department store of its kind, it carries exclusive labels like Louis Vuitton and Burberry. Completed in 1912, the building itself is impressive, with a large circular staircase at the main entrance. On the fifth floor is Tudor Hall, the city's first music hall.

MAP 2: 1307 rue Ste-Catherine W., 514/842-7711, www.ogilvycanada.com; 10am-6pm Mon.-Wed., 10am-9pm Thurs.-Fri., 9:30am-6:30pm Sat., 11am-6pm Sun.

Tiffany & Co.

CLOTHING AND SHOES

Marie Saint Pierre

Montrealer Marie Saint Pierre is a leading figure in Canadian fashion, and her creations are available in high-end boutiques from New York to Paris. This boutique on the ritzy rue de la Montagne is her flagship store. Working with a mostly neutral palette, she focuses on texture, volume, and shape, and the results are stunningly modern. The boutique itself has a strong feel, with concrete floors and smoke-like murals, though the low lighting gives it a softer touch.

MAP 2: 2081 rue de la Montagne, 514/281-5547, www.mariesaintpierre.com; 10am-6pm Mon.-Wed., 10am-8pm Thurs.-Fri., 10am-5pm Sat., noon-5pm Sun.

Off the Hook

Off the Hook is an independent menswear retailer, founded in 1999, right in the heart of the Ste-Catherine strip. It carries a variety of brands—tending, now, toward athleisure and understated streetwear—and also has a partnership with shoe manufacturer Vans. It carries accessories like shoes and backpacks as well as clothing.

MAP 2: 1021 rue Ste-Catherine W., 514/499-1021, www.offthehook.ca; 10am-6pm Mon.-Wed. and Sat., 10am-8pm Thurs.-Fri., noon-6pm Sun.

ACCESSORIES AND JEWELRY

Tiffany & Co.

This iconic jeweler needs no introduction. You'll find the company's most coveted collections and pieces by their most prized designers. Known for its craftsmanship and beauty, Tiffany is synonymous with family heirlooms and life's greatest events. Opened in 2012, this location on the opulent stretch of Sherbrooke is housed in the same building as the Ritz, appropriate company for the world's most beloved jewelers.

MAP 2: 1290 rue Sherbrooke W., 514/842-6953, www.tiffany.ca; 10am-9pm Mon.- Fri., 9:30am-6:30pm Sat., 11am-6pm Sun.

ANTIQUES AND KITSCH

Antiquités Foley L'Ecuyer

Old traveling trunks and luggage are elegantly stacked along the walls of this beautifully decorated store, with black-and-white photos hanging on the walls. You'll feel as though you've just entered the corridor of a family about to go on vacation. Set designers are in love with this place, as are those with a thing for classic nostalgia pieces. The owner-operator is friendly and accommodating, but it's best to call ahead to double-check the day's hours.

MAP 2: 1896 rue Notre-Dame W., 514/932-8461; 11am-5pm Mon.-Sat., 1pm-4pm Sun.

Grand Central Inc.

The ceiling here is dripping in chandeliers. Owners Wayne and Gordon Downs have an eye for those from the 18th and 19th centuries, and at dusk, the view from outside is stunning, giving it a romantic and old-timey feel. Though lighting is their specialty—beyond chandeliers they have a range of floor lamps, desk lamps, and table lamps—they also have the furniture to match your early-20th-century hurricane lamp.

MAP 2: 2448 rue Notre-Dame W., 514/935-1467, www.grandcentralinc.ca; 9:30am-5:30pm Mon.-Fri., 11am-5pm Sat.

BOOKS AND MUSIC

Cheap Thrills

Established in 1971, Cheap Thrills harmoniously brings books and music together in this second-floor mecca, a stone's throw from McGill University. Specializing in jazz, avant-garde, experimental, and blues albums, they also stock the latest rock and indie rock albums on vinyl and CD. No matter what you're looking for they likely have it, since their stock of vinyl and CDs is over 10,000. The selection of used books is so vast it almost reaches the ceiling.

MAP 2: 2044 rue Metcalfe, 514/844-8988, www.cheapthrills.ca; 11am-6pm Mon.-Wed. and Sat., 11am-9pm Thurs.-Fri., noon-5pm Sun.

Paragraphe

A long-time independent bookstore, Paragraphe was bought out by Québécois company Archambault in the mid-aughts. Somehow, though, it's managed to retain its charm and the feel of a neighborhood bookstore. Kitty-corner to McGill University and on the northern tip of downtown, it always has a good selection of fiction and nonfiction to browse. A long-time favorite with authors—Yann Martel in particular drops in when he's in town—it hosts readings and book launches throughout the year.

MAP 2: 2220 ave. McGill College, 514/845-5811, www.paragraphbooks.com; 8am-9pm Mon.-Fri., 9am-9pm Sat.-Sun.

BATH, BEAUTY, AND SPAS

Murale

The Canadian answer to Sephora, Murale is a one-stop beauty store with internationally recognized brands and emerging beauty labels. The first Murale to open in Canada, it's on the ground level of Place Ville-Marie. Über-sleek and futuristic looking, the entirely white store has a high-gloss shine to it, and the vibe is super modern. Alongside beauty and fragrance experts, Murale has a pharmacist and a dermatological skin-care center, which offers facials and other services.

MAP 2: 1 Place Ville-Marie, 514/875-1593, www.murale.ca; 10am-6pm Mon., 8am-6pm Tues.-Wed., 8am-9pm Thurs.-Fri., 10am-6pm Sat.

Paragraphe

DEPARTMENT STORES

La Baie

A Canadian colonial institution, La Baie was first founded in 1670 as the Hudson's Bay Company and controlled much of North America's fur trade. By the early 20th century, it had morphed into one of the biggest chain department stores in Canada. Housed in a grand redbrick building that was constructed in 1891, the Bay's seven floors offer everything from kids' shoes to perfumes, housewares to electronics. Fans of Canadiana should pick up an iconic Hudson's Bay blanket.

MAP 3: 585 rue Ste-Catherine W., 514/281-4422, www.thebay.com; 10am-8pm Mon.-Tues., 10am-9pm Wed.-Fri., 9am-7pm Sat., 10am-7pm Sun.

Henri Henri, a city institution

ACCESSORIES AND JEWELRY

✪ Henri Henri

To those who say "I don't suit hats," Henri Henri's answer is that a person who doesn't suit hats simply doesn't have a head. Founded by Honorius Henri and Jean-Maurice Lefebvre in 1932, the store remains devoted to hats, and they've got everything from straw Pith helmets to Panamas, bowler hats, and tricorns. Part of this store's charm is its appearance, from the window displays and 1930s-style awning to the all-wood interior, with hats tucked away in cubbies. The service is genuine and thorough.

MAP 3: 189 rue Ste-Catherine E., 514/288-0109, www.henrihenri.ca; 10am-6pm Mon.-Fri., 10am-5pm Sat.-Sun.

Maison Birks

It may not have a movie with its name in the title, but Maison Birks is Canada's answer to Tiffany's—even their boxes are a particular shade of blue. Founded in 1879, this store opened on rue Ste-Catherine in 1894. You'll find men picking out an engagement ring, women trying on a pair of sapphire earrings, or family members picking out a keepsake for the newborn. It's worth popping in to see the store's turn-of-the-20th-century grandeur.

MAP 3: 1240 Place Philips, 514/397-2511, www.maisonbirks.com; 10am-6pm Mon.-Wed., 10am-9pm Thurs.-Fri., 10am-5pm Sat., noon-5pm Sun.

THRIFT AND VINTAGE

Eva B

Quirky and chaotic, this huge secondhand store feels like it goes on for miles, with entire sections dedicated to menswear, leather jackets, cowboy boots, dresses, hats, and even a costume trunk full of gloves. A favorite with students and those who love hunting for a good deal, the shop has a laid-back yet intense atmosphere,

SECONDHAND STYLE

Eva B is a quirky thrift-store-meets-café.

Montréal is full of *friperies* (secondhand shops), and each has its own interpretation of what secondhand means. Many boutiques deal exclusively with authentic pieces, while others sell goods on consignment or resell donations.

Head up to the Mile End to scope out a trinity of *friperies,* all within a few blocks of each other. **Local 23, Annex Vintage,** and **Citizen Vintage** offer some of the best vintage shopping in the neighborhood. Local 23 and Annex deal exclusively in secondhand: boots, fur hats, blouses, belts, and big 1980s earrings, as well as a large selection of menswear. Citizen Vintage offers a curated collection of secondhand duds.

Connoisseurs of vintage will get a kick out of **Friperie St-Laurent.** With elegant window displays full of hatboxes and trench coats, Friperie St-Laurent deals in vintage finds from the 1940s-1970s. It's a great place to look for a fur stole or a leather jacket; the men's selection usually outweighs the women's, though they do have a great collection of accessories. Pieces here are timeless, so you're likely to find a gem.

It's all about the hunt at **Eva B.** This sprawling boutique on the lower Main has been among the top go-to places for vintage for the past decade. Racks of leather and jean jackets are flanked by rows of vintage cowboy boots. Selection and prices run the gamut. If you're willing to dig, there's a trunk or two full of goodies to sort through. They've also got a small café at the front.

thanks to the sheer volume of stuff to dig through. They also serve coffee and snacks—including homemade lemonade in summer.

MAP 3: 2013 blvd. St-Laurent, 514/849-8246, www.eva-b.ca; 11am-7pm Mon.-Sat., noon-6pm Sun.

GIFT AND HOME
✪ Papeterie Nota Bene

A stationery-lover's dream, this airy, classic art-stationery shop carries notepads, agendas, pens, paper, giant calendars, and everything in between, from the top-quality international companies all over the world, including Lamy pencils, Atoma notebooks, Faber Castell, and graph-paper notebooks from Sweden's elusive Whitelines. The store motto is "think with your hands." A mezzanine level serves as an art gallery, with work by local artists featured regularly. (Grab a glass of wine next door at Pullman if the timing works out!)

MAP 3: 3416 ave. du Parc, 514/485-6587, www.nota-bene.ca; 11am-7pm Mon.-Fri., 11am-6pm Sat., noon-5pm Sun.

BOOKS AND MUSIC
The Word

In the heart of the McGill student neighborhood, this tiny lopsided house was once a laundry. In 1973, Adrian King-Edwards and his wife started an underground bookstore out of their apartment living room, and when the laundry went up for rent, they moved the shop next door. It specializes in secondhand academic books, so literature lovers will swoon at the shop's selection, which includes titles by local authors. You could, and should, spend hours browsing the shelves.

MAP 3: 469 rue Milton, 514/845-5640, www.wordbookstore.ca; 10am-6pm Mon.-Wed., 10am-9pm Thurs.-Fri., 11am-6pm Sat.

Quartier Latin and the Village

Map 4

SHOPPING DISTRICTS AND CENTERS
Rue St-Denis

The vibe of the stores on rue St-Denis, the major Francophone shopping district, is distinctly different from that on St-Laurent, even though they consist of similar elements—independent boutiques and a mishmash of restaurants and furniture stores. Because this is the French side of the city, it is no surprise that cafés and restaurants are more plentiful. You'll find jewelers, boutiques, and clothing shops as well as Québécois chains and outposts for the Gap, John Fluevog, Lululemon, Lush, MAC, and Urban Outfitters.

MAP 4: Between blvd. de Maisonneuve and ave. Mont-Royal

ANTIQUES AND KITSCH
Antiquités Seconde Chance

Dwindling vintage stock has caused prices to rise in the last few years, but Seconde Chance keeps things budget-friendly with their kitschy but well-selected finds. Design students are frequent shoppers here, looking for inspiration or to sift through the awesome selection of Expo 67 memorabilia, which includes everything from drinking glasses to travel bags.

MAP 4: 1691 rue Amherst, 514/523-3019, www.secondechance-retro.com; 11am-5pm Tues.-Sat.

Boutique Spoutnik

With lime-green walls and a packed floor-space, Spoutnik stands out among its rue Amherst brethren. The store offers everything from lamps adorned with mosaics and bizarre geometric wall hangings to clustered bubble light-fixtures that would make even Lady Gaga lustful. There's a

rue St-Denis

definite 1960s and '70s feel, with lots of stainless-steel lamps and Formica kitchen tables, but you'll also find more classic goods, like elegant teak desks and simple chandeliers. Prices vary greatly, but something should fit your budget.

MAP 4: 2120 rue Amherst, 514/525-8478, www.boutiquespoutnik.com; noon-5pm Tues.-Sat.

Plateau Mont-Royal   Map 5

SHOPPING DISTRICTS AND CENTERS

Boulevard St-Laurent

Independent boutiques (mainly fashion, with some *friperies* thrown in) start at the corner of boulevard St-Laurent and rue Sherbrooke and extend steadily north. Historically the dividing line between the western (English) and eastern (French) sides of the city, St-Laurent has stores with a real mix of influences, so you can pick up anything from a $400 pair of shoes to a vegetable steamer to an authentic lava lamp. Farther north, the boutiques change from clothing to housewares and furniture. Between rue Rachel and avenue du Mont-Royal there's a concentration of Québec-designed and -made furniture stores.

MAP 5: Between rue Sherbrooke and rue St-Viateur

CLOTHING AND SHOES

✪ Kanuk

Kanuk was established in 1974 by outdoor enthusiasts who realized the only way to get a winter coat warm enough for Québec's climate was to make it themselves. Specializing in coats, accessories, and other outerwear, this Plateau store is brightly lit and spacious. There are 35 parka models to choose from in a range of colors. A coat may be pricey—windbreakers run around $200, and parkas start at over $600—but it will last you a lifetime. The staff will help you figure out the type and fit that will work for you.

MAP 5: 485 rue Rachel E., 514/287-4494, www.kanuk.com; 10am-6pm Mon.-Wed., 10am-9pm Thurs.-Fri., 10am-5pm Sat.-Sun.

Deuxième Peau

The minimal decoration in this small, ground-floor boutique, which specializes in swimwear and lingerie, lets the prettiness of the garments stand out. Supporting women of all shapes and sizes, bras come in sizes AA to G from European brands like Marie Jo, Princess Tam-Tam, Simon Pérèle, Aubade, and Chantal Thomas. Swimwear includes pieces from Seafolly and Sunfair. Though they will happily measure you to determine proper bra size, owner Zoé Mitsakis's keen eye is better than any tape measure.

MAP 5: 4457 rue St-Denis, 514/842-0811, www.deuxiemepeau.com; 10:30am-6pm Mon.-Wed., 10:30am-9pm Thurs.-Fri., 10:30am-5pm Sat., noon-5pm Sun.

Ibiki

Minimal is the best way to describe both the decor and the clothing for sale at Ibiki. The store's aim is to sell menswear and womenswear that'll become a prized possession. The spacious two-story store on the Main features brands such as Oak NYC, Helmut Lang, and Paloma Wool. It also carries well-priced accessories and magazines.

MAP 5: 4357 blvd. St-Laurent, 514/509-1675, www.ibiki.co; noon-6pm Sun.-Wed., noon-7pm Thurs.-Fri., 11am-6pm Sat.

J. Schreter

In 1929, Joseph Schreter immigrated to Canada from Romania and began peddling his wares; 90 years later, J. Schreter is still a family business—but now it takes up 10,000 square feet of prime retail real estate on the Main. The store carries shoes, backpacks, and clothes in midrange brands like Vans, Zanerobe, Venque, Ben Sherman, Fjall Raven, Toms, and dozens of others.

MAP 5: 4358 blvd. St-Laurent, 514/845-4231, www.schreter.com; 9:30am-6pm Mon.-Wed., 9:30am-7pm Thurs.-Fri., 9:30am-5pm Sat., noon-5pm Sun.

Lustre

Owner/designer Yasmine Wasfy creates both the Lustre line and her own eponymous label, which can be found in this independent boutique full of one-of-a-kind pieces. Designs are fresh and young—think of a well-tailored shift with a cutout back or an on-trend polka dot crop top. The store's decorations, art, and accessories have a vintage feel. It carries sizes 0-18, and the service is sweet and friendly—Wasfy herself can sometimes be found doling out tailoring advice.

MAP 5: 4068 blvd. St-Laurent, 514/288-7661, www.lustreboutique. ca; noon-7pm Mon.-Wed., noon-9pm Thurs.-Fri., 11am-6pm Sat., noon-6pm Sun.

ACCESSORIES AND JEWELRY
M0851

The minimalist leather creations from this Montréal-based brand may have leaked beyond the boundaries of the city—they have stores in Toronto, Vancouver, and Japan—but they remain a strong part of the city's design scene. Known for its bags (once you've seen one, you'll notice the style anywhere), this boutique also sells other leather goods, including outerwear. The open-concept store on the Main, with wooden shelves and unfinished floors, is always welcoming.

MAP 5: 3526 blvd. St-Laurent, 514/849-9759, www.m0851.com; 10am-6pm Mon.-Wed., 10am-7pm Thurs., 10am-9pm Fri., 10am-6pm Sat., 11am-5pm Sun.

Oz Bijoux

Working mostly in sterling silver, jeweler Monic Dahan creates unique handmade pieces—if they're meant to recall Dorothy and Oz, they just as easily bring up images of Alice in Wonderland. At this St-Denis boutique, plain white walls are filled with glass display cases, and there is a huge semicircle display case in the middle. The displays show off the intricacy of the work, which features natural stones like onyx, turquoise, and quartz crystals. The staff is knowledgeable.

MAP 5: 3870 rue St-Denis, 514/845-9568, www.ozbijoux.com; 10am-7pm Mon.-Fri., 9am-6pm Sat.

CHILDREN'S STORES
✪ La Grande Ourse

Practically all the toys sold at La Grande Ourse (the Great Bear, or Ursa Major) are made of wood and crafted by local artisans. The store's aim is to inspire children to use their imagination during play. There are pull-along toys and rocking horses for toddlers, and kitchen sets, sailboats, and dollhouses for older children. The small store is full of wonder and excitement, and the staff is willing to answer parents' questions or play with the little ones.

MAP 5: 263 ave. Duluth E., 514/847-1207, www.lagrandeourse.jimdo.com; noon-6pm Tues.-Thurs., noon-9pm Fri., noon-5pm Sat.-Sun.

THRIFT AND VINTAGE
Friperie St-Laurent

Arbiters of vintage style should stop at this *friperie* on the Main. Elegant yet quirky window displays entice you into the well-laid-out store full of cubbies and glass shelves, on which accessories are artfully displayed. A vintage soundtrack with jazz and 1960s pop completes the atmosphere. The staff are usually decked out in vintage finds and will help you find some as well. It's a great place to pick up a leather jacket or a silk tie from the 1940s.

MAP 5: 3976 blvd. St-Laurent, 514/842-3893; 11am-6pm Mon.-Wed., 11am-9pm Thurs.-Fri., noon-6pm Sat.-Sun.

Kimono Vintage

Located in a corner spot in a quiet residential neighborhood, Kimono Vintage is a truly unique spot featuring recycled ("upcycled," if you must) vintage kimonos made into wallets, chain purses and pouches, tableware, *temari* balls and dolls, *tabi* socks, and gorgeous, high-quality kimonos.

MAP 5: 783 rue de Bienvielle, 514/522-5000, www.kimonovintage.com; noon-6pm Tues.-Sat.

Friperie St-Laurent

ANTIQUES AND KITSCH

✪ Kitsch 'n' Swell

This midcentury-modern fairyland of kitsch offers vintage and vintage-style clothing (plus sizes available) amidst fringed light fixtures and hook-rugs of flamenco dancers. Once you've pulled yourself away from the pin-up clothing, check out the array of unique items that could easily work in your home, like a teak side table, a set of themed highball glasses, or tiki cocktail mugs.

MAP 5: 3972 blvd. St-Laurent, 514/358-6336, www.boutiquekitschnswell. com; 11am-6pm Mon.-Wed., 11am-8pm Thurs.-Fri., 11am-5pm Sat.-Sun.

La Boutique du Collectionneur

Bird cages, horseshoes, antique lighting, old postcards, paintings, prints, glassware, vintage pornography, Roman coins—this shop is chockablock with interesting finds rooted out on the extensive travels of the father and son duo who own and run the shop.

MAP 5: 4569 blvd. St-Laurent, 514/282-4141, www.couleurs.qc.ca; 10am-6pm Mon.-Fri., noon-5pm Sat.-Sun.

GIFT AND HOME

✪ Arthur Quentin

Couples in the know come here to pick out their wedding registry. The selection is classic yet unconventional, with many products imported from France. The store comprises three distinct mini-stores: a British-style haberdashery, cookware, and tableware. These mini-boutiques help you keep your focus as you browse everything from high-end linens to Le Creuset cookware to canister sets and fine bone china. All three rooms are modest in size and filled to capacity, so each demands a bit of concentration.

MAP 5: 3960 rue St-Denis, 514/843-7513, www.arthurquentin.com; 10am-6pm Mon.-Fri., 10am-5pm Sat., noon-5pm Sun.

Chez Farfelu

Best described as a five-and-dime on steroids, Chez Farfelu has a definite nostalgic feel with its rows of lollipops and candy machines along with notebooks and coffee mugs emblazoned with 1960s comic-strip heroes. It also stocks a bunch of jewelry and novelty items, like blow-up chairs shaped like frogs, pillows shaped like cat and dog heads, and midcentury-modern-style alarm clocks. This spot used to have a sister location for their tamer houseware goods, but the two stores have merged.

MAP 5: 843 ave. du Mont-Royal E., 514/528-6251; 10am-9pm Mon.-Fri., 9am-5pm Sat., 10am-5pm Sun.

3 Femmes et 1 Coussin

Specializing in tableware, 3 Femmes et 1 Coussin offers dinnerware lines, many imported directly from Europe. The styles range from classic to quirky, including lines by Stolze and Vista Alegre. To show off the white china, the walls are beautifully covered in bright damask prints, and the simple layout ensures the china stays unbroken. The glassware is often bright and bubbly, though you can also find classic standards like champagne flutes, grappa glasses, and cognac snifters.

MAP 5: 783 rue Gilford, 514/987-6807, www.3f1c.ca; 10am-6pm Tues.-Wed., 10am-7pm Thurs.-Fri., 10am-5pm Sat.

BOOKS AND MUSIC

✪ Aux 33 Tours

Beloved by locals, this shop specializes in Japanese record pressings—each stamper is used for only 10,000 pressings before it gets retired—and they carry just about every type of music you can think of, including an impressive collection of hardcore and metal albums. It's not unusual to see early morning lines of people waiting to get gig tickets or spend their hard-earned cash on the annual Record Store Day. They've got a pretty swell collection of CDs, too.

MAP 5: 1373 ave. du Mont-Royal E., 514/524-7397, www.aux33tours.com; 10am-7pm Mon.-Wed., 10am-9pm Thurs.-Fri., 10am-6pm Sat.-Sun.

Beatnick Music

Die-hard record collectors and vinyl fanatics come from far and wide to check out the selection at Beatnick. There's an online store, but nothing beats heading into this cavern of sound and listening to a rare Northern Soul album on the turntables. Everything revolves around the album, from the walls full of vinyl to the fastidiously organized shelves. The staff's knowledge is encyclopedic and their tastes individual. Of course, they also carry CDs and the latest albums, usually on vinyl.

MAP 5: 3770 rue St-Denis, 514/842-0664, www.beatnickmusic.com; 11am-7pm Mon.-Wed., 11am-9pm Thurs.-Fri., 11am-6pm Sat.-Sun.

Paul's Boutique

Started with just 100 vinyls and 20 CDs in 2001, Paul's Boutique has since grown to 20,000 vinyls and has taken over two floors of a shabby house on Mont-Royal, filled to the rafters with every kind of music and music paraphernalia. The shop is named for the store's owner, not the iconic Beastie Boys album—though the band has visited. The staff can be grumpy (and occasionally capricious with the hours), but don't take it personally.

MAP 5: 112 ave. du Mont-Royal E., 514/284-7773; noon-6pm Mon.-Wed. and Sat.-Sun., noon-9pm Thurs.-Fri.

ARTS AND CRAFTS
Coop Saint-Laurent des Arts

Tucked into a basement just off boulevard St-Laurent, this nook of a shop manages to pack in an impressive stock of pens, papers, brushes, and canvases at reasonable prices. The staff is knowledgeable and friendly—no need to feel intimidated if you're just looking for some half-decent pencil crayons.

MAP 5: 10 rue Villeneuve E., 514/289-1009, www.coopstlaurent.com; Mon.-Fri. 10am-7pm, 10am-6pm Sat., noon-5pm Sun.

GOURMET TREATS
Epicerie Unique

While it might be a stretch to call Epicerie Unique gourmet—it feels more like a classic *dépanneur* (corner store) than an upscale cheese or chocolate shop—it finds a home in this guide for its prodigious beer selection and proximity to Parc Jeanne-Mance. You see where we're going with this, right? Pop by Epicerie Unique before getting some takeout on the Main, and then make your way over to the park for open-air picnic dining.

MAP 5: 4901 blvd. St-Laurent, 514/439-8939; 11am-11pm Mon.-Sun.

Sabor Latino-Andes

When the owners realized that just as many people were popping in for a quick bite as were coming to get their groceries, they renovated this place to make the hot food the centerpiece, and now there's a cute dining area. They carry at least 2,500 Latin American products, everything from hot sauces, beans, and corn meal to arepas (corn cakes). Stop in for your favorite salsa and get Peruvian, Colombian, or Salvadoran tamales while you're at it. Check out their sister location at 435 rue Belanger in Little Italy.

MAP 5: 4387 blvd. St-Laurent, 514/848-1078, www.saborlatino.ca; 8am-7pm Mon.-Wed., 9am-9pm Thurs.-Fri., 9am-7pm Sat., 10am-6pm Sun.

La Vieille Europe

The intoxicating smell of cheese and coffee hits you as soon as you walk into this veritable institution. With over 300 cheeses and 30 types of coffee, this is the go-to place for Montréal chefs and foodies looking for that particular ingredient. It specializes in products from France, Germany, Eastern Europe, Scandinavia, and England, so you can pick up pickled herring, sauerkraut, camembert, and black currant jam all at the same place. They also have sandwiches at the deli counter.

MAP 5: 3855 blvd. St-Laurent, 514/842-5773; 8am-6pm Mon.-Wed. and Sat., 7:30am-8pm Thurs.-Fri., 9am-5pm Sun.

BATH, BEAUTY, AND SPAS

Espace Nomad

Offering traditional and holistic massages (including pre-natal options) and organic body treatments, Espace Nomad is one of only a few green spas in the city. It's on the Main in the heart of the Plateau. The atmosphere is relaxed, but the surroundings are distinctly more modern and design-oriented than some places, with vibrantly colored walls contrasting with earth-tone furniture. Organic treatments include body wraps and scrubs, and they offer private yoga classes. Prices start at $85 for an hour-long massage and organic treatments.

MAP 5: 4650 blvd. St-Laurent, 514/842-7279, www.espacenomad.ca; 10am-6pm Mon., 10am-10pm Tues.-Sat., 10am-9pm Sun.

Mile End and Petite-Italie Map 6

CLOTHING AND SHOES

✪ Boutique Unicorn

It can be hard to find a name that works in both French and English, so when boutique owners Mélanie Robillard and Amélie Thellen finally stumbled on Unicorn the name stuck. Since opening in 2008, it has become a hit with fashionable Franco and Anglo women. Full of modern classics, the store recently expanded to include a room dedicated to shoes and accessories. The boutique is devoted to local and Canadian designers.

MAP 6: 5135 blvd. St-Laurent, 514/544-2828, www.boutiqueunicorn.com; noon-6pm Mon.-Wed., noon-8pm Thurs.-Fri., 11am-5pm Sat.-Sun.

✪ Les Étoffes

Started by a chic young couple, this boutique on the Main carries menswear and womenswear from contemporary, hard-to-find labels like Australia's Lover and Montréal's own Naked and Famous Jeans. There's a modern aesthetic to the store, but it also has a welcoming warmth, thanks to the rich, dark-blue walls and wooden fixtures. There's a real sense of timelessness in the pieces on sale here.

MAP 6: 5253 blvd. St-Laurent, 514/544-5500; noon-6pm Tues.-Wed., noon-7pm Thurs.-Fri., noon-5pm Sat.-Sun.

Atelier B.

Atelier B. is a workshop/boutique featuring the label's seasonal collections for men and women. The store has an industrial feel with gunmetal gray cabinets and drawers throughout. The space is open and has lots of room for browsing. Atelier B.'s simple and clean design aesthetic matches perfectly with the decor. If you're looking for wardrobe staples like winter coats or well-tailored shirts, this place is ideal. All merchandise is made on the premises at the back of the store.

MAP 6: 5758 blvd. St-Laurent, 514/769-6094, www.atelier-b.ca; noon-6pm Tues.-Wed., noon-8pm Thurs.-Fri., noon-5pm Sat.-Sun.

Billie

The floor-to-ceiling glass storefront of this boutique gives you a full view of the lovely finds inside. Elegant but youthful, the decor consists of small, cabin-style cubbies, a long dresser topped with perfectly selected accessories, and a luxurious satin-walled changing room that makes you feel as though you've stepped into a Chanel purse. Pieces are from designers ranging from Wildfox to Maison Scotch, but the look is distinctly soft and feminine, with occasional edgier pieces.

MAP 6: 1012 ave. Laurier W., 514/270-5415, www.billieboutique.com; noon-6pm Mon.-Wed., noon-9pm Thurs.-Fri.,10am-5pm Sat., noon-5pm Sun.

La Canadienne

This shoe and accessory maker's flagship store on Laurier is big and glossy, with lots of windows and a sleek gray interior. The go-to brand for stylish and functional winter boots, it also carries sandals, espadrilles, heels, coats, and bags, all made in Canada and Italy with the same attention to detail and practicality.

MAP 6: 273 ave. Laurier W., 514/270-8008, www.lacanadienneshoes.com; 10am-6pm Mon.-Wed., 10am-7pm Thurs.-Fri., 10am-5pm Sat., 11am-5pm Sun.

Général 54

Dedicated to local designers, Général 54 sells goods from Alison Wonderland, Isolde, Erin Templeton, Umbrella Collective, Maboue, and many more. Artfully curated antique furniture doubles as display cases for handmade leather goods, while jewelry pieces are often pinned on the wall and you'll find silk-screened pillowcases coming out of old hatboxes. The atmosphere is low-key, with local indie rock or classic oldies playing in the background, and the staff is always ready to offer a hand or an opinion.

MAP 6: 5145 blvd. St-Laurent, 514/271-2129, www.general54.ca; 11am-6pm Mon.-Wed., 11am-8pm Thurs.-Fri., 11am-5pm Sat.-Sun.

CHILDREN'S STORES
Boutique Citrouille

Started by a couple of Parisian parents, Boutique Citrouille (Pumpkin Store) sells marionettes, dolls, costumes, maps, and figurines, as well as toys from Meccano, Kapla, and Playmobil. This midsize space is so chockablock with exciting toys it's a miracle any parent can pull their child (or themselves, for that matter) out of here.

Anyone with a weakness for old-fashioned toys will immediately fall for this place. Best to set yourself a budget before entering!

MAP 6: 1126 rue Bernard W., 514/948-0555, www.boutiquecitrouille. com; 10am-5pm Mon.-Thurs. and Sat., 10am-7pm Fri., noon-5pm Sun.

Comme des Enfants

Like the name suggests, this shop offers clothes, books, and toys for kids and babies. Chic and pricey, everything here makes childhood seem like a quaint French movie. If you're expecting—or know someone who is—they have a range of adorable mobiles, swings, bunting, and blankets, any of which would make the perfect gift.

MAP 6: 122 rue Bernard W., 514/564-8334, www.commedesenfants.com; 11am-6pm Tues.-Fri. 11am-5pm, Sat.-Sun.

Annex Vintage

THRIFT AND VINTAGE
Annex Vintage

From boots to jackets, wide belts from the 1980s, and more than a few plaid shirts for men, the Annex offers vintage goods in the Mile End. Run by those who manage Général 54 and Local 23, it draws hipsters and thrift lovers of any age. Filled with finds like chests of drawers, wooden rocking chairs, and old luggage, the store has a homey, nostalgic feel. Music is usually indie rock, though CBC talk radio often sets the mood.

MAP 6: 56 rue St-Viateur W., 514/271-2129; noon-6pm Mon.-Wed., noon-7pm Thurs.-Fri., 11am-6pm Sat.-Sun.

Citizen Vintage

Citizen Vintage has a distinctly curated feel. The all-white space, with great high ceilings, also gives it an airy feel, rare for secondhand stores in this town. Popular with men and women, the shop has a dedicated menswear section as well as seating for tired shoppers to stop and rest a while. Lara and Becky, the shop's owners, founded the space with eco-conscious fashion in mind, recycling and upselling pieces to encourage their style-conscious clientele to eschew fast fashion.

MAP 6: 5330 blvd. St-Laurent, 514/439-2774, www.citizenvintage.com; 11am-6pm Mon.-Wed. and Sat.-Sun., 11am-7pm Thurs.-Fri.

Ex Voto

Homemade pins, patches, candles, jewelry, and perfumes, as well as hand-picked vintage clothes, line this bright, quirky shop. It's a great place for gifts, if there's someone in your life who would love to receive socks printed with lit matches, pastel-colored mountain candles, cat-printed tote bags, handmade prints, vintage sunglasses, or a pink ball cap saying, "I Owe You Nothing." If it's raining, you'd do well to pick up a stylish duck-head umbrella.

MAP 6: 6534 blvd. St-Laurent, 514/544-8230, www.exvoto.ca; noon-6pm Mon.-Wed., noon-7pm Thurs.-Fri., 11am-6pm Sat., noon-5pm Sun.

Local 23

Boots and shoes line the windowsill of this secondhand store, and a huge seasonal selection lines the walls. It's divided by item (menswear, skirts, dresses, blouses) and pleasingly organized by color. You'll find scores such as vintage fur hats or berets come winter. An old record player has been transformed into a jewelry display case, and luggage adds a bit of old-time flavor. It's staffed by vintage-savvy young women who will help you dig through the latest finds.

MAP 6: 23 rue Bernard W., 514/270-9333, http://local23mtl.blogspot.ca; noon-6pm Mon.-Wed. and Sat.-Sun., noon-7pm Thurs.-Fri.

ANTIQUES AND KITSCH

Monastiraki

Monastiraki is difficult to classify. Part gallery, part antiques shop, part comics shop, and all kitsch, it's unlike any store you've been in. It's owned by local artist, cartoonist, and all-around nice guy Billy Maveras, who knows the merchandise inside and out and has organized the antiques, collectibles, and knickknacks to make them organized and easily accessible. Find a gift for an artsy friend or something to frame once you get home.

MAP 6: 5478 blvd. St-Laurent, 514/278-4879, www.monastiraki.blogspot. com; noon-6pm Wed., noon-8pm Thurs.-Fri., noon-5pm Sat.-Sun.

Style Labo

Style Labo specializes in vintage and throwback furniture, often reclaimed from industrial and school buildings (co-owner Anne Defay, originally from France, restores pieces herself). Also selling lighting, home decorations (including antlers), clocks, and other bric-a-brac, this spot hits a comfortable note between high and low end. You might find a vintage globe or pair of skates—or, if you're an office supply enthusiast, a vintage in-and-out tray, pencil sharpener, or even a manual desk calendar.

MAP 6: 5595 blvd. St-Laurent, 514/658-9910, www.stylelabo-deco. com; 11am-6pm Mon.-Wed., 11am-7pm Thurs.-Fri., noon-5pm Sat., 1pm-5pm Sun.

GIFT AND HOME

Café Domo

Located just north of St-Zotique on Clark, this tiny café and design shop serves up equal amounts of Montréal nostalgia and great coffee. Metro light boxes, Expo 67 kitsch, posters, books, and bags—this spot has it all. Not to mention, the proprietor is super friendly—stop in to get caffeinated and learn a little about Montréal's history.

MAP 6: 6712 rue Clark, 514/971-6489; 7:30am-5pm Mon.-Tues. and Thurs., 7:30am-5pm Wed., 7:30am-6pm Fri., 11am-6pm Sat.

Jamais Assez

Jamais Assez

Practical and modern are two traits belonging to most of the goods in this bright, open, and modern store. But there is also a fair amount of whimsy in what they stock, like a yellow bookcase custom-made for your collection of *National Geographic* magazines, a rocking horse in the shape of a dodo bird, or a designer kitty litter box. Most goods are made in Montréal or Québec, and the staff is very knowledgeable about where their products are from.

MAP 6: 5153 blvd. St-Laurent, 514/509-3709, www.jamaisassez.com; 11am-6pm Mon.-Wed., 11am-8pm Thurs.-Fri., 10am-5pm Sat., noon-5pm Sun.

Les Touilleurs

Styled to look like a cross between an art gallery and a dream kitchen, Les Touilleurs displays its wares along white walls, stacked on butcher-block tables, and neatly put away in perfect cubbies. From cookware to tableware, small kitchen appliances like old-fashioned scales to scoops for your coffee canister, this store has the chicest stuff for your kitchen. Owners François Longré and Sylvain Côté also offer cooking workshops, and the staff will give you insider tips on their favorite restaurants.

MAP 6: 152 ave. Laurier W., 514/278-0008, www.lestouilleurs.com; 10am-6pm Mon.-Wed., 10am-7pm Thurs.-Fri., 10am-5pm Sat., 11am-5pm Sun.

BOOKS AND MUSIC

✪ Drawn & Quarterly

Possibly one of the best bookstores on the continent, Drawn & Quarterly is the physical extension of the art and graphic novel publishing house of the same name. Located in a turn-of-the-20th-century building, it has a cozy, old-store feel with tables full of books, low and accessible wooden shelves, and exposed bricks. The staff couldn't be sweeter. It carries graphic

novels and comics, gorgeous art books, literature, and kids' books. It's also a popular spot for book launches.

MAP 6: 211 rue Bernard W., 514/279-2224, www.drawnandquarterly.com; 11:30am-6pm Mon.-Tues., 11am-9pm Wed.-Sat., 11am-7pm Sun.

Drawn & Quarterly

180g

Here in Mile-Ex, we like our cafés. We like them so much that we cram them into bookstores, bike shops, and, why not, record stores! This vinyl emporium and coffee shop (they also have soup and sandwiches) is in a mid-size industrial garage space. Staff are close-knit and sometimes play Mario Kart, projected onto the walls, on their breaks.

MAP 6: 6546 Waverly St., 438/386-4121; 9am-5pm Mon.-Wed., 9am-7pm Thurs.-Fri., 11am-6pm Sat.-Sun.

Phonopolis

Carrying new and used vinyl and CDs, Phonopolis has a great collection of indie rock, obscure bands and labels, and vintage finds. Located next door to Drawn & Quarterly, it's also a good spot to find out what shows are

There is little that brings Montrealers together more than a craft fair. Held throughout the year, with an abundance around the holidays, these fairs take all shapes and sizes, with vendors traveling from all over to attend.

The biggest show of all, attracting international vendors, is **Le Salon des Mètiers d'Art** (www.metiers-d-art.qc.ca/smaq, Dec., free), which takes at Place Bonaventure come winter. It houses over 400 professional exhibitors and the 200,000 people who come to take it all in. Running throughout December, the fair encompasses traditional and artisan crafts, such as blown-glass jewelry, felted winter accessories, and handmade bed linens.

After Mètiers, **Souk at SAT** (www.souk.sat.qc.ca) is the second most popular pre-Christmas craft fair. Attracting a diverse clientele of hipsters and suburban parents, this show always strikes a perfect balance of vendors, with an emphasis on local producers. Greeting cards and ceramics are on sale, as is the work of emerging designers. The only trick with this fair is walking away with gifts for anyone but yourself. This place gets packed, so if you want to browse without heating up, check your winter coat before you shop.

Held during the weeklong September music festival Pop Montreal, **Puces POP** (www.popmontreal.com) attracts a hipster crowd of shoppers and sellers with young crafters coming from all over Canada and the United States to participate. It's usually held in a church basement, and there's a definite nostalgic feel to the whole event, but the work on sale is top-notch and includes everything from cupcakes to screen prints, from natural beauty products to toys. A pre-Christmas edition is usually held mid-December, with a third event in the spring.

Organized by the Montreal Gem and Mineral Club, the **Annual Gem and Mineral Show** (www.montrealgemmineralclub.ca) takes place every fall. Vendors from across North America descend bearing precious gems, minerals, fossils, carvings, tools, books, and beading supplies.

coming up in the city—you can pick up tickets for acts at La Sala Rossa or Bar le Ritz PDB.

MAP 6: 207 rue Bernard W., 514/270-4442, www.online.phonopolis.ca; 11am-7pm Mon.-Sat., 11am-6pm Sun.

ARTS AND CRAFTS
Effiloché

This knitting and sewing space is one of a handful along a sheltered, just-beginning-to-gentrify strip of St-Hubert. While its name means unraveled in English (to continue the vocab lesson, *le porc effiloché* means "pulled pork"), it's a quaint space, jam-packed with wools in an appetizing range of colors and textures, as well as embroidery threads, needles, and fabrics. In the summertime, they move the party onto the street, knitting and crafting on a makeshift terrace next to the curb.

MAP 6: 6260 rue St-Hubert, 514/276-2547, www.effiloche.com; 11am-7pm Tues.-Fri., 11am-5pm Sat.-Sun.

Lozeau

This family-owned and -operated business goes back to 1927, when it was started by founder Leo Laurent Lozeau as a wedding photography and film-processing business. Now, it is the go-to place for everything related to photography, videography, lighting, and drones. Whether you're looking to have film photos developed, get your old SLR repaired, or buy a new light meter, the knowledgeable, bilingual staff can help you out.

MAP 6: 6229 rue St-Hubert, 514/274-6577, www.lozeau.com; 9am-6pm Mon.-Wed., 9am-9pm Thurs.-Fri., 9am-5pm Sat., 10am-5pm Sun.

Au Papier Japonais

A seriously beautiful store, with soft lighting and reels of *washi* tape hanging off the wall, Au Papier Japonais— or the Japanese paper store, as locals call it—carries over 500 different kinds of Japanese paper. They also stock paper from Nepal, India, Mexico, and Montréal, as well as journals, photo albums, and even kimonos. Check out the workshop schedule—they offer book-binding courses on everything from Coptic-style to accordion-style to Japanese-style.

MAP 6: 24 ave. Fairmount W.,
514/276-6863, www.aupapierjaponais.com;
10am-6pm Mon.-Sat., noon-4pm Sun.

GOURMET TREATS
Café Saint-Henri

Technically a coffee shop (Mile End and Little Italy are absolutely full of them), Café Saint-Henri also sells its own coffee and espresso roasts in small and large bags—rich, West Coast-worthy coffees with balanced flavors that you can take home for yourself or to give as a gift to your favorite coffee snob. Bonus: If you buy a large bag, you'll receive a free espresso. Check out its sister stores downtown and in Saint-Henri.

MAP 6: 260 Place du Marché du Nord, 514/507-9696, www.sainthenri.ca; 7:30am-6pm Mon.-Thurs. and Sat., 7:30am-7pm Fri.

Chocolats Privilège

Made fresh every day or two, the chocolates at this shop on the edge of Marché Jean-Talon are mouthwateringly good. Try the candied oranges dipped in chocolate, the boozy cherries, or anything salted—you really can't go wrong. Near Easter, Christmas, Halloween, and other chocolate-friendly holidays, Chocolats Privilège is the ideal place to pick up an upscale bunny or Christmas tree. Check out its sister store at Marché Atwater.

MAP 6: 7070 rue Henri-Julien, 514/276-7070, www.chocolatsprivilege.com; 9am-6pm Mon.-Wed. and Sat., 9am-8pm Thurs.-Fri., 9am-5pm Sun.

Fromagerie Hamel

The moment you step in, you'll be greeted by the heady, slightly sweat-socky smell of good cheese. Established in 1961, Hamel is one of the best-stocked *fromageries* in the city. Take a number to pick a cheese or three from the well-staffed display case of world cheeses, or have a taste at the sample counter and pick up local yogurts, ricotta, parmesan, or weekly special cheeses. Hamel also sells upscale spices and herbs, crackers, and very good chocolate.

MAP 6: 220 rue Jean-Talon E., 514/272-1161, www.fromageriehamel.com; 9am-6pm Mon.-Wed., 9am-7pm Thurs., 8am-8pm Fri., 8am-6pm Sat., 8:30am-5pm Sun.

Geneviève Grandbois

Chocolatier Geneviève Grandbois's tiny boutique with its steel walk-up counter is reminiscent of an ice cream shop. Stepping up to the window, you make your selection from a precise menu that includes chocolates from places like Madagascar, Cuba, and Tanzania, and from flavors like chai, extra-virgin olive oil, and maple syrup. Your order comes to you perfectly packaged in a neat little box and ready to eat. Locals pop in for a hot chocolate or rich ice cream.

MAP 6: 162 rue St-Viateur W., 514/394-1000, www.chocolatsgg.com; 10am-6pm Mon.-Wed. and Sat., 10am-9pm Thurs.-Fri., 10am-5pm Sun.

Maison de Thé Camellia Sinensis

When you visit the Marché Jean-Talon, be sure to stop in at this shoebox-sized tea library, complete with a rolling library ladder. It smells delicious, and the knowledgeable staff can help you find whatever you're looking for. They also have good taste in music (mostly post-rock, think Tortoise or Boards of Canada), and they'll most likely offer you a sample of tea. Looking for a gift? Purchase one of their unique teapots, mugs, or cups.

MAP 6: 7010 ave. Casgrain, 514/271-4002, www.camellia-sinensis.com; 10am-6pm Mon.-Wed., 10am-7pm Thurs.-Fri., 9am-6pm Sat., 9am-5pm Sun.

Milano

Around for over 50 years, Milano is *the* place to get things like olive oil, balsamic vinegar, and panettone. The setup is different than pretty much any other grocery store: Instead of aisles, it's set up with little islands around the store overflowing with packages of imported Italian coffee, 10 different kinds of arborio rice, and jars of roasted vegetables. They also have a mean selection of cheeses at great prices, bulk foods and spices, and stove-top espresso makers.

MAP 6: 6862 blvd. St-Laurent, 514/273-8558; 8am-6pm Mon.-Wed., 8am-9pm Thurs.-Fri., 8am-5pm Sat.-Sun.

WHERE TO STAY

Vieux-Montréal 216
Centre-Ville 219
Centre-Ville Est 222
Quartier Latin and the Village 224
Plateau Mont-Royal 225
Mile End and Petite-Italie 227

Because it's a large North American city, Montréal has hotels with all the amenities travelers are used to, like air-conditioning in the summer and standard double beds. Some, however, follow a more European model and offer a single queen-size bed for double occupancy. Breakfast is usually, but not always, included. And those expecting a daily buffet may be disappointed with some hotels that offer a simple continental breakfast with fresh pastries, coffee, and juice instead. If breakfast at the hotel is going to set you back more than $10 per person, you can most likely find a more palatable and affordable breakfast option not far from your accommodation.

a room at Le 9 et Demi

Though most hotel websites can be trusted to give authentic photos, it is always a good idea to check visitor review sites like www.tripadvisor.ca for feedback before booking. Tired-looking decor might have been recently updated, or a five-star hotel might no longer be up to standard.

Parking in the city can be a hassle, and expensive, so double-check to make sure your hotel offers parking or at the very least a reasonably close alternative. Street parking is usually safe, but watch out for unusual parking rules—like having to move the car for an hour each day. Finding a spot close to the hotel isn't always easy.

CHOOSING WHERE TO STAY

Montréal has accommodations for any size budget. But depending on the time of year, you might find you're paying for more than what you're getting. There's no

HIGHLIGHTS

✪ **BEST-KEPT SECRET:** The huge rooms, quiet luxury, and minimalist design of **Hôtel Gault,** tucked away in a quiet corner of Old Montréal, make it perfect if you're looking for your own private paradise in the city (page 216).

✪ **MOST ROMANTIC HOTEL:** The opulent Louis XIV-inspired decor and charming Old Montréal setting of **Pierre du Calvet** make it perfect for a couple's weekend away (page 216).

✪ **BEST DESIGN:** One of the first boutique hotels in the city, **Hôtel St-Paul** has bold interiors that remain cutting edge, and the location is unbeatable (page 217).

✪ **MOST HISTORICAL ROOM:** Yoko Ono and John Lennon holed up in room 1742 of the **Fairmont Queen Elizabeth** during their famous 1969 peace protest. Request the same suite and make your own history (page 219).

✪ **BEST CLASSIC HOTEL:** The top-hatted doormen, sharply dressed staff, and afternoon tea at the opulent **Ritz-Carlton** are guaranteed to transport you to a different era (page 219).

✪ **MOST LIKELY TO MAKE YOU EXTEND YOUR STAY:** Designed with comfort in mind, **Hôtel Le Germain** makes you feel like you're entering your own private loft. The hotel also boasts a 24-hour gym, a four-star restaurant, and panoramic views of the city (page 220).

✪ **BEST CONTEMPORARY HOTEL:** The **Hotel 10 Montréal** has a sleek, modern design and stunning Gaudí-like art nouveau architecture that will make you feel like you're stepping into a luxury European hotel (page 222).

✪ **BEST BUDGET BOUTIQUE HOTEL:** Wonderfully located and with sharp contemporary decor, **Hotel Zero1** raises the bar on affordable luxury (page 222).

✪ **BEST LGBTQ-FRIENDLY INN:** **Sir Montcalm** is a charming B&B in the heart of the Village. With its exquisitely designed rooms, this hotel offers an oasis in the city (page 224).

PRICE KEY

$	Less than CAN$150 per night
$ $	CAN$150-300 per night
$ $ $	More than CAN$300 per night

disputing that Vieux-Montréal is the ideal location, as there's nothing quite like walking out of your hotel and onto the cobblestone streets. However, it's one of the more expensive areas in the city, so staying here might not fit every budget.

Some of the best rates can be found in the suburbs or close to the airport. But even though public transit is generally fast and efficient, there's little reason to stay so far outside of the city center. If you're booking online double-check the address before hitting the confirmation button.

The farther north of rue Sherbrooke you go, the harder it is to find accommodations. Though a few hotels are available in the Plateau, residential areas like the Mile End and Little Italy offer very few options, most of which are independently run bed-and-breakfasts or rental apartments.

Hostels can be found throughout the city. Though dorms are popular with student travelers, a number of the hostels offer private rooms and cater to more mature travelers.

Vieux-Montréal

Vieux-Montréal is perhaps the crown jewel of places to stay in Montréal. With boutique hotels, some centuries old, the neighborhood offers a taste of Europe in North America. You'll pay for the privilege, but if you're looking for high-end accommodations, this is where to stay.

Centre-Ville

Most of the international chain hotels are concentrated on rue Sherbrooke between University and avenue du Parc, but there are lots of other options, including smaller inns, hostels, and independent hotels, usually found in the eastern or western end of the downtown core. Centre-Ville is a great place to stay if you're looking for a mix of modern amenities and fair prices. You'll be close enough to travel to Vieux-Montréal without paying steep prices, but you'll also be close to the art and culture institutions downtown and in Centre-Ville Est.

Centre-Ville Est

Centre-Ville Est straddles the line between Centre-Ville and the Quartier Latin both geographically and conceptually. You'll find chains here, and you'll also find hostels and a few boutique hotels. Most prices are reasonable. You'll be within walking distance of Vieux-Montréal and the Quartier Latin.

Quartier Latin and the Village

A student hub, the Quartier Latin is full of budget options and the rowdier, party-on-your-doorstep crowd that usually comes with them. Still, larger hotels and smaller, intimate boutique-style inns can be found here, and all are within walking distance to downtown and the Plateau, making it a great choice for those who want to see the city by foot, bike, or Métro. A little farther east, the Village is home to LGBTQ-friendly B&B options.

Plateau Mont-Royal

Jam-packed with cute parks and restaurants, the charming Plateau is a great place to stay if you want to experience the city like a local. Most of the hotels, hostels, and B&Bs are small, though, so book well in advance.

Mile End and Petite-Italie

Mile End and Little Italy are, in some respects, ideal places to stay—Mile

WHERE TO STAY IF . . .

Depending on how you plan to spend your time, some neighborhoods will be better home bases than others.

YOU ONLY HAVE A WEEKEND
Stay in **Centre-Ville,** within a stone's throw of the city's contemporary cultural institutions and its historical heart, Vieux-Montréal.

YOU WANT OLD-WORLD CHARM (AND DON'T MIND PAYING FOR IT)
Book a room overlooking the cobblestone streets in **Vieux-Montréal,** where fresh air and gorgeous views take the edge off city living.

YOU WANT TO PARTY
You won't be alone in **Centre-Ville Est** or the **Quartier Latin,** adjoining neighborhoods home to a wide variety of nightlife spots.

YOU'RE TRAVELING ON A BUDGET
You'll find low-cost options in the **Quartier Latin,** but it's worth checking out hostels in other neighborhoods, too.

YOU'RE LOOKING FOR AN LGBTQ-FRIENDLY B&B
Check out the **Village.** In fact, B&Bs throughout the city tend to be quite LGBTQ-friendly and are often run by queer couples.

YOU AREN'T REALLY A CITY PERSON
Check out **Plateau Mont-Royal.** B&Bs and boutique hotels dot the eastern part of the neighborhood, and you'll find peace, quiet, and serenity in a spot close to Parc La Fontaine.

COFFEE SHOPS AND INDIE CULTURE ARE YOUR THING
Stay in **Mile End** (or the northern edge of **Plateau Mont-Royal**) and avail yourself of vintage shops, boutique eats, and indie arts and music.

YOU'RE A SERIOUS FOODIE
Find an Airbnb in **Petite-Italie.** You'll be close to Marché Jean-Talon and a short Métro ride away from the gems of the Plateau.

End is full of independent culture and Little Italy is a foodie's paradise. But precious **few official hotels** and hostels exist here. To get close to the Mile End, check out what's available along the north edge of the Plateau or head to **Airbnb.** Prices are usually quite reasonable, and you might get bonuses like kitchen access. Listings mostly come from the city's older rental housing, meaning they may not be accessible or have air-conditioning.

ALTERNATIVE LODGING OPTIONS

Airbnb has a thriving presence in Montréal, offering a wide range of affordable options in every conceivable neighborhood. If you want to stay in the **Mile End** or **Little Italy** during peak season, Airbnb may in fact be your only option. In the **Plateau** and **Vieux-Montréal,** Airbnb opens up a world of charming, exposed-brick city rentals—allowing you to set up a home base in the city as if you're a local. Many B&Bs list themselves on Airbnb.

Rental housing in Montréal is often on the older side, making it charming but not generally equipped with air-conditioning. Montréal law requires Airbnb hosts to register with the city and follow certain rules and regulations. To stay on the right side of the

The Fairmont Queen Elizabeth was most famously home to John Lennon and Yoko Ono's 1969 "Bed-In."

law, inquire with a potential host to double-check that their listing conforms to Montréal's guidelines and requirements.

If you're booking last-minute and find yourself with few options, staying near the Pierre Trudeau International Airport might be a good near-last resort. There are about a dozen chain hotels out near the airport, some of which offer airport shuttles (handy to get to the 747 Express bus that you'll take into the city). Most are reasonably priced and, unlike city hotels, offer free parking.

Camping and RV park options exist if you're willing to go a bit off the beaten track. For camping options, first check out SEPAQ (Societé des Etablissements Plein-Air du Québec), which offers booking access across the province to campsites, cabins, and even a lodge, including at national parks close to Montréal like Oka, Îles-de-Boucherville, and Mont-Saint-Bruno. There are KOAs (Kampgrounds of America) west and south of Montréal offering RV camping sites, cabin accommodations, and tent sites, as well as other amenities like mini-golf, fire pits, and tourist shuttles. Farther out, there are great options in the Laurentians (Laurentides in French), Mauricie, Mont Orford, Frontenac, and Mastigouche.

✪ Hôtel Gault $$$

A 19th-century cotton factory owned by Andrew Gault became Hôtel Gault, one of the most scenic, serene, and discreet—it's popular with celebrities—boutique hotels in the city. The 30 spacious rooms (300-1,050 square feet each) come complete with movable ergonomic workstations and heated ceramic bathroom floors, a welcome luxury for Montréal winters. The hotel is also pet-friendly and treats its guests to a very high level of personalized service: If you requested to be welcomed by a particular kind of brandy your first stay, it will greet you again on your second.

MAP 1: 449 rue Ste-Hélène, 514/904-1616, www.hotelgault.com

the lobby bar at Pierre du Calvet

✪ Pierre du Calvet $$$

Just in front of Chapelle Notre-Dame-de-Bon-Secours, this ancestral mansion, built in 1725, is one of the oldest hotels in Montréal. The four-poster beds and wardrobes were hand-crafted in Central America; they bear the fleur de lis and the lion (symbols of France and England) as well as the owner's Trottier family coat of arms. With a gorgeous lobby bar, walled-in terrace, sumptuous dining room, and studies on every level, this nine-room *maison* feels a bit like you've lucked into staying in a living museum.

MAP 1: 405 rue Bonsecours, 514/282-1725, www.pierreducalvet.ca

Auberge du Vieux-Port $$$

Overlooking the waterfront, this boutique *auberge* (inn) offers luxury rooms and an accommodating concierge service. The hotel is decorated with rustic touches—exposed ceiling beams, wrought-iron balconies—so the feel is more homey than modern, like visiting a friend's summer home. The in-house restaurant, Taverne Gaspar, boasts both a rooftop terrace (with a panoramic view of the river) and a downstairs bistro, complete with remnants of the city's original fortifications.

MAP 1: 97 rue de la Commune, 888/660-7678, www.aubergeduvieuxport.com

Hôtel Le St-James $$$

Madonna, Victoria Beckham—this is where the celebrities stay when in Montréal. Decorated with lovingly preserved antiques, four-poster beds, and marble-accented bathrooms, the St-James has gone to great lengths to create a luxurious, European atmosphere. Located on the cusp of Vieux-Montréal and the modern Quartier

International, this former merchants bank still has many of its defining features, including John Hammond's 1930 murals, which are an ode to hydroelectric energy, and the idiosyncratic window treatments that grace each of the building's eight floors. If you are looking for a unique spa experience, theirs is located in the bank's former vault.

MAP 1: 355 rue St-Jacques, 514/841-3111, www.hotellestjames.com

Hôtel Nelligan $$$

Occupying four buildings that date back to the 1850s, this hotel features an indoor Mediterranean-style atrium and has a more traditional approach than some of the other boutique hotels in the area. The dark-wood furniture and earthy palette give each of their 105 rooms (including 59 suites and two penthouses) a sophisticated gravitas. The hotel's facade is a modest Montréal greystone, blending in to its Old Montréal environs, but enter and you'll be surprised to find their rooftop terrace offers some of the best views (and cocktails) in the city. Breakfast and parking are included in the room cost.

MAP 1: 106 rue St-Paul W., 514/788-2040, www.hotelnelligan.com

W Hotel $$$

The 1960s-modernist architecture of the converted Banque du Canada building gives this high-fashion, world-class hotel a sort of timeless edge and allows it to blend in seamlessly with the existing structures in the Quartier International. Though some aspects of the place might make your eyes roll—the Whatever/Whenever service is better known by its typical name, *concierge*—the W does provide an upscale, modern environment in a neighborhood better known for its cozy, historical charm.

MAP 1: 901 rue du Square-Victoria, 514/395-3100, www.whotels.com

✪ Hôtel St-Paul $$

As you enter the sleek lobby of this Beaux-Arts building, you'll notice the large marble fireplace, which seems to appear almost out of nowhere. The warm, monochromatic and minimalist decor, accented with leather, suede, and fur (a nod to Québec's past and the frigid winters) made it one of the first "design" hotels in the city. Even if you're not staying, pop into The Hambar, the hotel's restaurant, for brunch or a drink and a peek at the gorgeous interior.

MAP 1: 355 rue McGill, 514/380-2222, www.hotelstpaul.com

LHotel Montreal $$

Situated on what was once "Canadian Wall Street," this Second Empire-style building, erected in 1870, was originally the Montréal City and District Savings Bank. The hotel has a focus on art; works by Warhol, Litchenstein, and Christo are on view throughout the premises, and each room is uniquely decorated, mixing modern decor with the existing architectural elements, such as the ceiling friezes. The hotel offers indoor parking—a key perk, especially if you're visiting in winter.

MAP 1: 262 rue St-Jacques, 514/985-0019, www.lhotelmontreal.com

Place d'Armes Hôtel and Suites $$

Mixing elements from their 1880 structure with contemporary design, this family-friendly hotel, which was the first of its kind to open in Vieux-Montréal, offers a fine balance of

Le Saint-Sulpice

classic and modern—brick walls and industrial lighting fixtures meet colonial furniture—giving it a cozy, yet luxurious atmosphere. Looking out onto Place d'Armes and the Notre-Dame Basilica, Aix Cuisine du Terroir restaurant's rooftop terrace offers stunning views. The hotel also has an in-house hammam spa. Take advantage of the complimentary cheese and wine during afternoon cocktail hour on Terrasse Place d'Armes.

MAP 1: 55 rue St-Jacques W., 514/842-1887, www.hotelplacedarmes.com

Le Saint-Sulpice $$

Just down the street from the Notre-Dame Basilica, this four-star luxury hotel retains the charm of its historical surroundings while offering contemporary construction—built in 2002 on the site of an old parking lot, the Saint-Sulpice is perfect for guests looking for creature comfort and spacious surroundings. Each of the hotel's 108 rooms is a suite with its own kitchenette. Offering a 24-hour concierge service, Le Saint-Sulpice is also pet-friendly. The dining room has a fireplace as well as an impressive wine cellar and, in the summer, opens onto a garden terrace.

MAP 1: 414 rue St-Sulpice, 514/288-1000, www.lesaintsulpice.com

L'Hôtel Champs-de-Mars $

On the eastern border of Vieux-Montréal, this establishment has a long history as a hotel. Built in 1889, it first opened its doors as Hôtel le Relais, and its street-level tavern soon became a popular meeting place for sailors and port workers (its rumored history as a bordello only adds to its seedy charm). Far from fancy, the hotel has a family-run feel, and its 26 rooms provide a great option if you'd like to stay in the historic quarter on a budget. It also offers a filling, delicious breakfast.

MAP 1: 756 rue Berri, 514/844-0767, www.hotelchampsdemars.com

AIRBNB

Montréal's residential neighborhoods—in particular the Plateau, Mile End, Mile-Ex, and Little Italy—are quickly becoming tourist attractions, especially among younger visitors. Problem is, these neighborhoods, especially Mile End, Mile-Ex, and Little Italy, aren't exactly jam-packed with options, so your best bet is to rent a room or an apartment via **Airbnb** (www.airbnb.com).

The province of Québec enacted a law that requires owners who frequently rent their property to obtain the certification that B&Bs are required to get. If you'd like to dip a toe in the sharing economy but appreciate the rules and regulations the law has to offer, you may want to inquire about certification with your potential host.

Centre-Ville   Map 2

✪ Fairmont Queen Elizabeth $$$

One of the most famous hotels in the city, the Fairmont Queen Elizabeth has been the temporary home of Queen Elizabeth II, Nelson Mandela, and Mikhail Gorbachev. And it was here in 1969 that Yoko Ono and John Lennon staged their infamous "Bed-In" in suite 1742 and wrote and recorded "Give Peace a Chance." Opened in 1958, this world-class luxury hotel is an imposing structure and has over 1,000 rooms, 100 of which are suites. A classic Montréal hotel, it is directly connected to the train station and is accessible through the Underground City.

MAP 2: 900 blvd. René-Lévesque W., 514/861-3511, www.fairmont.com

✪ Ritz-Carlton $$$

Opened in 1912 on posh rue Sherbrooke, the Ritz-Carlton is still "La Grande Dame" of Montréal hotels, as it's the only Canadian hotel of its era still in existence, and it's still the top choice for those who can afford it. The luxury hotel still has a wrought-iron awning and top-hatted doormen that greet guests on the rich, blue carpet, and the imposing Beaux-Arts building is as elegant as when it first opened. If you can't quite afford the price tag for a night's stay, stop by the Dom Perignon bar, located in the hotel's famed Palm Lobby.

MAP 2: 1228 rue Sherbrooke W., 514/842-4212, www.ritzcarltonmontreal.com

the Ritz-Carlton

Le Mount Stephen $$$

In the heart of Montréal's Golden Square Mile, this contemporary luxury hotel offers 90 rooms and sky-loft suites. Comprising a modern building incorporated behind the greystone club of Lord Mount Stephen, a former Canadian Railway president, this hotel blends old and new, traditional and modern—you'll feel like you're visiting Lord Stephen's era but also have access to valet parking. Feeling peckish? Check out Bar George, Le Mount Stephen's cozy high-end gastropub.

MAP 2: 1440 rue Drummond, 514/313-1000, www.lemountstephen.com

✪ Hôtel Le Germain $$

Once an office building, this austere concrete structure—certainly a product of the 1970s—was renovated in 1999 to become Hôtel Le Germain. Totally redesigned to give its clients the feel of entering their own private loft, the boutique hotel's decoration is all dark wood, earth tones, and glass. With a full gym, spa, and restaurant, all staffed by experienced practitioners in their fields, their facilities are considered some of the best in the city. Panoramic views of Montréal only add to the hotel's charm.

MAP 2: 2050 rue Mansfield, 514/849-2050, www.germainmontreal.com

Château Versailles

Château Versailles $$

An intimate hotel in four grand old townhouses on the western end of downtown, Château Versailles is a great option if you're looking for a cozy but lavish atmosphere. Each room and suite is uniquely decorated, giving the hotel the feel of an old manor house. The decor itself falls somewhere between contemporary and classic, with big, heavy furniture, modern art, and opulent touches like gilded mirrors. They also serve afternoon tea, are pet-friendly, and offer a babysitting service.

MAP 2: 1659 rue Sherbrooke W., 514/933-3611, www. chateauversaillesmontreal.com

L'Hôtel le Crystal $$

Located in the heart of downtown, looking out over the Centre Bell, this gleaming glass tower boasts 131 spacious suites, all with flat-screen TVs. Contemporary in design, the furnishings are modern and monochromatic. Amenities include a pool and spa. Since it's kitty-corner to the Centre Bell, members of the Canadiens are sometimes residents here, so don't be surprised if you bump into one of them in the elevator or hot tub.

MAP 2: 1100 rue de la Montagne, 514/861-5550, www.hotellecrystal.com

Marriott Château Champlain $$

With 38 floors, the Château Champlain is the tallest hotel in the city and one of the most interesting architecturally. Designed by Roger D'Astous and Jean-Paul Pothier, it was completed in time for Expo 67. It was set apart by its arched windows, which won it an astute nickname: "the cheese grater." Now owned by Marriott, it's lobby features a golden ceiling made up of numerous domes. Similar opulent touches can be found throughout the hotel. Located on the outer edge of downtown, it looms over the Cathédrale Marie-Reine-du-Monde.

MAP 2: 1050 rue de la Gauchetière W., 514/878-9000, www. montrealchateauchamplain.com

Le Méridien Versailles $$

Among the grandiose buildings of the city's Golden Square Mile, Le Méridien Versailles is a boutique hotel set in a striking, modern building. With its classic but relaxed decor (think overstuffed couches and lots of light), it offers a modern take on comfort. Located downtown but away from the hustle and bustle of the area's noisier streets, Le Méridien's amenities include a 24-hour gym, a spa, and valet services. Guests can also access bike rentals on-site: $10 for a three-hour rental, which is a better rate than you'll find elsewhere.

MAP 2: 1808 rue Sherbrooke W., 514/933-8111, www. lemeridienversailleshotel.com

Sofitel Montréal $$

Set on the Golden Square Mile, close to McGill University and the Musée des Beaux-Arts, it may be part of a chain but French-owned Sofitel is one of the sleekest and most stylish hotels in the downtown core. Tall and lean with huge windows, its ultramodern design continues inside with a minimalist decor, stained-glass windows in the lobby, and contemporary art throughout. This is a European chain, so room sizes are slightly smaller than their North American counterparts, but, on the plus side, it's pet friendly.

MAP 2: 1155 rue Sherbrooke W., 514/285-9000, www.sofitel.com

Auberge les Bon Matins $

This lively, adorable bed-and-breakfast features fireplaces, exposed brick walls, and a great location close to Centre Bell. If you're tired of city chains, Auberge Les Bon Matin's European, country-chic character— think midway between staying at someone's house and staying at a regular hotel—will do the trick. You're afforded the perfect mix of privacy and company, and the all-you-can-eat hot breakfast makes the mornings that much sunnier.

MAP 2: 1401 ave. Argyle, 514/931-9167, www.bonmatins.com

L'Hôtel Espresso $

This former Days Inn in the heart of downtown, within walking distance to Vieux-Montréal and close to the Métro, has been mostly renovated and brought up to date. Warm earth tones are found throughout the hotel, from the lobby to the rooms, which have a comfortable but sleek and modern feel with parquet floors and crisp white duvets. Amenities include a 24-hour gym, sauna, reasonably priced on-site massage facilities, and an outdoor pool in summer. It's a fairly bare-bones hotel, but the price is right if you're staying downtown on a budget.

MAP 2: 1005 rue Guy, 514/938-4611, www. hotelespresso.ca

✪ Hotel 10 Montréal $$

A great mix of old and new, Hotel 10 has some of the most stunning architecture in the city. On the corner of St-Laurent and Sherbrooke, it is the perfect distance between downtown and the Plateau. Originally built in 1914 by Joseph-Arthur Godin, the art nouveau-style building was the first poured-concrete structure in North America. Incorporating the existing structure into the new design, Hotel 10 balances sleek design and decor with old-world charm. The friendly and bilingual staff is always helpful, and the in-house bar has a great outdoor terrace and is a popular hangout.

MAP 3: 10 rue Sherbrooke W., 514/843-6000, www.hotel10montreal.com

Holiday Inn Select $$

There's a lot of European flavor in Montréal hotels, but this place is a little different. Located in Chinatown on the edge of Vieux-Montréal, it has an Asian theme. As the rooftop pagodas indicate, the Far East aesthetic runs throughout, with a water garden and more pagodas and paper lanterns in the foyer. The rooms are standard, with queen-size beds, TVs, and windows onto Vieux-Montréal or Chinatown. Kitty-corner to the Métro, but right next to a highway, it's within walking distance to downtown and the Vieux-Port, and visitors can take advantage of the indoor pool, gym, and spa services.

MAP 3: 999 rue St-Urbain, 514/878-9888, www.yul-downtown.hiselect.com

✪ Hotel Zero1 $

This stylish boutique hotel, converted from a former university residence building, is right near the Quartier des Spectacles, with views overlooking Chinatown and Vieux-Montréal. The design is clean and sleek with lots of concrete, dark wood, and punches of yellow and white to lighten the mood. All rooms come with a mini-kitchenette, and the majority offer unobstructed views of the city's skyline. Get some fresh air on the third-floor patio or enjoy your morning coffee in the ground-floor atrium. The hotel has a restaurant, the Z Tapas Lounge, and it's close to many eateries.

MAP 3: 1 blvd. René-Lévesque E., 514/871-9696, www.zero1-mtl.com

Hotel Zero1

Hotel Quartier des Spectacles $

In the heart of the Quartier des Spectacles, this boutique budget hotel is on a small block populated by sex shops and tattoo parlors. Once inside, you'll find exposed brick walls, a tidy reception area, and comfortable,

HOSTELS

If you're looking for alternatives to the swanky boutique hotels of Old Montréal and the hotel chains of downtown, there are great hostels and bed-and-breakfasts in the city.

VIEUX-MONTRÉAL

Those looking to stay in Vieux-Montréal without the hefty price tag should look no further than **Auberge Alternative du Vieux-Montréal** (358 rue St-Pierre, 514/282-8069, www.auberge-alternative.qc.ca; $19-27 dorm room, $52-98 private room). This converted warehouse retains the arched windows and high ceilings of its 1875 construction. Decorated with an eclectic collection of found or made objects, the hostel's dorms and private rooms are brightly colored, enlivening the old stone walls. Conveniently located in the western part of Vieux-Montréal, close to rue McGill, it's easily accessible by Métro and within walking distance to downtown. It is three floors up to the reception area, so be prepared to lug your bags.

Visitors looking to be close to the downtown action should check out **Auberge L'Apéro** (1425 rue Mackay, 514/316-1052, www.aubergeapero.com; $14-25 dorm room), an affordable, popular alternative to less-than-favorable cheaper hotels. Clean and minimally decorated, it is relatively small, with only 30 beds available in an old building built in the 1880s. It boasts an outdoor terrace as well as knowledgeable and bilingual staff.

QUARTIER LATIN

The center of activity for Francophone students, the Latin Quarter has a number of hostels, though if you're well out of university, choose carefully; the area and the hostels themselves can get rowdy. Location-wise it is perfect, a stone's throw from the Plateau and close to downtown. All the choices have a truly French vibe.

Your best choice for the Quartier Latin, and possibly the city, is the **M Montreal** (1245 rue St-Andre, 514/845-9803, www.m-montreal.com; $27-40 dorm room, $124-180 private room). With exposed brick walls, modern decor, TVs in just about every room, a bumping bar, and complimentary breakfast, this hostel is one of the best in the city for young travelers.

Offering private rooms and small apartments, **Auberge de Jeunesse Alexandrie** (1750 rue Amherst, 514/525-9420, www.alexandrie-montreal.com; $21-30 dorm room, $65-104 private room) in the Latin Quarter is in the center of the action and a good choice for those traveling in small groups. The same goes for **SameSun Montréal Central** (1586 rue St-Hubert, 514/843-5739, www.samesun.com; $27-33 dorm room, $95-125 private room), though it has more of a student vibe with an outdoor terrace and in-house restaurant and bars.

PLATEAU MONT-ROYAL

For a more residential location, the Plateau is perfect. Once you get used to the laid-back pace and tree-lined streets, you might not want to venture downtown. Close to Parc La Fontaine in the eastern Plateau and open June-August, **La Gîte du Parc Lafontaine** (1250 rue Sherbrooke E., 514/522-3910, www.hostelmontreal.com; $24 dorm room, $65-74 private room) offers private rooms or dormitory beds in a classic-style townhouse. If you're visiting at a different time of year, check out **La Gîte du Plateau** (185 Sherbrooke E., 514/284-1276, www.hostelmontreal.com; $18 and up dorm room, $48-86 private room), which is run by the same people, offers the same amenities, and is closer to the downtown core.

clean rooms. It is superbly located within walking distance of both Old Montréal and the Plateau; the one drawback would be just how close you want to be to the action. During the summer months (June to late August), this area is the heart of the festival season, and things can get rowdy.

MAP 3: 17 rue Ste-Catherine W., 514/849-1619, www.hotelquartierdesspectacles.com

Quartier Latin and the Village

Map 4

✪ Sir Montcalm $$

This ultra-chic bed-and-breakfast in the Village—think matte black walls, sleek white linens, and ambient lighting—caters to the LGBTQ community and will also draw anyone and everyone with an eye for design. It's a perfect blend of comfortable yet polished. Perks include a day pass to the local gym, access to the gorgeous terrace in summer, and a filling four-course breakfast. Close to Vieux-Montréal and the Métro, it's an urban oasis that's sure to please.

MAP 4: 1453 rue Montcalm, 514/522-7747, www.sirmontcalm.com

Auberge Hotel Le Jardin d'Antoine $

Around the corner from the Métro and the bus station and within walking distance to the main shopping district and the Plateau, this hotel—a cozy cross between a chain and a B&B—makes navigating the city super simple. The rooms have a cozy, country vibe (paisley quilts and wrought-iron bed frames) as well as free Wi-Fi and air-conditioning, a savior come summer. The room rate includes a generous buffet breakfast.

MAP 4: 2024 rue St-Denis, 514/843-4506, www.aubergelejardindantoine.com

Auberge Le Pomerol $

Auberge Le Pomerol is not a huge hotel, but it's conveniently located and quite affordable for its rooms, location, and amenities. The modestly sized rooms are minimally decorated, with a smattering of contemporary touches.

The staff is friendly, helpful, and fully bilingual. It's within walking distance to the Village, Vieux-Montréal, the Quartier des Spectacles, and the Plateau. The continental breakfast is delivered to your room in a picnic basket.

MAP 4: 819 blvd. de Maisonneuve E., 514/526-5511, www.aubergelepomerol.com

Sir Montcalm

Celebrities Hotel $

The Celebrities Hotel is a well-loved, movie-themed hotel in the Latin Quarter. Situated in an old Victorian mansion built in 1897, the house has been renovated to turn it into a small boutique hotel with themed rooms: the urban, the Geisha, the Marilyn, earth and water, the African, the Moroccan, and the Trocadero. Portraits of Audrey Hepburn and Marilyn Monroe abound.

MAP 4: 1095 rue St-Denis, 514/849-9688, www.celebritieshotelmontreal.com

Chateau de L'Argoat $

On the edge of the Quartier Latin and the Plateau, this hotel's friendly service is matched by its colorful, old-school rooms featuring contemporary Québec art. The hotel's classic exterior opens onto to a mishmash of rooms and lounges—some of which have a bit of a '90s vibe, others more of a 19th-century one. Free parking and all-you-can-eat continental breakfast sweeten the deal.

MAP 4: 534 rue Sherbrooke E., 514/842-2046, www.hotel-chateau-argoat.com

Hôtel St-Denis $

Built in the 1920s—and originally known as Hotel Pennsylvania—L'Hôtel St-Denis is in the center of the action, not far from downtown and only a block away from the Berri-UQÀM Métro station. The rooms are your standard hotel fare; some guests might find the rooms to be noisy in the summer due to the air-conditioners. Parking is available just around the corner and Wi-Fi is free for guests. Breakfast isn't included at the hotel, but since it's next to cafés and restaurants, finding a good meal is hardly a problem.

MAP 4: 1254 rue St-Denis, 514/849-4526, www.hotel-st-denis.com

La Loggia $

On Amherst in the center of the Village, this charming bed-and-breakfast is in a three-story early-20th-century townhouse. Its five rooms are all uniquely decorated with antique chairs, modern art, and personal touches, like vibrant cushions or Persian rugs, all of which give it a homey vibe. Close to the Plateau and Berri Métro station, the hotel offers packages that include private yoga classes, personal trainer sessions, or a course in sculpture. Breakfast is made with local, fair-trade, and organic ingredients and is served on the terrace in the summer.

MAP 4: 1637 rue Amherst, 514/524-2493, www.laloggia.ca

Plateau Mont-Royal   Map 5

L'Hôtel de l'Institut de tourisme et d'hôtellerie du Québec $$

This hotel, training ground for future hotel and restaurant staff, has 42 rooms, 24-hour desk service, and a concierge to help with travel needs. Most rooms have their own balcony, and all rooms are reachable via the elevators, which are adorned with notable 3-D murals from 1975, created by the late local artist Claude Théberge. Ideally located in the Plateau, it is within walking distance to downtown and is directly above a Sherbrooke Métro station. The hotel offers secure

L'Hôtel de l'Institut de tourisme et d'hôtellerie du Québec

bike parking (free) and car parking (for an additional fee).

MAP 5: 3535 rue St-Denis, 514/282-5120, www.ithq.qc.ca

Anne Ma Soeur Anne $

In the heart of the Plateau, this clean, no-frills hotel features 17 rooms—some facing onto the busy rue St-Denis and others onto a quiet courtyard. Most rooms are outfitted with Murphy beds, and all have kitchenettes; a couple of suites with private terraces are suitable for families. Continental breakfast, consisting of croissants, jam, and orange juice, is available to be delivered via basket to your door in the morning. This hotel is perfect for budget travelers looking to put their dollars toward Montréal's restaurants and spirits. Parking doesn't come with the rooms, though there's a municipal lot nearby.

MAP 5: 4119 rue St-Denis, 514/281-3187, www.annemasoeuranne.com

Auberge de la Fontaine $

Offering 21 rooms and suites that look out onto Parc La Fontaine, this hotel is intimate, but not quite as intimate as a B&B. The location is perfect, and if you wake up early enough, you'll be able to start your day with the complimentary continental breakfast buffet. Like most spots in the Plateau, Auberge de la Fontaine does not offer much parking, so book a spot ahead of time or leave your car at home (street parking is bananas in Montréal anyways).

MAP 5: 1301 rue Rachel E., 514/597-0166, www.aubergedelafontaine.com

Gingerbread Manor $

Just off of Carré St-Louis between St-Denis and St-Laurent, this charming bed-and-breakfast in a Victorian three-story townhouse built in 1885 is a different way to see the city. With large bay windows, original molding, and an attached carriage house, it harkens back to a bygone golden age. Treat yourself by booking the Frotenac, a spacious room with original stained-glass windows, or the Champlain, on the top floor, with an amazing bay window and view of Mont Royal's Cross. A hot breakfast includes croissants, homemade jam, and fruit salad. Parking is available upon request and for an additional fee.

MAP 5: 3445 ave. Laval, 514/597-2804, www.gingerbreadmanor.com

Auberge de la Fontaine

Like a Hotel $

As its name suggests, Like a Hotel is not *quite* a hotel. Instead of a front desk, you check in virtually; visitors pay a reasonable rate for privacy and autonomy but forgo room service and maid service, which are not offered. Suites are spacious, well-decorated, and feature fully equipped kitchens. They usually have pull-out couches or Murphy beds, making them perfect for family trips. Like a Hotel offers three more locations in Montréal: another location in Plateau Mont-Royal, one in Vieux-Montréal, and one downtown.

MAP 5: 54 Rue Prince Arthur E., 514-868-8419, www.likeahotel.com

Pensione Popolo $

The owners of music venues Casa del Popolo and La Sala Rossa also own a small, European-style *pensione* consisting of one apartment that can sleep up to 10 people and four rooms, half with shared baths and half with private baths. Ideally located on the border of the Plateau and Mile End, it's perfect for the self-sufficient traveler looking for a no-frills bed. Guests also get 25 percent off tapas and two free passes per room to see bands playing at the Sala Rossa during their stay.

MAP 5: 4871 blvd. St-Laurent, 514/284-0122, www.casadelpopolo.com

Shézelles $

Covered in ivy in the summer, Shézelles is a homey, sunny B&B with a West Coast feel. Rent a room upstairs—you'll share a couple of impeccably clean bathrooms—or call dibs on the ground-level suite, which features a Jacuzzi tub popular with honeymooners. (My personal favorite is the sky room, on the top floor—you'll need to open and close a trapdoor to enter, but the rooftop terrace is worth the climb!)

MAP 5: 4272 Rue Berri, 514/849-8694, www.shezelles.com

Mile End and Petite-Italie   Map 6

Le 9 et Demi $

Le 9 et Demi is a clean, warm, welcoming B&B with a bit of a hostel sensibility (guests are welcome to make use of the kitchen), located in a gorgeous old building dating from 1900 on St-Denis. Just a hop from the Beaubien Métro station, this is the perfect place to stay if you'd like to be close to Little Italy and the Marché Jean-Talon but have the option of one quick Métro trip to get downtown. It features five rooms, one of which is a suite; prices are quite reasonable and bathrooms are shared.

MAP 6: 6529 rue St-Denis, 514/842-4451, www.le9etdemi.com

DAY TRIPS

Mont-Tremblant 231
Lower Laurentians 236
Cantons de l'Est 242

One of the greatest things about Montréal is its proximity to nature. Montrealers are always heading out of the city for some antiquing, apple-picking, or cycling in the Cantons de l'Est (Eastern Townships in English) or leaving the office en route to some of the best skiing on the East Coast and a cozy chalet weekend in the Laurentides (the Laurentians).

Chez Trudeau, a down-to-earth diner with a great sign in Granby

Depending on which way you leave the island—to the mountains in the north or to the valleys in the south—you're headed for some diverse geography. To the southeast, you'll find lowlands, lakes, and rolling hills, populated with wineries and towns, each with its own—often British-influenced—style. Located 80 kilometers from Montréal and bordering on New Hampshire and Vermont, certain parts of the Eastern Townships can seem almost indistinguishable from their American counterparts. The covered bridges, Victorian gingerbread houses, and antiques stores give it a certain Anglophone touch you don't always see elsewhere in the province.

This was a predominantly English area until the 1970s, and English and French are spoken so fluently here it can be hard to figure out the native from nonnative speakers. Driving out of the city, you'll pass three unique Monteregian hills. Mont Saint-Hilaire, Rougemont, and Yamaska explode out of the flatlands; these mini-mountains, created by what many think may have been intrusions of long extinct volcanoes, are now accessible ski stations in the winter.

Leave Montréal to the north and you'll soon be in thick, dense boreal forests and driving through the foothills of the Laurentian mountains, first colonized in the mid-1800s. It was a priest, Antoine Labelle, who saw the area's potential and pushed to exploit it. Saddened by the number of French Canadians moving south

HIGHLIGHTS

✪ **MOST MULTICULTURAL COTTAGE COUNTRY:** Jewish, Francophone, and English populations pioneered the summer existence of **Sainte-Agathe-des-Monts,** and to this day all three cultures are evident in the town, making it the most culturally diverse in the region (page 237).

✪ **BEST ROCK CLIMBING:** Experienced and inexperienced climbers alike come to **Parc Régional Val-David and Val-Morin,** the site of the best rock climbing in Québec as well as some delicately preserved ecology (page 239).

✪ **BEST PLACE TO SEE THE LEAVES IN FALL:** There's no better way to see the seasons change than by riding or walking along the **Parc Linéaire Le P'tit Train du Nord,** which is 230 kilometers long and cuts through the Laurentians (page 239).

✪ **BEST KID-FRIENDLY SIGHT:** More than 1,000 animals call the **Granby Zoo** home. With unique attractions like Hippo River, it's a great day out for the kids (page 242).

✪ **BEST CHILDREN'S MUSEUM:** Interactive exhibits at the **Museum of Science and Nature** in Sherbrooke beautifully mix history and art (page 243).

✪ **BEST SUMMER STAGE:** Located in the picturesque town of Knowlton, **Theatre Lac Brome** is one of the most respected English summer stages in the province, with performances of classic and contemporary plays (page 244).

✪ **BEST PLACE TO TUNE UP YOUR GREGORIAN CHANT:** Located on the banks of Lake Memphremagog, **Abbaye Saint-Benoît-du-Lac** is home to 50 monks who produce some of the tastiest cheese and gourmet goods in the region. A bonus: They'll also let you pray with them and join in a little Gregorian chant three times a day (page 246).

✪ **MOST LIKELY TO GIVE YOU VERTIGO:** One of the longest pedestrian suspension bridges in the world can be found at the **Parc de la Gorge-de-Coaticook.** The bridge sits 50 meters above the gorge (page 247).

✪ **MOST UNEXPECTED WAY TO EXPLORE THE REGION:** Few people associate Québec with wine, so following **La Route des Vins** to the many wineries in the region will give you a totally different perspective on the region and its geography (page 247).

✪ **BEST PLACE TO HIT THE SLOPES:** It's the scenery that stays with you after you've slalomed your way down the 60 picturesque alpine trails at **Ski Mont Sutton** (page 249).

Day Trips

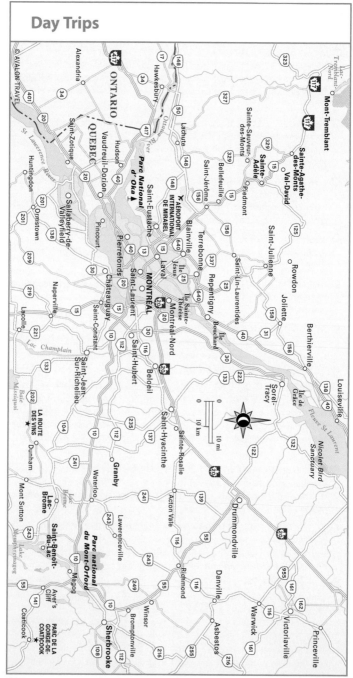

© AVALON TRAVEL

230

of the border for work, he convinced mills and logging companies and their workers to move north into the mountains. The opening of the northern railway Petit Train du Nord in the late 1800s also pushed development.

Today, this region remains particularly close to the hearts of many Montrealers, and it has become a popular place to retire. Amid the woods and the lakes and mountains are cottage towns and, of course, some of the most accessible ski slopes in the province.

PLANNING YOUR TIME

Though all of these excursions from Montréal can be made in a day by car, those who have the time should think about staying a night or two in the region for more exploring. The Laurentians, approximately an hour's drive north of the city, in particular offer different types of escapes, and you could spend weeks hiking the various trails, canoeing some of the area's bigger lakes, and camping out in a different area each night.

The Cantons de l'Est, meanwhile, are great for a day out of town or a romantic getaway; it all depends on what you're looking for. Camping is popular. The quaint inns and many towns to explore allow for a more relaxed visit, and because it's barely a 90-minute drive from the city, it's ideal for those on a short stay. This region is great to hit if you have a bit of time when traveling between Montréal and Québec. If you want to make a stop on your way out of the city, the town of Chambly, with its 18th-century fort, is a great place for a pit stop.

Weekends are always busiest no matter the time of year or whether you're heading north or to the southeast. If you're flexible in your travel times, avoid the crowds and opt for a midweek excursion, then head back to the city for the weekend. Between December 15 and March 15 snow tires are the law for any vehicle registered in the province, so if you're driving a rental you'll be covered. But if you've got your own set of wheels, sticking to major (read, plowed) roads and avoiding dirt tracks is the safest bet. Many of the roads, especially those that lead to out-of-the-way, privately owned chalets and cottages, rely on local residents to shovel and plow them.

Mont-Tremblant

With its lakes, streams, mountains, and untamed wilderness, Mont-Tremblant is one of the most popular destinations in the Laurentians. A 90-minute drive from Montréal, it boasts a national park and an internationally renowned resort that attracts tourists year-round.

Autumn is an ideal time to head up to the mountains and catch the tremendous colors of the leaves as they turn. The mixed Laurentian forest, with its boreal and big woods species, is one of the most diverse in the world, and its beauty is undeniable.

This is considered the premier ski and snowboarding region in Eastern Canada, and during winter (generally December to March) sport enthusiasts and those just wanting to kick back in an Icelandic sweater with a drink next to a roaring fire flock to the region. Though the biggest draw is the resort itself, where you can spend an entire vacation and never get bored, it's also worth visiting the region's many heritage buildings and churches, all of which can be discovered in the old towns.

Though it's possible to visit Mont-Tremblant in a day (provided you rise early and stay late), you'd be advised to stay at least a night to get the most out of the region, especially if you plan on doing outdoor activities.

SIGHTS AND RECREATION

Mont-Blanc

Just over an hour's drive from Montréal is Mont-Blanc (1006 Route 117, St-Faustin-Lac-Carré, 800/567-6715, www.skimontblanc.com, 9am-4pm Mon.-Fri., 8:30am-4pm Sat.-Sun. and holidays late Nov.-early Apr., $52 adult), the second-highest mountain in the Laurentians. Boasting 42 trails, including 5 expert trails, it also has a major ski school and is one of the more affordable hills in the region, perfect for beginners and pros. An on-site spa is the perfect answer to a day on the slopes.

Mont-Tremblant National Park

Smack dab in the middle of the Laurentian mountains, Mont-Tremblant National Park (819/688-2281, www.sepaq.com/pq/mot, daily 24 hours, weather permitting, $7 adult, $3 child) is the biggest and oldest of the province's national parks. Measuring 1,500 square kilometers, it boasts six rivers, 400 lakes and streams, and 40 diverse animal species, including wolves and moose. The park is so vast that it contains four different sectors, accessible from different entrances:

deer on a mountain overlooking the village of Mont-Tremblant

La Diable, La Pimbina, L'Assomption, and La Cachée. Each sector offers unique activities, so do some research beforehand to see what might be best for you. Each sector also has its own visitors center—drop in when you arrive to learn about the park and its wildlife, including wildlife spottings or warnings.

Mont-Tremblant, which literally means "trembling mountain," is a popular holiday spot year-round; kayaks and canoes traverse the rivers and streams, while pedal boats and rowboats share the lakes with fishers and swimmers. Over 150 kilometers of hiking trails are available as well as 59 kilometers of mountain-biking tracks. These turn into cross-country skiing and snowshoeing trails in the winter. Unique to the park is the Via Ferrata du Diable, a mix of hiking and climbing that takes you through part of the park that is not accessible otherwise.

If there's one northern pastime you have to indulge in, it's dogsledding. Not far from the park's Diable entrance is Nordic Adventure Dog Sledding (Place St-Bernard, 819/681-4848, www.tremblantactivities.com, $143). The guides will teach you how a powerful team of eight harnessed huskies is steered and stopped before you hop on the sled to experience the ride firsthand. The ride winds up mountains, across frozen lakes, and through thick forest with a quick stop for hot chocolate to warm you up. Reservations are required.

Mont-Tremblant Resort

Just next door to the national park is Mont-Tremblant Resort (1000 chemin des Voyageurs, Mont-Tremblant, 888/738-1777, www.tremblant.ca, 8:30am-3:30pm daily late Nov.-mid-Apr., $87 adult), the premier ski resort in Eastern Canada and one of the best-known spots in the region. The first lodge and ski lift opened here in 1939, and no one has looked back since. The view from the mountain remains just as stunning now as then, and you can see the whole countryside from atop the 95 runs and numerous lifts. Acres of ramps, rails, and jumps are also available. Come for the day or stay overnight in one of the resort's brightly colored, Disney-fied versions of a mountain town. In summer, activities like biking and hiking take over the hills.

Ville de Mont-Tremblant

The actual village from which everything else got its name, the town of Mont-Tremblant (877/425-2434, www.villedemont-tremblant.qc.ca) is a nice change of pace from the hustle and bustle of the resort. Established in the late 1800s, Mont-Tremblant was one of many new villages founded by Father Antoine Labelle, who encouraged city folk to colonize the country. Since the late 1930s it has become a popular village, and the stores and restaurants reflect that. Take a stroll down the main strip, or pop into the Maison des Arts et de la Culture Saint-Faustin (1171 rue de la Pisciculture, 819/688-2676, www.maisondesarts.ca, 11am-5pm Wed.-Sun.) to see the latest in the region's arts. Those visiting in the summer can get a taste of local life at Le Marché d'Été de Mont-Tremblant (1875 chemin du Village, 9am-1pm Sat. early July-early Sept.), the seasonal local market.

RESTAURANTS

There are tons of restaurants in and around Mont-Tremblant Resort, but there are also plenty of independently run places worth checking out—many of them located in old converted houses—only a 10- to 15-minute drive away. If you head into downtown Mont-Tremblant, stop at Couleur Café (415 rue Léonard, 819/681-0723, www.couleurcafe.ca, 7:30am-5pm daily, $6-8) for a coffee—it's fair-trade and roasted on-site.

Not far away, Seb l'Artisan Culinaire (444 rue St-Georges, 819/429-6991, www.resto-seb.com, 6pm-11pm Thurs.-Mon., table d'hôte $50) is modern yet romantic. This converted old house is the setting for dishes made with fresh local ingredients, like lamb gnocchi and local pork with kimchi, beets, and bok choy. The food is hearty but delicate, and the wine list is full of soon-to-be favorites.

Those lusting after some Québec duck or seafood should head to Le Cheval de Jade (688 rue de St-Jovite, 819/425-5233, www.chevaldejade.com, 5pm-10pm Tues.-Sat., $25-40), with delicacies like bouillabaisse, scallops, and black cod on the menu. Situated in a house that was built in 1925, the restaurant has an elegant, relaxed vibe. Though known for seafood, Le Cheval de Jade also offers a unique specialty, duckling *à la Rouennaise,* a French dish in which the duck carcass is squeezed in a "duck press" that extracts the juices. A hard-to-find delicacy, even in France, it's a must for any hard-core foodie. Call ahead to make a reservation for the dish, which serves two for $100.

There's no better place to dig into traditional, hearty Québécois grub than in the backcountry, surrounded by woods and mountains. Southeast of the ski hills is La Tablée des Pionniers (1357 rue St-Faustin, Saint-Faustin-Lac-Carré, 855/688-2101, www.latableedespionniers.com, 8:30am-2pm Sat.-Sun. in the sugar season). This traditional Québec sugar shack serves dishes such as eggs and sausages in maple syrup, baked beans, and maple taffy; it's sure to put you in the best kind of food coma.

HOTELS

When it comes to hotels in Mont-Tremblant, the obvious choice is the Fairmont Mont-Tremblant (3045 chemin de la Chapelle, 866/540-4415, www.fairmont.com/tremblant, $250-525), with its luxurious rooms, great views, and the convenience of skiing down the mountain and right up to your hotel. The spa and the restaurant with a roaring winter fire are the icing on the cake.

Built in 1942 by Joe and Mary Ryan, the founders of the Mont-Tremblant Resort, Château Beauvallon (6385 Montée Ryan, 888/681-6611, www.chateaubeauvallon.com, $200 and up) is equally as luxurious as the Fairmont but off the well-beaten path. Offering 70 different suites, Beauvallon has a secluded feel; it offers in-room breakfast and, for dinner, a steak and sushi bar.

Many of the best places to stay are small inns a few minutes away from the mountain. Looking out over Lac Mercier and adjacent to the P'tit Train du Nord bike trail, the Auberge la Porte Rouge (1874 chemin du Village, 819/425-3505, www.aubergelaporte-rouge.com, $184 and up) looks and feels more like a friend's cottage than a midsize inn. Six rentable chalets sleep 4-16 people, and the auberge offers packages and activities to suit your needs.

If bed-and-breakfasts are more your thing, the Crystal Inn (100 Joseph Thibault, 819/681-7775, www.crystal-inn.com, $120 and up) offers an intimate and unique experience. Each of the four suites is decorated according to the healing powers of different crystals—agate, amethyst, sun stone—and each room has its own fireplace and is decorated with hand-painted murals. Breakfast (contact them ahead of time if you have dietary restrictions) and a session at the in-house nature spa are also included.

If you prefer to be self-sufficient, check out the stylish and modern chalets available for rent from Côté Nord Tremblant (210 Chemin des Ecorces, Lac-Supérieur, 888/624-6097, www.cotenordtremblant.com, $200 and up), just outside of Mont-Tremblant. The lake views and proximity to hiking, snowshoeing, and skiing make the chalets a perfect spot for a rural getaway, and the accommodations will be easier on your pocketbook if you're traveling with a group.

INFORMATION AND SERVICES

Covering all aspects of the area, including the resort and the old Mont-Tremblant village, Tourisme Mont-Tremblant (877/605-4746, www.mont-tremblant.ca) has all the information you need to get your bearings in the area. Local maps and even package deals are accessible on the website, and it also has links to the chamber of commerce and detailed information on getting to and from the area. Once there, the Tourist Information Bureau (5080 Montée Ryan, 9am-5pm daily) will be able to help you with anything else.

GETTING THERE
BY AIR
Boutique airline Porter (888/619-8622, www.flyporter.com) offers direct flights to Mont-Tremblant International Airport from the Billy Bishop Airport in Toronto; Air Canada (888/247-2262, www.air-canada.com) offers flights between Pearson Airport in Toronto and Mont-Tremblant International Airport.

All international and national flights to Montréal arrive at Pierre Trudeau International Airport (www.admtl.com) in Dorval. A shuttle bus service offered by Skyport (877/605-4746, www.skyportinternational.com, $100 one-way) departs Trudeau for Mont-Tremblant during skiing season, mid-December to mid-April. Check the website for exact rates and times.

BY BUS
A coach is available daily from Montréal's main bus terminal, Gare d'Autocars (1717 rue Berri, 514/842-2281, www.gamtl.com). The trip with Galland (514/333-9555, $65 round-trip) takes just under three hours and will deposit you at a gas station/convenience store an easy walk to town.

BY CAR
Driving from Montréal to Mont-Tremblant couldn't be simpler. Take Highway 40 West to Highway 15 North and drive straight for about 90 minutes. After Sainte-Agathe, Highway 15 becomes Route 117 North; continue until you get to Mont-Tremblant.

GETTING AROUND
The easiest way to get around Mont-Tremblant is by car. If you don't have your own, there is a Discount Car Rental (1270 Route 117, 844/562-2886, www.discountcar.ca) agency at the edge of town. Public buses are available for $3 per ride; the schedule and routes can be found on the chamber of commerce's website (www.ccdemont-tremblant.com).

Lower Laurentians

Even closer to the city than Mont-Tremblant, about an hour or so drive from downtown, there are different areas to be explored that are perfect for an entire day, or even just an afternoon. Still part of the Laurentians, the geography overall is slightly flatter, and though a few ski hills can still be found, you won't find bigger mountains than those in the north. Instead, the Lower Laurentians are populated with towns and villages and summer homes laid out along the shores of freshwater lakes. Forests and low mountains still define the area, but it's the lakes and villages that set it apart.

Many of the places could be visited individually in a day, or if you get an early start or stay out late, a few places that are closer together, like Sainte-Agathe-des-Monts and Val-David, are doable in a single day. If you want to take advantage of the area but only have a day to spare, pick a single town and spend the day exploring by foot. Returning to the city along smaller roads is also a great way to feel like you're getting the most out of your day.

SIGHTS AND RECREATION
Oka

Northwest of the city, just off the island, is Oka National Park (2020 chemin Oka, 450/479-8365, www.sepaq. com/pq/oka, $10 adult). Easily accessible (it's about a 45-minute drive east of the city), it offers outdoor recreation year-round. June-September locals flock to the beaches on the shores of Lac des Deux-Montagnes for a swim or to try their hand at windsurfing, one of the lake's popular sports. Another

one of the park's biggest draws is the wetlands, where marshes mingle with the boreal forest. Explore them by walking the Grande Baie trail or canoeing through the Rivière des Serpents. In 1742, the Sulpicians defined their presence in this area when they built the Way of the Cross. Revisit the stone structures and chapels by walking the 4.5-kilometer Calvaire d'Oka path. In winter, the park offers 47 kilometers of cross-country skiing trails and 16 kilometers of snowshoeing. Throughout summer the park is accessible by Route 644 in the east and Highway 640 in the west, with the latter closed during winter.

The Marina d'Oka (257 rue des Anges, 450/479-8323, mid-May-mid-Oct.) is one of the more picturesque marinas in the area. Located on Lac des Deux-Montagnes, accessed by downtown Oka, the marina has a small shop that sells boating accessories and decorative items, as well as seafaring wear. Shand Thai (261 rue des Anges, 450/479-9957, www.shandthai.com, 4pm-close Thurs.-Sun. Apr. and Sept., 4pm-close Mon.-Fri., 3pm-close Sat.-Sun. early May-late Aug., 4pm-close Fri.-Sun. Oct.-late Mar.), which serves Thai and Cambodian food right next to the marina, is a great place to grab a bite and look out over the water.

Saint-Sauveur

Head north out of the city and in less than an hour you'll hit Saint-Sauveur. Incorporated in 1855, the village and the surrounding ski hills have since become a weekend destination. There's still a feel of an old downtown main street, though the houses have been turned into restaurants and stores, many of them are dedicated to sports gear and winter wear, with a few dedicated to antiques.

Those looking to nab a bargain are likely to find it at the city's many outlet stores. Nike, Diesel, Guess, La Senza, and Reebok can all be found at Les Factoreries (100 ave. Guindon, 450/240-0880, www.factoreriestanger. com, 10am-6pm Mon.-Wed., 10am-9pm Thurs.-Fri., 10am-5pm Sat.-Sun.).

The town also plays host to a yearly celebration of music and dance. Around since the early 1990s, the Festival des Arts de Saint-Sauveur (www.fass.ca, late July-early Aug.) has everything from contemporary to hip-hop dance and traditional music from around the world. Many of the events are free.

Also in summer, Parc Aquatique du Mont Saint-Sauveur (350 ave. St-Denis, 450/227-4671, www.parcaquatique.com, $37 adult, $30 youth, $17 child) is one of the area's biggest attractions. One of Canada's largest water parks, it features rafting, a wave pool, a tidal-wave river, and slides. It also has lots of non-water fun like alpine slides and zip-lining.

Thanks to a few hard-working snow machines, Mont-Saint-Sauveur (350 rue St-Denis, 450/277-4671, www. montsaintsauveur.com, Dec.-late Apr., $55) has one of the longest winter seasons in the country, with hills and snowboard runs open well into April. The hills also have nighttime lighting for after-work runs, and the latest attraction is a year-round alpine roller coaster.

✪ Sainte-Agathe-des-Monts

Continue farther north on Route 117 and you'll reach the quaint town of Sainte-Agathe-des-Monts (www.

a church in Saint-Sauveur

ville.sainte-agathe-des-monts.qc.ca), established in 1849. Situated on Lac des Sables, it's one of the most popular cottage towns in the region. By the 1860s it was a thriving, mostly Francophone community that eventually grew to include many Anglophone residents. Today, it's one of the most diverse towns in the region, with a large population of Jewish summer residents who were originally drawn here in the early part of the 20th century, not only for the town's proximity to Montréal but also for the good, clean mountain air (part of Mordecai Richler's *The Apprenticeship of Duddy Kravitz* was set here). For a fair number of years one of the town's main draws was its benefits for the ill and convalescing and those suffering from tuberculosis. The Laurentian and Mount Sinai Sanatoriums were both here, and you can see their influences reflected in the architecture of old homes equipped with large covered balconies and solariums.

At the end of the main street (rue Principale)—lined with the original Catholic church and restaurants and boutiques that have been refurbished to capture their original glory—you'll find the Lac des Sables and the Croisières Alouette (866/326-3656, www.croisierealouette.com, late May-mid Oct., $22). A staple in the area since the 1940s, these 50-minute cruises give you a bit of context by pointing out historical sites, celebrity homes, and features of the landscape. They're especially nice in fall when the leaves are multicolored.

Val-David

Few towns in this region have the same hippie commune vibe as Val-David (www.valdavid.com), which is slowly but surely drawing a younger crowd. Nestled in the Laurentians, this former mill town has become known for the amateur artists who work and live here. The town offers self-guided tours that point out public art works and take you to artist studios. Since the town is highly concentrated, it's fairly easy to get around, with many of the sites next door to each other. The Centre d'Exposition de Val-David (2495 rue de l'Église, 819/322-7474, www.culture.val-david.qc.ca, 11am-5pm daily summer, 11am-5pm Wed.-Sun. winter) holds exhibits by local and regional artists with exhibitions changing regularly.

Those interested in the history of the town's architecture can guide themselves around the various historical buildings, including Magasin Général Alexis-Guindon (2475 rue de l'Église), a general store built in 1919 that remains virtually unchanged, and La Maison Narcisse et Olivier Ménard (1235 chemin du 7e Rang), an old-school log house (now a private residence) built in 1850.

the river bordering Val-David

✪ Parc Régional Val-David and Val-Morin

For the best climbing on the country's east coast head to the Dufresne Sector of the Parc Régional Val-David and Val-Morin (1165 chemin du Condor, 888/322-7030, www.parcregional.com). The site of the first ever rock-climbing competition in Québec, the park now has over 500 routes, including walls for those just beginning to learn and walls that'll challenge those who've been doing it for a lifetime. Dedicated to preserving the local ecosystem—it was created largely by locals—it is also a great place to bird-watch, check out the native plants, hike through in the summer, and cross-country ski in the winter.

✪ Parc Linéaire Le P'tit Train du Nord

After drawing people to the region in the mid-1800s, Antoine Labelle's second feat was the construction of a railway (built between 1891 and 1901) that carried visitors and holiday makers from the outer reaches of the city all the way into the northern Laurentians. It was this advancement that allowed the area to grow. Made obsolete 100 years later by highways and cars, the old railway is now the Parc Linéaire Le P'tit Train du Nord (800/561-6673, www.laurentians.com/parclineaire), a 230-kilometer-long recreational trail running from Saint-Jérôme to Mont-Laurier.

Providing a north-south crossing, it's most used by cyclists in the summer, many of whom spend days exploring the region. If cycling's not your bag, inline skating and hiking are also permitted on the trail and will still let you see the beauty of the area and the stunning vistas the trail offers. In winter, snowmobiling is allowed between Labelle and Mont-Laurier, and cross-country skiing is possible between Saint-Jérôme and Val-David. All along the trail, the old railway stations have been converted into cafés, repair shops, and information centers. There are campsites along the way, and the park will help you arrange baggage transport.

Village du Père Noël

The spirit of Christmas, and Santa himself, can be found throughout the summer and holiday season at Village du Père Noël (987 Morin, 819/322-2146, www.noel.qc.ca, 9am-5pm daily June-late Aug. and Labor Day weekend, 10am-5pm daily mid-Dec.-early Jan., except Dec. 25, $20 adult and child). This outdoor children's play park offers a ton of activities for kids ages two and up. A tree house, electrical train, goat run, zip line, and slides are open no matter the weather, and kids will get a kick out of Santa's house, where they can meet the man himself.

RESTAURANTS

Before heading out for a morning of apple-picking in Oka, warm up with a coffee and a pastry. Chocolaterie Mathilde Fays (47 rue Notre-Dame, Oka, 514/622-9411, www.chocolateriemf.com, 10am-6pm Mon.-Fri., 10am-5pm Sat.-Sun., $5-30) has a sunny, rustic patio and also sells handmade chocolates—you really can't go wrong.

A quick drive outside of Oka, Au Pied de Cochon Sugar Shack (11382 Rang de la Fresnière, Saint-Benoît-de-Mirabel, http://cabane.aupieddecochon.ca, open during the harvest season, prices vary) is a meaty, mapley, prix-fixe treat. You'll need to make reservations well ahead of time to secure a spot, but it's well worth it.

Orange & Pamplemousse (120 rue Principale, Saint-Sauveur, 450/227-4330, www.orangepamplemousse.com, 8am-2:30pm Mon.-Tues., 8am-2:30pm and 5pm-9pm Wed.-Thurs. and Sun., 8am-2:30pm and 5pm-9:30pm Fri.-Sat., $20) in Saint-Sauveur is a modern bistro with an outdoor patio in summer. They serve breakfast staples like eggs Benedict and crêpes and dynamic dinner fare like poutine and grilled jumbo shrimp, all at reasonable prices.

For more classic bistro fare, there's **La Bohème** (251 rue Principale, Saint-Sauveur, 450/227-6644, www.resto-boheme.com, Wed.-Sun. 5pm-10pm, $30-60), a dark, cozy neighborhood staple with a bar that's often busy. Dishes include mussels and fries and New York steak.

Restaurant Au Petit Poucet

In Val-David there's no better place to find a hearty breakfast than **Restaurant Au Petit Poucet** (1030 Route 117, Val-David, 819/322-2246, www.aupetitpoucet.ca, 6:30am-4pm daily, $10-20), which serves Canadian and Québécois fare in a cozy, cabin-like environment. Try the maple-smoked ham, *tourtière* (meat pie), and split-pea soup, and for dessert, try a tableside pulled-maple treat—you bring an appetite, they'll bring the snow.

HOTELS

When it comes to spending the night in **Oka National Park** (2020 chemin Oka, 450/479-8365, www.sepaq.com/pq/oka) the only accommodation choice you have is your tent or theirs. That being said, the park does offer rental Huttopia tents ($102 per night and up), which are large enough for a family of four and have a kitchen, two bunk areas, and even wood floors—perfect if you're not in the mood for roughing it. You can reserve tents through the park's website.

In the middle of Saint-Sauveur Valley and overlooking the ski hill is **Hotel St-Sauveur** (500 chemin des Frênes, 450/227-1800, www.hotelst-sauveur.ca, $109-309), a modern hotel that mixes cozy, antique-style furnishings and minimal design. It's a great option, especially if you're traveling in a group. Each unit has a fireplace, balcony, and a kitchen where you can whip up your own breakfasts.

Reminiscent of an old ski chalet—peaked roofs, stone walls in the foyer—the **Manoir Saint-Sauveur** (246 chemin du Lac Millette, Saint-Sauveur, 800/361-0505, www.manoir-saint-sauveur.com, $169-350) is in the middle of the village, with views overlooking the slopes. Those staying in summer can hang out at the outdoor pools or play a round of tennis before heading off for an afternoon hike. Luxuriously decorated rooms are all fitted with an espresso

PICK YOUR OWN: APPLE ORCHARDS

Vergers (apple orchards) flourish in Québec, and from September to late October the Eastern Townships are full of different varieties of apples ready to be picked. The perfect afternoon outing, especially if you're with the kids, apple-picking offers a great escape from the city as well as a closer look at the leaves in all their autumn glory. Orchards can be found throughout the Townships, but a few are just a short drive from Montréal. Though most orchards are open throughout the week in high season, call ahead if you're unsure of times, since opening hours are often dependent on weather conditions.

- **Cidrerie et Verger Léo Boutin:** 710 Rang de la Montagne, Mont Saint-Grégoire, 450/346-3326, www.vergerboutin.com, 8am-6pm daily Sept.-Oct., 9am-5pm daily Nov.-Aug.

- **Verger Biologique Maniadakis:** 1150 Route 209, Franklin Centre, 514/946-3414, www.vergerbiologique.com, 1pm-4pm Mon.-Fri., 10am-6pm Sat.-Sun. (offering organic apples and pears)

- **Verger du Flâneur:** 1161 La Petite Caroline, Rougemont, 450/469-0505, 9am-5pm daily Sept.-Oct.

- **Verger du Flanc Nord:** 835 chemin Rouillard, Mont Saint-Hilaire, 450/464-7432, www.vergerduflancnord.com, 8am-7pm daily mid-Aug.-mid-Nov.

- **Verger du Pavillon de la Pomme:** 1130 Sir Wilfrid Laurier, Mont Saint-Hilaire, 450/464-2654, www.pavillondelapomme.com, 9am-6pm daily

- **Vergers et Cidrerie Denis Charbonneau:** 575 Rang de la Montagne, Mont Saint-Grégoire, 450/347-9184, www.vergersdc.qc.ca, store open 9am-7pm daily, check website for seasonal picking schedule

machine, Wi-Fi, and views of the surrounding hills.

Staying true to the area's roots, Auberge du Lac des Sables (230 rue St-Venant, Sainte-Agathe-des-Monts, 800/567-8329, www.aubergedulac.com, $169-300), with its back to the forest and with a view of the lake, exudes good, clean mountain air. Though the interior design is nothing spectacular, large windows and lake views more than make up for it.

INFORMATION AND SERVICES

Each town has its own tourist center with all the information you need for the town and surrounding area. Oka National Park's Discovery and Information Center (450/479-8365, www.sepaq.com/pq/oka, 8am-5pm daily mid-May-mid-Oct.) is at the northeastern corner of the park, and the Oka National Park's Le Littoral Visitors Centre (450/479-8365, www.sepaq.com/pq/oka, 8am-4pm daily year-round, closing hours later in summer), which has a ski shop, waxing room, first-aid services, and a restaurant, is in the southwest.

Saint-Sauveur's tourist office (3 rue Filion, Saint-Sauveur, 450/227-3417, 11am-7pm Sat.-Sun. May-Oct., www.valleesaintsauveur.com) covers all aspects of the region. The Sainte-Agathe-des-Monts Tourist Information Office (24 rue St-Paul, 888/326-0457, www.sainte-agathe.org, 9am-6pm daily) is open year-round.

In Val-David, road maps, brochures, and souvenirs are all available at the Val-David tourist office (2525 de l'Église, 888/323-7030, ext. 4325, 9am-5pm daily mid-May-mid-Oct. and mid-Dec.-mid-Mar., hours vary rest of year).

GETTING THERE AND AROUND

BY BUS

All of the Laurentians can be reached from the city with Galland (514/333-9555) coach lines. Trips (and tickets) are available daily from Montréal's main bus terminal, Gare d'Autocars (1717 rue Berri, 514/842-2281, www.gamtl.com). The same coach that takes you to Mont-Tremblant will also take you to Saint-Sauveur in about 1.75 hours ($30 round-trip), Val-David in 2.25 hours ($42 round-trip), and Sainte-Agathe-des-Monts in 2.5 hours ($46 round-trip).

BY CAR

Driving is by far the easiest and fastest way to get here and get around, especially if you want to see more than one village or are taking equipment like ski gear. From Montréal, take Highway 40 West to Highway 15 North and watch out for the signposts. All of the towns are easily accessible off of Highway 15 (which eventually becomes Route 117 North). To get to Oka, take Highway 15 to Highway 13, then head west on Highway 640; road signs will help you along the way.

Cantons de l'Est

Southeast of the city, you'll find the low, rolling hills, flatlands, and picturesque towns of the Cantons de l'Est (the Eastern Townships). Traditionally the home of the Abenaki First Nation, the Eastern Townships were later colonized by the United Empire Loyalists, who sided with the British during the American Revolution. Though many of the town's roots started with the Loyalists, it wasn't until the turn of the 19th century that immigration from the United States exploded, especially by wealthy folk looking for a place to build their dream summer home. This distinct patrimony sets the Eastern Townships apart from the rest of the province, and it can still be seen today in the architecture, culture, and language.

Interesting towns and villages can be found throughout the region. You can easily visit one or two in a day. Depending on what sights you're attracted to, an afternoon or day in the region is enough time to get the overall feel of the place. If you want to do more serious exploring, it's better to spend at least one night in one of the many towns, and a weekend is ideal for those interested in cycling around the region or exploring the many wineries.

SIGHTS

GRANBY

One of the bigger towns on the Eastern Townships map, Granby (www.ville.granby.qc.ca) has a lovely old main street (called rue Principale) that you can stroll along, browsing the shops and cafés and seeing some of the area's older architecture. Built on the textile, lumber, and dairy businesses, it is one of the more commercial towns, but the main attraction is the Granby Zoo.

✪ Granby Zoo

The Granby Zoo (1050 blvd. David-Bouchard, 877/472-6299, www.zoogranby.ca, 10am-7pm daily late

RIDE THE ORFORD EXPRESS

Russia may have the Trans-Siberian Railway, but the Eastern Townships have the Orford Express (720 rue Minto, Marché de la Gare, 866/575-8081, www.orfordexpress.com, Wed.-Sun. May-late Oct., $50-125). Mixing a little sightseeing with snack options or a gourmet meal, the train takes you through the countryside of the Eastern Townships. Options range from a quicker two-hour tour to a more leisurely four-hour tour.

The train ride offers views of the region that you might not get otherwise. The train consists of three restaurant-coach cars; each is decorated to recall the good old days of rail travel, with white tablecloths, soft lighting, and sumptuous curtains on the windows of the main car. The latest edition to the trains is the lounge car, with panoramic windows that give you an unobstructed view of the landscape.

Several different journeys, covering different meals, are available, including a weekend brunch outing, a couple of lunch options, and a dinner outing. The Express train offers a cocktail, and you may buy finger food on-board. The food is gourmet—smoked salmon frittatas, Angus beef steaks, duck terrine. Advance notice is required for allergies and dietary restrictions.

May-Aug., 10am-5pm Sat.-Sun. Sept.-Oct., $40 adult, $27 child) is home to over 1,000 animals. Watch the hippopotamuses swimming underwater in the Hippo River, feed the sharks, see the gorillas in their very own valley, and get to know the kangaroos as they hop around.

SHERBROOKE

The largest city in the Eastern Townships and the region's commercial center, Sherbrooke (www.ville.sherbrooke.qc.ca) has a downtown core filled with shops and restaurants. First settled by Loyalists in 1793, it was originally an English-speaking town, but today the majority of the city's 200,000 residents are Francophones. It also has a large student population and is the home of two universities, the Francophone Université de Sherbrooke and the Anglophone Bishops University, which became part of the city in 2002 when Lennoxville merged with Sherbrooke.

✪ Museum of Science and Nature

Some of the best sights in the city are the many museums. Kids (and parents) get a chance to learn about

southern Québec's natural surroundings at the Museum of Science and Nature (225 rue Frontenac, 819/564-3200, www.naturesciences.qc.ca, 9am-5pm Wed.-Sun. early Sept.-mid-June, 9am-6pm daily mid-June-early Sept., $13 adult, $9 child), where interactive exhibits teach kids about everything from river ecology to renewable energy.

the Museum of Science and Nature

Musée des Beaux-Arts de Sherbrooke

Situated in the old Eastern Township Bank, the Musée des Beaux-Arts de Sherbrooke (241 rue Dufferin, 819/821-2115, www.mbas.qc.ca, noon-5pm Tues.-Sun., $10 adult) has a

243

diverse collection of works dating from the 19th up to the 21st century from both Canadian and Québécois artists.

La Société d'Histoire de Sherbrooke

Discover the history of the town and the people who created it through the permanent exhibits at La Société d'Histoire de Sherbrooke (275 rue Dufferin, 819/821-5406, www.his-toiresherbrooke.org, 9am-noon and 1pm-5pm Tues.-Fri., 1pm-5pm Sat.-Sun., call ahead to double-check hours, $7). The center also offers tours, including a self-guided one of the downtown streets ($7 with iPod and map) and a tour of the Frontenac Power Station ($3).

Réseau Riverain

Explore the area's riverside with a stroll (or ride) along the Réseau Riverain. This bike and walking path runs alongside the Magog River for 18 kilometers, connecting both with the Route Verte as well as with a network of over 130 kilometers of bike trails that circle Sherbrooke. Starting at Blanchford Park, the Magog leg takes you through the Magog River Gorge and has panels all along the pathway pointing out interesting points and historical facts.

Lion d'Or

Beer fans should pop into the Lion d'Or (2 rue de College, Lennoxville, 819/562-4589, www.lionlennoxville.com, 3pm-1am Mon., 3pm-3am Tues.-Thurs. and Sat., 11:30am-3am Fri.) for a well-pulled pint of Lion's Pride, the pub's flagship dark brown brew. It opened in 1973, and they started brewing their own in 1986, making the Lion d'Or the oldest microbrewery in Québec.

LAC BROME

Surrounding the lake of the same name, the town of Lac Brome is made up of seven smaller villages. One of the more popular tourist destinations is the village of Knowlton, whose downtown core is full of restaurants, boutiques, antiques dealers, and cafés, which are set in restored Victorian buildings.

The town is also known for the Lac Brome duck. Reared in the area, the duck is found on menus throughout the region and is celebrated with the yearly Duck Festival (www.ca-nardenfete.ca), which takes place in the month of September. Visitors are given the chance to taste the world-renowned duck, enjoy concerts and the farmers market, and watch a winner waddle its way to victory at the duck race.

Brome County Historical Museum

Stop into the Brome County Historical Museum (130 chemin Lakeside, 450/243-6782, www.brome-museum.com, 10am-5pm daily mid-May-Canadian Thanksgiving, $8 adult, $5 senior and student) in the center of town to check various artifacts connected to the area's past, including a rare World War I Fokker plane.

✪ Theatre Lac Brome

During the summer months, Theatre Lac Brome (9 Mont-Echo, Knowlton, 450/242-2270, www.theatrelacbrome.ca) becomes one of the best summer stages in the province, presenting works in English and French, from classics like *Candide* and *Around the World in 80 Days* to pieces by Canadian playwrights and its own commissioned works. Other events,

BORDER CROSSING: STANSTEAD, QUÉBEC

Stanstead is one of those rare places actually located on a border—the division line between the United States and Canada literally cuts right through the town.

Settled in the 1790s by the Taplin family, who came north from New England looking for affordable land, Stanstead and its counterpart, Derby Line, Vermont, have always had a long and intertwined history. On Canusa Street, the border cuts right down the middle, so the homes on the south side are in America and those on the north side are in Canada, with the U.S. and Canadian Customs situated at the west end of the street. The stone building now facing Customs was once a post office; cut in two by the border, it was the only international post office in the world, with two different counters: one serving Vermont and the other serving Québec.

One of the town's greatest attractions is the **Haskell Free Library and Opera House** or **La Bibliotheque Gratuite de Haskell** (93 Caswell Ave., Derby Line, VT, and 1 rue Church, Stanstead, QC, 819/876-2471, www.haskellopera.com, 9am-5pm Tues.-Wed. and Fri., 9am-6pm Thurs., 9am-2pm Sat.). A gift of Martha Stewart Haskell in memory of her late husband, who was a prominent merchant, the cultural center was deliberately built across the border in order to give residents of both sides equal access to culture and the arts.

The library is on the first floor and the music hall on the second, with the original notion that one would pay for the other. Opened in 1904, it is unlike anywhere else; where else can you watch a performance where one-half of the audience and the performers on stage are in another country entirely?

Though the border might be one of the more interesting things about the town, it's not the only thing. It's called the Capital of Granite, and many of Montréal's most famous buildings, including Sun Life (1155 rue Metcalfe), were made with granite from the nearby quarry. And like many towns in this region, it is unbelievably picturesque, with historical homes and scenic surroundings. The only difference is, when you go for a stroll in the town, you need your passport.

including musical performances, happen throughout the year.

NORTH HATLEY

Sitting on the northern shore of Lake Massawippi, North Hatley is one of the most beautiful towns in the region. A popular summer resort, it first attracted aristocrats, savvy businessmen, and other rich, mostly American tourists in the mid-1800s. The town's popularity grew even more with the opening of the railway in the 1880s, and it became a haven for many American playboys during Prohibition. Today, much of that history remains in the architecture, with many of the grand old homes converted into hotels and bed-and-breakfasts.

Though the year-round population is under 1,000, it is home to a few antiques shops, artist studios, folk art shops, and a few galleries, including **Galerie Jeannine Blais** (102 rue Main, 819/842-2784, www.galeriejeannineblais.com, 10am-5pm daily mid-June-Oct., 10am-5pm Thurs.-Mon. Nov.-mid-June), devoted entirely to art naïf.

English plays take over the summer stage at **Théâtre Piggery** (215 chemin Simard, 819/842-2431, www.piggery.com), and musical acts can be seen all year. If you're traveling with kids, check out **L'Épopée de Capelton** (5800 chemin Capelton, 819/346-9545, www.capelton.ca, 9am-5pm Sat. late May-mid-June, 9am-5pm daily late June-late Aug., 9am-5pm Labour Day weekend, $31 adults, $27 youth, $21 child), a copper mine now open for tours. In summer, cool off on the shores of the lake with a dip or a day out boating. North Hatley is a quiet town, and there isn't much in the

Try the famous cheeses of Abbaye Saint-Benoît-du-Lac.

way of sights, but that hasn't stopped it from being one of the most sought-after places in the region; those thinking of visiting and staying should book well in advance.

SUTTON

Nowhere is the historical influence of the United Empire Loyalists more prominent than in Sutton. Located about 20 minutes from the U.S. border (its neighbor is Richford, Vermont), this small town is a unique spot in the Eastern Townships, with a quaint town center that's full of remnants of British architecture. It is at the base of Mount Sutton, a popular skiing spot. Visitors can explore the town's heritage by taking a tour of the Township Trail (www.chemindescantons.qc.ca), which invites you to follow in the footsteps of the town's early settlers, who first arrived here in 1802. A four-kilometer-long walking tour will show you many important sites and point out certain architectural influences. Pick up a map at the Sutton Tourist Office (24-A rue Principale S., Sutton, 800/565-8455, 11am-4pm Mon.-Thurs., 10am-4pm Fri., 10am-5pm Sat.-Sun.).

✪ ABBAYE SAINT-BENOÎT-DU-LAC

Founded in 1912, overlooking Lake Memphremagog, Abbaye Saint-Benoît-du-Lac (819/843-4080, www.st-benoit-du-lac.com, church 5am-8:30pm daily, shop 9am-10:45am and 11:50am-4pm Mon.-Sat.) is home to more than 50 monks who continue to work and live here. Designed by Dom Bellot, the abbey is known throughout the province for the monks' cheeses—they make 10 different types, including Blue Ermite and Fontina—jams, cider, and other goods that are made on the premises. Those looking for a quiet place for contemplation can stay at the men's hostel; there's a women's hostel in a nearby nunnery. The public is invited to join the monks in daily prayer and Gregorian chant (7:30am, 11am, and 5pm daily).

COATICOOK

In the southernmost part of the Eastern Townships, bordering on the United States, is the town of Coaticook. Though the town is full of quaint buildings, there are few sights; instead, people come for the scenic surroundings and its *fromageries* (cheese shops).

✪ Parc de la Gorge-de-Coaticook

Parc de la Gorge-de-Coaticook (135 rue Michaud, 888/524-6743, www.gorgedecoaticook.qc.ca, 9am-5pm Mon.-Fri., 9am-6pm Fri.-Sat. summer, 10am-4pm Mon.-Fri., 9am-4pm Sat.-Sun. winter, hours vary by activity, especially the Foresta Lumina) is best known for its magnificent suspension bridge, one of the longest pedestrian suspension bridges in the world. It sits 50 meters above the gorge. There is more to this park than the breathtaking views (though admittedly they are the main attraction). Hiking and mountain-biking trails are available throughout the summer, and at nighttime, the Foresta Lumina illuminates the forest with lanterns and sparkling lights. In winter, the main attractions are snowshoeing and sledding. Stay at one of the park's campsites, or rent one of the on-site cabins.

Cheese

Coaticook is well known for its cheeses, and Fromagerie La Station (440 chemin de Hatley, Compton, 819/835-5301, www.fromageri-elastation.com, 9:30am-5pm daily June-Nov., 10am-5pm Thurs.-Sun. Dec.-May) specializes in raw or-ganic milk cheese and gives tours of their workshop and farm. Try the freshest goat cheese you'll ever taste at Domaine de Courval (825 chemin de Courval, Waterville, 819/837-0062, noon-5pm Thurs.-Mon.). This artisanal *fromagerie* has five different flavors of rich but delicate cheese, as well as two aged varieties and a triple cream. A map of all the local *fromageries* is available at the tourist office.

✪ LA ROUTE DES VINS

Not far from the U.S. border, in the Brome-Missisquoi lowlands, you'll find over 140 kilometers of wineries. Inaugurated in 2003, La Route des Vins (888/811-4928, www.laroutedes-vins.ca) takes you through the valleys and bends of a picturesque region with a winery at almost every corner. Twenty-two wineries can be found on this route, and maps can be picked up at the region's tourist centers. All of the wineries are open June-October, with some of them open throughout the year. Drive a route, or, if you're feeling ambitious, cycle it!

Québec's specialty is ice wine, a dessert wine that is semi-sweet and produced from grapes that have been frozen on the vine. Vignoble Chapelle Ste-Agnès (2565 chemin Scenic, Sutton, 450/583-0303, www.vindeglace.com, Wed. and Sun. 1:30pm June-Oct., reservations required otherwise, $25 tasting tour) has a monastic feel with its Romanesque stone chapel and vaulted stone cellars.

With no entrance fee and a peaceful nature trail, Domaine des Cotes d'Ardoise (879 rue Bruce, Dunham, 450/295-2020, www.cotesdardoise.com, 10am-5pm Mon.-Thurs., 10am-6pm Fri.-Sun. May-Oct., 11:30am-4:30pm Fri.-Sun. Nov.-May) is the perfect place to stop for a picnic or purchase a snack from the café, before tasting the winery's reds, whites, and rosés.

Domaine du Ridge (205 chemin Ridge, St-Armand, 450/248-3987, www.domaineduridge.com, daily 10am-6pm May-Oct., 9am-5pm Mon.-Fri. Nov.-Apr., tastings $12-25) produces a broad range of whites and reds, even some ice wines. You'll probably find yourself taking a bottle or two of Clos du Maréchal to go.

A unique selection of wines and ciders is available to taste at Val Caudalies (4921 rue Principale, Durham, 450/295-2333, www.val-caudalies.com, 10am-5pm Mon.-Fri., 10am-6pm Sat.-Sun. May-early Nov., by reservation only Nov.-Apr., tastings $2 and up), where they make everything from rosé to ice cider, cider liqueur, and Vidal semi-dry white wine. Visitors are invited to pick apples and grapes in the vineyards and orchards.

Your eye will likely be caught by the large glass bottles lining the roof at Vignoble d'Orpailleur (1086 rue Bruce, Dunham, 450/295-2763, www. orpailleur.ca, 9am-5pm daily May-Oct., 10am-4:30pm daily Nov.-Apr., tour with tasting $10-15). The bottles contain one of their specialties, La Part des Anges, a sweet wine that ages on the roof's edge for 24 months. In addition to ice wine and a tasty Vin Gris, they also produce a brut, one of the few places in the area to do so.

The only producer of chardonnay in Québec is Vignoble Les Pervenches (150 chemin Boulais, 450/293-8311, www.lespervenches. com, 10am-4pm Wed.-Sun. June-Oct., free, self-guided tours). It's also one of the few organic wineries in the region. Along with chardonnay, they produce two varieties of red using traditional methods.

RECREATION
BICYCLING

Spanning 5,000 kilometers and linking all parts of the province, the Route Verte (800/567-8356, www.routeverte. com), initiated in the late 1990s, is the ultimate cyclist's dream. Most of the major cycling trails in Québec, like those that travel alongside the St-Lawrence River or head deep into the Laurentians, are part of this linking route. The proximity of the towns in the Eastern Townships and the area's lower-lying lands, however, make it an ideal spot to use the Route Verte, even for the most occasional of bikers. Bring your own ride with you or rent one for the day from rental outlets in Lac Brome, Sherbrooke, Orford, Sutton, and Granby.

SKIING

Ski hills can be found not too far from the city; they are great for hitting the runs after work or for a day-long outing.

Not too far from the town of Magog is Mont-Orford (4380 chemin du Parc, 866/673-31, www.orford.com, 8am-4:30pm Mon.-Fri., 9:30am-4:30pm Sat.-Sun. Dec.-Apr., $129 day pass), one of the best skiing spots in the province. With the fourth highest summit in Québec, it consists of three mountains (Orford, Giroux, and Alfred Desrochers) and 61 trails.

Rising over the western shores of Lake Memphremagog, Owl's Head (40 chemin du Mont Owl's Head, 800/363-3342, www.owlshead.com, 8:30am-4pm daily Dec.-Apr., $49 day pass) offers 45 trails of varying difficulty, with the majority in the intermediate range, and is about 80 minutes outside of Montréal.

Even closer to the city, about a 45-minute drive away, is Ski Bromont

(150 Champlain, 866/276-6668, www.skibromont.com, 9am-4pm daily Dec.-Apr., $55 day pass). Taking over Mont Brome, Mont Spruce, and Pic du Chevreuil, it is the largest illuminated alpine ski resort in North America, making it ideal for night runs. In the summer (June-Sept.), the same hills are home to an extensive water park.

In the winter, downhill skiing is a favorite activity.

✪ Ski Mont Sutton

Opened in 1960, Ski Mont Sutton (671 Maple C.P. 1850, 866/538-2545, www.montsutton.com, 10am-4pm Mon.-Fri., 9am-5pm Sat.-Sun. Dec.-Apr., $62 day pass) was started by a family who wanted to pursue their favorite pastime. Nowadays it's one of the most popular ski resorts in the area and with good reason. A little over an hour's drive from the city, it has 60 trails that cut through the woods, giving it a tranquil atmosphere. It offers ski packages for weekday visits.

RESTAURANTS

In Sherbrooke, check out Siboire (80 du Dépôt, Sherbrooke, 819/565-3636, www.siboire.ca, 7am-3am daily, $20), a microbrewery located in the downtown core. The high ceilings and open floor plan make it a welcoming place to grab a pint. Four permanent beers and two seasonal types are made on the premises. You can also enjoy them on the sidewalk *terrasse*. For a sweet treat, head over to Savoroso (720 place de la Gare, Sherbrooke, 819/346-2206, www.savoroso.com, 10am-6pm daily winter, 10am-10pm daily summer, $10) in the train station market. A popular place for gelato in the summer, it also serves up coffees, pastries, sandwiches, and salads, making it perfect for a light lunch.

In Knowlton, pick up some fresh, homemade bread at Panissimo (291a chemin Knowlton, Knowlton, 450/242-2412, www.panissimo.ca, 8am-4pm Thurs.-Sun., $10), where they specialize in traditional French baguettes and aromatic focaccia, as well as seasonal delicacies.

As the saying goes, when in Brome . . . you have to try Lac Brome duck. There's no better place to taste it than at Knowlton's Le Relais (286 chemin Knowlton, Knowlton, 450/242-6886, www.aubergeknowlton.ca/relais, 11am-10pm daily, $25). Located in Auberge Knowlton, it has an entire menu dedicated to the local delicacy, as well as standard dishes.

North Hatley's Pilsen (55 rue Main, North Hatley, 819/842-2971, www.pilsen.ca, 11:30am-3am daily) is one of the livelier restaurants in the area. Located on the water, this pub and restaurant serves classic pub grub like bangers and mash as well as finer selections like grilled salmon and ribs. Get a taste of local ingredients and cooking at the upscale Plaisir Gourmand (2225 Rte. 143, North Hatley, 819/838.1061, www.plaisirgourmand.com, 6pm-close Thurs.-Sat. Oct.-June, 6pm-close

Wed.-Sat. June-Oct.); go for gold with the seven-course tasting menu or opt for à la carte selections like braised lamb and roast boar.

After a day on the hills or hiking the trails, there's nothing better than a satisfying meal. The chef at Sutton's Auberge des Appalaches (234 chemin Maple, Sutton, 450/538-5799, www.auberge-appalaches.com, 6pm-close Fri.-Mon.) uses local ingredients to create delectable bistro dishes, such as rabbit lasagna and bison burgers. The restaurant has a homey, rustic feel and a wine list that includes local favorites.

Anyone who grew up in Québec likely has a soft spot for Coaticook Ice Cream (1000 rue Child, Coaticook, 800/846-7224, www.laiteriedecoaticook.com, 8am-6pm Mon.-Sat. Oct.-Mar., 8am-8pm Mon.-Wed., 8am-9pm Thurs.-Sat., 11am-8pm Sun. Apr.-May, 8am-10pm Mon.-Sat., 11am-10pm Sun. June-Sept.). Established in 1940, the small business has grown to become one of the biggest in the region, but they still make it the way they used to, with real cream. Their *bar laitier,* or ice cream bar, is open year-round and has all the latest flavors on hand for you to choose from, as well as other products for you to check out, like their Capricook goat cheese and Québec cheddar.

HOTELS

A century-old house makes sleeping in Sherbrooke a welcoming experience at Le Marquis de Montcalm (797 rue Générale-Montcalm, Sherbrooke, 819/823-7773, www.marquisdemontcalm.com, $109-159). The five rooms at this bed-and-breakfast are charmingly decorated with antiques and personal touches like the hand-painted mural in the Place de Voges room.

Built in 1849, Auberge Knowlton (286 chemin Knowlton, Knowlton, 450/242-6886, www.aubergeknowlton.ca, $130-170) has been fully renovated but still holds much of that old-world charm, with hardwood floors and country pine furniture. Looking out on Lac Brome, it's got one of the best views in the village. It's also pet-friendly.

Auberge du Joli Vent (667 chemin Bondville, Lac Brome, 866/525-4272, www.aubergedujolivent, $135-155) is a great little bed-and-breakfast with charming, brightly colored rooms and a fine-dining restaurant on-site. Surrounded by nature, the B&B even has an outdoor pool, which is great when traveling with kids.

North Hatley's reputation as a place for vacationing aristocrats is safe with Auberge La Raveaudière (11 chemin Hatley, North Hatley, 819/842-2554, www.laraveaudiere.com, $115-175), an elegant guesthouse in an old Victorian home. Along with seven guest rooms it has two acres of gardens, a comfortable living room, and a large, open patio. It backs onto the local golf course.

Just outside of North Hatley on Lake Massawippi is Manoir Hovey (575 chemin Hovey, North Hatley, 800/661-2421, www.manoirhovey.com, $250-820), one of the most charming inns in the region. Modeled after George Washington's Mount Vernon home, it was built at the turn of the 20th century and has 40 comfortably luxurious rooms, a pool, two beaches, touring bikes, an exercise room, and complimentary haute-cuisine dinners and breakfasts.

On a hill, up a winding, ice-prone driveway sits Domaine Tomali-Maniatyn (377 chemin Maple, Sutton, 450/538-6605, www.maniatyn.com, $150-180), a striking bed-and-breakfast that's designed to charm. Though it's not far from the ski hills of Mont Sutton, the quiet is undeniable. The large chalet has suites available with views overlooking the countryside. An indoor saltwater pool and hearty, homemade breakfast seal the deal.

North of Coaticook is Le Bocage (200 Moe's River Rd., Compton, 819/835-5653, www.lebocage.qc.ca, $100-250), a charming Victorian home that's been converted into a welcoming four-room bed-and-breakfast. Handmade quilts lie atop pine bed frames, giving the place a country farm feel. Breakfast is served in a cozy, stone-walled dining room or outside on the terrace.

INFORMATION AND SERVICES

Coming from Montréal, stop off at the Regional Tourist Office (Autoroute 10, exit 68, 866/472-6292, www.easterntownships.org, 8:30am-4:30pm Mon.-Fri., 8:30am-5pm Sat.-Sun. mid-Aug.-late June, 8:30am-6pm daily July-mid-Aug.), the first center in the Eastern Townships region. Though some towns have their own tourist centers, larger centers can be found in Granby (111 rue Denison E., Place de la Gare, Granby, 800/567-7273, 9am-5pm daily June-Sept.), Sutton Tourist Office (24-A rue Principale S., Sutton, 800/565-8455, 11am-4pm Mon.-Thurs., 10am-4pm Fri., 10am-5pm Sat.-Sun.), Sherbrooke (785 rue King W., 800/561-8331, www.destinationsherbrooke.com, 9am-5pm Mon.-Sat., 9am-3pm Sun. mid-Aug.-mid-June, 9am-7pm daily mid-June-mid-Aug.),

and Coaticook (137 rue Michaud, 866/665-6669, www.tourismecoaticook.qc.ca, 10am-4pm Sat.-Sun. late May-late June, 10am-8pm daily late June-early Sept., 10am-4pm Mon.-Thurs., 10am-8pm Fri.-Sun. early Sept. to Canadian Thanksgiving).

GETTING THERE AND AROUND

BY BUS

A coach is available daily from Montréal's main bus terminal, Gare d'Autocars (1717 rue Berri, 514/842-2281, www.gamtl.com). Limocar (limocar.ca) takes travelers to Sherbrooke ($66 round-trip), Magog ($60 round-trip), Granby ($40 round-trip), and Sutton ($45), among other towns, several times per day.

BY CAR

The simplest way to travel to the Eastern Townships and around is by car. Head out of Montréal by the Champlain Bridge, then head for Autoroute 10 East. The roads are clearly marked with signs for the Cantons de l'Est, but they can sometimes come up quickly, so keep your eyes peeled. Once on Autoroute 10 all the towns are easily accessible; it's just a matter of watching for the right exits.

Once you've arrived, getting from one town to the next is just as simple. Many of the small, country roads are signposted, ensuring you get from Lac Brome to North Hatley by the quickest way possible. Depending on where you are, you might have to get back on Autoroute 10 to reach your next destination.

BACKGROUND

The Landscape..252
History..255
Government and Economy...260
People and Culture..262
The Arts..267

The Landscape

GEOGRAPHY

Québec is Canada's largest province. It covers an area of 1,540,681 square kilometers, basically the size of France, Germany, Belgium, Spain, Portugal, and a couple Switzerlands put together, all in all an enormous territory. For the most part, it is filled with boundless forests and innumerable lakes (some say more than 400,000), vestiges of the huge Sea of Champlain that flooded the area 10,000 years ago.

Québec's geography can be divided into three main regions. The Canadian Shield goes from the extreme north down to the plain of the St-Lawrence River and includes the Laurentian Mountains, said to be the oldest mountain range in the world. The Appalachians, at the south of that plain, turn the landscape into a green and hilly area characteristic of the Eastern Townships region and extend down to the United States. Southwest of Montréal, the Eastern Townships, also known as the Cantons de l'Est, are a predominantly Francophone tourist region, with Anglophone minority pockets left over from post-American Revolution United Empire Loyalist settlements.

Laurentian landscape

A rift valley between these two antediluvian geological formations, the St-Lawrence is a 1,200-kilometer-long river that takes its source from the Great Lakes and ends up in the world's largest estuary. The majority of Québec's residents live along the banks of the river, and it's also the center of Québec's development. Looking out over the landscape from the window of a plane, you can see (along with the sprawling cities of Montréal and Québec) the rural landscape divided into narrow rectangular tracts of land extending from the river: These patterns denote the seigneurial land system, designed to allow each parcel access to water; they date back to the settlement of 17th-century Nouvelle France (New France).

The second largest and second most populated city in Canada (after Toronto) and the largest in Québec, Montréal's metropolitan area has a population of just over four million. Standing at the confluence of the St-Lawrence and Ottawa Rivers, it is set on an island of 500 square kilometers, 50 kilometers long and 15 kilometers wide at its widest. North of the island is the suburb of Laval, and beyond that the Laurentian Mountains; south of it, across the St-Lawrence, you'll find the south-shore cities of Longueil and Brossard. Smaller islands surround Montréal, such as Île des Sœurs and Île Bizard; most of the islands are now suburban communities. South of the Vieux-Port, what used to be several little islands were consolidated into Île Sainte-Hélène for the Expo 67. Next to it, Île Notre-Dame was built from scratch with 15 million tons of rocks excavated from the construction of the Métro in 1965.

The most prominent geographical feature of the island, from which it takes its name, is the triple-peaked hill Mont-Royal. Though locals like to call it a "mountain," its highest point reaches only 232 meters. Except for the plateau surrounding the diminutive peak, the rest of the city is flatter than flat. The opening of the Lachine Canal in 1824 and its enlargement over the 19th century permitted ships to bypass the unnavigable Lachine Rapids, making Montréal a major port and linking the St-Lawrence to the Great Lakes, all of which turned the city into a booming economic center.

As in most North American cities, one of the biggest problems facing Montréal is traffic. The city's two main bridges off the island, Pont Jacques-Cartier and Pont Champlain, are chronically congested, a problem that worsens each year. The City of Montréal does not include all the boroughs located on the island. In fact, several boroughs, including Dorval, Mount Royal, and Westmount, refused to merge with the rest of the city at the beginning of the 21st century and remain politically independent. This can sometimes get in the way when dealing with topics like city infrastructure, library systems, and dog licensing.

CLIMATE

"Mon pays ce n'est pas un pays, c'est l'hiver" (My country is not a country, it's winter) sang Québec's premier *chansonnier* (singer-songwriter), Gilles Vigneault. Truer words have never been spoken, especially regarding the six months during which winter takes over, changing the landscape and affecting the mood of its resigned inhabitants. Yes, wintertime temperatures have an average of -10°C in Montréal and can drop down to -30°C. However, the winters aren't as harsh, cold, and snowy as they used to be, thanks to global warming. But the freezing wind, blowing *poudreuse* (drifting snow) everywhere like a tempest in the desert, is probably the toughest thing about being here in the winter. When the temperatures dip to bone-chilling proportions, make sure to cover up everything from your nose to your toes or you could end up with frostbite.

Approximately three meters of snow fall every winter, but sometimes there's more. Snowstorms are frequent and can last up to a day if not more. Snow removal can be interesting to watch if you're a tourist and have never seen it before. The sidewalk and road snowplows can also be deadly, so be careful, especially when walking at night.

Despite being harsh and long, winters in Québec are also sunny, with a bright luminosity that can sometimes be blinding. Because of the length of the season, stoical locals have adopted a "if you can't beat 'em, join 'em" attitude in order to survive, and you'll be surprised to see just how active Quebeckers can be in winter, putting on their skates and snowshoes after every snowstorm, sometimes going to work on cross-country skis and pulling their kids in toboggans along the sidewalks. There is no need to say that winter has had a major cultural impact on this society; its influence is apparent in everything from the architecture to the invention of Montréal's Underground City.

Of course, Québec isn't just about winter, and people are often surprised to see just how hot and humid the summers are, with temperatures often reaching 35°C. After having complained about the cold all winter, locals curse the heat and turn their air-conditioners on full blast.

Autumn and spring are shorter in Québec, but in many ways they are the most impressive seasons. In spring, the snow melts away, revealing new blossoms, while autumn has a particular beauty as the trees change to a rainbow of colors before shedding their leaves.

PLANTS AND ANIMALS

The best place to explore Québec's rich and diverse fauna and flora is in the national parks. National parks offer interpretive materials and guides to help you understand just exactly what it is you're surrounded by.

Since Montréal is a city, there's not much chance to run into a moose or a black bear while getting a pint of milk at the *dép* (short for *dépanneur*, meaning corner store). But the city has Parc du Mont-Royal, with protected fauna and flora, where you might see animals that can be exotic for some: red and gray squirrels, chipmunks, and raccoons. If you're really lucky wandering through the park on a quiet day, you might also glimpse a fox.

Montréal is remarkably green for its size, with trees lining just about every side street. Originally part of the Laurentian forest ecosystem, the vegetation has changed over time due to urbanization. A good example of this is Mont-Royal, originally made up exclusively of red oaks and sugar maples. The introduction in the 1960s and '70s of the Norway maple, which is more resistant to city pollution, has considerably changed the face of the beloved mountain. And today, they've overtaken much of the sugar maple; this is most visible in the fall when, instead of turning bright red the way sugar maples do, the Norway maples turn yellow.

Today, Canada is undergoing a process of truth and reconciliation with First Nations, Métis, and Inuit peoples. (The Métis are a post-contact indigenous people; their culture came about through a mix of mostly Cree, French, and Scottish traditions and new traditions in the Prairies region.) The idea is to make amends for historical and ongoing colonial policies—many violent—that had negative and lasting impacts on indigenous peoples.

Indigenous peoples, seeking self-determination and nation-to-nation relationships, are also leading cultural and linguistic renaissances in their communities across the country. When you visit, keep an eye out for gorgeous indigenous art—sculpture, painting, beadwork—but do a little research to ensure that you're purchasing an item that is made by an indigenous person and will support their indigenous culture (there are a lot of commercial knock-offs out there!).

History

EARLY INHABITANTS

Long before its European takeover, the North American continent was home to indigenous people for thousands of years. Historians date the population back to at least 12,000 years ago—though it may date back much further. One theory posits that hunting tribes crossed the Bering Strait in pursuit of game from Siberia. Those tribes then scattered all over the land, developing diverse ways of life as they adapted to different environments. By the time explorers arrived, the area that would eventually become known as the St-Lawrence valley was populated by the nomadic Algonquin and sedentary Iroquoian peoples, who lived off game, fish, and crops, and were particularly well adapted to their environment.

EUROPEAN ARRIVAL

When it comes to the "discovery" of Canada, French explorer Jacques Cartier's name usually pops up. But the truth is that by the time he finally made it to Québec in 1534, Newfoundland's coastline had been periodically cruised by explorers and fishermen from different nations—the Vikings had sailed its coast and even put down a few roots 500 years before.

What Jacques Cartier did that other Europeans didn't was explore the interior of the river, a river that he named in honor of the saint on the calendar the day he reached it: St-Lawrence. Sent by the king of France, Francis I, with the mandate of finding gold and—the typical request of the day—a passage to Asia, the sailor explored the region thoroughly, visiting Iroquoian villages Stadacona (Québec) and, farther upstream, Hochelaga, in present-day Montréal. After many voyages, he found neither gold nor Asia, bringing home instead a bunch of made-up stories told by fabulist natives and a handful of rocks he thought were diamonds (a popular French saying of the time was "*faux comme un diamant du Canada*" (fake as a Canadian diamond). Deemed by the French to be inhospitable and dull, what we know today as Canada remained unvisited and almost forgotten by Cartier's nation for half a century.

NOUVELLE FRANCE (NEW FRANCE)

Two things rekindled the French interest in this part of the world: the fur trade and an appetite for colonial expansion. In addition to these two motives, the Catholic Church saw an opportunity to spread the gospel to the indigenous population and sent missionaries along on the expedition. Seeing promise in the new European fashion of fur hats and coats, trading companies quickly formed, including the Compagnie des Cent-Associés, which set up outposts around Québec where First Nations people and French settlers could trade.

In 1608, Samuel de Champlain set up the first permanent European trading post in an abandoned Iroquoian village that Jacques Cartier had visited 80 years before, building a wooden fort he called l'Abitation de Québec (*kebec* in Algonquin means "where the river narrows"). That first winter, most of the settlers died of scurvy and harsh weather, but the colony continued even though it faced numerous difficulties and was slow to grow. In 1635 (the year Samuel de Champlain, the Father of New France, died), the population was slightly more than 300 settlers, a fair number of them Catholic missionaries. Some of these missionaries organized the Société Notre-Dame de Montréal and, in 1642, decided to establish an evangelizing mission near the deserted village of Hochelaga. Called Ville-Marie, it would eventually become Montréal.

While colonists cleared forests and cultivated the land, the thriving fur trade attracted a different kind of young explorer, one daring enough to go farther and farther into the continent seeking bearskins, mink furs, and, above all, the popular and coveted beaver pelts. Called *coureurs des bois* (wood runners, or woodsmen), these adventurers are legendary figures in Québec, since they represent a life of freedom and a particular connection with nature that characterized the colonization of the continent. These *coureurs* also paved the way for the explorers and voyageurs to whom we owe the exploration of the regions of the Great Lakes and the Mississippi Valley, much of which they claimed for the French. These explorers left their mark on places all over the United States, including Detroit, St. Louis, and Baton Rouge.

The commercial relations brought on by the trade helped the French secure alliances with the Hurons, who in exchange for the pelts received copper and iron utensils, alcohol, and rifles. This alliance put the French colony in the middle of a bloody war when the English-backed Iroquois Five Nations launched an offensive campaign to wipe out the Hurons, their long-time enemies. The war lasted 25 years, seriously affecting both the First Nations and the French colony.

TOWARD DEFEAT

The conflicting commercial and political interests of the French and English caused a succession of intercolonial wars. In 1713, following a military defeat in Europe, the Treaty of Utrecht resulted in France relinquishing control of Newfoundland, Acadia, and Hudson Bay, something that considerably hurt New France's fur trade and jeopardized its colony. This date marks the beginning of the end for New France, even if it took another 50 years for the British to secure power, a takeover that seemed inevitable considering the difference in population. Indeed, on the eve of the final battle,

When things started looking really bad for the British during the American Revolution, colonists who wanted to remain loyal to the British crown were offered free land (no matter that much of it was Indigenous territory, not really England's to give) and safe passage to other—non-rebelling—parts of the British colonies.

Called United Empire Loyalists because of their unyielding devotion to King George III, many chose to escape north, settling in the regions of southern Ontario and Québec. So many immigrated to the province, close to 50,000, that it sent the Québécois into a breeding frenzy and kicked off the *revanche des berceaux*, the "revenge of the cradle."

By 1791 so many loyalists had arrived in the country that the government signed the Constitutional Act, dividing the province in two: Upper Canada, which would eventually become Ontario, and Lower Canada, the province of Québec.

Though many Loyalists and descendants of Loyalists eventually moved out of the province, their influence can still be seen in the Eastern Townships, where covered bridges, clapboard houses, and Victorian gingerbread moldings are the norm.

there were 60,000 French living in a huge territory, surrounded by two million British colonists living in the narrow strip of the 13 colonies.

The final showdown happened on September 13, 1759, on an open field by Cap-Diamant, now called the Plains of Abraham, in present-day Québec City. After a two-month-long siege, the French army, led by General Montcalm, was attacked by surprise early in the morning. General Wolfe and the British army used a dried-up old creek to climb the cliff, something everyone thought was impossible. The Battle of the Plains of Abraham, which sealed the fate of French North America, was bloody, lasted barely 20 minutes, and cost the lives of both generals. One year after, Montréal capitulated and thus France lost all of its colonies in North America, leaving behind a small population of deeply rooted French Catholics in an ocean of British Protestants.

BRITISH REGIME

Though at first they tried to assimilate the French minority by imposing British Common Law and having them swear an oath to the British king, the victors decided that it was wiser to accommodate the French, wanting to

secure their allegiance as social unrest and rebellion smoldered in the south. In order to cement the support of the French-Canadians, England wrote up the Act of Québec in 1774, recognizing both the French language and French civil law, and granting them freedom of religion. These concessions succeeded in preventing the French-Canadians from joining the rebels in the south who started the American Revolution a year later.

At the end of that war, in 1783, 50,000 United Empire Loyalists (British Loyalists) had fled the United States for the province of Québec, many of them settling into the Eastern Townships region. To accommodate these Loyalists, who were an English minority in a French-speaking majority, a new Constitutional Act was signed in 1791, dividing the province in two: Upper Canada (which would eventually become Ontario) and Lower Canada (the province of Québec). The names Upper and Lower Canada were given according to their location on the St-Lawrence River.

The 19th century was marked by the power struggles between the Francophones and the Anglophones in Lower Canada. The elected French-Canadian representatives were constantly at odds with the colonial British executive and legislative powers. Over the years, the nationalist and reformist Parti Canadien denounced the untenable situation, ending up in an armed insurrection. The Patriots War (Guerre des Patriotes) of 1837-1838 was immediately crushed, and an emissary was sent from London to study the problems of this wayward colony.

The solution proposed by Lord Durham was radical: Make every effort to assimilate French-Canadians. This was the impetus behind the Union Act, laid down by the British government in 1840. Along with unifying Upper and Lower Canada and giving them an equal political power—despite the fact that Lower Canada was much more populated—it also made English the only official language, despite the fact that the vast majority were French-speakers. These new laws and the constant arrival of English-speaking immigrants prompted a major exodus of Francophones, many of whom immigrated to the United States.

CONFEDERATION

The troubled politics of the subsequent years coupled with a dire economic situation prompted leaders of Upper and Lower Canada to unify. The British North America Act, signed in 1867, is the constitutional act that solidified Canada as an independent nation that would eventually stretch from the Atlantic to the Pacific.

It also created the two-level structure of government, in which power is split between the federal and provincial levels. Even though Québec's minority status was deepened by it, the new structure granted the province jurisdiction over education, civil

law, and culture, among other things. Québec maintained a central importance in the evolution of the country, and, before long, a French-Canadian, Wilfrid Laurier, became prime minister of Canada. Elected in 1896, he was the first of many Québécois, including Pierre Elliot Trudeau and Jean Chrétien, who would lead the country—most recently, Justin Trudeau was elected prime minister.

Faced with a prodigious period of economic growth at the beginning of the 20th century, Prime Minister Laurier declared it "Canada's century." The prediction fell short, though, when the Great Depression disrupted economic and social progress in Québec for many years. World War II finally put an end to the economic doldrums, and, in fact, Québec came out of the war economically stronger than ever before and ready for social change, as the anarchist manifest *Refus Global* (Total Refusal), signed by artists and writers, made clear.

Despite this exciting new energy and mind-set, the province would remain under the spell of Maurice Duplessis and his conservative party (Union Nationale) for another 15 years. In spite of its considerable economic growth, this period is often referred to as "La Grande Noirceur" (The Great Darkness), the last obstacle before real transformation.

THE QUIET REVOLUTION AND CONTEMPORARY TIMES

After the death of Maurice Duplessis in 1959, Québec was ripe for change, and the Liberal Party government of Jean Lesage was elected the year after, kicking off what would be dubbed the Révolution Tranquille (Quiet

Revolution), a wide range of bold economic and social reforms. The most important result of these reforms is the secularization of society, putting an end to the centuries-long overarching power of the church in every aspect of Québécois society. Education, health care, and social services were no longer under the control of the church as the state began to take over.

The most ambitious economic project of the time, the nationalization of the province's electric companies under Hydro Québec is a powerful symbol of that new ambition. The Quiet Revolution also witnessed the rise of nationalism. Jean Lesage's Liberal government election slogan, *maîtres chez nous* (masters in our own home), meant to put a stop to the unbridled selling of the province's natural resources to foreign business interests.

Montréal hosted two major international events that still define its identity: the 1967 World's Fair (Exposition Universelle—Terre des Hommes) and the Summer Olympic Games in 1976. The sentiment of empowerment at the time exacerbated enthusiasm for the idea of a stronger autonomy within the Canadian federation, and more and more people became attracted by the idea of building a new country instead, some groups even falling into extremism. Thus, the Front de Liberation du Québec (FLQ), founded in 1963, used terrorist tactics against the Québec and national governments and businesses with the aim of establishing a socialist independent country.

In 1970, during the October crisis, when the FLQ kidnapped Québec Labour Minister Pierre Laporte and eventually killed him, Pierre Elliot Trudeau, then Canadian prime minister, launched the War Measures Act against Québec dissidents, putting the country under martial law to much public controversy. After that, the FLQ declined drastically and eventually disappeared.

Despite these radical actions and a certain support the FLQ gained with the public, the majority of pro-sovereigntists preferred moderate nationalism. In 1967, René Lévesque, a rising star of the Liberal government, quit the party and founded the Parti Québécois (PQ). Soon after, in 1976, a stunning and unexpected victory brought the PQ to power, putting the question of sovereignty at the forefront of political and social life of Québec society for decades. Bill 101 in 1977 made French the only official language of Québec. In 1980 Lévesque's government launched a referendum on the issue of independence, losing when the "no" side won with 60 percent of the vote. In time, the tensions with the federal government became aggravated, mostly over constitutional matters and Québec's refusal to ratify the repatriated Canadian constitution in 1982.

In 1995, a second referendum campaign was launched. This time the results were extremely close, and Canada held its breath: 49.4 percent of Quebeckers voted "yes" and 50.6 percent voted "no," underlining the deep division of the population over the issue.

However, the national question has faded in importance over the last 20 years, with public attention drifting toward other public matters like the environment and economy. In 2003, the PQ was ousted from power after 10 years, and the Québec Liberal Party, resolutely federalist, was elected. Led by Premier Jean Charest, they were voted in for a third term in 2009.

Thanks to political unrest related to the rising costs of tuition, the PQ regained political power with a minority government in the autumn 2012 election. They lost to the Liberals again in 2014, in large part due to a bill the PQ introduced in 2013 called the Charter of Values, which would have, among other things, limited the wearing of "conspicuous" religious symbols by state personnel—small crosses would have been fine, but Jewish workers would not have been able to wear kippot, and Muslim women would not have been able to wear the hijab. The bill was met with some support as well as a strong backlash, and the Liberals took power in the next election.

Contemporary Québec is a province in flux: Multicultural and multi-linguistic, it is influenced by particularly French conceptions of secularism and free speech, as well as values that underscore the importance of a pluralistic society. Particularly for Francophone Québécois, it is increasingly important to find a balance between supporting and ensuring the strength and longevity of Francophone culture and the French language, while ensuring that newcomers to the province can thrive and be culturally recognized and supported here. Over the past generation, major gains have been made in cities like Montréal, where traditionally Anglophone Montrealers have embraced learning French, and French has increasingly become the language of business—this shift in power has allowed for a positive shift in cultural commingling. Of course, there are still tensions, and much work to be done, but visitors to Montréal, and the province, will mostly just notice the citizens' warmth and cultural vibrancy.

Government and Economy

POLITICS

Canada's political system is modeled after the British parliamentary system it historically inherited. Central in the government organization is the House of Commons, sitting in Ottawa, a democratically elected body consisting of 338 members known as Members of Parliament (MPs). Each MP in the House of Commons is elected by simple plurality in an electoral district, also known as a riding. Federal elections are called within five years of the previous election or when the government loses a confidence vote.

The leader of the party that won the most seats generally becomes the new prime minister and forms the new government. Canada being a federation, this political structure is reproduced for every province. Therefore, each has its own parliament. In Québec, the provincial government is called the Assemblée Nationale, and its 125 elected members sit in Québec City, the province's capital. The Canadian Constitution divides the power between federal and provincial governments. For example, defense, postal services, and international relations are under federal jurisdiction, while education, health, and natural resources are under provincial jurisdiction. Since the Constitution is not always clear about these divided powers, constitutional conflicts arise, a situation that has been particularly true between Québec and the federal government.

Canada is also a constitutional monarchy. People are often surprised to know that there is a queen in Canada: Queen Elizabeth II of England is the Canadian head of state. Though her role is mostly formal and symbolic, she does have a representative in Canada acting on her behalf: the governor general. She is represented by the lieutenant-governor in the provinces.

Though this first-past-the-post governmental structure favors a two-party system, in Canada's case, five parties make up the federal government: the right-leaning Conservative Party, centrist Liberal Party, left-leaning NDP (New Democratic Party), the Bloc Québécois (the Québec sovereigntist party), and the Green Party (environmentalists who are relatively new on the scene and usually don't hold many seats). In major political battles, the Conservatives and Liberals are generally the front-runners, but the NDP and Bloc Québécois are instrumental to how government is run and what bills are passed in the House of Commons.

From 2006 to 2015, the Conservative party, under the leadership of Stephen Harper, formed the federal government, ruling alternately with a majority rule and a minority rule. In 2015, facing growing public criticism over issues like non-renewable energy, press freedom, and senator expense scandals, the Harper Conservatives were ousted in favor of the Liberal Party under the leadership of Justin Trudeau, whose father, Pierre Elliott Trudeau, served as the prime minister of Canada 1968-1979 and again 1980-1984. The Liberals,

who have a majority government, were elected on promises to develop renewable energy strategies, work on reconciliation with indigenous peoples in Canada, and change the electoral system from first-past-the-post to some form of proportional representation. (So far on shaky ground in terms of *keeping* those promises, it's anyone's guess as to what will take place next election year.)

On the provincial stage, two parties have been exchanging power for half a century: the centrist, federalist Québec Liberal Party, and the sovereigntist Parti Québécois founded by René Lévesque. In the 1980s and '90s, the Parti Québécois (PQ) became the center of international attention when it organized two referendums on Québec sovereignty. The consecutive defeats of the PQ in these referendums and in recent elections has laid the sovereigntist question aside for the time being, and the Liberals are currently in power.

ECONOMY

Since the beginning, Québec's natural resources have been the major asset in the province's economy. Vast forests, mining resources, rich agricultural land, and a huge potential for hydroelectricity—because of all the lakes—make this province, like much of Canada, good for a primary, resource-based economy. Historically everything began with the fur trade, kicking off the European colonization of the territory and sustaining it for over a century. In the 19th and most of the 20th centuries, wood, pulp, and paper industries took the lead and are still, along with the mining sector and hydroelectricity production, the most important sectors of Québec's economy.

The government plays an important role in the economy and is the largest employer in the province. Despite the trend toward more privatization, this strong state involvement reaches a certain consensus in the population and is considered essential due to the small size of its economy. Government-owned Hydro Québec, the world's leader in hydroelectricity, remains a national pride, and dams and development projects in the north are thoroughly followed by the population. Another economic national jewel is aerospace and railway maker Bombardier, a world-class company started 70 years ago by Joseph Bombardier, the inventor of the snowmobile.

Once the undisputed economic center of Canada, Montréal lost its predominance to Toronto 40 years ago and now plays second fiddle to "the city that works." Even if most of Montréal's defenders would say this relative decline was caused by the massive fleeing of Anglophone businesses after the PQ reached power in 1976, you have to admit that the demographic and economic trends were already on track at the time. The last episode in this rivalry between the two cities was the acquisition of the Bourse de Montréal (Montréal Stock Exchange) by the Toronto Stock Exchange in 2007.

Despite this relative decline, however, Montréal thrives with high-class industries like aerospace (Bombardier, Pratt & Whitney, etc.) and information technology companies. In 1997, Ubisoft, a major French video game publisher, opened (with government funds) a subsidiary in Montréal, establishing itself in the new hip area Mile End. This studio, responsible for developing games like *Prince of Persia* and *Assassin's Creed,* is now one of the world's largest, with over 1,700 employees, making the city a central hub for that industry. Tourism and other creative industries also thrive in Montréal—the government is quite supportive of the arts, making the city a great home for both artists and visitors.

People and Culture

INDIGENOUS PEOPLES

Québec's first inhabitants were indigenous peoples. Ten different First Nations, as well as the Inuit in the northern part of what is now Québec, have made their homes here for tens of thousands of years. Today, after centuries of harsh colonial policies, indigenous peoples represent a small but growing part of the population. Three-quarters of indigenous peoples in Québec live on reserves throughout the province: The Mohawk reserves Kahnawake and Kanesatake in the Montréal region and the Wendat-Huron reserve Wendake north of Québec City are some of the bigger ones. Though some indigenous peoples live in areas where they can hunt and fish, many reserves preclude following a traditional way of life, and the federal government has not honored commitments to ensure their livelihood—or sometimes even provide basics like access to food and clean drinking water.

One of the most important political events of the past decades was the Oka Crisis: For two months in the summer of 1990, Mohawks barricaded one of the main bridges into Montréal, protesting land claims and issues of self-government. The incident forced native issues to the forefront, and in recent years nation-to-nation agreements have granted indigenous peoples more autonomy—though there is still much work to be done if Canada is to honor its treaties and work in good faith with indigenous peoples.

FRANCOPHONES

The vast majority of the Québécois people are descendants of the settlers who arrived between 1608 and 1759. From the 60,000 French-Canadians in 1759 there are now seven million living in Canada. Part of the reason Québec has such a strong cultural and social heritage is because of the population's demographics. In the late 18th century with the arrival of the United Empire Loyalists, the French-Canadians became nervous at the idea of being overpopulated by the English-speaking contingent. One response to this immigration was something that would later be called the *revanche des berceaux* (revenge of the cradle), which saw the families of French-Canadians growing larger by the year. Of course, the province's Catholic background helped, and throughout the years Québécois families were typically large and women had an average of 8 children (Céline Dion is from a family of 14 kids). In the 1970s, however, the birthrate dropped considerably, and it remains one of the lowest in the world.

Though today the province is experiencing a baby boom, it is a mere blip compared to the numbers in the mid-20th century. Much of the growth to the province's Francophone population now comes from immigration.

ANGLOPHONES

The first Anglophone immigrants arrived after the British conquest in 1759. Most of them were well-to-do Protestant merchants, forever forging the stereotype of the rich Anglophone. However, this wasn't always the case; one of the most important groups of immigrants was the working-class Irish, who arrived in the province as early as the founding of New France. The biggest wave of Irish immigrants came 1815-1860, driven from Ireland by the potato famine. They came to the province by the boatload, disembarking at Grosse-Île, an island off the shores of Québec City that was set up as a reception center. During the summer of 1847, thousands died during a typhus epidemic, and the orphaned children were adopted by Québec families. It is estimated that a staggering 45 percent of Quebeckers have Irish ancestry, even if most of them don't know it. In Québec City many immigrant families were relegated to the slum-like dwellings in Petite Champlain, while in Montréal they congregated in places like Griffintown and Point-Saint-Charles closer to the banks of the river.

The arrival of the United Empire Loyalists between 1783 and the beginning of the 19th century shaped not only the Eastern Townships, where most of them settled, but also the future of the country. They fled the United States in such great numbers as to facilitate the division of the province into Upper and Lower Canada. The 19th century also saw the largest number of immigrants from the British Isles, many of whom would put down roots in Montréal and, in the case of the Scots, found McGill University.

In the 1970s, after the rise to power of the PQ and the October Crisis in particular, many English-speakers left Québec, often settling in Ontario. Nowadays, they make up only 10 percent of the total population of the province and live mostly in Montréal. The west end of the city has the most prominent English boroughs: Westmount, Notre-Dame-de-Grâce (NDG), and Montréal-West. Of the English-speakers who did stay, the vast majority are now bilingual.

QUEBECKERS OF OTHER ETHNIC ORIGINS

Immigration from countries other than Britain and France began in earnest in the 20th century. Canada's growing ethnic diversity is particularly obvious in Montréal, whose history has been defined by successive waves of immigrants. After World War II, the majority of immigrants arrived from Italy, Greece, and Portugal, communities that continue to have a stronghold in neighborhoods like the Mile End and Little Italy. For the most part, these immigrants aligned themselves with the Anglophone community, raising Québec's perennial concerns over French language subsistence. In 1977, the Parti Québécois passed Bill 101—among other things, the children of newcomers were required to attend French schools. Immigration demographics began to change in the latter part of the century, and the 1970s and '80s saw exiles from Vietnam and Haiti join the ranks, followed more recently by North African, Middle Eastern, Chinese, and Central European immigrants. Many immigrants now arrive speaking French,

and the government funds programs for those who don't so that they may, with financial support, acquire French proficiency.

Québec also has a large Jewish community, whose roots can be traced all the way back to the British conquest, while a large Hassidic community can be found in the Mile End and Outremont.

LGBTQ COMMUNITY

The first recorded gay establishment in North America, Moise Tellier's apples and cake shop, opened in Montréal in 1869. Like all LGBTQ communities, Montréal's has faced discrimination and hardships, one of the most crucial being a raid in October 1977, during which 144 men were arrested. Those arrests, however, led to a 2,000-person-strong protest the following day. It's this show of political support and acceptance that Montréal has become known for.

Today, there are queer establishments and events all over the city. There is also massive support both within the city and community for younger members of the LGBTQ community.

Fierté Montréal Pride is the city's pride festival, which takes place in the summer. Montréal also hosts dance parties throughout the year aimed at the gay community, including Black and Blue, a weekend-long party that's been going strong for over 20 years. Though the Village is known as being the city's premier gay neighborhood, the Plateau, Mile End, and Saint-Henri are also home to significant queer populations.

RELIGION

There is no denying the influence of the Catholic Church on the history

King Louis XIV of France might have banned Jews from entering the colony of Nouvelle France, but Québec's Jewish roots can be traced back for centuries.

The first Jewish people to settle in Québec were members of the British army who arrived after the initial conquest. Several are thought to have been a part of General Jeffery Amherst's battalion, four of whom were officers. Of those officers at least one, Aaron Hart, remained in Canada, settling in Trois-Rivières and eventually becoming a wealthy landowner. One of his sons, Ezekiel Hart, later became the first Jew to be elected to public office in the British Empire.

Though the Jewish community in Montréal numbered little more than 200, the Spanish and Portuguese Synagogue of Montréal opened its doors in 1768 and became the first non-Catholic house of worship in the province. In Québec City the first known Jewish inhabitant was Abraham Jacob Franks, who settled in the city in 1767, but it wasn't until 1892 that the Jewish population in Québec City had enough members to warrant a proper synagogue. In the interim, however, they had founded a number of institutions, including the Québec Hebrew Sick Benefit Association, the Québec Hebrew Relief Association for Immigrants, and the Québec Zionist Society. By 1905, Québec City's Jewish population numbered 350.

As anti-Semitism mounted in Europe, over 155,000 Jews resettled in Canada, many of them in Montréal, where they became storekeepers, tradespeople, and workers in the city's numerous garment factories. The history of one of the city's greatest streets, boulevard St-Laurent, can be traced back to the immigrant families who worked and lived along the Main or in the factories nearby. Jewish businesses left an indelible mark on the city, and many of Montréal's most recognizable symbols—the smoked-meat sandwich, the bagel—come from that strong Jewish lineage.

At the end of World War II approximately 40,000 Holocaust survivors came to Canada, and in 1947, the Workmen's Circle and Jewish Labour Committee started the Tailors Project, aimed at bringing Jewish refugees to Montréal in the needle trades. Jewish immigration continued to expand in Québec, especially in the 1950s when North African Jews fled the continent, settling in Québec City and Montréal, where their French language would be an asset.

The community today is concentrated in Montréal, in areas such as Hamstead, Côte-St-Luc, and Outremont, with a large Hassidic community in the Mile End. Though Québec City still has a Jewish community, the majority of the province's Jewish population lives in Montréal, and in fact, many of the city's most recognizable figures come from this community, including literary giants Irving Layton and Mordecai Richler, poet and musician Leonard Cohen, and psychologist and linguist Steven Pinker.

of Québec, and almost every street corner features a three-story high cathedral, though today many of them have been converted into condos. Instrumental in the founding of the nation and throughout most of its history, the Catholic Church only really began to lose its prominence in the 1960s and '70s. For the most part, Francophones remain Catholic (though most are non-practicing) and Anglophones are Protestant, but there are also diverse religions encompassing Muslims, Jews, Hindus, and Sikhs.

LANGUAGE

The language issue is arguably the most important for Québécois Francophones. They can be very touchy about how other people view their language, be it toward other Francophones who consider *joual* (Canadian French slang) a mere dialect, or toward people who obstinately refuse to make any efforts to speak French. Don't be afraid, though; they're usually not hard to please, and using a mere *bonjour* (hello) or *merci* (thank you) is the safest way to gain their respect. They will often switch to

English (even broken English) if they see you struggling.

After the British conquest in 1759, even though language, religion, and other rights were granted to the French community, Francophone citizens were barred from political and economical power for a long time. This linguistic exclusionism, in which access to the upper levels of business and power was barred to the French-Canadians, lasted well into the 20th century. In fact, until the 1970s, English-speakers were the minority that ran many of the businesses and held positions of power in the province.

The Quiet Revolution in the 1960s, however, helped to change all that as it fostered nationalist sentiment, which reached a peak when the Parti Québécois was elected in 1976. In 1977, Bill 101 was passed, asserting the primacy of French on public signs across the province, and apostrophes were removed from store fronts in the 1980s to comply with French usage. English is allowed on signage as long as it's half the size of the French lettering. Despite the debate that surrounded the bill when it was first implemented, many believe it has helped to preserve the language.

Anyone with a good ear will likely be able to tell that there's a big difference between the French spoken here and the French in France. The French here is said to be an evolved version of the French spoken in the 17th and 18th centuries in France, partially preserved due to its geographical isolation. The language spoken in everyday life is full of funny expressions and syntax. Depending on where you are in the province, some accents may be harder to understand than those in the cities.

Unlike in France where they've integrated English terms like "weekend" into regular usage, Québec—surrounded by Anglos and Anglo culture—is much more ardent about the preservation of the language. That's not to say English words aren't in common usage in Québec; there is simply a heightened awareness of them. The Office Québécoise de la Langue Française is an institution whose mandate is to translate new words, typically those related to IT or technology, into a French equivalent. For example, in Québec, email is *courriel,* the French contraction of electronic mail, and Québec's stop signs are also written in French, with the word *arrêt* at their center, though even in France the signs read "stop."

Montréal is the largest French-speaking city outside of Paris, and at least 57 percent of Montrealers, and 43 percent of Québécois, speak both official languages. Young Montrealers are less concerned with language issues than past generations, and many, especially those that come from immigrant families, speak more than two languages.

The Arts

MUSIC

Without a doubt, the province's best-known recording artist is Céline Dion. Born in the small town of Charlemagne 30 kilometers from Montréal, she was a mega-star in Québec and France when she was just a teenager and well before she started singing in English. Although she was criticized at first by her Francophone fan base for "selling out," her world-wide success is now a huge source of pride for the province, and fans now love (and buy) her English albums just as much as her French ones.

The province's second biggest export, music-wise, is Montréal's Arcade Fire, who took over the airwaves in 2004 with their infectious indie rock anthems and haven't looked back. Despite their rock star status—they've shared the stage with everyone from David Byrne to David Bowie—they remain active in the community, and many of the group's members play in other Montréal bands. Their success in the early 2000s was also part of a bigger Montréal indie rock explosion, with bands like The Dears, Wolfe Parade, and the Unicorns, among others. The scene has continued to grow since then and is constantly evolving. In recent years Francophone bands like Malajube, Radio Radio, and Karkwa—who won the 2010 Polaris Music Prize, Canada's largest for an "indie" band—have been gaining fans across the language divide. Godspeed You! Black Emperor and Cœur de Pirate are two other favorite local acts, beloved for their craft and creativity.

Poet and singer/songwriter Leonard Cohen, who died in 2016, was one of the city's most-loved inhabitants, and many of his melancholy and soulful compositions were inspired by the city, including the song *So Long Maryanne.* Grammy Award-winning artist Rufus Wainwright is also from Montréal, though he now resides in New York. Mixing symphonic sounds with a pop mentality, his sweeping compositions are utterly unique and catchy. His sister, Martha Wainwright, also a musician, is somewhat less experimental in her style, but continues to push the boundaries of pop. On one of her more recent albums *(Sans Fusils, Ni Souliers, à Paris)* she sings the songs of Edith Piaf. Of course, it helps when you have good genes, and the Wainwrights have them in spades: Their father is American folk singer Loudon Wainwright III, and their mother is Kate McGarrigle; Kate and her sister Anna are two of the biggest folk singers in the province. Since the 1960s, the McGarrigle sisters have sung and written in both French and English.

It wasn't until the 1960s that modern music really started to hit its stride in the province. Québec held a festival of experimental music in 1961, and by the mid-1960s, the symphony was starting to attract a larger audience. It was also the heyday of folk singers or *chansonniers* like Félix Leclerc and Gilles Vigneault. Leclerc in particular had been singing and writing for a long time, even finding success in Paris, before returning to find the same success at home. Singing about themes like nature and celebrations has made him one of the most revered musicians in the province.

CINEMA

After being under religious censorship during the first half of the 20th century, Québec cinema really kicked off in the 1960s, when a generation of directors formed the National Film Board (NFB). This film board gave them a platform, and they started to make movies mostly about the Québécois identity. Part of the enthusiastic social transformations that were happening in arts in this period, they shot documentaries and features that gained international recognition, despite their local flavor. Experiments in documentary film led to the Direct Cinema genre, which included Pierre Perreault's *Pour la Suite du Monde,* a vivid documentary about the ancestral beluga hunt in Isle-aux-Coudres, and Michel Brault's *Les Orders,* a rendition of the October crisis of 1971.

In the 1970s, a number of feature films gained wide critical acclaim and today are seen as part of a golden age in Québec cinema. Among these are *La Vraie Vie de Bernadette* by Gilles Carle (1972), *J.A. Martin Photographe* by Jean Beaudin (1977), and Frank Mankiewicz's *Les Bons Débarras* (1979). Most important of all is Claude Jutra's 1971 movie *Mon Oncle Antoine,* a coming-of-age story set in the rural Québec of the 1940s, which is considered to be one of the greatest Canadian films.

The Québec film industry is seen as the strongest in the country, and Québec films regularly win top accolades at the Genie Awards, which are the Canadian film industry awards. Québec's French cinema has a stronger character than its English counterpart, which often struggles to differentiate itself from American cinema.

With movies like *Le Déclin de l'Empire Américain* (1986) and *Jésus de Montréal* (1988), Denys Arcand is probably the best-known Québécois director. *Les Invasions Barbares* (2003), a poignant critique of the aging generation of the Quiet Revolution, won the Oscar for Best Foreign Film and was Best Screenplay at Cannes. Other stand-out directors have been scooped up by Hollywood, including Jean-Marc Vallée, best known for *Dallas Buyers Club,* and Denis Villeneuve, who directed *Arrival.* Newcomer Xavier Dolan has been recognized at the Cannes Film Festival for his films *J'ai Tué Ma Mère, Les Amours Imaginaries, (Heartbeats), Lawrence Anyways,* and *It's Only the End of the World,* and has set the course for a new generation of filmmakers.

LITERATURE

After Paris, Montréal has the most French-language writers in the world, many of whom have been translated into English. Playwright and author Michel Tremblay wrote *Chroniques du Plateau,* which has made him one of the most prolific and well-recognized authors in the province. His stories about working-class French-Canadians in the 1960s, written almost entirely in *joual* (colloquial Canadian French), defined the writing of his generation. Other important writers include Émile Nelligan, Hubert Aquin, Dany Laferrière, Marie-Claire Blais, and Anne Hébert, whose *Kamouraska* looks at treachery and love in 19th-century Québec. Gabrielle Roy's *The Tin Flute* tells the tale of a young woman in working-class Verdun during the Depression.

English-language Montréal literature has pretty much been defined, and reigned over, by the acerbic wit of Mordecai Richler, who continues to be one of the strongest voices

The 20th century saw a number of literary stars from many of the city's communities debut with unimaginable success. The most prominent of those was poet and musician **Leonard Cohen**, who died in 2016. Born in Westmount, a well-to-do and predominantly English neighborhood, Cohen went on to study at McGill University before publishing his first book of poetry, *Let Us Compare Mythologies,* in 1956. In 1964 he published the novel *The Favourite Game,* a semi-autobiographical book about a boy growing up in Montréal. Tracing Cohen's adolescence from primary through high school and university, you'll find many recognizable places and streets that in some cases remain unchanged.

Another Jewish-Canadian writer who became known for his semi-autobiographical tales of Montréal is **Mordecai Richler.** Where Cohen grew up on the affluent side of the city, Richler was born on rue St-Urbain, a working-class, mostly Jewish neighborhood in the Mile End. One of his most well-known novels, *The Apprenticeship of Duddy Kravitz,* revolves around the neighborhood, and you can still visit many of the places mentioned in the book—and in some cases shown in the movie (starring Richard Dreyfuss)—including the timeless St-Viateur Bagel Shop. His last novel, *Barney's Version,* which became an acclaimed film of the same name in 2010, was set and filmed here, though his criticisms of home and country make him a bit of a contentious figure with Francophone Montrealers, and some argue that the city should do more to recognize his literary contributions.

Life in the French community of the Plateau is vividly brought to life in the work of novelist and playwright **Michel Tremblay**, the preeminent Québécois writer of his time and famous for his 1965 play *Les Belles-Sœurs.* Tremblay's creations perfectly evoke life in the working-class neighborhood in the 1950s and '60s, right down to his use of *joual,* colloquial speech.

Born in Winnipeg, Manitoba, to a French-Canadian family, **Gabrielle Roy** eventually settled in Montréal, where she published her novel *Bonheur d'Occasion* in 1945 to rave reviews and a prestigious prize. Published in English two years later as *The Tin Flute,* it tells the story of a young woman during World War II struggling with poverty and ignorance in the working-class neighborhood of Saint-Henri. Even today it remains one of the few novels to accurately describe the struggles of the neighborhood and its inhabitants.

More recently, Montréal's vibrant culture and reasonable rents have made it a popular locale for poets, novelists, and nonfiction writers like Ann Carson, Sina Queyras, Guillaume Morrissette, Carmine Starnino, Saleema Nawaz, Rawi Hage, Heather O'Neill, Erin Mouré, and others. Check out the event listing at bookstore Drawn & Quarterly for old favorites and new discoveries; for reading series, try Resonance Reading Series, Writers Read Concordia, and the Atwater Poetry Project.

in Anglophone literature, even after his death in 2001. His novels *The Apprenticeship of Duddy Kravitz, Son of a Smaller Hero,* and *St-Urbain's Horseman* defined not only the city's Jewish population but the city itself.

The witty and poignant novels and short stories of Mavis Gallant continued to weave their way through Montréal, despite the fact that she'd long since emigrated to France.

New writers include Rawi Hage, who moved to Montréal in 2001 and whose 2006 novel *De Niro's Game* was nominated for the Scotiabank Giller Prize, and Heather O'Neill, whose 2006 novel *Lullabies for Little*

Criminals won the Hugh MacLennan Prize for Fiction.

VISUAL ARTS

Early-Québec art can be divided into two subject matters: landscapes and religion. The province's first painters were Catholic missionaries who used paintings and engravings to convert indigenous peoples. Since many of the works were by priests and nuns, they have a particularly naïve quality, a trend that continues in Québécois art. The first great Québécois painters emerged in the 19th century and included Théophile Hamel, known for portraits of explorers; Dutch-born

Cornelius Krieghoff, who depicted settlers and images of the wilderness; and Ozias Leduc, whose portrait *Boy with Bread* is one of the defining images of Québécois art.

Work continued to be defined by snowy city-scapes and bucolic farmland until the modern era of Canadian painting was ushered in by Paul-Émile Bourduas, John Lyman, and Alfred Pellan in the 1940s. Bourduas was the most prolific and outspoken of all three and developed a radical style of surrealism that came to be identified with a group called the Automatistes.

In 1948 Bourduas published the manifesto *Refus Global* (Global Refusal), rejecting traditional social, artistic, and psychological norms of Québécois society and the religious and bucolic art that defined it. The manifesto called instead for an untamed liberation of creativity and championed abstract art.

Canadian art and Québec's artistic community were never the same again. Automatiste artist Jean-Paul Riopelle would soon emerge as the movement's newest driving force, and his abstract works, called "grand mosaics," would become world renowned.

The 1960s and '70s were defined by artists like Claude Tousignant and Guido Molinari, whose abstract works used hypnotic geometric shapes and unusual color combinations to almost psychedelic proportions.

Some of Québec's biggest contemporary artists include David Altmejd, known for mixed-media pieces that incorporate various materials—everything from a decapitated werewolf head to shards of broken mirrors—into something cohesive and anthropomorphic. Valérie Blass also plays with a mix of materials and human yet non-human forms. Adnad Hannah's film and photographic works play with traditional art history. Melanie Authier, born in Montréal, is an abstract painter whose playful, colorful style evokes Turner-like landscapes and weather events. Two of the province's biggest artists are collectives: The work of BGL plays with conventional objects or pop culture icons in unconventional ways—a melted Darth Vader, or a motorcycle covered with snow in the middle of a gallery floor. Cooke et Sasseville play with similar ideas, and one of their works involves a giant flamingo laying its head down on train tracks.

DANCE AND THEATER

The established Québécois culture and the province's bohemian disposition help nurture a particularly diverse arts scene in both languages.

French theater is some of the best in the world, while English theater struggles to keep the pace. The country's top performing arts educational institution, the National Theatre School of Canada, is found in the Plateau, attracting Canada's most promising playwrights and stage actors in either language.

An innovative contemporary dance scene in the province has fostered internationally recognized companies like La La La Human Steps, O Vertigo, and Fondation Jean-Pierre Perreault, as well as the careers of dancers and choreographers Margie Gillis, Marie Chouinard, and Benoît Lachambre. Montréal institutions like Agora de la Danse, Tangante, and Studio 303, are dedicated exclusively to emerging dance artists. Québec also supports two classical ballet companies, Les Grands Ballets Canadiens de Montréal and Le Ballet de Québec.

ARCHITECTURE IN QUÉBEC

When settlers first arrived in Québec their main concern was with security; with that in mind all of the first towns started out as fortified enclosures. These were made of wood or stone and designed in the five-pointed Vauban style. By the end of the French regime, New France closely resembled provincial towns in the old country, with hospitals, convents, colleges, and churches whose steeples peeked out over the walls.

Early-1700s inhabitants had trouble adapting their homes to the cold weather, and many froze to death before the colony got it right. The design was altered and structures were made of rubble stone instead of wood, with small casement windows that were few and far between. The number of rooms in the house matched the number of chimneys. In 1721, wooden houses with mansard roofs were banned after a devastating fire, and stone firewalls and attic floors covered in terracotta tiles became the standard.

Although the British conquest took place in 1759, it wasn't until the 1780s that English influence could be seen in architecture around the province. A few high-ranking officials started building homes in the popular Palladian and Regency styles, with open-air porticoes and Italian columns. The Regency balconies and windows allowed for a perfect mix between inside and out, while also stopping the snow from blocking windows and doors in winter. Roofs became less slanted so the snow no longer fell directly on your head as you closed the door on your way out. All buildings during this period, commercial or residential, resembled country homes. Commercial buildings were set up to look like homes in part because the Catholic Church disapproved of the expansion of commerce.

The industrialization of the province led to an architectural style that would forever define Montréal: the duplexes and triplexes with circular exterior staircases. Built between 1900 and 1930, these economical structures were meant to accommodate large families. With outdoor staircases to save on heating and space, and balconies reminiscent of rural galleries, they also gave inhabitants the feel of a personal entrance. Covered in either limestone or brick, each had decorative touches like a cornice, Tuscan columns, or art nouveau-inspired windows. Over 100 years later, these unique staircases and multiple-family dwellings continue to thrive in the city and define its architectural identity.

THE CIRCUS

Cirque du Soleil is undoubtedly the most famous Québécois circus, founded in Baie-Saint-Paul in the early 1980s by a group of street performers. These stilt-walkers, jugglers, and fire-eaters banded together to create a performance platform, since the circus tradition didn't exist in the province at the time. In the years since then, they've become part of a rich circus culture they helped to create. Two schools dedicated to the circus arts are located in Montréal: the National Circus School, established in 1981, and TOHU, established in 2004.

Cirque Éloize, established in 1993, is another professional company situated in Montréal that is quickly following in the footsteps of Cirque du Soleil when it comes to pushing boundaries and innovation. They bring an edginess and dance sensibility to their shows, which can be seen throughout the world. This dedication to circus arts also means that the province has some of the best street performers in the world, who are especially visible during festival season.

ESSENTIALS

Transportation 272
Visas and Officialdom 275
Conduct and Customs 276
Tips for Travelers 277
Health and Safety 278
Information and Services. 280

Transportation

Pierre Trudeau International Airport

GETTING THERE

AIR

All international and in-country flights to Montréal arrive at Pierre Trudeau International Airport (514/394-7377, www.admtl.com) in Dorval.

The cheapest way to get from the airport to downtown is to take the 747 Express. The ride on this elongated city bus costs $10, and the ticket can then be used on other STM buses and Métros throughout the city. The bus takes passengers from the airport to nine downtown intersections, including Berri-UQÀM, the largest Métro station in the city. The bus runs 24 hours a day, 365 days a year, and takes 45-70 minutes depending on traffic and construction. During rush hour and bad weather, give yourself an extra 90 minutes of leeway.

A taxi from the airport to downtown will cost you $40 before tip. All taxis charge the same rate for destinations inside the downtown perimeter.

RAIL

Montréal's train station, Gare Centrale (895 rue de la Gauchetière W., 514/989-2626), is in the downtown core and is a major hub for Canada's VIA Rail trains (888/842-7245, www.viarail.ca). Amtrak (800/872-7245, www.amtrak.com) has a daily train heading to and from New York City, and though the ride is long—it clocks in at approximately 10 hours—it's a scenic one alongside the Hudson River.

BUS

Montréal's central bus terminal, the Gare d'Autocars (1717 rue Berri, 514/842-2281, www.gamtl.com), is in the Quartier Latin and has a restaurant, shops, an information booth, and electronic ticket dispensers, which are often faster than lining up at the ticket counter. It connects with the Berri-UQÀM Métro station, a major junction for the city's subway lines. Taxis are always lined up outside the exit on rue Berri.

the Square Victoria–OACI Métro entrance, a 1967 gift from Paris

CAR

Like most major Canadian cities, Montréal is accessible via the Trans-Canadian Highway, which crosses the island with two parallel routes. The southern part of the island can be traversed on Route 20 (Route 720 leads to downtown), the northern part of the island on Route 40; both have exits leading to downtown, including St-Laurent and St-Denis.

From the United States, to drive across the border from New York, you can take I-87 or I-89 north. From Massachusetts via New Hampshire and Vermont, take Route 55. At the border, all travelers must present a valid passport, and drivers must show the car's registration.

GETTING AROUND
PUBLIC TRANSPORTATION

Montréal's Métro and bus system is run by the STM (Société de Transport de Montréal, 514/786-4636, www.stm.info). The Métro is quick, safe, and efficient and consists of four lines. It is easy to navigate. A single fare on both bus and Métro is $3.25; 10 tickets will set you back $27. Each single ticket is valid for transfers for 120 minutes. If you're in town for a short stay and plan to take the Métro often in one day, get the unlimited day pass for $10; on the weekend, get the unlimited weekend pass, which is valid from 4pm on Friday afternoon to 5am Monday morning for $13.75. Sales are cash only at the ticket booth, but you can use both debit and credit cards at the automated machines. The Métro runs from 5am to 1am; check individual stations for last train times.

Métro and bus tickets are interchangeable, but if you want to get on the bus and don't have a ticket, make sure you have exact change. Once you've paid for your bus ticket, make sure to take a transfer (which will look like a regular ticket), especially if you're heading to the Métro or want to take another bus. Buses run all night long on many major streets, including Sherbrooke, Mont-Royal, St-Laurent, St-Denis, and avenue du Parc, but the night-bus number is often different from the daytime number, so double-check with the driver before you hop on.

DRIVING

In Montréal it is illegal to make a right-hand turn on a red light. Once you're off-island, it is fair game, but not in the city. Full of one-way streets and busy boulevards, Montréal is an easy city to navigate by car. But traffic, especially during rush hour or during construction (most of the time), gets a little out of hand. Parking can also be a real pain in the city, especially on quiet residential streets, where permits, usually for residents only, are required. Free parking downtown is especially hard to come by, but meters start around $3 per hour. Most of the meters are now automated and each parking spot is given a specific number; you punch that number into the machine and then place the receipt on your dashboard. You can also pay online or through an app, P$ Mobile Service—available for iPhone and Android users—which allows you to extend your parking time or pay when you're in a rush. If you don't see a machine but see a number on the spot, you're not looking far enough; some machines can be half a block away.

For a city that gets such cold winters, underground parking lots are hard to find, though the majority of them exist downtown and offer reasonable day rates. Parking, underground or otherwise, isn't always included with the price of your hotel, so double-check before you book. Overall, driving in the city can be a time waster; it's best to use a car just for side trips and excursions.

The speed limit on Canadian highways is 100 kilometers per hour (km/h), and it's 50 km/h on city streets

unless otherwise noted. U.S. citizens don't need an international license and neither do drivers from England or France. If your driver's license is in a language other than English or French, you need an International Driver's Permit; see the Québec government website (www.saaq.gouv.qc.ca) for more information. Members of AAA (American Automobile Association, www.aaa.com) are covered under the Canadian equivalent CAA (www.caa.ca). Gasoline is more expensive than in the United States, so fill up before crossing the border.

Rental Cars

Many of the large rental companies (Avis, Budget, Discount, Enterprise) are available in Montréal. The minimum age to rent a vehicle is 25, and rates run the gamut from $34 per day to $60 depending on time of year. If you're renting from downtown to head out of the city on weekends, plan ahead; many Montrealers have the same idea.

TAXIS

Montréal has a ton of different taxi companies, including Taxi Champlain (514/271-1111) and Taxi Co-op (514/725-9885). The initial charge is $3.30, each kilometer adds $1.60, and each minute of waiting is $0.60. Tip is usually 10-15 percent. Some drivers know the city well, others not so much, so make sure you have your destination with the cross street written down to show the driver, especially if it's a word you're unsure how to pronounce.

BICYCLING

Between April and November Bixi bikes (www.bixi.com) are available around the city. These are one of the fastest ways to get around and are easy to use. Swipe your credit card to get a number code, then type that number code into the bike of your choice to unlock it, and you're ready to ride. When you get to your destination return the Bixi to a station and make sure it is locked in. A 24-hour rental will cost you $5 as long as you keep your individual trips under 30 minutes; after that, a charge of $3-6 for each subsequent 30-minute period will apply. A $30 per month plan is available through the website.

Visas and Officialdom

PASSPORTS AND VISAS

All visitors must have a valid passport or other accepted secure documents to enter the country, even those entering from the United States by road or train. Citizens of the United States, Australia, New Zealand, Israel, Japan, and most western European countries don't need visas to enter Canada for stays up to 180 days. U.S. permanent residents are also exempt. People who travel regularly between Canada and the United States can consider getting a Nexus membership; details are available online (www.cbsa-asfc.gc.ca/prog/nexus).

Nationals from South Africa, China, and about 150 other countries must apply for a temporary resident visa, or visitor visa, in their home country. Full details can be found at Citizen and Immigration Canada (888/242-2100 within Canada, www.cic.gc.ca). Single-entry visitor visas are valid for six months and cost $100; multiple-entry visas last for up to 10 years, as long as a single stay doesn't last for longer than six months, and cost $100. A separate visa is required if you intend to work in Canada.

CUSTOMS

Depending on how long your stay in Canada is, you're allowed to take various amounts of goods back home without paying any duty or import tax. There is a limit on the amount of tobacco and liquor you can bring back duty-free, and some countries have a limit on perfumes. For exact amounts, check with the customs department in your home country. Also check the Canadian Border Services Agency (505/636-5064, www.cbsa-asfc.gc.ca) for details on bringing in and taking home goods.

There are very strict rules on bringing plants, flowers, food, and other vegetation into the country, so it's not advisable to bring them. If you're 18 years or older, you're allowed to bring into the country 50 cigars or 200 cigarettes, as well as 1.14 liters of liquor, 1.5 liters of wine, or 24 cans or bottles of beer. If you bring more, you'll face a hefty fine. Those traveling with their pets should check with the Canadian Food Inspection Agency (www.inspection.gc.ca) to see what is required. If you're traveling from the United States with your cat or dog, for example, you'll need a rabies vaccination certificate that meets certain requirements, and you will need to pay inspection fees.

Conduct and Customs

MOVING DAY

While the rest of the country celebrates Canada Day, the nation's national holiday, on July 1, Québécois move. It is the unofficial moving day for renters across the province—this is the day most leases change hands—and it is usually a hot, sweaty day with cars, vans, trucks, SUVs, and even bikes loaded to the hilt and headed for new digs. It's also not uncommon to see people simply schlepping their belongings by foot.

Don't even think about renting a car on July 1, as there won't be any left. A thrifter's paradise, the aftermath of the move leaves sidewalks and alleyways littered with discarded belongings and unwanted junk, which may turn out to be your treasure.

ALCOHOL

As in most Canadian provinces, if you're looking for good wine or spirits, you have to get it at the SAQ (Société des Alcools de Québec, www.saq.ca), the store run by the provincial liquor board. Found all over the city, they carry a wide selection of wine and spirits and a small selection of imported beer. Québec differs from most other provinces in that beer and wine can also be purchased in your local grocery and corner stores.

The selection of wine and beer varies from store to store; both the *dépanneur* (corner store) and the grocery store carry generally lower-quality wine than you'll find at the SAQ (Montrealers commonly use the term "*dép* wine" to denote overpriced cheap-quality wine—though that's not always the case). If you're looking for beer, however, a *dép* is your best bet. If you don't find the brand you're looking for, just step into the fridge yourself; it might look like just another display case, but step through the camouflaged door and you're in beerville. Drinking age in Québec is 18, and stores stop selling alcohol at 11pm.

STRIP CLUBS

Montréal is known for its strip clubs, a long and proud tradition that's been part of the city's landscape since the early 20th century. They are as out in the open as you can get, with many of them slotted in between shops on rue Ste-Catherine. Super Sexe, one of the larger clubs in the city, is hard to miss since its facade is adorned with an illuminated mural of flying women in capes and bikinis.

There are over 40 strip clubs in the city, both full-contact and non-contact. Full-contact dances are legal in Québec, and popular. Dancers work on a freelance basis, which allows them to work at any club they'd like.

Montréal embraces its position as a sex-positive city. It's not unusual to see women in strip clubs, and one of the most popular clubs in town, for both men and women, is Café Cleopatra, which has a popular drag cabaret on the second floor.

Make sure to follow the rules set out by each club, and respect the dancers—a little tipping and goodwill will get you a long way!

TIPPING

Tips and service charges aren't covered in the bill; instead a 15-20 percent tip should be added to the total bill at restaurants and bars at which you

In Québec, swearing is its own language. Instead of being derived from naughty sexual innuendo, swear words generally come from Catholicism and its practices. Originating in the early 19th century, many of the swear words or *sacres* developed out of a frustration at the church that seemingly controlled everything. The church is much less influential since the Quiet Revolution of the 1960s, and though the swear words are still in use, they are no longer as powerful and have become part of common language. Even English-speakers get into the habit, especially when talking with Québécois friends.

Among the most popular *sacres* and the ones you'll likely hear the most are *crisse* (Christ), *tabarnak* (from tabernacle), *ostie* (from host), and *sacrement* (from sacrament). Like all good swear words, however, they work best when used together, as in *criss d'ostie de tabarnak,* which defies translation.

Another word you might hear is *fucké,* which, weirdly enough, has nothing to do with the English pejorative; instead it means strange or bizarre, as in *"ce film était vraiment fucké,"* or "that film was really weird."

run a tab. When you order a drink at a bar, you're usually expected to pay when the drink is brought to you; a $1-2 tip for drinks is the standard. Tip the same for valet parking attendants, bellhops at the hotel, and coat-check attendants. Housekeeping staff should be tipped $3-5.

SMOKING

Since May 2006, smoking is illegal in bars, cafés, clubs, and restaurants and not permitted in enclosed public spaces. Outdoors on the sidewalk or on a restaurant's or bar's patio is fair game. Some hotels, however, still have smoking and non-smoking options, though it's becoming rarer. There are a few cigar bars, including Whisky Café, where smoking indoors is allowed due to specialized ventilation systems. You must be 18 years or older to buy tobacco in Québec.

Tips for Travelers

TRAVELING WITH CHILDREN

The plentiful kid-friendly activities in Montréal will tucker any kid out by the end of the day. Top choices include ice-skating and tobogganing in winter, and wading pools and bike rides along the canal in summer. Public parks with playgrounds can be found throughout the city and are perfect for blowing off some steam. However, some of the sleeker, cooler boutique hotels might not be the most fun for the kids. Children are also given half-price or free entry to most museums and attractions; some venues offer family rates. Hotels can often recommend babysitting services if none are available in-house.

WOMEN TRAVELERS

Montréal is a relatively safe city and women should feel at ease traveling alone. Still, the usual rules apply, and women should avoid walking alone on quiet streets and dimly lit areas, such as Mont-Royal, late at night. Violence is far less prevalent here than in the States, but if you are attacked or sexually assaulted call

911 or the Sexual Assault Center (514/934-4504 in Montréal).

LGBTQ TRAVELERS

Québec is one of the top destinations for gay travelers. In 1977 Québec became the second political entity (after Holland) to include a non-discrimination clause on the basis of sexual orientation in its charter of rights. Gay marriage is legal in Québec, and attitudes toward homosexuality in the province are generally open and accepting.

Montréal is the queer capital, and Tourisme Montréal (www.tourisme-montreal.org) has an LGBTQ mini-site with suggestions for hotels, restaurants, meet-ups, and beyond. CAEO Québec (www.caeoquebec.org) offers services for Montréal's English-speaking LGBTQ community and is behind Gay Line (888/505-1010), a help line that offers information on accommodations, services, and events.

Though there are several LGBTQ publications, monthly magazine *Fugues* (www.fugues.com) is the most comprehensive and has information on everything from hotels to saunas and upcoming gay events. It's available for free at racks around the city.

ACCESS FOR TRAVELERS WITH DISABILITIES

Most public buildings, including tourist offices, museums, and sights, are wheelchair accessible. Métro stations, however, are usually not accessible; instead almost all major bus routes are serviced by NOVA LFS buses adapted for wheelchairs. See www.stm.info for full details about your journey.

Access to Travel (www.accessto-travel.gc.ca) is a guide to accessible transportation across the country.

Kéroul (514/252-3104, www.keroul.qc.ca) specializes in tourism for people with disabilities. The association publishes *Québec for All* magazine, which lists 1,000-plus hotels, restaurants, museums, and theaters that are accessible. *The Accessible Road,* an online tool, offers information on everything from the most accessible top sights to how to get a handicapped parking sticker.

Health and Safety

HOSPITALS AND CLINICS

Canadians have free health care, but it's not free for visitors, so get travel insurance before you leave your home country. Montréal has high-ranking hospitals, but the emergency room wait can be lengthy, and if you're not a Canadian citizen, the treatment could be pricey (though not compared to U.S. hospitals).

Emergency rooms can be found in Montréal at Montréal General Hospital (1650 ave. Cedar, 514/934-1934), CHU Sainte-Justine (3175 chemin De la Côte-Saint-Catherine, 514/345-4931), and the Montréal Children's Hospital (1001 blvd. Decarie, 514/412-4400).

For minor maladies, visit walk-in clinic CLSC (514/527-2361, www.santemontreal.qc.ca); the one closest to downtown Montréal is at Guy-Concordia Métro station (1801 blvd.

If you want to fit in among the locals during winter's deep freeze you need two things: a parka and a pair of Sorel boots.

- **Parka:** When it comes to parkas, there are two schools: The younger generation goes for a selection from Canada Goose, while many mature Québécois opt for the Kanuk. Both are made in Canada and offer that important balance of warmth without too much puffiness. When buying a parka the goal is to avoid the "Michelin Man" look: Don't buy white and stay away from anything that has a ringed effect. Make sure it's got a fur- or faux fur-trimmed hood and covers your bum—good coverage is essential, especially when you want to take a crazy carpet down Mont-Royal.

- **Boots:** Made with a heavy insulated rubber sole and sturdy leather, Sorel winter boots have been a Canadian staple since 1959. Introduced to the market by Kaufman Footwear of Kitchener, Ontario, the boots were an instant hit. Originally they were made in Canada, but the company was bought by Columbia Sports in 2000. Though the boots are no longer Canadian owned and made, there is still a strong connection to their Canadian heritage. The ingenious construction of a thermal, waterproof sole paired with a more stylish upper is ideal for city life when 99.9 percent of the time you're walking through freezing gray slush.

- **Fur:** Another popular winter material in Québec is fur, and it's not unusual to see both men and women covered in fur from head to toe. If you find fur offensive, try to suppress your inner activist and instead take a deep breath—see that? Your nose is now completely frozen. Fur in Québec is less about style and more about survival and heritage, and many of the furs have been passed down through family members.

de Maisonneuve W., 514/934-0354), or call to find the closest one. Though the clinics will be glad to help you, you will have to pay cash to see a doctor; they don't take debit or credit.

If you're feeling unwell and just want some advice, call the health hotline (811) from any landline to speak with a nurse 24 hours a day.

PHARMACIES

The two big pharmacy chains in Montréal, Pharmaprix (www.pharmaprix.ca) and Jean Coutu (www.jeancoutu.com), both offer late-night services at various locations. Pharmaprix (1500 rue Ste-Catherine W., 514/933-4744, 8am-midnight daily) also has a 24-hour location north of Mont-Royal (5122 chemin de la Côte-des-Neiges, 514/738-8464). Jean Coutu (1675 rue Ste-Catherine W., 514/933-4221, 8am-midnight Mon.-Fri., 9am-midnight Sat.-Sun.) is another option.

EMERGENCY SERVICES

The fire department, police, and ambulance can all be reached by dialing 911. When in doubt, you can reach the operator by dialing 0. There's also the Poison Center (800/463-5060) if you're worried about something you've ingested.

CRIME AND HARASSMENT

Montréal is relatively safe and violent crime is rare. Tourists are more likely to be the targets of pickpockets at crowded bars, markets, and Métro stations. Cars with out-of-province license plates are also targets for theft, so make sure not to leave anything of value in the car and to remove your car registration and identification papers. Pedestrians should be careful, especially late at night when drivers don't always heed stop signs.

Information and Services

MONEY

Prices quoted in this book are in Canadian dollars. Canadian coins come in 5-cent (nickel), 10-cent (dime), 25-cent (quarter), $1 (loonie), and $2 (toonie) pieces. Paper money comes in $5 (blue), $10 (purple), $20 (green), $50 (red), and $100 (brown). In 2013, the government phased out the penny, so most companies round up their prices to the closest 5 cents. The Canadian dollar's value is sometimes much lower than the American dollar and sometimes trades at a few cents off par; www.xe.com has the most current rates.

the loonie, a $1-coin featuring a loon, and the toonie, a $2-coin featuring, well, a bear

ATMS

ATMs are all around the city, not just in banks. Though if you're getting money out from a foreign account, the safest way is to get it from a proper bank machine, to avoid fraud. Most banks charge you an additional fee when you withdraw a currency different from that of your home country as well as the original transaction fee. Check your daily withdrawal limit, so you don't get caught short.

CHANGING MONEY

Counters dedicated solely to exchanging money are becoming rarer and rarer. It's much simpler just to head to the bank; you'll find plenty in Montréal on rue Ste-Catherine, boulevard St-Laurent, and rue St-Denis. Foreign-exchange desks can also be found at the main tourist office and at the airport. Try Calforex (1230 Peel, 514/392-9100).

CREDIT CARDS

Major international credit cards are accepted at most stores, hotels, and restaurants. Carrying a credit card means you don't have the worry of carrying cash, and it also gives you excellent exchange rates. Visa and MasterCard are the most widely accepted, though certain places also accept American Express and, more rarely, Diners Club.

MAPS AND TOURIST INFORMATION

Airports have information offices open year-round. Information for Montréal can be obtained from Tourisme Montréal (877/266-5687, www.tourism-montreal.org). For Québec province info, visit Bonjour Québec (www.bonjourquebec.com).

Montréal has two main tourist offices. Centre Infotouriste (1255 rue Peel, 9am-6pm daily) will help you rent boats or cars, plan a city tour, and even reserve a hotel room. Though not as big, Old Montréal Tourist Office (174 rue Notre-Dame E., 9am-7pm daily June-Sept., 10am-6pm daily Oct., 10am-6pm Thurs.-Mon. Feb.-Apr.) is also helpful.

COMMUNICATIONS AND MEDIA

PHONES

Thanks to the massive popularity of cell phones, public pay phones are becoming almost impossible to find. If you do manage to find one, a single local call will set you back $0.50. Though many are coin operated, some also accept phone cards and credit cards. The main area code for Montréal is 514, though some newer numbers have the 438 area code. When dialing local numbers, you must include the area code.

Toll-free numbers begin with 800, 866, or 888 and must be preceded by a 1. Most of these numbers work in both Canada and the United States, but some may work only in a specified province. Dialing 0 for the operator or 911 for emergency services is free of charge from landlines and public phones, but calling 411 for directory assistance will cost you.

Cell Phones

Tribrand model cell phones working on GSM 1900 and other frequencies are the only foreign cell phones that will work in Canada, and you will probably need to purchase a local SIM card—but check with your phone service provider for details. If your phone doesn't work, it might be worth picking up an inexpensive phone at an electronics store and getting a pay-as-you-go plan. Travelers from the United States will likely have service, though roaming charges will probably apply; check with your provider for details.

Mobile Apps

Montréal has mobile apps that you can download for free for both Android and iPhone. If you're using public transit to get around, the STM mobile app will help you navigate Montréal's buses and subway system. DistrictMontréal will clue you in to what's happening and what events to catch on your visit.

INTERNET SERVICES

Numerous cafés offer free Wi-Fi; you can register for free at Île Sans Fil (www.ilesansfil.org) and find out where you can get online with your laptop. Visit www.zapquebec.org for free Wi-Fi in Québec. If you left your computer at home and can't check your email at your hotel, your best bets are the local libraries.

In Montréal, the Grand Bibliothéque (475 blvd. de Maisonneuve E., 514/873-1100, www.banq.qc.ca, 10am-10pm Tues.-Fri., 10am-6pm Sat.-Sun.) offers free Internet access as well as Wi-Fi. Atwater Library (1200 Atwater, 514/935-7344, www.atwaterlibrary. ca, 10am-8pm Mon. and Wed., 10am-6pm Tues. and Thurs.-Fri., 10am-5pm Sat.) offers Internet services for $4 per hour as well as free Wi-Fi access.

Most hotels, though not all, offer free Wi-Fi access, and the majority also have public computers.

MAIL SERVICES

There are dozens of postal outlets located across Montréal. If you know the postal code of the place you're staying, you can look up the closest branch to you at www.canadapost.ca or call Canada Post (866/607-6301) for general information. Many outlets are located in Pharmaprix branches.

NEWSPAPERS AND PERIODICALS

Montréal's only English-language daily paper is the *Montréal Gazette* (www.montrealgazette.com), which covers local and national news as well as arts and politics.

The Globe & Mail (www.globeandmail.com) and the *National Post* (www.nationalpost.com) are the country's two national papers, and while both cover national and international events as well as the arts, the *Globe* leans more to the center-left and the *Post* to the right.

For French readers there's the federalist *La Presse* and separatist-leaning *Le Devoir,* both of which cover the news and art of the entire province, not just the Francophone community (though that's a large part of it). There's also *Le Journal de Montréal,* a tabloid paper that mainly covers local events. And in Québec there's *Le Soleil,* a great little paper with a focus on events in the capital. There's also the Francophone alternative weekly *Voir* (www.voir.ca), in both a Montréal and Québec version, great for getting the latest scoop on what's going on in town or for scoping out their restaurant reviews.

L'actualité is the Québec monthly news magazine, *Maclean's* is Canada's most well-known news magazine, and *The Walrus* is the country's best-known general interest magazine.

TELEVISION

The main public-radio and television stations are run by the Canadian Broadcasting Corporation. The CBC is the English-language component and Radio-Canada is the French-language component; both are revered for their long broadcast history. The other major English-language network is the Canadian Television Network (CTV), which broadcasts both Canadian and U.S. programs as well as nightly newscasts.

For Francophone audiences there's Télé-Québec (TVA) and V (formally TQS), both of which broadcast news programs, movies, and shows from France, as well as dubbed American sitcoms and dramas.

RADIO

There are both Francophone and Anglophone radio stations in Montréal. Many young, English-speaking Montrealers are fans of CBC Montréal 1 (88.5 FM), the area's version of NPR. It has educational and cultural programs, and CBF (95.1 FM) is its French counterpart. Fans of Led Zeppelin hear them on heavy rotation on CHOM (97.7 FM); though it also plays alternative music, it's primarily classic rock. CKUT (90.3 FM) is a nonprofit station that plays an eclectic mix of music and news stories. CISM (89.3 FM) is Université de Montréal's station, with a focus on indie and Francophone tunes. CJFM (95.9 FM) is Virgin Radio playing Top 40 hits all day long, and TSN 690 Montréal (690 AM) is your classic AM sports station.

WEIGHTS AND MEASURES
ELECTRICITY

Like the United States and Japan, Canada uses 110/120-volt, 60-cycle electrical power. Canadian electrical goods have a plug with two flat, vertical prongs and sometimes a third rounded prong, which acts as a ground. Travelers from outside North America should bring a plug adapter for small appliances; a voltage converter may also be necessary.

MEASUREMENTS

Canada uses the metric system of measurement. Distances are measured in kilometers, liquids in liters and milliliters, but height, strangely enough, is measured in feet.

TIME

Montréal is on eastern standard time (EST/EDT), the same as New York and Toronto. Canada switches to daylight saving time (one hour later than standard time) from the second Sunday in March to the first Sunday in November. "Spring forward, fall back," is a simple way to remember how to set your clocks properly. In Québec the 24-hour clock is used for most schedules, including movies and trains.

RESOURCES

Glossary

l'Abitation: the first settlement (habitation)

allongé: a long espresso coffee, the French name for an Italian *lungo*

Allophone: an immigrant to Canada whose native language is neither French nor English

Anglophone: a native English speaker

Bill 101: a Québec law that deals with French and English language issues

boîte à chansons: a place where you can hear singer/songwriters *(chansonniers)* play

boréal: the type of forest that is found in the province of Québec

branchée: plugged in, which translates to hip, or cool, in the French vernacular

brasserie: a brewery or pub

brioche: a type of sweet, eggy French bread

cabane à sucre: a sugar shack; this is where you go to see maple syrup tapped from trees and to eat maple-drenched treats

café: where you buy coffee as well as the word for the drink itself; usually refers to an espresso

café filtre: drip coffee

calèche: a horse-drawn carriage

casse-croûte: Québécois snack bar, known for serving cheap, working-class fare. It's at *casse-croûtes* that Québécois snacks like poutine and *guédilles* were first created.

chansonnier: a folk singer/songwriter

côte: hill; if a street has *"côte"* in its name, it's on a hill

coureurs de bois: early fur hunters and adventurers who helped explore North America

dépanneur: meaning "to help out"; a convenience store in Québec, commonly referred to as a *dép.*

First Nations: indigenous nations in Canada other than the Métis and Inuit

Francophone: a native French speaker

frites: French fries

guédille: a sandwich served in a hot dog roll, similar to a lobster roll (though fillings vary). They are commonly found at *casse-croûtes.*

Inuit: northern indigenous peoples

joual: a popular form of slang

loonie: Canadian one-dollar coin

Métis: a post-contact Indigenous group in Canada

Nouvelle France: the name given to Québec by the French; it also means New France

pâté chinois: a meat, potato, and vegetable pie similar to shepherd's pie

patriotes: the name given to patriots who led an uprising against the government in 1837; it's used today to denote those who are against federal rule

pogo: corn dog (from a popular brand name in Canada)

pont: a bridge

poudreuse: blowing snow

poutine: crispy French fries covered with fresh cheese curds and smothered in gravy—the unofficial food of Québec

quai: quay that juts out into the water

Quebecker: English name for all native citizens of the province of Québec

Québécois: the name for the Francophone population in the province as well as the language they speak; can also be the French term for all native citizens of the province of Québec

Refus Global (Total Refusal): a manifesto of a group of Québec artists that radically changed the face of modern Québec art

sacres: the name for Québécois swear words

sandwicherie: a place that makes sandwiches

sans gluten: gluten-free

sloche: slush made from melted snow

sovereigntists: those who want Québec to separate from the rest of Canada

stimés: hot dog with a steamed bun

Sulpicians: society of Catholic priests founded in Paris in 1641 who were part

of the founding of Québec

table d'hôte: a fixed-price meal

terrasse: an outdoor patio; terrace

terroir: food products that come from the area, as in *terroir* cooking

tire sur la neige: maple syrup that has been frozen on snow, a popular treat during the sugaring-off season

toastés: hot dog with a toasted bun

toonie: a Canadian two-dollar coin

tourtière: a meat pie made with everything from pork and beef to game

végétalien: vegan

végétarien: vegetarian

viennoiseries: pastries and sweet breads usually eaten at breakfast

vieux: old, as in Vieux-Montréal (Old Montréal) and Vieux-Port (Old Port)

French Phrasebook

If you're uncomfortable about breaking out your rusty 10th-grade French, relax. You might not even crease the spine of this phrasebook, since just about everyone in Montréal understands English, even if they're not adept at speaking it. Even if you do feel confident with your French, the Québécois accent will take some getting used to, and the language you hear on the street won't have much to do with the words you read in this phrasebook. The Québécois also have a tendency to speak very fast, so don't be afraid to ask someone to slow down if you're having trouble understanding.

As has been explained throughout the guide, language is a central issue in Québec, so a good rule of thumb is to be polite; the Québécois are especially receptive to people who are at least trying to speak a little French, and they're always encouraging. Throw in a few easy

French words here and there, like *bonjour* or *merci,* and try to start all your conversations in French, and you'll be well on your way.

PRONUNCIATION

French is known for being difficult to pronounce. When it comes to phonetic pronunciation, French is as bad as English. Most of the spellings and the pronunciations don't have much in common, which can make learning French difficult. Here are a few guidelines to get you started.

VOWELS

Vowels in French can be confusing for an English speaker: the "a" is **e,** the "e" is **i,** and the "u" is from outer space. Here is the secret:

a pronounced a, as in "cat"

i pronounced ee, as in "free"

y pronounced the same way as **i**

o pronounced ah, as in "dog," or oh, as in "bone"

u This vowel has always been a tough one for English-speakers. The closest you can get would be to put your lips and tongue in position to say "oh" and try to say "ee" instead. Something like the ew in "stew" is not that far off.

e pronounced uh, as in "about." Before two or more consonants, it is pronounced eh as in "set." At the end of a word, such as *chaise* (chair), **e** is silent, except in words of one syllable like *je* (I), where it is pronounced "uh."

VOWEL GROUPS

To make things harder, French assembles certain letters to produce new sounds.

ai pronounced eh, as in "set," as well as **ei**

au pronounced oh, as in "bone," as well as **eau**

eu pronounced uh, as in "about." It is sometimes spelled **œu**, as in *œuf* or *sœur*

oi pronounced wa, as in "wagon"

ou pronounced oo, as in "foot"

NASAL VOWELS

A typical aspect of French speech is nasal vowels, vowels pronounced through both the mouth and nose. They are as difficult for English-speakers to reproduce as the **u** and will require quite a bit of phonetic gymnastics before you get it right.

an, am pronounced ahn, as in "aunt"

en, em pronounced pretty close to ahn, combined with the on of "honk"

in where the a of "bag" is nasalized as in "anchor." You'll find more or less the same sound in many different spellings, such as **im, un, um, yn, ym, ain, aim, ein,** and **eim**

on, om pronounced on, as in "long"; a nasalized **o**

ACCENTS

French has five different accents that stick to vowels and make French as exotic to read as it is to hear: In French they are called *accent aigu* (´), *accent grave* (`), *accent circonflexe* (^), *accent tréma* (¨), and the *cédille* (ç), which is only used with the letter **c.**

The circumflex and grave accents appear as **è, à, ù, ê, â, û, î,** and **ô.** Except for **ê** and **è,** which are pronounced eh as in "set," and **ô,** which always sounds like oh as in "bone," the accents don't change the pronunciation of the letters; they are mere decoration.

The acute accent, as in **é,** is pronounced ay as in "day," but shorter. The cedilla makes **c** sound like **s.**

Last but not least, the dieresis (*tréma*) separates two vowel sounds, such as **ï** in *naïve,* which is not pronounced nev, but as two separate syllables, na-ive.

CONSONANTS

Most French consonants are similar to their English equivalents, even though there are a few differences. For example, *some* final consonants are silent; rather than pronouncing *vous* as "vooz," you'd say "voo." In general the following consonants are usually silent: **b, d, g, m, n, p, t, x,** and **z. S** is always silent in plurals but often pronounced otherwise. Others are generally pronounced: **c, f,** and **l. R** is usually pronounced, except in the endings **er** and **ier.**

c pronounced k as in "kick" before **a, o,** or **u,** and s as in "set" before **e, i,** or **y.** Combine **c** and **h,** as in *chance* (luck), and it is pronounced like sh as in "ship"

g pronounced g as in "god," except when placed before **e, i,** or **y,** when it is pronounced zh as in "measure." Combine it with **n,** as in *vigne* (vine), and it is pronounced like ny in "canyon"

h	always silent
j	pronounced zh as in "measure"
ll	pronounced y as in "yes," in words like *famille*
r	emphasized more strongly than in English and comes from the far back of the throat

BASIC EXPRESSIONS

Hello *Bonjour*

Hi *Salut*

Good-bye *Au revoir/Salut*

Good morning/afternoon *Bonjour*

Good evening *Bonsoir*

Good night *Bonne nuit*

How are you? (courteous) *Comment allez-vous?*

How are you doing? (colloquial) *Ça va?*

Fine, thank you. *Ça va bien, merci.*

And you? *Et vous?*

See you later. *À plus tard/À bientôt.*

Nice to meet you. *Enchanté.*

Yes *Oui*

No *Non*

Please *S'il vous plaît*

Thank you *Merci*

You're welcome *Bienvenu/De rien*

Excuse me *Excusez-moi*

Sorry *Pardon/Désolé* (*pardon* is for small mistakes, like bumping into someone; *désolé* is best used if you've made a larger error)

What's your name? *Comment vous appelez-vous?*

My name is . . . *Je m'appelle . . .*

Where are you from? *D'où venez-vous?*

I'm from . . . *Je viens de . . .*

Do you speak English? *Parlez-vous anglais?*

I don't speak French. *Je ne parle pas français.*

I don't understand. *Je ne comprends pas.*

I don't know. *Je ne sais pas.*

Can you please repeat? *Pourriez-vous répéter?*

What's it called? *Ça s'appelle?*

Would you like . . . ? *Voulez-vous . . . ?*

TERMS OF ADDRESS

In French, the most polite way to address a stranger is by using the *vous* form of "you," as opposed to *tu*, even though *vous* is the plural second person. Montréal is a less formal place, linguistically, than Paris, but it never hurts to err on the side of politesse.

I *je*

you *tu*

he *il*

she *elle*

we *nous*

you (plural) *vous*

they *ils/elles* (*ils* is for a group of men, or a mixed group; *elles* is for a group of women)

Mr./Sir *monsieur*

Mrs./Madame *madame*

Miss *mademoiselle* (best used only for young girls—*madame* is preferable for anyone you'd refer to as "Ms." in English)

young man *jeune homme*

young woman *jeune fille*

child *enfant*

brother/sister *frère/sœur*

father/mother *père/mère*

son/daughter *fils/fille*

husband/wife *mari/femme*

friend *ami/amie*

boyfriend/girlfriend *copain/copine*

married *marié/mariée*

single *célibataire*

divorced *divorcé/divorcée*

QUESTIONS

When? *Quand?*

What? *Quoi?*

What is it? *Qu'est-ce que c'est?*

Who? *Qui?*

Why? *Pourquoi?*

How? *Comment?*

Where is . . . ? *Où est . . . ?*

What's it called? *Ça s'appelle?*
Would you like . . . ? *Voulez-vous . . . ?*

GETTING AROUND

Where is . . . ? *Où est . . . ?*
How far away is . . . ? *À quelle distance est . . . ?*
How can I get to . . . ? *Puis-je aller à . . . ?*
bus *bus*
car *voiture*
train *train*
bus station *la station d'autobus*
train station *la gare de trains*
airport *l'aéroport*
What time do we leave? *À quelle heure est le départ?*
What time do we arrive? *À quelle heure arrive-t-on?*
a one-way ticket *un aller simple*
a round-trip ticket? *un aller retour*
Can you take me to this address? *Pourriez-vous m'emmener à cette adresse?*
north *nord*
south *sud*
east *est*
west *ouest*
left/right *gauche/droite*
straight ahead *tout droit*
entrance *entrée*
exit *sortie*
first *premier*
last *dernier*
next *prochain*

ACCOMMODATIONS

Are there any rooms available? *Avez-vous des chambres disponibles?*
I'd like to make a reservation. *J'aimerais faire une reservation.*
I want a single room. *J'aimerais une chambre simple.*
Is there a double room? *Y a-t-il une chambre double?*
private bathroom *salle de bains privée*

key *clé*
one night *une nuit*
Can you change the sheets/towels? *Pourriez-vous changer les draps/les serviettes?*
Could you please wake me up? *Pourriez-vous me réveiller?*
Is breakfast included? *Est-ce que le petit déjeuner est inclus?*

FOOD

to eat *manger*
to drink *boire*
breakfast *déjeuner*
lunch *dîner*
dinner *souper*
Can I see the menu? *Puis-je voir le menu?*
We're ready to order. *Nous sommes prêts à commander.*
Can I have some more wine? *Puis-je avoir un peu plus de vin?*
Can you bring me the bill please? *Pourriez-vous apporter l'addition?*
Is the service/the tip included? *Est-ce que le service est compris?*
I'm a vegetarian. *Je suis végétarien.*
It was delicious. *C'était délicieux.*
hot *chaud*
cold *froid*
sweet *sucré*
salty *salé*
bread *pain*
toast *rôtis*
rice *riz*
Enjoy! *Bon appétit!*

MEAT AND FISH

meat *viande*
beef *bœuf*
sweetbreads (veal) *ris de veau*
pork *porc*
lamb *agneau*
sweetbreads (lamb) *ris d'agneau*
chicken *poulet*

ham *jambon*
fish *poisson*
salmon *saumon*
mussels *moules*
oysters *huîtres*
shrimp *crevette*
tuna *thon*
rare *saignant*
medium *à point*
well done *bien cuit*
roasted *rôti*
boiled *bouilli*
grilled *grillé*
fried *frit*

EGGS AND DAIRY

milk *lait*
cream *crème*
butter *beurre*
cheese *fromage*
ice cream *crème glacée*
egg *œuf*
hard-boiled egg *œuf dur*
over-easy eggs *œufs tournés*
scrambled eggs *œufs brouillés*
poached egg *œuf poché*

VEGETABLES AND FRUITS

vegetables *légumes*
carrot *carotte*
tomato *tomate*
potato *patate/pomme de terre*
cucumber *concombre*
pepper *poivron*
mushrooms *champignons*
eggplant *aubergine*
peas *petits pois*
cabbage *chou*
apple *pomme*
pear *poire*
banana *banane*
orange *orange*
lemon *citron*
grape *raisin*
strawberry *fraise*
blueberry *bleuet*
raspberry *framboise*

SEASONING AND SPICES

sugar *sucre*
salt *sel*
black pepper *poivre*
onion *oignon*
garlic *ail*
olive oil *huile d'olive*
vinegar *vinaigre*
cinnamon *cannelle*
basil *basilic*
parsley *persil*
mint *menthe*
ginger *gingembre*

DRINKS

drinks *boissons*
beer *bière*
wine *vin*
wine list *la carte des vins*
cheers! *à votre santé!/santé!*
water *eau*
ice *glace*
juice *jus*
filtered coffee *café filtre*
coffee with milk *café au lait*
black coffee *café noir*

SHOPPING

money *argent*
ATM *guichet automatique*
credit card *carte de crédit*
to buy *acheter*
to shop *magasiner*
I don't have change. *Je n'ai pas de monnaie.*
more *plus*
less *moins*
a good price *un bon prix*
sales *soldes*
How much does it cost? *Combien ça coûte?*
That's too expensive. *C'est trop cher.*
discount *rabais*
Can I try it on? *Est-ce que je peux l'essayer?*
It's too tight. *C'est trop serré.*
It's too big. *C'est trop grand.*

Can I exchange it? *Est-ce que je peux l'échanger?*

HEALTH AND SAFETY

Can you help me? *Pouvez-vous m'aider?*

I don't feel well. *Je ne me sens pas bien.*

I'm sick. *Je suis malade.*

Is there a pharmacy close by? *Y a-t-il une pharmacie pas loin?*

Can you call a doctor? *Pouvez-vous appeler un docteur?*

I need to go to the hospital. *Je dois aller à l'hôpital.*

medicine *médicament*

condom *condom, préservatif*

Is this neighborhood safe? *Est-ce que ce quartier est sécuritaire?*

Help! *À l'aide!/Au secours!*

Call the police! *Appeler la police.*

thief *voleur*

COMMUNICATIONS

to talk, to speak *parler*

to hear, to listen *écouter, entendre*

to make a phone call *faire un appel téléphonique*

cell phone *cellulaire*

What's your phone number? *Quel est ton numéro de téléphone?*

What's your email address? *Quelle est ton adresse électronique?*

collect call *appel à frais virés*

Do you have Internet? *Avez-vous Internet ici?*

post office *bureau de poste*

letter *lettre*

stamp *timbre*

postcard *carte postale*

NUMBERS

0 *zéro*

1 *un*

2 *deux*

3 *trois*

4 *quatre*

5 *cinq*

6 *six*

7 *sept*

8 *huit*

9 *neuf*

10 *dix*

11 *onze*

12 *douze*

13 *treize*

14 *quatorze*

15 *quinze*

16 *seize*

17 *dix-sept*

18 *dix-huit*

19 *dix-neuf*

20 *vingt*

21 *vingt-et-un*

30 *trente*

40 *quarante*

50 *cinquante*

60 *soixante*

70 *soixante-dix*

80 *quatre-vingt*

90 *quatre-vingt dix*

100 *cent*

101 *cent un*

200 *deux cent*

500 *cinq cent*

1000 *mille*

2000 *deux mille*

TIME

What time is it? *Quelle heure est-il?*

It's 2 o'clock. *Il est deux heures.*

It's 2:15. *Il est deux heures et quart.*

It's 2:30. *Il est deux heures et demie.*

It's 2:45. *Il est deux heures quarante-cinq.*

in two hours *dans deux heures*

now *maintenant*

before *avant*

after *après*

late *tard*

early *tôt*

When? *Quand?*

DAYS AND MONTHS

day *jour*

night *nuit*
morning *matin*
afternoon *après-midi*
yesterday *hier*
tomorrow *demain*
today *aujourd'hui*
week *semaine*
month *mois*
year *année*
Monday *lundi*
Tuesday *mardi*
Wednesday *mercredi*
Thursday *jeudi*
Friday *vendredi*
Saturday *samedi*
Sunday *dimanche*
January *janvier*
February *février*
March *mars*
April *avril*
May *mai*
June *juin*
July *juillet*
August *août*

September *septembre*
October *octobre*
November *novembre*
December *décembre*

SEASONS AND WEATHER

season *saison*
spring *printemps*
summer *été*
autumn *automne*
winter *hiver*
weather *temps/météo*
sun *soleil*
It's sunny. *Il fait du soleil.*
rain *pluie*
It's raining. *Il pleut.*
snow *neige*
It's snowing. *Il neige.*
snowstorm *tempête de neige*
ice *glace/verglas*
It's hot. *Il fait chaud.*
It's cold. *Il fait froid.*

Suggested Reading

HISTORY AND GENERAL INFORMATION

Dickinson, John A., and Brian Young. *A Short History of Québec*. Montréal: McGill-Queen's University Press, 1993, revised 2008. Originally written in 1992, this book is now into its fourth edition and offers a comprehensive overview of the province's social and economic development from pre-European to modern times. This latest edition includes reflections on the Bouchard-Taylor Commission on Accommodation and Cultural Differences, which examined attitudes toward immigration and immigrants in the province.

Fox, Joanna. *Montréal's Best Terrasses*. Montréal: Véhicule Press, 2012. One of Montréal's greatest attributes is its outdoor dining options. Restaurant reviewer and food industry insider Joanna Fox gives readers the lowdown on 60 of the city's best patios, with a selection to suit all tastes and budgets.

Grescoe, Taras. *Sacré Blues: An Unsentimental Journey through Quebec*. Toronto: Macfarlane Walter & Ross, 2001. Montréal author Taras

Grescoe's modern account of Québec explores the stranger side of the province's pop culture, takes readers to a Francophone country-and-western festival, meets up with UFO-obsessed followers of Raël, and, of course, deconstructs a Montréal Canadiens hockey game. The book won the Québec Writers' Federation First Book Award and the Mavis Gallant Prize for Nonfiction in 2001.

Jenish, D'Arcy. *The Montreal Canadiens: 100 Years of Glory*. Toronto: Doubleday Canada, 2008. Published to coincide with the hockey team's 100th anniversary, this is the definitive history of the team—from the days of their first Stanley Cup win to the return of former player Bob Gainey as general manager. Even if you're not a fan, this book provides an insider's look at one of the NHL's most storied teams.

Lacoursière, Jacques, and Robin Philpot. *A People's History of Québec*. Montréal: Baraka Books, 2009. First published in French, this concise book looks at the history of the province through the people who discovered, explored, and inhabited it. The focus is on day-to-day life and offers little-known details, like the despicable "mixed dancing" at times of celebration and early settlers' love of *charivari,* a loud, rambunctious party through the streets.

FICTION AND MEMOIRS

Carrier, Roch. *The Hockey Sweater.* Montréal: Tundra Books, 1979. This semi-autobiographical children's picture book is one of the most memorable Canadian stories. It tells the tale of a boy in small-town Québec who orders a Canadiens hockey sweater from the Eaton's catalogue only to receive a Toronto Maple-Leaf jersey. Full of subtle comments on Québec and the rest of Canada, it's a touching story that has been immortalized by an NFB film.

Cohen, Leonard. *The Favourite Game.* New York: Vintage, 1963. In this semi-autobiographical book, protagonist Lawrence Breavman wanders through the Montréal streets with his best friend and confidant, Krantz, reminisces about his years at summer camp, and tries to understand the death of his father.

Doucet, Julie. *365 Days: A Diary.* Montréal: Drawn & Quarterly, 2008. Born and raised in Montréal, comic artist Julie Doucet first gained recognition as an artist for her zine *Dirty Plotte,* a funny, demented take on her own life experiences. This book offers an intimate look at the artistic community Doucet surrounded herself with in her early days and the experience of an artist in Montréal.

Hage, Rawi. *Cockroach*. Toronto: House of Anansi Press, 2009. IMPAC-Dublin award-winner Rawi Hage's second effort, *Cockroach* tells the tale of a struggling immigrant living in Montréal's underbelly. Hage, who is originally from Lebanon, brings a unique perspective and an adept eye to the Montréal experience.

MacLennan, Hugh. *Two Solitudes.* Toronto: McClelland & Stewart, 1945. The title of this book has become emblematic of the country's French/

English cultural and linguistic divide. Set between World War I and 1939, the book takes place in Saint-Marc-des-Érables, a small Québec town, and the booming, predominantly English city of Montréal. Centered on Paul Tallard, a Québécois at home with both languages, the book follows him on a quest to find his own identity and a way of defining the Canadian experience.

O'Neill, Heather. *Lullabies for Little Criminals*. Toronto: Harper Perennial, 2006. Heather O'Neill was born and (mostly) raised in Montréal, and her debut novel tells the story of Baby, a 12-year-old girl growing up in the seedy area of lower Saint-Laurent with her young, well-meaning junkie father. There is a touching humanity to O'Neill's writing, and her depiction of Montréal in all its real, gritty glory is fascinating.

Proulx, Monique. *Les Aurores Montréales*. Toronto: Douglas & McIntyre, 1997. Twenty-seven short stories make up this collection that takes place in pre- and post-referendum Québec. Weaving in and out of Montréal, the stories look at the lives of Quebeckers and how they are affected by the changing times.

Richler, Mordecai. *Son of a Smaller Hero*. Paris: André Deutsch, 1955. From Mile End's Jewish ghetto to the bed of a downtown non-Jewish woman, this book follows prodigal son Noah Adler as he searches to find his identity in the neighborhoods and communities that make up Montréal.

Tremblay, Michel. *Les Belles Sœurs*. Vancouver: Talonbooks, revised ed., 1992. Arguably the most important Québécois writer of his generation, Tremblay was only 23 years old when he wrote this play in 1965. First presented in 1968 at Théâtre du Rideau Vert, it ushered in a new era of Québécois theater. Written in *joual* (working-class slang), the play is set in the triplexes of Montréal's Plateau and follows the exploits of an extended family.

Internet Resources

An Endless Banquet
www.endlessbanquet.squarespace.com
A Montréal couple closely connected with the food scene—she's a chef at the FoodLab, he's a former restaurant critic—gives readers the lowdown on restaurants and food happenings around the city. From the best late-night burger to the best place to blow $200 on a meal, they've got you covered.

Bonjour Québec
www.bonjourquebec.com
The province's official tourism website has comprehensive information on anything and everything to do with the province, from national parks to kid-friendly fun.

Cult Montréal
www.cultmontreal.com
This website and bimonthly publication gives you the goods on the city's

cultural happenings and covers everything from news stories to movies, music, art events, and restaurant reviews.

Montréal Eater
www.montreal.eater.com
A website that covers the eating habits and news of cities all over North America has a Montréal version. Expect everything from exclusive interviews with local chefs to review round-ups.

MTL Blog
www.mtlblog.com
From best-of-Montréal lists to news and lifestyle journalism, this youth-focused website has you covered.

Said the Gramophone
www.saidthegramophone.com
Though not exclusively Montréal-based (one of the writers lives in Toronto), this music blog offers an interesting insider take on the Montréal music scene.

Tourism Montréal
www.mtl.org
The official tourism site for the city also has bloggers dedicated to specific aspects of the city—gay, nightlife, women's interests—that keep the site fresh and interesting.

Voir
www.voir.ca
The online component to the Francophone alternative weekly, Voir has event listings, restaurant reviews, and sections focusing on visual arts, books, music, and cinema.

Index

A

Abbaye Saint-Benoît-du-Lac: 229, 246
accessibility: 278
accessory shopping: Centre-Ville 193;
    Centre-Ville Est 195; Plateau Mont-
    Royal 199
accommodations: 211-227; Centre-Ville
    219-221; Centre-Ville Est 221-223;
    highlights 212; hostels 223; Mile End
    and Petite-Italie 227; Plateau Mont-
    Royal 225-227; Quartier Latin and
    the Village 224-225; reservations for
    23; tips on choosing 211-215; Vieux-
    Montréal 216-219; see also Hotels
    Index
activities: best bets 17; Centre-Ville
    178-179; Greater Montréal 182-186;
    highlights 174; Mile End and Petite-
    Italie 181-182; Plateau Mont-Royal
    179-181; spectator sports 186; Vieux-
    Montréal 175-178
African music: 169
Agora de la Danse: 149, 156
Airbnb: 214
air travel: 22, 272
alcohol: 276
Aldred Building: 60
alfresco dining: 11, 118
alleyways, green: 11, 85
Les Alouettes de Montréal: 174, 180
amusement parks: 93
Anglophone culture: 263
animals: 254
antiques: Centre-Ville 193; Knowlton 244;
    Mile End and Petite-Italie 206; Plateau
    Mont-Royal 201; Quartier Latin and
    the Village 197; rue Amherst 80
apple orchards: 241
apps, mobile: 281
Arab culture: 27, 171
architecture: general discussion 271;
    Biosphère 91; Centre Canadien
    d'Architecture 39, 70-71; Chapelle
    Notre-Dame-de-Bon-Secours 65;
    Church of Saint-Michael and Saint-
    Anthony 85; Dorchester Square 73; La
    Grande Bibliothèque 44, 79; Habitat
    67 68; Haskell Free Library and Opera
    House 245; highlights 60; Hotel 10
    Montréal 43; Hôtel de Ville 67; Marché

Atwater 90; Marché Bonsecours 64;
    Musée du Château Ramezay 67; Le
    Musée Dufresne-Nincheri 163; Place
    d'Armes 61; Pointe-à-Callière Musée
    d'Archéologie et d'Histoire 63; rue
    St-Denis 82; Saint Joseph's Oratory 87;
    Stade Olympique 95-96; St. Lawrence
    Warehouse and water tower 52; UQÀM
    (Université de Québec à Montréal) 78;
    see also churches and temples
art/craft stores: 202, 208-209
Articule: 161
arts and culture: 148-172; general
    discussion 267-271; calendar of events
    24-27, 165-172; Centre-Ville 153-154;
    Centre-Ville Est 155-157; Greater
    Montréal 163-164; Haskell Free Library
    and Opera House 245; highlights 149;
    Mile End and Petite-Italie 48, 161-163;
    Mont-Tremblant 233; Plateau Mont-
    Royal 159-161; Quartier des Spectacles
    77; Quartier Latin and the Village 157-
    158; Val-David 238; Vieux-Montréal
    150-152
Arts Building: 72
L'Astral: 156
ATMs: 280
Auberge la Porte Rouge: 15, 234
L'Autre Montréal: 66
Avenue du Mont-Royal: 81

B

bagels: 10, 123
banking: 280
bars: Centre-Ville 135-136; Centre-Ville
    Est 136-137; Mile End and Petite-Italie
    144-146; Plateau Mont-Royal 141;
    Quartier Latin and the Village 138;
    Vieux-Montréal 132-133
Basilique Notre-Dame-de-Montréal: 7, 12,
    13, 16, 18, 28, 57, 58-61
Bateau-Mouche: 177
Battat Contemporary: 161
beaches: Greater Montréal 182; Oka
    National Park 236; Vieux-Montréal 176
beauty stores: 191, 194
beer: BYOB restaurants 113; craft beer
    barhopping 146; Festival Mondial de
    la Bière 26, 167; Lion d'Or 244; picnic
    law 118

Belgo Building: 19, 40, 42, 149, 155
Bell Centre: 75
Belvédère Camillien-Houde: 86
Belvedere Kondiaronk: 14, 89
Bessette, Brother André: 88
La Bibliotheque Gratuite de Haskell: 245
biking: 184-186; Bixi 22, 180; Centre-Ville 179; Greater Montréal 182; guided tours 24; Mont-Tremblant National Park 233; Parc de la Gorge-de-Coaticook 247; Parc Linéaire Le P'tit Train du Nord 239; Route Verte 181, 248; top experience 10, 175; transportation 274-275; Vieux-Montréal 175
Biodôme: 18, 96
Biosphère: 15, 54, 57, 91
Bixi: 14, 15, 19, 22, 180
Blue Metropolis Literary Festival: 25, 166
boating: dinner cruises 23; Oka National Park 236; Parc Jean-Drapeau 92; Vieux-Montréal 177
Bonsecours Basin: 17, 177
bookstores: Centre-Ville 194; Centre-Ville Est 197; Mile End and Petite-Italie 207; Plateau Mont-Royal 201-202
boulevard St-Laurent: 15, 81
Bourgeoys, Marguerite: 65
British history: 255-257
Brome County Historical Museum: 244
budget travel tips: 19
bus travel: 22, 24, 273
BYOB restaurants: 113

C

Café Saint-Henri: 52, 84, 209
Canadian Grand Prix: 23, 174, 186
Cantons de l'Est: 242-251
Cao Dei Temple of Montreal: 53
Ça Roule Montréal: 174, 175
car racing: 186
Carré Saint-Louis: 81
car travel: 22, 273, 274
Casino de Montréal: 94
Cathédrale Marie-Reine-du-Monde: 38, 74
cell phones: 281
Centaur Theatre: 152
La Centrale Galerie Powerhouse: 15, 159
Centre Bell: 34, 75
Centre Canadien d'Architecture: 39, 70-71
Centre des Sciences de Montréal and IMAX Telus Theatre: 17, 150
Centre d'Exposition de Val-David: 238
Centre d'Histoire de Montréal: 150

Centre-Ville: accommodations 211, 219-221; activities 178-179; arts and culture 153-154; map 314-315; neighborhood overview 34-39; nightlife 135-136; restaurants 106-110; shops 191-194; sights 69-75; walking tour 36-39
Centre-Ville Est: accommodations 221-223; arts and culture 155-157; map 316-317; neighborhood overview 40-43; nightlife 136-138; restaurants 110-111; shops 195-197; sights 76-78
Chalet du Mont-Royal: 87, 89
Chapelle Notre-Dame-de-Bon-Secours: 13, 32, 65
Château Apartments: 60
cheese: 247
Chiesa della Madonna della Difesa: 52, 84
children's stores: 199, 204-205
children, traveling with: 277
Chinatown: 40, 43, 77
chocolate: 38
churches and temples: Abbaye Saint-Benoît-du-Lac 246; Cathédrale Marie-Reine-du-Monde 74; Chapelle Notre-Dame-de-Bon-Secours 65; Chiesa della Madonna della Difesa 84; Church of Saint-Michael and Saint-Anthony 85; Église St-Pierre-Apôtre 80; Saint Joseph's Oratory 87
Church of Saint-Michael and Saint-Anthony: 51, 85
cigarettes: 277
Cimetière Mont-Royal: 89
Cimetière Notre-Dame-des-Neiges: 88, 90
cinema: general discussion 268; Centre-Ville 154; Plateau Mont-Royal 160-161; Quartier Latin and the Village 158
Cinéma Banque Scotia: 154
Cinema du Parc: 160
Cinema L'Amour: 161
Cinémathèque Québécoise: 44, 149, 158
Cineplex Odeon: 154
circus: 151, 164, 271
Cirque du Soleil: 15, 23, 149, 151, 271
Cirque Éloize: 151, 271
Cité Mémoire: 66
City Hall: 67
climate: 253-254
climbing: 239
clinics, health: 278-279
Clock Tower Beach: 176
clothing: 279
clothing/shoe stores: Centre-Ville 193; Mile End and Petite-Italie 203-204;

Plateau Mont-Royal 198; Vieux-Montréal 189-190
Club Soda: 156-157
Coaticook: 247
cocktail hour: 136
comedy: 26, 169
communications: 281
concert venues: Centre-Ville 154; Centre-Ville Est 156; Mile End and Petite-Italie 162-163; Plateau Mont-Royal 160; Quartier Latin and the Village 157
contemporary history: 258-260
Corona Theatre: 154
craft beer: 146
craft fairs: 208
La Crêperie du Marché: 13, 84
crime: 279
Croix du Mont-Royal: 87, 89
cross-country skiing: 182, 183
cuisine: cheese 247; Duck Festival 244; food tours 24; local specialties 10, 115, 123; Montréal en Lumière 166; see also dining; Restaurants Index
cursing: 277
customs and immigration: 275

D

dance: general discussion 270; Centre-Ville Est 156; Festival des Arts de Saint-Sauveur 237; Festival TransAmériques 167; Plateau Mont-Royal 159
dance clubs: Plateau Mont-Royal 143; Quartier Latin and the Village 140; Vieux-Montréal 134
day trips: 228-251
department stores: 192, 195
DHC/ART: 149, 151
dietary restrictions: 109
digital arts festival: 25
dining: alfresco 118; picnic law 11, 118; reservations 22; see also cuisine; Restaurants Index
dinner cruises: 23
dog sledding: 233
Domaine de Courval: 247
Domaine des Cotes d'Ardoise: 247
Domaine du Ridge: 248
Dorchester Square: 37, 73
Drapeau, Jean: 95
dress: 279
drinking: 276
driving: 273, 274
drumming: 87
Duck Festival: 244
Dufresne Sector: 239

E

Éco Musée du Fier Monde: 157
economy: 261-262
Église St-Pierre-Apôtre: 80
electricity: 282
Elektra: 25, 167
emergency services: 279
English explorers: 256
L'Épopée de Capelton: 245
European immigration: 255
events: general discussion 24-27, 165-172; top experience 11, 165
Expo 67: 68, 91, 95, 259

F

family activities: Biodôme 96; Bonsecours Basin 177; Centre des Sciences de Montréal and IMAX Telus Theatre 150; L'Épopée de Capelton 245; Granby Zoo 242-243; La Grande Roue de Montréal 24, 113; Insectarium de Montréal 97; itinerary 16-18; Jean-Drapeau Aquatic Complex 183; Museum of Science and Nature 243; Parc Aquatique du Mont Saint-Sauveur 237; Planétarium Rio Tinto Alcan 97; La Ronde 93; shopping 199, 204-205; SOS Labyrinthe 177; travel tips 277; Vieux-Montréal 28; Village du Père Noël 239; Voiles en Voiles 178
Fantasia Film Festival: 27, 169
Les Fantômes du Vieux-Montréal: 66
farmers markets: 22, 48, 83, 244
Ferris wheels: 24, 93, 177
Festival des Arts de Saint-Sauveur: 237
Festival du Monde Arabe: 27, 171
Festival du Nouveau Cinéma: 171
Festival International de Jazz de Montréal: 24, 26, 40, 165, 168-169
Festival International Nuits d'Afrique: 169
Festival Mondial de la Bière: 26, 167
festivals: see events
Festival St-Ambroise Fringe de Montréal: 25, 166
Festival TransAmériques: 167
La Fête des Neiges: 20, 25, 165
Fierté Montréal Pride: 27, 170
film festivals: 25, 27, 169, 171
First Nations people: general discussion 262; La Guilde 70, 153; history 255; Place Jacques-Cartier 66
Fitz and Folwell: 66, 174, 179
food: see cuisine; dining; Restaurants Index
football: 180

Les FrancoFolies de Montréal: 26, 77, 165, 167
Francophone culture: 167, 263
free admission days: 22, 24
Free Montréal Tours: 66
French history: 255-257
French phrasebook: 285-291
French theater: 152
Fringe festivals: 25, 166
Fromagerie Hamel: 52
Fromagerie La Station: 247

G

Galerie Jeannine Blais: 245
Galerie Simon Blais: 162
Galerie Yves Laroche: 162
galleries: Centre-Ville 153; Centre-Ville Est 155; Mile End and Petite-Italie 161-162; Plateau Mont-Royal 159; Vieux-Montréal 151
gardens: green alleyways 85; Jardin Botanique 94; Parc La Fontaine 82-83
Gare Centrale: 22, 272
Gare d'Autocars: 22, 235
Gare Windsor: 60
geodesic domes: 91
geography: 252-253
George-Étienne Cartier monument: 14, 86
Gesù Centre de Créativité: 155
gift and home stores: Centre-Ville Est 196; Mile End and Petite-Italie 206-207; Plateau Mont-Royal 201; Vieux-Montréal 190-191
Glen LeMesurier's Twilight Sculpture Garden: 52
glossary: 284-285
gluten-free food: 109
gourmet food stores: 202-203, 209-210
government: 260-261
Granby: 242-243
Granby Zoo: 229, 242-243
La Grande Bibliothèque: 44, 57, 79
La Grande Roue de Montréal: 13, 17, 20, 24, 177
Grand Prix Cyclistes: 181
Les Grands Ballets Canadiens de Montréal: 149, 156
Grand Séminaire de Montréal: 70
gratuities: 276
Greater Montréal: activities 182-186; arts and culture 163-164; family activities 18; map 324-325; neighborhood overview 54-55; restaurants 129; sights 86-97

Gregorian chanting: 246
Grey Nuns: 62
Griffintown: 24, 134, 263
Guidatour: 66
La Guilde: 70, 153

H

Habitat 67: 13, 33, 60, 68
harassment: 279
Haskell Free Library and Opera House: 245
Havre aux Glaces: 17, 90
health: 278-279
Heavy MTL: 26, 169
Héritage Montréal: 66
hiking: 247
historic sights: Basilique Notre-Dame-de-Montréal 58-61; Centre d'Histoire de Montréal 150; Grand Séminaire de Montréal 70; Main, the 81; Maison de Mère d'Youville 62; Maison Papineau 65; Maison Saint-Gabriel 163; Musée du Château Ramezay 67; Oka National Park 236; Place d'Armes 61; Place Jacques-Cartier 66; Pointe-à-Callière Musée d'Archéologie et d'Histoire 63; rue St-Paul 64; Saute Moutons 177; Sherbrooke 243, 244; Sir George-Étienne Cartier National Historic Site 150; Vieux-Port 63-64
Hochelaga-Maisonneuve: 94
hockey: Centre Bell 75; Montréal Canadiens 34, 178-179; reservations 23; season 27
Holocaust memorials: 163
home decor stores: see gift and home stores
Hop-On Hop-Off Double Decker Tour: 66
hospital history: 159
hostels: 223
Hôtel de Ville: 67
hotels: see accommodations; Hotels Index

I

ice-skating: Centre-Ville 178; Greater Montréal 183; Lac aux Castors 87, 183; Plateau Mont-Royal 180; Vieux-Montréal 177
ice wine: 247
Igloofest: 20, 25, 165
Île Notre-Dame: 54, 91, 253
Île Sainte-Hélène: 54, 91, 253
Image+Nation: 172
immigrant culture: 264
immigration: 21, 275

indigenous peoples: 255, 262
Insectarium de Montréal: 18, 97
Internet services: 281
itineraries: 12-20; best-of itinerary 12-15; budget travel 19; family travel 16-18; winter travel 20

JKL

Jardin Botanique: 15, 18, 57, 94
jazz: 168-169
Jean-Drapeau Aquatic Complex: 174, 183
jewelry stores: Centre-Ville 193; Centre-Ville Est 195; Plateau Mont-Royal 199
Jewish people: 265
Just for Laughs: 23, 26, 40, 77, 165, 169
kayaking: 182
Knowlton: 244
Lac aux Castors: 17, 20, 183
Lac Brome: 244-245
Lac des Sables: 237
Lachine Canal: 17, 90, 175, 184
Lachine Canal Bike Path: 175
language: 265-266
language resources: 285-291
Laurentians: 236
LGBTQ travel tips: general discussion 278; cultural overview 264; Fierté Montréal Pride 27, 170; Image+Nation 172; Quartier Latin and the Village 44, 140; rue Ste-Catherine Est 79;
libraries: 44, 79
Linton, the: 60
Lion d'Or: 244
literary festivals: 25, 166
literature: 268-269
Little Burgundy: 24
lounges: Mile End and Petite-Italie 146; Plateau Mont-Royal 142; Vieux-Montréal 133-134
Lower Laurentians: 236-242

M

Magasin Général Alexis-Guindon: 238
MAI: 159
MainLine Theatre: 159
Main, the: 81
Maison de Mère d'Youville: 33, 62
Maison des Arts et de la Culture Saint-Faustin: 233
Maison Narcisse et Olivier Ménard: 238
Maison Papineau: 65
Maison Saint-Gabriel: 163
Le Mal Nécessaire: 43
maps: general discussion 280; Centre-Ville 314-315; Centre-Ville Est 316-317; Greater Montréal 324-325; Mile End and Petite-Italie 322-323; Plateau Mont-Royal 320-321; Quartier Latin and the Village 318-319; Vieux-Montréal 312-313
Marché Atwater: 14, 17, 90
Marché Bonsecours: 20, 64
Marché d'Été de Mont-Tremblant: 233
Marché Jean-Talon: 9, 13, 15, 48, 52, 57, 83
Marina d'Oka: 236
markets: Marché Atwater 90; Marché Bonsecours 64; Marché des Éclusiers 103; Marché d'Été de Mont-Tremblant 233; Marché Jean-Talon 83
McGill University: 36, 71-72
measurements: 283
media: 281
medical services: 278-279
metric system: 283
Métro: 22, 273
Métropolis: 157
Mile End and Petite-Italie: accommodations 211, 227; activities 181-182; alfresco dining 118; arts and culture 161-163; biking 185; map 322-323; neighborhood overview 48-53; nightlife 144-147; restaurants 122-129; shops 203-210; sights 83-84; walking tour 50-53
Mile-Ex: 48
military sights: 92
mobile apps: 281
money: 280
Mont-Blanc: 232
Mont-Orford: 248
Montréal Canadiens: 20, 23, 27, 34, 178
Montréal en Lumière: 20, 25, 166
Montréal Holocaust Memorial Museum: 88, 163
Montréal Impact: 186
Montréal Museums Pass: 24
Montréal Roller Derby League: 186
Montréal World Film Festival: 171
Mont-Royal: 20, 253
Mont-Royal Métro station: 14, 81
Mont-Saint-Sauveur: 237
Mont-Tremblant: 231-235
Mont-Tremblant National Park: 15, 17, 232-233
Mont-Tremblant Resort: 15, 233
mountain biking: 233
Mount Royal Park: 183
Moving Day: 276
Mural Festival: 162, 165, 168
murals: 162

Musée d'Art Contemporain: 40, 76
Musée des Beaux-Arts de Montréal: 9, 14, 34, 39, 57, 69
Musée des Beaux-Arts de Sherbrooke: 243
Musée des Hospitalières de l'Hôtel Dieu: 159
Musée du Château Ramezay: 67
Le Musée Dufresne-Nincheri: 163
Musée Marguerite Bourgeoys: 65
Musée McCord: 72
Museum of Science and Nature: 229, 243
museums: Centre-Ville 153; Greater Montréal 162; Musée d'Art Contemporain 76; Musée des Beaux-Arts de Montréal 69; Musée Marguerite Bourgeoys 65; Plateau Mont-Royal 159; Quartier Latin and the Village 157; Sherbrooke 243; Stewart Museum 92; Vieux-Montréal 149
music: general discussion 267; Centre-Ville 154; Centre-Ville Est 137, 156; festivals 25, 26, 27, 167, 237; Mile End and Petite-Italie 146; Plateau Mont-Royal 143; Sunday Tam-Tam 87; Vieux-Montréal 135
music stores: Centre-Ville 194; Centre-Ville Est 197; Mile End and Petite-Italie 207; Plateau Mont-Royal 201-202
Mutek: 170

N

Le National: 157
national parks: 232-233, 236
neighborhoods: 28-53; Centre-Ville 34-39; Centre-Ville Est 40-43; Mile End and Petite-Italie 48-53; Plateau Mont-Royal 46-47; Quartier Latin and the Village 44-45; Vieux-Montréal 28-33
Never Apart: 84, 149, 161
New City Gas: 131, 134
New France: 256
newspapers: 282
nightlife: 130-147; Centre-Ville 135-136; Centre-Ville Est 136-138; highlights 131; Mile End and Petite-Italie 48, 144-147; Plateau Mont-Royal 141-144; Quartier Latin and the Village 138-141; Vieux-Montréal 132-135; see also Nightlife Index
Nordic Adventure Dog Sledding: 233
North Hatley: 245-246
Notre-Dame-des-Neiges Cemetery: 90

O

Oka National Park: 17, 236
Old Montréal: see Vieux-Montréal
L'Olympia: 158
Olympics of 1976: 95
Olympic Village: 60
Opéra de Montréal: 156
Orchestre Symphonique de Montréal: 156
Orford Express: 243
Osheaga Music and Arts Festival: 23, 27, 170
Outremont: 48
Owl's Head: 248

P

paintings: 269
Palais des Congrès: 60
Parc Aquatique du Mont Saint-Sauveur: 237
Parc de la Gorge-de-Coaticook: 229, 247
Parc de la Petite-Italie: 181
Parc du Mont-Royal: 9, 13, 14, 17, 54, 57, 86, 183
Parc Jean-Drapeau: 15, 17, 54, 91
Parc Jeanne-Mance: 179
Parc La Fontaine: 15, 17, 18, 19, 20, 82, 180
Parc Linéaire Le P'tit Train du Nord: 229, 239
Parc Outremont: 51
Parc Régional Val-David and Val-Morin: 229, 239
Parisian Laundry: 154
passes: 23
Passport MTL: 23
passports: 21, 275
people-watching: general discussion 14; Avenue du Mont-Royal 81; Café Olimpico 14, 128; Carré Saint-Louis 82; George-Étienne Cartier monument 14, 86; Marché Atwater 14, 90; Mont-Royal Métro station 14, 81; Place des Arts 14, 76
performing arts: general discussion 270; Centre-Ville Est 155-156; French theater 152; Greater Montréal 164; North Hatley 245; Parc La Fontaine 83; Plateau Mont-Royal 159; rue St-Denis 82; Theatre Lac Brome 244; Vieux-Montréal 152
periodicals: 282
Petite-Italie: see Mile End and Petite-Italie
pharmacies: 279
Phi Centre: 149, 151
phone services: 281

phrasebook: 285-291
picnicking: Parc Jeanne-Mance 179; picnic law 11, 118; Plateau Mont-Royal 46
Pierre Trudeau International Airport: 22, 272
Piknic Électronik: 25, 92, 167
Pizza Mia: 17, 90
Place d'Armes: 13, 16, 30, 61
Place des Arts: 14, 19, 40, 43, 76-77
Place Jacques-Cartier: 13, 31, 65-66
Place Ville-Marie: 74-75
Planétarium Rio Tinto Alcan: 18, 97
planning tips: 21-27
plants: 254
Plateau Mont-Royal: 14; accommodations 211, 225-227; activities 179-181; alfresco dining 118; arts and culture 159-161; biking 175; map 320-321; neighborhood overview 46-47; nightlife 141-144; restaurants 114-122; shops 198-203; sights 81-83
Pointe-à-Callière Musée d'Archéologie et d'Histoire: 17, 57, 63
politics: 260-261
Pop Montreal: 27, 165, 171
Port, Old: see Vieux-Port
poutine: 10, 115
Prohibition-era nightlife: 139
public transit: 22, 273

QR

Quartier des Spectacles: 40, 77
Quartier International: 62
Quartier Latin and the Village: accommodations 211, 224-225; arts and culture 157-158; map 318-319; neighborhood overview 44-45; nightlife 138-141; restaurants 112-114; shops 197-198; sights 78-80
Les Quartiers du Canal: 24
Québec geography: 252-253
Quiet Revolution: 258-259
radio: 282
reading, suggested: 291-293
recreation: see activities
Redpath Museum of Natural History: 37, 153
religion: 264-265
Rencontres Internationales du Documentaire Montréal: 27, 171-172
Rendez-vous du Cinéma Québécois: 25, 166
rental cars: 274
Réseau Riverain: 244

reservations: 22
resources, Internet: 293-294
restaurants: Centre-Ville 106-110; Centre-Ville Est 110-111; Greater Montréal 129; highlights 99; Mile End and Petite-Italie 122-129; Plateau Mont-Royal 114-122; Quartier Latin and the Village 112-114; Vieux-Montréal 100-105; see also Restaurants Index
Revolutionary War history: 257
Rialto Theatre: 162
rock climbing: 239
Rogers Cup: 186
roller derby: 186
romantic sights: general discussion 15; Belvédère Camillien-Houde 86; Bota Bota 15, 191; Jardin Botanique 15, 94; La Route des Vins 15, 247; Marché Jean-Talon 15, 83; Parc La Fontaine 15, 180; Pierre du Calvet 15, 216
La Ronde: 15, 93
rooftop bars: 136
La Route des Vins: 15, 247
Route Verte: 181, 248
rue Amherst: 80
rue Crescent: 34
rue St-Denis: 14, 44, 82
rue Ste-Catherine Est: 44, 57, 79
rue St-Paul: 12, 16, 64

S

safety: 278-279
Sainte-Agathe-des-Monts: 229, 237
Saint-Henri: 24, 129, 184
Saint Joseph's Oratory: 8, 13, 14, 54, 57, 60, 87
Saint-Sauveur: 236
Sala Rossa: 160
SAT (Société des Arts Technologiques): 77, 157
Saute Moutons: 177
sculpture: 52, 87
season, travel tips by: 21
Seb l'Artisan Culinaire: 15, 234
secondhand stores: 195, 196
Segal Centre for the Performing Arts: 88, 149, 164
seminaries: 70
Sherbrooke: 243-244
shoe stores: see clothing/shoe stores
shopping districts: Centre-Ville 191; Plateau Mont-Royal 198; Quartier Latin and the Village 197
shops: 187-210; Centre-Ville 191-194; Centre-Ville Est 195-197; highlights

188; Mile End and Petite-Italie 203-210; Plateau Mont-Royal 198-203; Quartier Latin and the Village 197-198; Underground City 73; Vieux-Montréal 189-191; *see also* Shops Index
sights: 56-97; Centre-Ville 69-75; Centre-Ville Est 76-78; Greater Montréal 86-97; highlights 57; Mile End and Petite-Italie 83-84; Plateau Mont-Royal 81-83; Quartier Latin and the Village 78-80; Vieux-Montréal 58-68
Silo #5: 13, 33, 64
Sir George-Étienne Cartier National Historic Site: 150
Sir George-Étienne Cartier statue: 87
Ski Bromont: 17, 248
skiing: Cantons de l'Est 248-249; Mont-Saint-Sauveur 236, 237; Mont-Tremblant Resort 233
Ski Mont Sutton: 17, 229, 249
sledding: 247
smoking: 277
snowshoeing: 182, 183, 247
soccer: 186
La Société d'Histoire de Sherbrooke: 244
Au Sommet observation deck: 13, 75
SOS Labyrinthe: 17, 177
Space for Life: 18, 97
spas: Centre-Ville 194; Plateau Mont-Royal 203; Vieux-Montréal 191
sports: 95, 186; *see also* hockey
Stade Olympique: 54, 57, 95-96
Stanshead, Québec: 245
Stewart Museum: 92
St. Lawrence River: 28, 185
St. Lawrence Warehouse and water tower: 52
strip clubs: 276
St-Viateur Bagel Shop: 15, 19, 51, 123
summer travel: 21
Sunday Tam-Tam: 87
Sun Life Building: 60
surfing: 176
Sutton: 246
swearing: 277
swimming: 183

T

taxis: 274
telephones: 281
television: 282
tennis: 186
theater: *see* performing arts
Theatre Berri: 158
Theatre Lac Brome: 229, 244

Théâtre Outremont: 162
Théâtre Piggery: 245
Théâtre Sainte-Catherine: 155
Aux 33 Tours: 188, 201
time zone: 283
tipping: 276
TOHU: 164
top experiences: 7-11; alleyways, green 11, 85; Basilique Notre-Dame-de-Montréal 7, 58-61; biking 10, 175; cuisine 10, 115, 123; dining/wining alfresco 11, 118; festivals 11, 165; Marché Jean-Talon 9, 83; Musée des Beaux-Arts de Montréal 9, 69; Parc du Mont-Royal 9, 86; Saint Joseph's Oratory 8, 87
Tour de la Bourse: 60
tourist information: 280
Tour Olympique: 96
tours, guided: 24, 66
tours, walking: Centre-Ville 36-39; Centre-Ville Est 42-43; Mile End and Petite-Italie 50-53; Vieux-Montréal 30-33
Township Trail: 246
traffic: 253
train travel: 22, 243, 272
transportation: Cantons de l'Est 251; Lower Laurentians 242; Montréal 22, 272-275; Mont-Tremblant 235
La Tulipe: 160
Le 2-22: 155

UV

Underground City: 20, 34, 73
Université de Montréal: 60
universities: Centre-Ville 34; McGill University 36, 71-72; Université de Montréal 60; UQÀM (Université de Québec à Montréal) 44, 78
UQÀM (Université de Québec à Montréal): 44, 78
Val Caudalies: 248
Val-David: 238
vegetarian/vegan food: 109
Vieux-Montréal: 16; accommodations 211, 216-219; activities 175-178; arts and culture 150-152; map 312-313; neighborhood overview 28-33; nightlife 132-135; restaurants 100-105; shops 189-191; sights 58-68; walking tour 30-33
Vieux-Port: 13, 16, 28, 63-64, 103
views, best: general discussion 13; Belvedere Kondiaronk 89; La Grande

Roue de Montréal 113; Parc du Mont-Royal 13, 86; Saint Joseph's Oratory 13, 87; Au Sommet observation deck 13, 74; Terrasse Place d'Armes 13, 113, 133; Vieux-Port 13, 63
Vignoble Chapelle Ste-Agnès: 247
Vignoble d'Orpailleur: 248
Vignoble Les Pervenches: 248
the Village: 15, 18; see also Quartier Latin and the Village
Village du Père Noël: 239
Ville de Mont-Tremblant: 233
Ville-Marie: 73
vintage shopping: 15, 19; Centre-Ville Est 195; Mile End and Petite-Italie 205-206; Plateau Mont-Royal 200; rue Amherst 80
visas: 22, 275
visual arts: see arts and culture
Voiles en Voiles: 17, 178

WXYZ
weather: 253-254
Week-ends du Monde: 169
Westmount Square: 60
wildlife viewing: 232-233
windsurfing: 236
wine: BYOB restaurants 113; Centre-Ville Est 137; picnic law 118; Plateau Mont-Royal 142; La Route des Vins 247; Vieux-Montréal 133
winter: 253-254
winter, dressing for: 279
winter itinerary: 20
winter travel: 21
women travelers: 277
writers, Montréal: 268-269
Youville Stables: 32, 62
zoos: 96, 242-243

Restaurants Index

L'Anecdote: 117
Avesta: 108
Le Ballpark: 126
La Banquise: 18, 109, 115, 116
Barroco: 103
Beauty's: 117
Bonny's: 108
Bottega Pizzeria: 125
Le Boucan: 109
Boulangerie Guillaume: 99, 128
Boustan: 70, 108
Brasserie T!: 110
Le Bremner: 103
Brit and Chips: 17, 104, 109
Burgers Royal: 103
Burgundy Lion: 109
Café des Chats: 121
Café Falco: 99, 128
Café Myriade: 70, 110
Café Névé: 121
Café Olimpico: 14, 15, 19, 51, 128
Café Replika: 122
Café Santropol: 14, 121
Café Titanic: 104
Le Cagibi: 109, 126
Camellia Sinensis: 113
Le Cartet: 17, 33, 104
Chez Bong: 43, 111
Chez Claudette: 109, 128
Chez José: 99, 109, 118

Chez L'Épicier: 101
Le Chien Fumant: 114
ChuChai: 109, 120
Le Club Chasse et Pêche: 13, 101
La Colombe: 113, 115
Comptoir 21: 126
Crew Café: 16, 20, 32, 99, 105
La Croissanterie Figaro: 127
Dépanneur le Pick-Up: 109
Dépanneur Le Pick-Up: 127
Dinette Triple Crown: 99, 124
Dunn's Famous Deli: 106
Étoile Rouge: 124
Europea: 106
L'Express: 14, 99, 116
Fairmount Bagel: 123
Fortune: 125
Les 400 Coups: 101
Gandhi: 102
Garage Beirut: 108
Garde Manger: 61, 104
Gibby's: 104
Gibeau Orange Julep: 60, 120
Graziella: 102
Icehouse: 117
Jardin Nelson: 17, 101
Joe Beef: 99, 106
Juliette et Chocolat: 20, 38, 114
Kaza Maza: 119
Kazu: 14, 99, 107

Kem CoBa: 99, 129
Khyber Pass: 119
Kitchenette: 113
Laloux: 116
Lawrence: 122
Leméac: 122
Liverpool House: 107
Lucca: 125
Mâche: 112
Maison Kim Fung: 110
Maison Publique: 114
Mangiafoco: 61, 102
Marché des Éclusiers: 33, 103
La Mie Matinale: 15, 113
Milos: 124
Miss Bánh Mì: 107
Moishes: 120
Muvbox Homard: 103
Négasaké: 117
Nora Gray: 108
Olive & Gourmando: 12, 105, 109
O'Thym: 112
Les Oubliettes: 109, 129
La Panthère Verte: 109, 126
Pastaga: 103
Patati Patata: 20, 109, 115, 116
Pâtisserie Harmonie: 42, 111
Pâtisserie Kouign Amann: 122

Le Petit Alep: 84, 125
Au Petit Extra: 112
Pho Saigon VIP: 107
Pho Tay Ho: 124
Au Pied de Cochon: 114, 115
Pikolo Espresso Bar: 111
Pintxo: 119
Pizzeria Napoletana: 84, 113, 125
Le Poisson Rouge: 113, 120
Pourquoi Pas Espresso Bar: 113
Qing Hua Dumpling: 19, 107
Le Quartier Général: 113, 115
Rotisserie Romados: 19, 118
St-Viateur Bagel Shop: 123
Sala Rosa: 119
SAT Labo Culinaire: 110
Schwartz's: 15, 99, 117
7Grains Bakery & Cafe: 18, 105
Sophie Sucrée: 109, 122
Stash Café: 102
Taco Box: 103
Toqué!: 15, 100
Tuck Shop: 99, 129
Vieux Vélo: 127
Aux Vivres: 14, 99, 109, 120
Volcanic Organic: 103
Wilensky's Light Lunch: 127

Nightlife Index

Alexandraplatz Bar: 53, 131, 144
L'Amère à Boire: 138
Arcade MTL: 131, 138
Le Bar Sans Nom: 145
Barfly: 141
Bar George: 135
Bar Le Ritz PDB: 147
Bar Plan B: 141
Barraca: 141
Big in Japan Bar: 20, 131, 141
Bily Kun: 142
Blizzarts: 142
Brutopia: 136
La Buvette Chez Simone: 142
Cabaret Mado: 140
Café Campus and Petit Campus: 143
Casa del Popolo: 15, 19, 131, 143
Le Cheval Blanc: 138
Circus After-Hours: 140
Club Unity: 140
Complexe Sky: 140
Le Confessional: 132

Coop Katacombes: 137
Le Date Karaoke: 140
Les Deux Pierrots: 135
Dieu du Ciel: 131, 144
La Distillerie no. 1: 136
Divan Orange: 143
Dolcetto: 133
Dominion Square Tavern: 131, 135
Else's: 15, 142
L'Escogriffe: 144
Les Foufounes Electriques: 137
Furco: 131, 136
Harricana: 84, 145
HELM: 145
Le Mal Nécessaire: 137
New City Gas: 131, 134
Notre Dames des Quilles: 131, 145
Nyks: 137
O Patro Vys: 144
Le Philémon Bar: 61, 132
Ping Pong Club: 145
Pit Caribou: 142

Pullman: 131, 137
Le Saint-Sulpice: 139
Le Sainte-Élisabeth: 137
Le Salon Daomé: 143
Sparrow: 146
Stereo: 140
Taverne Gaspar: 133, 136
Terrasse Nelligan: 133

Terrasse Place d'Armes: 13, 61, 133, 136
Terrasses Bonsecours: 13, 133
Les Trois Brasseurs: 136, 139
Velvet Speakeasy: 134
Vices et Versa: 146
Whisky Café: 146
Wunderbar: 13, 134

Shops Index

Annex Vintage: 196
Annual Gem and Mineral Show: 208
Antiquités Foley L'Ecuyer: 193
Antiquités Seconde Chance: 197
Arthur Quentin: 188, 201
Atelier B.: 204
La Baie: 195
Beatnick Music: 202
Billie: 204
Bota Bota: 15, 33, 188, 191
Boulevard St-Laurent: 198
Boutique Citrouille: 204
Boutique Denis Gagnon: 189
Boutique du Collectionneur: 201
Boutique Spoutnik: 197
Boutique Unicorn: 188, 203
Café Domo: 206
Café Saint-Henri: 52, 84, 209
Cahier d'Exercices: 189
La Canadienne: 204
Centre Eaton: 191
Cheap Thrills: 194
Chez Farfelu: 201
Chocolats Privilège: 52, 84, 209
Citizen Vintage: 196, 205
Clusier Habilleur: 189
Comme des Enfants: 205
Coop Saint-Laurent des Arts: 202
Les Cours Mont-Royal: 191
Deuxième Peau: 198
Drawn & Quarterly: 15, 19, 188, 207
Dubarry Fourrures: 189, 190
Effiloché: 208
Epicerie Unique: 202
Espace Nomad: 203
Espace Pepin Maison: 190
Les Étoffes: 188, 203
Eva B: 195
Ex Voto: 205
Friperie St-Laurent: 196, 200
Fromagerie Hamel: 209

Général 54: 204
Geneviève Grandbois: 209, 209
Grand Central Inc.: 194
La Grande Ourse: 188, 199
Harricana by Mariouche: 190
Henri Henri: 43, 188, 195
Holt Renfrew: 70, 192
Ibiki: 198–199
Jamais Assez: 206
J. Schreter: 199
Kanuk: 188, 198
Kimono Vintage: 200
Kitsch 'n' Swell: 15, 188, 201
Local 23: 196, 206
Lozeau: 208
Lustre: 199
M0851: 199
Maison Birks: 195
Maison de Thé Camellia Sinensis: 84, 210
La Maison Ogilvy: 70, 192
Marie Saint Pierre: 70, 193
Milano: 210
Monastiraki: 206
Murale: 194
Off the Hook: 193
180g: 207
Oz Bijoux: 199
Papeterie Nota Bene: 188, 196
Au Papier Japonais: 209
Paragraphe: 194
Paul's Boutique: 202
Phonopolis: 207
Puces POP: 208
rue St-Denis: 197
rue Ste-Catherine: 34, 192
Sabor Latino-Andes: 202
Salon des Mètiers d'Art: 208
Scandinave Les Bains Vieux-Montréal: 191
Souk at SAT: 208
SSENSE: 190

Style Labo: 206
Aux 33 Tours: 188, 201
3 Femmes et 1 Coussin: 201
Tiffany & Co.: 193

Les Touilleurs: 207
U&I: 190
La Vieille Europe: 203
The Word: 197

Hotels Index

Anne Ma Soeur Anne: 226
Auberge de la Fontaine: 226
Auberge du Vieux-Port: 216
Auberge Hotel Le Jardin d'Antoine: 224
Auberge Le Pomerol: 224
Auberge les Bon Matins: 221
Celebrities Hotel: 224
Chateau de L'Argoat: 224
Château Versailles: 220
Fairmont Queen Elizabeth: 212, 219
Gingerbread Manor: 226
Holiday Inn Select: 222
L'Hôtel Champs-de-Mars: 218
L'Hôtel le Crystal: 220
L'Hôtel Espresso: 221
L'Hôtel de l'Institut de tourisme et
    d'hôtellerie du Québec: 225
Hotel 10 Montréal: 43, 212, 222
Hôtel Gault: 212, 216
Hôtel Le Germain: 212, 220
Hôtel Le St-James: 216

Hôtel Nelligan: 217
Hotel Quartier des Spectacles: 222
Hôtel St-Denis: 225
Hôtel St-Paul: 212, 217
Hotel Zero1: 212, 222
LHotel Montreal: 217
Like a Hotel: 226
La Loggia: 225
Marriott Château Champlain: 220
Le Méridien Versailles: 221
Le Mount Stephen: 219
Le 9 et Demi: 227
Pensione Popolo: 227
Pierre du Calvet: 15, 212, 216
Place d'Armes Hôtel and Suites: 217
Ritz-Carlton: 37, 212, 219
Le Saint-Sulpice: 218
Shézelles: 227
Sir Montcalm: 212, 224
Sofitel Montréal: 221
W Hotel: 217

Photo Credits

All photos © Andrea Bennett except title page photo: © Eudaemon | Dreamstime; page 2 (top) © Will Keats-Osborn; page 4 (top) © Will Keats-Osborn, (bottom) © Will Keats-Osborn; page 5 © Meunierd | Dreamstime; page 6 © Demerzel21 | Dreamstime; page 8 © Meunierd | Dreamstime; page 9 (top) © Mario Beauregard | Dreamstime, (middle) © Michel Bussieres | Dreamstime, (bottom) © Songquan Deng | Dreamstime; page 10 (top) © Zhao Qin | Dreamstime, (bottom) © Bhofack2 | Dreamstime; page 11 (top) © Will Keats-Osborn, (middle) © Michel Bussieres | Dreamstime, (bottom) © Will Keats-Osborn; page 12 © Demerzel21 | Dreamstime; page 13 © Will Keats-Osborn; page 16 © Will Keats-Osborn; page 18 © Espace pour la vie/Raymond Jalbert.; page 19 © Will Keats-Osborn; page 21 © Will Keats-Osborn; page 23 © Will Keats-Osborn; page 26 © Will Keats-Osborn; page 29 © Will Keats-Osborn; page 35 (top) © Will Keats-Osborn, (middle) © Will Keats-Osborn, (bottom) © Will Keats-Osborn; page 37 (top) © Will Keats-Osborn, (bottom) © Will Keats-Osborn; page 38 © Will Keats-Osborn; page 39 © Michel Bussieres | Dreamstime; page 41 (top) © Will Keats-Osborn, (bottom) © Will Keats-Osborn; page 47 (top) © Will Keats-Osborn, (bottom) © Will Keats-Osborn; page 52 © Andrea Bennett; page 53 © Will Keats-Osborn; page 55 © Nik Bennett; page 59 © Meunierd | Dreamstime; page 63 © Will Keats-Osborn; page 67 © Will Keats-Osborn; page 68 © Will Keats-Osborn; page 69 © Will Keats-Osborn; page 72 © Will Keats-Osborn; page 73 © Will Keats-Osborn; page 75 © Will Keats-Osborn; page 82 © Will Keats-Osborn; page 83 © Will Keats-Osborn; page 84 © Will Keats-Osborn; page 85 © Will Keats-Osborn; page 86 © Martine Oger | Dreamstime; page 92 © Will Keats-Osborn; page 94 © Espace pour la vie/Raymond Jalbert; page 98 © Will Keats-Osborn; page 102 © Will Keats-Osborn; page 103 © Will Keats-Osborn; page 106 © Will Keats-Osborn; page 107 © Will Keats-Osborn; page 111 © Will Keats-Osborn; page 115 © Will Keats-Osborn; page 118 © Christian Ouellet | Dreamstime; page 123 © Elena Elisseeva | Dreamstime; page 132 © Will Keats-Osborn; page 134 © Will Keats-Osborn; page 135 © Will Keats-Osborn; page 143 © Andrea Bennett; page 150 © Will Keats-Osborn; page 153 © Will Keats-Osborn; page 155 © Will Keats-Osborn; page 159 © Will Keats-Osborn; page 165 © Mario Beauregard | Dreamstime; page 166 © Mario Beauregard | Dreamstime; page 168 © Paul Mckinnon | Dreamstime; page 170 © Mario Beauregard | Dreamstime; page 173 © Meunierd | Dreamstime; page 175 © Zhao Qin | Dreamstime; page 176 © Will Keats-Osborn; page 177 © Vlad Ghiea | Dreamstime; page 189 © Will Keats-Osborn; page 190 © Will Keats-Osborn; page 195 © Will Keats-Osborn; page 196 © Will Keats-Osborn; page 200 © Will Keats-Osborn; page 205 © Will Keats-Osborn; page 206 © Will Keats-Osborn; page 215 © Will Keats-Osborn; page 218 © Hotel le Saint Sulpice; page 219 © Will Keats-Osborn; page 220 © Will Keats-Osborn; page 222 © Will Keats-Osborn; page 226 © Will Keats-Osborn; page 232 © Mont Tremblant; page 243 © Destination Sherbrooke; page 246 © Abbaye St-Benoît-du-Lac; page 249 © Mont Tremblant; page 252 © Olivier Vancayzeele | Dreamstime; page 272 © Le Cong Duc Dao | Dreamstime

Acknowledgments

I owe a debt of gratitude to friends and past coworkers whose love of Montreal informed my own. In particular, I'd like to thank Amelia Schonbek and the staff of Fitz & Follwell, who first helped me find my feet in the city and learn many interesting story snippets about its past and present.

A huge thank you to my partner Will, who provided feedback on city walks and took many of the better photos in this volume, and to my father, Nik, whose keen eye and desire to Instagram every last corner of the Old Port and Old Montréal also came in handy at photo selection time.

Montréalers are a notoriously gregarious, friendly bunch, and I was welcomed with helpful information at every corner. Particular thanks are owed to the proprietors and staff of Le 9 et Demi, Gingerbread Manor, the ITHQ, Shézelles, Pierre du Calvet, Destination Sherbrooke, Le Saint-Sulpice, Le Café des Chats, Strom Spa Nordique, Hôtel Gault, Mont Tremblant, Éspace pour la vie, and Abbaye Saint-Benoît-du-Lac.

Finally, many thanks to everyone at Avalon Travel for the opportunity to write this book. It has been a pleasure to work with editors Kathryn Ettinger and Leah Gordon, photo editor Rue Flaherty, and all the folks working behind the scenes in copy-editing, acquisitions, marketing, and everything else that goes into making a book a book!

SEE MAP 2

Station Place-d'Armes

RUE VIGER

AVE VIGER

Quartier International 6

RUE SAINT ANTOINE

RUELLES DES FORTIFICATIONS

RUELLES DES FORTIFICATIONS

RUE SAINT JACQUES

Place d'Armes 8

SEE MAP2

RUE NOTRE DAME

Basilique Notre-Dame-de-Montréal

VIEUX-MONTRÉAL

Rue St-Paul

RUE RÉCOLLETS

RUE DE L'HÔPITAL

RUE SAINT SACREMENT

RUE LE ROYER

RUE BRESOLES

Pointe-à-Callière Musée d'Archéologie et d'Histoire

Youville Stables

Maison de Mère d'Youville

PLACE D'YOUVILLE

RUE WELLINGTON

RUE MARGUERITE D'YOUVILLE

To New City Gas and Darling Foundry

Marché des Éclusiers

RUE DE LA COMMUNE

PROMENADE DU VIEUX-PORT

DISTANCE ACROSS MAP
Approximate: 1 mi or 1.6 km

0 — 200 yds
0 — 200 m

RESTAURANTS

3	B1	Toqué!
5	B1	Crew Café
14	B5	Le Club Chasse et Pêche
16	B5	Les 400 Coups
22	C1	Brit and Chips
25	C1	Café Titanic
29	C2	Garde Manger
37	C3	Mangiafoco
49	C4	Jardin Nelson
50	C5	Chez L'Épicier
54	C5	Le Bremner
55	C5	7Grains Bakery & Cafe
61	D1	Olive & Gourmando
63	D1	Graziella
64	D1	Le Cartet
67	D2	Gibby's
69	D2	Barroco
70	D2	Gandhi
72	D2	Stash Café

NIGHTLIFE

1	B1	Wunderbar
10	B3	Terrasse Place d'Armes
23	C1	Le Confessionnal
31	C2	Dolcetto
33	C3	Le Philémon Bar
34	C3	Terrasse Nelligan
42	C4	Velvet Speakeasy
45	C4	Taverne Gaspar
47	C4	Les Deux Pierrots
78	D5	Terrasses Bonsecours
81	E1	New City Gas

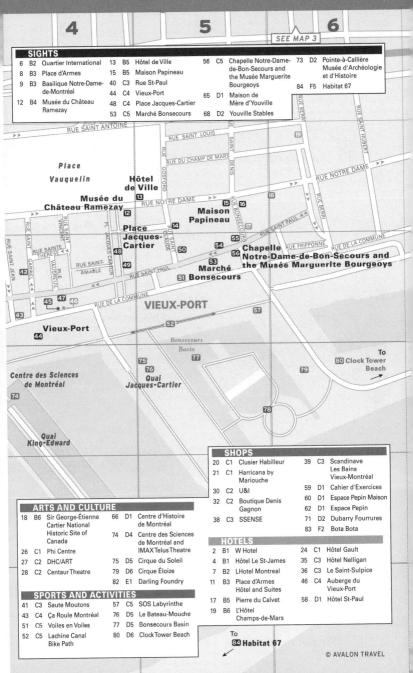

SEE MAP 3

SIGHTS

6	B2	Quartier International
8	B3	Place d'Armes
9	B3	Basilique Notre-Dame-de-Montréal
12	B4	Musée du Château Ramezay
13	B5	Hôtel de Ville
15	B5	Maison Papineau
40	C3	Rue St-Paul
44	C4	Vieux-Port
48	C4	Place Jacques-Cartier
53	C5	Marché Bonsecours
56	C5	Chapelle Notre-Dame-de-Bon-Secours and the Musée Marguerite Bourgeoys
65	D1	Maison de Mère d'Youville
68	D2	Youville Stables
73	D2	Pointe-à-Callière Musée d'Archéologie et d'Histoire
84	F5	Habitat 67

ARTS AND CULTURE

18	B6	Sir George-Étienne Cartier National Historic Site of Canada
26	C1	Phi Centre
27	C2	DHC/ART
28	C2	Centaur Theatre
66	D1	Centre d'Histoire de Montréal
74	D4	Centre des Sciences de Montréal and IMAX Telus Theatre
75	D5	Cirque du Soleil
79	D6	Cirque Éloize
82	E1	Darling Foundry

SPORTS AND ACTIVITIES

41	C3	Saute Moutons
43	C4	Ça Roule Montréal
51	C5	Voiles en Voiles
52	C5	Lachine Canal Bike Path
57	C5	SOS Labyrinthe
76	D5	Le Bateau-Mouche
77	D5	Bonsecours Basin
80	D6	Clock Tower Beach

SHOPS

20	C1	Clusier Habilleur
21	C1	Harricana by Mariouche
30	C2	U&I
32	C2	Boutique Denis Gagnon
38	C3	SSENSE
39	C3	Scandinave Les Bains Vieux-Montréal
59	D1	Cahier d'Exercices
60	D1	Espace Pepin Maison
62	D1	Espace Pepin
71	D2	Dubarry Fourrures
83	F2	Bota Bota

HOTELS

2	B1	W Hotel
4	B1	Hôtel Le St-James
7	B2	LHotel Montreal
11	B3	Place d'Armes Hôtel and Suites
17	B5	Pierre du Calvet
19	B6	L'Hôtel Champs-de-Mars
24	C1	Hôtel Gault
35	C3	Hôtel Nelligan
36	C3	Le Saint-Sulpice
46	C4	Auberge du Vieux-Port
58	D1	Hôtel St-Paul

To **84 Habitat 67**

© AVALON TRAVEL

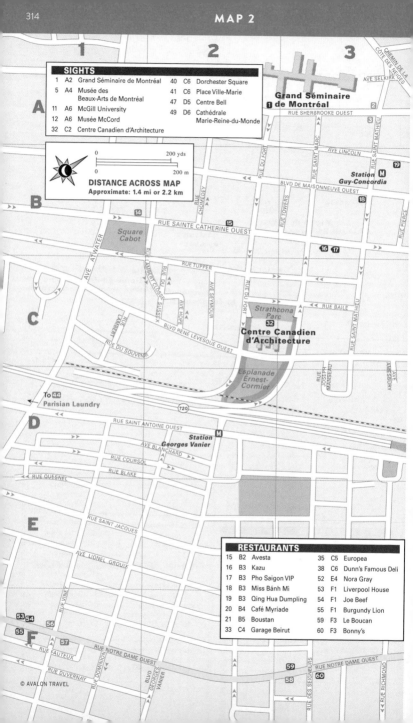

SIGHTS

1	A2	Grand Séminaire de Montréal	40	C6	Dorchester Square
5	A4	Musée des Beaux-Arts de Montréal	41	C6	Place Ville-Marie
			47	D5	Centre Bell
11	A6	McGill University	49	D6	Cathédrale
12	A6	Musée McCord			Marie-Reine-du-Monde
32	C2	Centre Canadien d'Architecture			

0   200 yds
0   200 m

DISTANCE ACROSS MAP
Approximate: 1.4 mi or 2.2 km

Grand Séminaire
de Montréal

RESTAURANTS

15	B2	Avesta	35	C5	Europea
16	B3	Kazu	38	C6	Dunn's Famous Deli
17	B3	Pho Saigon VIP	52	E4	Nora Gray
18	B3	Miss Bánh Mi	53	F1	Liverpool House
19	B3	Qing Hua Dumpling	54	F1	Joe Beef
20	B4	Café Myriade	55	F1	Burgundy Lion
21	B5	Boustan	59	F3	Le Boucan
33	C4	Garage Beirut	60	F3	Bonny's

© AVALON TRAVEL

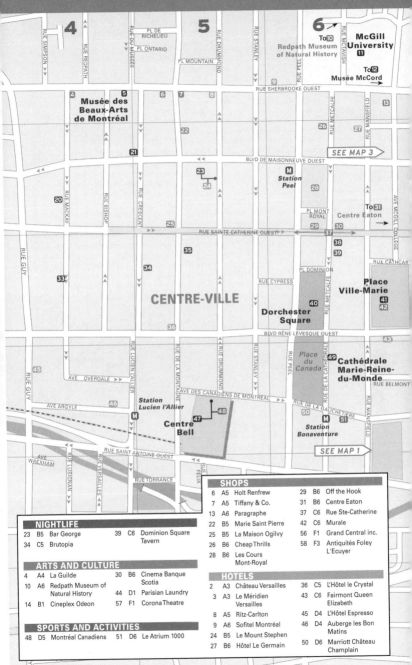

4 A4 La Guilde

5 Musée des Beaux-Arts de Montréal

Musée des Beaux-Arts de Montréal

McGill University

Redpath Museum of Natural History

Musée McCord

Station Peel

Centre Eaton

CENTRE-VILLE

Place Ville-Marie

Dorchester Square

Place du Canada

Cathédrale Marie-Reine-du-Monde

Centre Bell

Station Lucien l'Allier

Station Bonaventure

SEE MAP 3

SEE MAP 1

NIGHTLIFE

23	B5	Bar George	39	C6	Dominion Square Tavern
34	C5	Brutopia			

ARTS AND CULTURE

4	A4	La Guilde	30	B6	Cinema Banque Scotia
10	A6	Redpath Museum of Natural History	44	D1	Parisian Laundry
14	B1	Cineplex Odeon	57	F1	Corona Theatre

SPORTS AND ACTIVITIES

48	D5	Montréal Canadiens	51	D6	Le Atrium 1000

SHOPS

6	A5	Holt Renfrew	29	B6	Off the Hook
7	A5	Tiffany & Co.	31	B6	Centre Eaton
13	A6	Paragraphe	37	C6	Rue Ste-Catherine
22	B5	Marie Saint Pierre	42	C6	Murale
25	B5	La Maison Ogilvy	56	F1	Grand Central inc.
26	B6	Cheap Thrills	58	F3	Antiquités Foley L'Ecuyer
28	B6	Les Cours Mont-Royal			

HOTELS

2	A3	Château Versailles	36	C5	L'Hôtel le Crystal
3	A3	Le Méridien Versailles	43	C6	Fairmont Queen Elizabeth
8	A5	Ritz-Carlton	45	D4	L'Hôtel Espresso
9	A6	Sofitel Montréal	46	D4	Auberge les Bon Matins
24	B5	Le Mount Stephen	50	D6	Marriott Château Champlain
27	B6	Hôtel Le Germain			

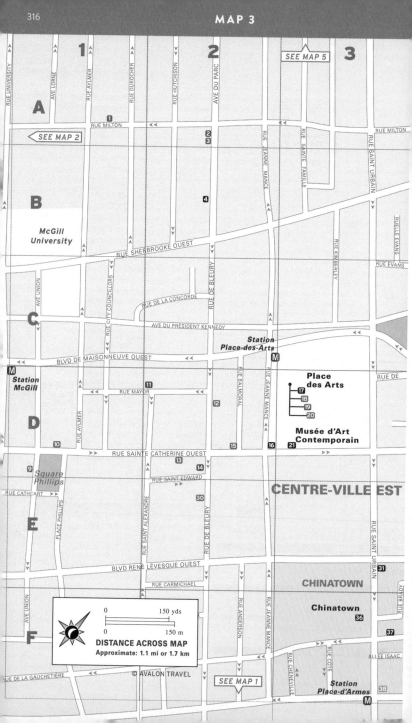

SIGHTS

17	D3	Place des Arts
21	D3	Musée d'Art Contemporain
36	F3	Chinatown

RESTAURANTS

4	B2	Pikolo Espresso Bar
16	D2	Brasserie T!
31	E3	Maison Kim Fung
32	E4	SAT Labo Culinaire
37	F3	Pâtisserie Harmonie
39	F4	Chez Bong

NIGHTLIFE

2	A2	Pullman
6	B5	La Distillerie no. 1
8	C4	Coop Katacombes
11	D2	Furco
14	D2	Nyks
26	D4	Les Foufounes Electriques
28	D5	Le Sainte-Élisabeth
35	E4	Le Mal Nécessaire

ARTS AND CULTURE

12	D2	Agora de la Danse
13	D2	Belgo Building
15	D2	L'Astral
18	D3	Opéra de Montréal
19	D3	Les Grands Ballets Canadiens de Montréal
20	D3	Orchestre Symphonique de Montréal
23	D4	Le 2-22
24	D4	Club Soda
25	D4	Métropolis
29	D5	Théâtre Sainte-Catherine
30	E2	Gesù Centre de Créativité
33	E4	SAT

SHOPS

1	A1	The Word
3	A2	Papeterie Nota Bene
7	C4	Eva B
9	D1	Maison Birks
10	D1	La Baie
27	D5	Henri Henri

HOTELS

5	B4	Hotel 10 Montréal
22	D4	Hotel Quartier des Spectacles
34	E4	Hotel Zero1
38	F3	Holiday Inn Select

SEE MAP 4

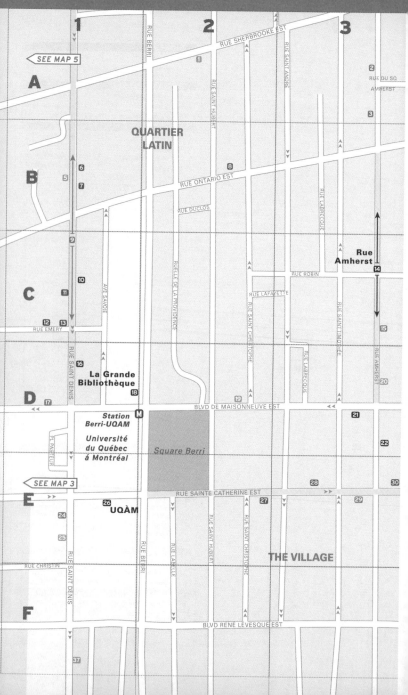

SEE MAP 5

1   **2**   **3**

RUE SHERBROOKE EST

A

RUE BERRI

RUE SAINT-HUBERT

RUE SAINT-ANDRÉ

RUE DU SQ

2

AMBERST

3

**QUARTIER
LATIN**

6

5

7

8

RUE ONTARIO EST

RUE LABRECQUE

RUE DUCLOS

9

RUELLE DE LA PROVIDENCE

**Rue
Amherst**

14

RUE ROBIN

10

AVE SAVOIE

RUE SAINT-CHRISTOPHE

RUE LAFAYETTE

RUE SAINT-TIMOTHÉE

C

11

RUE AMHERST

15

12   13

RUE EMERY

16

RUE SAINT-DENIS

**La Grande
Bibliothèque**

18

RUE LABRECQUE

20

D   17

19

BLVD DE MAISONNEUVE EST

**Station M
Berri-UQAM**

21

**Université
du Québec
á Montréal**

Square Berri

22

SEE MAP 3

28

30

RUE SAINTE-CATHERINE EST

E

26 **UQÀM**

27

29

24

RUE SAINT-HUBERT

RUE SAINT-CHRISTOPHE

25

RUE SAINT-DENIS

RUE BERRI

RUE LASALLE

THE VILLAGE

RUE CHRISTIN

F

BLVD RENÉ-LÉVESQUE EST

37

SIGHTS

14	C3	Rue Amherst
18	D1	La Grande Bibliothèque
26	E1	UQÀM
34	E4	Rue Ste-Catherine Est
38	F4	Église St-Pierre-Apôtre

RESTAURANTS

4	A6	Au Petit Extra
10	C1	Mâche
12	C1	Camellia Sinensis
16	D1	Juliette et Chocolat
21	D3	O'Thym
22	D3	Pourquoi Pas Espresso Bar
36	E6	La Mie Matinale
39	F5	Kitchenette

NIGHTLIFE

6	B1	L'Amère à Boire
7	B1	Arcade MTL
8	B2	Le Cheval Blanc
11	C1	Le Saint-Sulpice
13	C1	Les Trois Brasseurs
27	E2	Stereo
28	E3	Circus After-Hours
30	E3	Cabaret Mado
31	E4	Club Unity
32	E4	Le Date Karaoke
35	E5	Complexe Sky

ARTS AND CULTURE

3	A3	Éco Musée du Fier Monde
17	D1	Cinémathèque Québécoise
24	E1	Theatre Berri
29	E3	L'Olympia
33	E4	Le National

SHOPS

2	A3	Boutique Spoutnik
9	C1	Rue St-Denis
15	C3	Antiquités Seconde Chance

HOTELS

1	A2	Chateau de L'Argoat
5	B1	Auberge Hotel Le Jardin d'Antoine
19	D2	Auberge Le Pomerol
20	D3	La Loggia
23	D4	Sir Montcalm
25	E1	Hôtel St-Denis
37	F1	Celebrities Hotel

Station Beaudry

Rue Ste-Catherine Est

Parc de Champlain

Église St-Pierre-Apôtre

0		100 yds
0		100 m

DISTANCE ACROSS MAP
Approximate: 1 mi or 1.6 km

© AVALON TRAVEL

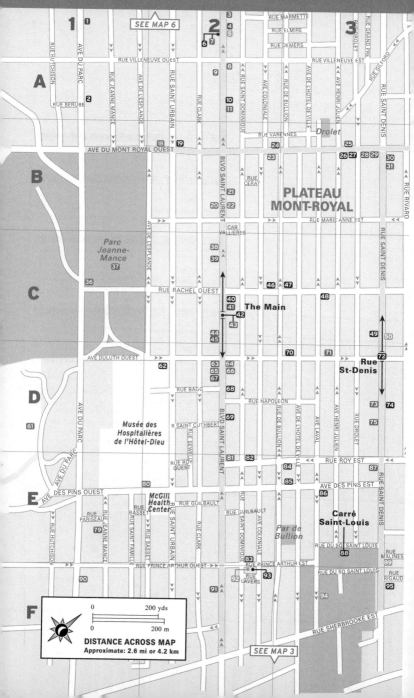

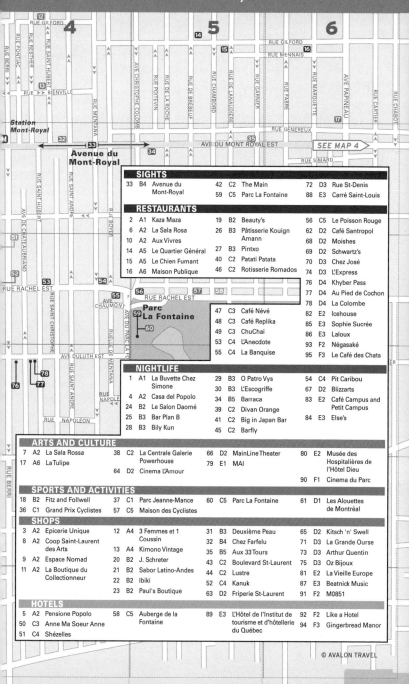

Station Mont-Royal

Avenue du Mont-Royal

Parc La Fontaine

SEE MAP 4 >

SIGHTS

33	B4	Avenue du Mont-Royal	42	C2	The Main	72	D3	Rue St-Denis
			59	C5	Parc La Fontaine	88	E3	Carré Saint-Louis

RESTAURANTS

2	A1	Kaza Maza	19	B2	Beauty's	56	C5	Le Poisson Rouge
6	A2	La Sala Rosa	26	B3	Pâtisserie Kouign Amann	62	D2	Café Santropol
10	A2	Aux Vivres	27	B3	Pintxo	68	D2	Moishes
14	A5	Le Quartier Général	40	C2	Patati Patata	69	D2	Schwartz's
15	A5	Le Chien Fumant	46	C2	Rotisserie Romados	70	D3	Chez José
16	A6	Maison Publique				74	D3	L'Express
			47	C3	Café Névé	76	D4	Khyber Pass
			48	C3	Café Replika	77	D4	Au Pied de Cochon
			49	C3	ChuChai	78	D4	La Colombe
			53	C4	L'Anecdote	82	E3	Icehouse
			55	C4	La Banquise	85	E3	Sophie Sucrée
						86	E3	Laloux
						93	F2	Négasaké
						95	F3	Le Café des Chats

NIGHTLIFE

1	A1	La Buvette Chez Simone	29	B3	O Patro Vys	54	C4	Pit Caribou
4	A2	Casa del Popolo	30	B3	L'Escogriffe	67	D2	Blizzarts
24	B2	Le Salon Daomé	34	B5	Barraca	83	E2	Café Campus and Petit Campus
25	B3	Bar Plan B	39	C2	Divan Orange	84	E3	Else's
28	B3	Bily Kun	41	C2	Big in Japan Bar			
			45	C2	Barfly			

ARTS AND CULTURE

7	A2	La Sala Rossa	38	C2	La Centrale Galerie Powerhouse	66	D2	MainLine Theater	80	E2	Musée des Hospitalières de l'Hôtel Dieu
17	A6	La Tulipe	64	D2	Cinema L'Amour	79	E1	MAI	90	F1	Cinema du Parc

SPORTS AND ACTIVITIES

18	B2	Fitz and Follwell	37	C1	Parc Jeanne-Mance	60	C5	Parc La Fontaine	61	D1	Les Alouettes de Montréal
36	C1	Grand Prix Cyclistes	57	C5	Maison des Cyclistes						

SHOPS

3	A2	Epicerie Unique	12	A4	3 Femmes et 1 Coussin	31	B3	Deuxième Peau	65	D2	Kitsch 'n' Swell
8	A2	Coop Saint-Laurent des Arts	13	A4	Kimono Vintage	32	B4	Chez Farfelu	71	D3	La Grande Ourse
9	A2	Espace Nomad	20	B2	J. Schreter	35	B5	Aux 33 Tours	73	D3	Arthur Quentin
11	A2	La Boutique du Collectionneur	21	B2	Sabor Latino-Andes	43	C2	Boulevard St-Laurent	75	D3	Oz Bijoux
			22	B2	Ibiki	44	C2	Lustre	81	E3	La Vieille Europe
			23	B2	Paul's Boutique	52	C4	Kanuk	87	E3	Beatnick Music
						63	D2	Friperie St-Laurent	91	F2	M0851

HOTELS

5	A2	Pensione Popolo	58	C5	Auberge de la Fontaine	89	E3	L'Hôtel de l'Institut de tourisme et d'hôtellerie du Québec	92	F2	Like a Hotel
50	C3	Anne Ma Soeur Anne							94	F3	Gingerbread Manor
51	C4	Shézelles									

© AVALON TRAVEL

MAP 6

RUE DE CASTELNAU OUEST

Station de Castelnau

JEAN TALON EST

PLACE DU MARCHE DE NORD

PLACE DU MARCHE DU NORD

AVE SHAMROCK

AVE MOZART EST

RUE JEAN TALON OUEST

Station Acadie

AVE JEAN TALON OUEST

AVE DE L'EPEE

AVE HUTCHISON

AVE DU PARC

AVE BEAUMONT

AVE MOZART OUEST

AVE BEAUMONT

RUE BELANGER

RUE DANTE

PETITE-ITALIE

AVE ALEXANDRA

RUE SAINT ZOTIQUE OUEST

RUE SAINT ZOTIQUE OUEST

RUE SAINT ZOTIQUE EST

300 yds

300 m

DISTANCE ACROSS MAP
Approximate: 2.2 mi or 3.6 km

AVE MANSEAU

AVE OUTREMONT

AVE DUCHARME

RUE BEAUBIEN OUEST

RUE BEAUBIEN EST

RUE BURELLE

AVE WISEMAN

AVE VAN HORNE

Station Outremont

AVE VAN HORNE

RUE HENRI IV

AVE DUVERGER

AVE MARSOLAIS

AVE BLOOMFIELD

AVE DE L'EPEE

RUE JEANNE MANCE

AVE DE L'ESPLANADE

RUE WAVERLY

RUE CLARK

RUE DE L'ARCADE

BLVD ROSEMONT

AVE STUART

AVE LAJOIE

AVE JOYCE

AVE BERNARD

RUE BERNARD OUEST

RUE LESAGE

Parc St Viateur

MILE END

Church of Saint-Michael and Saint-Anthony

AVE LAVIOLETTE

AVE SAINT JUST

AVE CHAMPAGNEUR

AVE QUERBES

AVE DUROCHER

AVE HUTCHISON

AVE SAINT VIATEUR OUEST

RUE SAINT URBAIN

RUE CLARK

BLVD SAINT LAURENT

RUE SWISS

RUE SAINT VIATEUR EST

RUE SAINT DOMINIQUE

AVE CASGRAIN

AVE DE GASPE

Parc Outremont

AVE DU PARC

AVE ELMWOOD

RUE GROLL

PL ELMWOOD

CHEMIN DE LA CÔTE SAINTE CATHERINE

AVE DE L'EPEE

AVE MCDOUGALL

RUE MAGUIRE

AVE FAIRMOUNT EST

Parc de St Michel

AVE FAIRMOUNT OUEST

RUE LABADIE

AVE CLERMONT

RUE JEANNE MANCE

AVE LAURIER OUEST

RUE CHARLES

Parc Lahaie

RUE BULLION

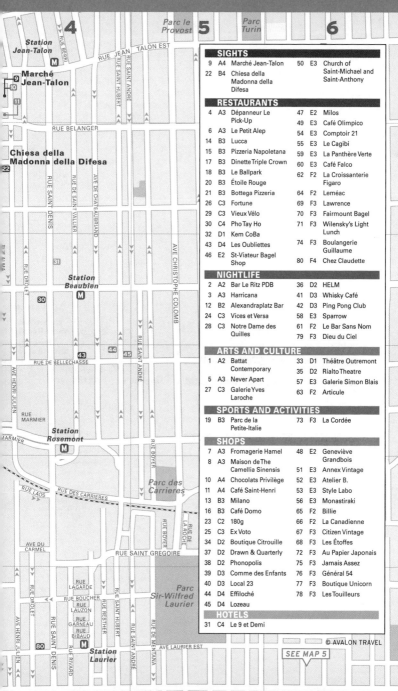

SIGHTS

| 9 | A4 | Marché Jean-Talon | 50 | E3 | Church of Saint-Michael and Saint-Anthony |
| 22 | B4 | Chiesa della Madonna della Difesa | | | |

RESTAURANTS

4	A3	Dépanneur Le Pick-Up	47	E2	Milos
6	A3	Le Petit Alep	49	E3	Café Olimpico
14	B3	Lucca	54	E3	Comptoir 21
15	B3	Pizzeria Napoletana	55	E3	Le Cagibi
17	B3	Dinette Triple Crown	59	E3	La Panthère Verte
18	B3	Le Ballpark	60	E3	Café Falco
20	B3	Étoile Rouge	62	F2	La Croissanterie Figaro
21	B3	Bottega Pizzeria	64	F2	Leméac
26	C3	Fortune	69	F3	Lawrence
29	C3	Vieux Vélo	70	F3	Fairmount Bagel
30	C4	Pho Tay Ho	71	F3	Wilensky's Light Lunch
32	D1	Kem CoBa	74	F3	Boulangerie Guillaume
43	D4	Les Oubliettes	80	F4	Chez Claudette
46	E2	St-Viateur Bagel Shop			

NIGHTLIFE

2	A2	Bar Le Ritz PDB	36	D2	HELM
3	A3	Harricana	41	D3	Whisky Café
12	B2	Alexandraplatz Bar	42	D3	Ping Pong Club
24	C3	Vices et Versa	58	E3	Sparrow
28	C3	Notre Dame des Quilles	61	F2	Le Bar Sans Nom
			79	F3	Dieu du Ciel

ARTS AND CULTURE

1	A2	Battat Contemporary	33	D1	Théâtre Outremont
5	A3	Never Apart	35	D2	Rialto Theatre
27	C3	Galerie Yves Laroche	57	E3	Galerie Simon Blais
			63	F2	Articule

SPORTS AND ACTIVITIES

| 19 | B3 | Parc de la Petite-Italie | 73 | F3 | La Cordée |

SHOPS

7	A3	Fromagerie Hamel	48	E2	Geneviève Grandbois
8	A3	Maison de The Camellia Sinensis	51	E3	Annex Vintage
10	A4	Chocolats Privilège	52	E3	Atelier B.
11	A4	Café Saint-Henri	53	E3	Style Labo
13	B3	Milano	56	E3	Monastiraki
16	B3	Café Domo	65	F2	Billie
23	C2	180g	66	F2	La Canadienne
25	C3	Ex Voto	67	F3	Citizen Vintage
34	D2	Boutique Citrouille	68	F3	Les Étoffes
37	D2	Drawn & Quarterly	72	F3	Au Papier Japonais
38	D2	Phonopolis	75	F3	Jamais Assez
39	D3	Comme des Enfants	76	F3	Général 54
40	D3	Local 23	77	F3	Boutique Unicorn
44	D4	Effiloché	78	F3	Les Touilleurs
45	D4	Lozeau			

HOTELS

| 31 | C4 | Le 9 et Demi |

© AVALON TRAVEL

SEE MAP 5

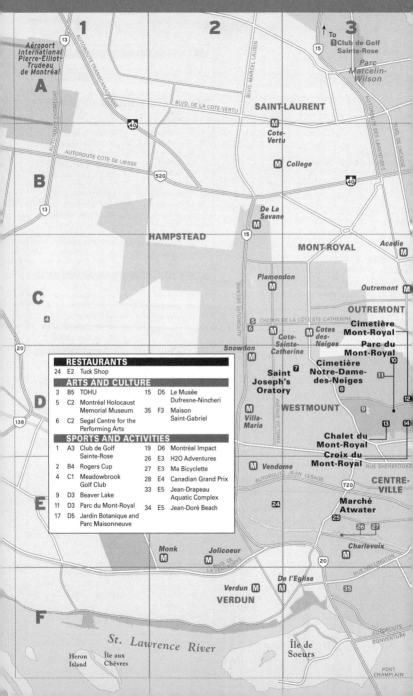

RESTAURANTS

| 24 | E2 | Tuck Shop |

ARTS AND CULTURE

3	B5	TOHU	15	D5	Le Musée
5	C2	Montréal Holocaust			Dufresne-Nincheri
		Memorial Museum	35	F3	Maison
6	C2	Segal Centre for the			Saint-Gabriel
		Performing Arts			

SPORTS AND ACTIVITIES

1	A3	Club de Golf	19	D6	Montréal Impact
		Sainte-Rose	26	E3	H2O Adventures
2	B4	Rogers Cup	27	E3	Ma Bicyclette
4	C1	Meadowbrook	28	E4	Canadian Grand Prix
		Golf Club	33	E5	Jean-Drapeau
9	D3	Beaver Lake			Aquatic Complex
11	D3	Parc du Mont-Royal	34	E5	Jean-Doré Beach
17	D5	Jardin Botanique and			
		Parc Maisonneuve			

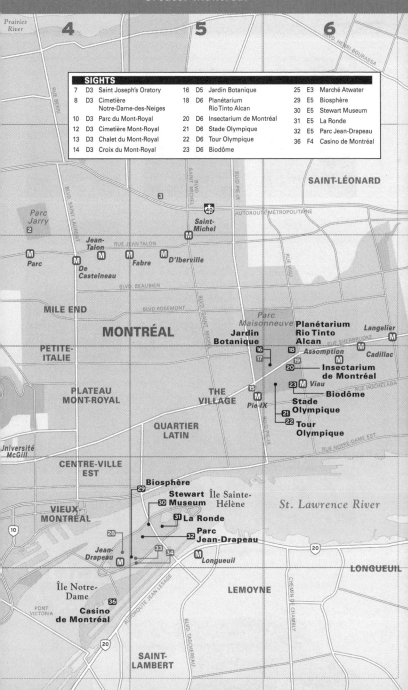

SIGHTS

7	D3	Saint Joseph's Oratory	16
8	D3	Cimetière Notre-Dame-des-Neiges	18
10	D3	Parc du Mont-Royal	20
12	D3	Cimetière Mont-Royal	21
13	D3	Chalet du Mont-Royal	22
14	D3	Croix du Mont-Royal	23

16 D5 Jardin Botanique
18 D6 Planétarium Rio Tinto Alcan
20 D6 Insectarium de Montréal
21 D6 Stade Olympique
22 D6 Tour Olympique
23 D6 Biodôme

25 E3 Marché Atwater
29 E5 Biosphère
30 E5 Stewart Museum
31 E5 La Ronde
32 E5 Parc Jean-Drapeau
36 F4 Casino de Montréal

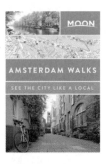
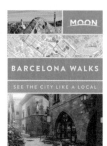

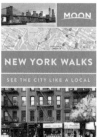
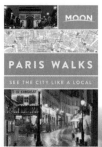

MAP SYMBOLS

■	Sights	⊛	National Capital	▲	Mountain	═══	Major Hwy
■	Restaurants	⊙	State Capital	✚	Natural Feature	───	Road/Hwy
■	Nightlife	○	City/Town	🌊	Waterfall	▒▒▒	Pedestrian Friendly
■	Arts and Culture	★	Point of Interest	♠	Park	▓▓▓	Tunnel
■	Sports and Activities	●	Accommodation	⩲	Archaeological Site	-------	Trail
▦	Shops	▾	Restaurant/Bar	❶	Trailhead	▪▪▪▪▪	Stairs
▦	Hotels	▪	Other Location	℗	Parking Area	▪▪▪▪▪	Ferry
						▬▬▬	Railroad

CONVERSION TABLES

°C = (°F - 32) / 1.8
°F = (°C x 1.8) + 32
1 inch = 2.54 centimeters (cm)
1 foot = 0.304 meters (m)
1 yard = 0.914 meters
1 mile = 1.6093 kilometers (km)
1 km = 0.6214 miles
1 fathom = 1.8288 m
1 chain = 20.1168 m
1 furlong = 201.168 m
1 acre = 0.4047 hectares
1 sq km = 100 hectares
1 sq mile = 2.59 square km
1 ounce = 28.35 grams
1 pound = 0.4536 kilograms
1 short ton = 0.90718 metric ton
1 short ton = 2,000 pounds
1 long ton = 1.016 metric tons
1 long ton = 2,240 pounds
1 metric ton = 1,000 kilograms
1 quart = 0.94635 liters
1 US gallon = 3.7854 liters
1 Imperial gallon = 4.5459 liters
1 nautical mile = 1.852 km

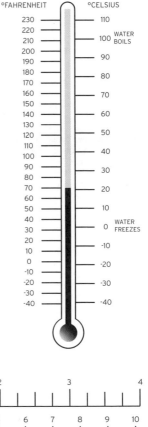

MOON MONTRÉAL
Avalon Travel
Hachette Book Group
1700 Fourth Street
Berkeley, CA 94710, USA
www.moon.com

Editors: Kathryn Ettinger, Leah Gordon
Series Manager: Leah Gordon
Copy Editor: Deana Shields
Graphics Coordinator: Rue Flaherty
Production Coordinator: Rue Flaherty
Cover Design: Faceout Studios, Charles Brock
Interior Design: Megan Jones Design
Moon Logo: Tim McGrath
Map Editor: Albert Angulo
Cartographers: Brian Shotwell and Larissa Gatt
Proofreaders: Rosemarie Leenerts, Caroline Trefler
Indexer: Rachel Kuhn

ISBN-13: 978-1-63121-492-9

Printing History
1st Edition — April 2018
5 4 3 2

Front cover photo: Place Jacques Cartier © Guido Cozzi / SIME / eStock Photo
Back cover photo: Basilique Notre-Dame-de-Montréal © Demerzel21 | Dreamstime.com

Printed in China by RR Donnelley